FREE Test Taking Tips Video/DVD Offer

To better serve you, we created videos covering test taking tips that we want to give you for FREE. **These videos cover world-class tips that will help you succeed on your test.**

We just ask that you send us feedback about this product. Please let us know what you thought about it—whether good, bad, or indifferent.

To get your **FREE videos**, you can use the QR code below or email freevideos@studyguideteam.com with "Free Videos" in the subject line and the following information in the body of the email:

a. The title of your product

b. Your product rating on a scale of 1-5, with 5 being the highest

c. Your feedback about the product

If you have any questions or concerns, please don't hesitate to contact us at info@studyguideteam.com.

Thank you!

ACS Organic Chemistry Study Guide

ACS Exam Prep and Practice Test

[Includes Detailed Answer Explanations]

Joshua Rueda

Written and edited by TPB Publishing.

ISBN 13: 9781637752029
ISBN 10: 1637752024

Table of Contents

Welcome

Dear Reader,

Welcome to your new Test Prep Books study guide! We are pleased that you chose us to help you prepare for your exam. There are many study options to choose from, and we appreciate you choosing us. Studying can be a daunting task, but we have designed a smart, effective study guide to help prepare you for what lies ahead.

Whether you're a parent helping your child learn and grow, a high school student working hard to get into your dream college, or a nursing student studying for a complex exam, we want to help give you the tools you need to succeed. We hope this study guide gives you the skills and the confidence to thrive, and we can't thank you enough for allowing us to be part of your journey.

In an effort to continue to improve our products, we welcome feedback from our customers. We look forward to hearing from you. Suggestions, success stories, and criticisms can all be communicated by emailing us at info@studyguideteam.com.

Sincerely,
Test Prep Books Team

FREE Videos/DVD OFFER

Doing well on your exam requires both knowing the test content and understanding how to use that knowledge to do well on the test. We offer completely FREE test taking tip videos. **These videos cover world-class tips that you can use to succeed on your test.**

To get your **FREE videos**, you can use the QR code below or email freevideos@studyguideteam.com with "Free Videos" in the subject line and the following information in the body of the email:

a. The title of your product
b. Your product rating on a scale of 1-5, with 5 being the highest
c. Your feedback about the product

If you have any questions or concerns, please don't hesitate to contact us at info@studyguideteam.com.

Quick Overview

As you draw closer to taking your exam, effective preparation becomes more and more important. Thankfully, you have this study guide to help you get ready. Use this guide to help keep your studying on track and refer to it often.

This study guide contains several key sections that will help you be successful on your exam. The guide contains tips for what you should do the night before and the day of the test. Also included are test-taking tips. Knowing the right information is not always enough. Many well-prepared test takers struggle with exams. These tips will help equip you to accurately read, assess, and answer test questions.

A large part of the guide is devoted to showing you what content to expect on the exam and to helping you better understand that content. In this guide are practice test questions so that you can see how well you have grasped the content. Then, answer explanations are provided so that you can understand why you missed certain questions.

Don't try to cram the night before you take your exam. This is not a wise strategy for a few reasons. First, your retention of the information will be low. Your time would be better used by reviewing information you already know rather than trying to learn a lot of new information. Second, you will likely become stressed as you try to gain a large amount of knowledge in a short amount of time. Third, you will be depriving yourself of sleep. So be sure to go to bed at a reasonable time the night before. Being well-rested helps you focus and remain calm.

Be sure to eat a substantial breakfast the morning of the exam. If you are taking the exam in the afternoon, be sure to have a good lunch as well. Being hungry is distracting and can make it difficult to focus. You have hopefully spent lots of time preparing for the exam. Don't let an empty stomach get in the way of success!

When travelling to the testing center, leave earlier than needed. That way, you have a buffer in case you experience any delays. This will help you remain calm and will keep you from missing your appointment time at the testing center.

Be sure to pace yourself during the exam. Don't try to rush through the exam. There is no need to risk performing poorly on the exam just so you can leave the testing center early. Allow yourself to use all of the allotted time if needed.

Remain positive while taking the exam even if you feel like you are performing poorly. Thinking about the content you should have mastered will not help you perform better on the exam.

Once the exam is complete, take some time to relax. Even if you feel that you need to take the exam again, you will be well served by some down time before you begin studying again. It's often easier to convince yourself to study if you know that it will come with a reward!

Test-Taking Strategies

1. Predicting the Answer

When you feel confident in your preparation for a multiple-choice test, try predicting the answer before reading the answer choices. This is especially useful on questions that test objective factual knowledge. By predicting the answer before reading the available choices, you eliminate the possibility that you will be distracted or led astray by an incorrect answer choice. You will feel more confident in your selection if you read the question, predict the answer, and then find your prediction among the answer choices. After using this strategy, be sure to still read all of the answer choices carefully and completely. If you feel unprepared, you should not attempt to predict the answers. This would be a waste of time and an opportunity for your mind to wander in the wrong direction.

2. Reading the Whole Question

Too often, test takers scan a multiple-choice question, recognize a few familiar words, and immediately jump to the answer choices. Test authors are aware of this common impatience, and they will sometimes prey upon it. For instance, a test author might subtly turn the question into a negative, or he or she might redirect the focus of the question right at the end. The only way to avoid falling into these traps is to read the entirety of the question carefully before reading the answer choices.

3. Looking for Wrong Answers

Long and complicated multiple-choice questions can be intimidating. One way to simplify a difficult multiple-choice question is to eliminate all of the answer choices that are clearly wrong. In most sets of answers, there will be at least one selection that can be dismissed right away. If the test is administered on paper, the test taker could draw a line through it to indicate that it may be ignored; otherwise, the test taker will have to perform this operation mentally or on scratch paper. In either case, once the obviously incorrect answers have been eliminated, the remaining choices may be considered. Sometimes identifying the clearly wrong answers will give the test taker some information about the correct answer. For instance, if one of the remaining answer choices is a direct opposite of one of the eliminated answer choices, it may well be the correct answer. The opposite of obviously wrong is obviously right! Of course, this is not always the case. Some answers are obviously incorrect simply because they are irrelevant to the question being asked. Still, identifying and eliminating some incorrect answer choices is a good way to simplify a multiple-choice question.

4. Don't Overanalyze

Anxious test takers often overanalyze questions. When you are nervous, your brain will often run wild, causing you to make associations and discover clues that don't actually exist. If you feel that this may be a problem for you, do whatever you can to slow down during the test. Try taking a deep breath or counting to ten. As you read and consider the question, restrict yourself to the particular words used by the author. Avoid thought tangents about what the author *really* meant, or what he or she was *trying* to say. The only things that matter on a multiple-choice test are the words that are actually in the question. You must avoid reading too much into a multiple-choice question, or supposing that the writer meant something other than what he or she wrote.

5. No Need for Panic

It is wise to learn as many strategies as possible before taking a multiple-choice test, but it is likely that you will come across a few questions for which you simply don't know the answer. In this situation, avoid panicking. Because most multiple-choice tests include dozens of questions, the relative value of a single wrong answer is small. As much as possible, you should compartmentalize each question on a multiple-choice test. In other words, you should not allow your feelings about one question to affect your success on the others. When you find a question that you either don't understand or don't know how to answer, just take a deep breath and do your best. Read the entire question slowly and carefully. Try rephrasing the question a couple of different ways. Then, read all of the answer choices carefully. After eliminating obviously wrong answers, make a selection and move on to the next question.

6. Confusing Answer Choices

When working on a difficult multiple-choice question, there may be a tendency to focus on the answer choices that are the easiest to understand. Many people, whether consciously or not, gravitate to the answer choices that require the least concentration, knowledge, and memory. This is a mistake. When you come across an answer choice that is confusing, you should give it extra attention. A question might be confusing because you do not know the subject matter to which it refers. If this is the case, don't eliminate the answer before you have affirmatively settled on another. When you come across an answer choice of this type, set it aside as you look at the remaining choices. If you can confidently assert that one of the other choices is correct, you can leave the confusing answer aside. Otherwise, you will need to take a moment to try to better understand the confusing answer choice. Rephrasing is one way to tease out the sense of a confusing answer choice.

7. Your First Instinct

Many people struggle with multiple-choice tests because they overthink the questions. If you have studied sufficiently for the test, you should be prepared to trust your first instinct once you have carefully and completely read the question and all of the answer choices. There is a great deal of research suggesting that the mind can come to the correct conclusion very quickly once it has obtained all of the relevant information. At times, it may seem to you as if your intuition is working faster even than your reasoning mind. This may in fact be true. The knowledge you obtain while studying may be retrieved from your subconscious before you have a chance to work out the associations that support it. Verify your instinct by working out the reasons that it should be trusted.

8. Key Words

Many test takers struggle with multiple-choice questions because they have poor reading comprehension skills. Quickly reading and understanding a multiple-choice question requires a mixture of skill and experience. To help with this, try jotting down a few key words and phrases on a piece of scrap paper. Doing this concentrates the process of reading and forces the mind to weigh the relative importance of the question's parts. In selecting words and phrases to write down, the test taker thinks about the question more deeply and carefully. This is especially true for multiple-choice questions that are preceded by a long prompt.

9. Subtle Negatives

One of the oldest tricks in the multiple-choice test writer's book is to subtly reverse the meaning of a question with a word like *not* or *except*. If you are not paying attention to each word in the question, you can easily be led astray by this trick. For instance, a common question format is, "Which of the following is...?" Obviously, if the question instead is, "Which of the following is not...?," then the answer will be quite different. Even worse, the test makers are aware of the potential for this mistake and will include one answer choice that would be correct if the question were not negated or reversed. A test taker who misses the reversal will find what he or she believes to be a correct answer and will be so confident that he or she will fail to reread the question and discover the original error. The only way to avoid this is to practice a wide variety of multiple-choice questions and to pay close attention to each and every word.

10. Reading Every Answer Choice

It may seem obvious, but you should always read every one of the answer choices! Too many test takers fall into the habit of scanning the question and assuming that they understand the question because they recognize a few key words. From there, they pick the first answer choice that answers the question they believe they have read. Test takers who read all of the answer choices might discover that one of the latter answer choices is actually *more* correct. Moreover, reading all of the answer choices can remind you of facts related to the question that can help you arrive at the correct answer. Sometimes, a misstatement or incorrect detail in one of the latter answer choices will trigger your memory of the subject and will enable you to find the right answer. Failing to read all of the answer choices is like not reading all of the items on a restaurant menu: you might miss out on the perfect choice.

11. Spot the Hedges

One of the keys to success on multiple-choice tests is paying close attention to every word. This is never truer than with words like *almost*, *most*, *some*, and *sometimes*. These words are called "hedges" because they indicate that a statement is not totally true or not true in every place and time. An absolute statement will contain no hedges, but in many subjects, the answers are not always straightforward or absolute. There are always exceptions to the rules in these subjects. For this reason, you should favor those multiple-choice questions that contain hedging language. The presence of qualifying words indicates that the author is taking special care with his or her words, which is certainly important when composing the right answer. After all, there are many ways to be wrong, but there is only one way to be right! For this reason, it is wise to avoid answers that are absolute when taking a multiple-choice test. An absolute answer is one that says things are either all one way or all another. They often include words like *every*, *always*, *best*, and *never*. If you are taking a multiple-choice test in a subject that doesn't lend itself to absolute answers, be on your guard if you see any of these words.

12. Long Answers

In many subject areas, the answers are not simple. As already mentioned, the right answer often requires hedges. Another common feature of the answers to a complex or subjective question are qualifying clauses, which are groups of words that subtly modify the meaning of the sentence. If the question or answer choice describes a rule to which there are exceptions or the subject matter is complicated, ambiguous, or confusing, the correct answer will require many words in order to be expressed clearly and accurately. In essence, you should not be deterred by answer choices that seem excessively long. Oftentimes, the author of the text will not be able to write the correct answer without offering some qualifications and modifications. Your job is to read the answer choices thoroughly and completely and to select the one that most accurately and precisely answers the question.

13. Restating to Understand

Sometimes, a question on a multiple-choice test is difficult not because of what it asks but because of how it is written. If this is the case, restate the question or answer choice in different words. This process serves a couple of important purposes. First, it forces you to concentrate on the core of the question. In order to rephrase the question accurately, you have to understand it well. Rephrasing the question will concentrate your mind on the key words and ideas. Second, it will present the information to your mind in a fresh way. This process may trigger your memory and render some useful scrap of information picked up while studying.

14. True Statements

Sometimes an answer choice will be true in itself, but it does not answer the question. This is one of the main reasons why it is essential to read the question carefully and completely before proceeding to the answer choices. Too often, test takers skip ahead to the answer choices and look for true statements. Having found one of these, they are content to select it without reference to the question above. Obviously, this provides an easy way for test makers to play tricks. The savvy test taker will always read the entire question before turning to the answer choices. Then, having settled on a correct answer choice, he or she will refer to the original question and ensure that the selected answer is relevant. The mistake of choosing a correct-but-irrelevant answer choice is especially common on questions related to specific pieces of objective knowledge. A prepared test taker will have a wealth of factual knowledge at his or her disposal, and should not be careless in its application.

15. No Patterns

One of the more dangerous ideas that circulates about multiple-choice tests is that the correct answers tend to fall into patterns. These erroneous ideas range from a belief that B and C are the most common right answers, to the idea that an unprepared test-taker should answer "A-B-A-C-A-D-A-B-A." It cannot be emphasized enough that pattern-seeking of this type is exactly the WRONG way to approach a multiple-choice test. To begin with, it is highly unlikely that the test maker will plot the correct answers according to some predetermined pattern. The questions are scrambled and delivered in a random order. Furthermore, even if the test maker was following a pattern in the assignation of correct answers, there is no reason why the test taker would know which pattern he or she was using. Any attempt to discern a pattern in the answer choices is a waste of time and a distraction from the real work of taking the test. A test taker would be much better served by extra preparation before the test than by reliance on a pattern in the answers.

Introduction to the ACS Organic Chemistry

Function of the Test

The ACS Organic Chemistry exam tests student knowledge within the field of organic chemistry. It covers information from a standardized, general two-term curriculum published by the American Chemical Society (ACS).

Organic chemistry is an ever-growing field of science that focuses on compounds that contain carbon. Most compounds studied in organic chemistry contain hydrogen along with carbon, but other elements such as nitrogen, silicon, oxygen, and halogens are not uncommon. By studying the nature of these compounds, organic science helps develop an understanding of their properties and interactions, and how these compounds can be used in a variety of fields by experts in both the public and private sectors. In government service, organic chemistry is used by many organizations such as the Department of Health (often through its subsidiary agency, the Food and Drug Administration), the Patent and Trademark Office, and the US Department of the Interior. In consumer industry, organic chemistry allows for the production of petroleum products such as fuels, plastics, fertilizers, and even some pharmaceuticals. Beyond this, organic chemistry has such a broad range of applications that it can be found in almost every major branch of industry.

Test Format and Scoring

The ACS Organic Chemistry test consists of 70 multiple-choice questions; all questions are grouped together in a single section. There is a 110 minute time limit for taking the test. Tests are administered by bona fide chemistry teachers and administrators in the high school setting; these are often the same instructors that taught the organic chemistry courses being tested.

The scoring for the test varies between test administrators. While it can be graded on a strict scale by the number of questions right or wrong (like most other tests throughout an organic chemistry course), it is normally scored either on a curve or based on the national percentage rank (normative scores) for the test as published as percentiles from ACS.

The American Chemical Society

The American Chemical Society provides guidance for organic chemistry education, and they produce examinations available for high school and college levels. The ACS was founded in 1876 for the advancement of chemistry research and enterprise. Today, with over 150,000 members, the ACS stands as one of the world's largest scientific societies, with members in 140 countries. ACS is a non-profit organization that bears a US congressional charter and publishes an ongoing library of peer-reviewed scientific journals, holds several regional and international conferences, and maintains the Chemical Abstracts Services (which funds the ACS by offering global chemical databases), alongside its chemistry education programs.

Study Prep Plan for the ACS Organic Chemistry Test

1 **Schedule** - Use one of our study schedules below or come up with one of your own.

2 **Relax** - Test anxiety can hurt even the best students. There are many ways to reduce stress. Find the one that works best for you.

3 **Execute** - Once you have a good plan in place, be sure to stick to it.

One Week Study Schedule

Day 1	Nomenclature
Day 2	Stereoisomerism
Day 3	Nucleophilic Addition at Carbonyl Groups
Day 4	Electrophilic and Nucleophilic Aromatic
Day 5	Oxidations and Reductions
Day 6	Practice Test
Day 7	Take Your Exam!

Two Week Study Schedule

Day 1	Nomenclature	Day 8	Electrophilic and Nucleophilic Aromatic
Day 2	Structure, Hybridization, Resonance, Aromaticity	Day 9	Free Radical Substitutions and Additions
Day 3	Acids and Bases	Day 10	Oxidations and Reductions
Day 4	Stereoisomerism	Day 11	Spectroscopy
Day 5	Nucleophilic Substitutions and	Day 12	Practice Test
Day 6	Nucleophilic Addition at Carbonyl Groups	Day 13	Answer Explanations
Day 7	Enols and Enolate Ion Reactions	Day 14	Take Your Exam!

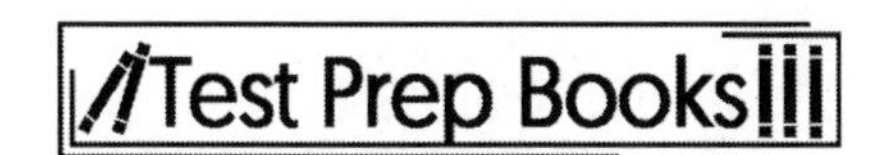

One Month Study Schedule

Day 1	Nomenclature	Day 11	Hydroboration-Oxidation: Forming Alcohols...	Day 21	Allylic Substitution Reactions
Day 2	Carbon Chains with Multiple Functional...	Day 12	Nucleophilic Addition at Carbonyl Groups	Day 22	Oxidations and Reductions
Day 3	Structure, Hybridization...	Day 13	1,2 and 1,4 Additions to a,b-unsaturated...	Day 23	Oxidative Reactions and Reagents
Day 4	Hybridization of Atomic Orbital...	Day 14	Nucleophilic Substitution at...	Day 24	Oxidation with Pyridinium Chlorochromate (PCC)
Day 5	Acids and Bases	Day 15	Reactions of Amides	Day 25	Spectroscopy
Day 6	Chemical Structure and Acidity...	Day 16	Enols and Enolate Ion Reactions	Day 26	Nuclear Magnetic Spectroscopy (NMR)
Day 7	Stereoisomerism	Day 17	Claisen-Condensation Reactions	Day 27	Synthesis and Analysis
Day 8	The Cahn-Ingold-Prelog...	Day 18	Electrophilic and Nucleophilic Aromatic...	Day 28	Practice Test
Day 9	Nucleophilic Substitutions...	Day 19	Electron-Donating and Electron-Withdrawing...	Day 29	Answer Explanations
Day 10	Electrophilic Additions	Day 20	Free Radical Substitutions...	Day 30	Take Your Exam!

Build your own prep plan by visiting:
testprepbooks.com/prep

Nomenclature

Chemical Nomenclature, Composition, and Bonding

Simple Compounds and Their Chemical Formulas

Chemical formulas represent the proportion of the number of atoms in a chemical compound. Chemical symbols are used for the elements present and numerical values. Parentheses are also sometimes used to show the number of combinations of the elements in relation to their ionic charges. An element's ionic charge can be determined by its location on the periodic table. This information is then used to correctly combine its atoms in a compound.

For example, the chemical formula for sodium chloride (table salt) is the combination of sodium (Na, ionic charge of +1) and chlorine (Cl, ionic charge of -1). From its placement on the periodic table, the electron valence of an outer shell can be determined: sodium has an ionic charge of +1, while chlorine has an ionic charge of -1. Since these two elements have an equal and opposite amount of charge, they combine in a neutral one-to-one ratio: $NaCl$. The naming of compounds depends mainly on the second element in a chemical compound. If it is a non-metal (such as chlorine), it is written with an "ide" at the end. The compound $NaCl$ is called "sodium chloride."

If the elements forming a compound do not have equal and opposite ionic charges, there will be an unequal number of each element in the compound to balance the ionic charge. This situation happens with many elements, for example, in the combination of nickel and oxygen into nickel oxide (Ni_2O_3). Nickel has a +3 ionic charge and oxygen has a -2 ionic charge, so when forming a compound, there must be two nickel atoms for every three oxygen atoms (a common factor of 6) to balance the charge of the compound. This compound is called "nickel oxide."

A chemical formula can also be written from a compound's name. For instance, the compound carbon dioxide is formed by the combination of carbon and oxygen. The word "dioxide" means there are two oxygen atoms for every carbon atom, so it is written as CO_2.

To better represent the composition of compounds, structural formulas are used. The combination of atoms is more precisely depicted by lining up the electron configuration of the outer electron shell through a Lewis dot diagram.

Types of Chemical Bonding

A chemical bond is a strong attractive force that can exist between atoms. The bonding of atoms is separated into two main categories. The first category, **ionic bonding,** primarily describes the bonding that occurs between oppositely charged ions in a regular crystal arrangement. It primarily exists between salts, which are known to be ionic. Ionic bonds are held together by the electrostatic attraction between oppositely charged ions. This type of bonding involves the transfer of electrons from the valence shell of one atom to the valence shell of another atom. If an atom loses an electron from its valence shell, it becomes a positive ion, or **cation**. If an atom gains an electron, it becomes a negative ion, or an **anion**. The Lewis electron-dot symbol is used to more simply express the electron configuration of atoms, especially when forming bonds.

The second type of bonding is covalent bonding. This bonding involves the sharing of a pair of electrons between atoms. There are no ions involved in covalent bonding, but the force holding the atoms

together comes from the balance between the attractive and repulsive forces involving the shared electron and the nuclei. Atoms frequently engage is this type of bonding when it enables them to fill their outer valence shell.

Mole Concept and Its Applications

The calculation of mole ratios of reactants and products involved in a chemical reaction is called "stoichiometry." To find these ratios, one must first find the proportion of the number of molecules in one mole of a substance. This relates the molar mass of a compound to its mass and this relationship is a constant known as **Avogadro's number** (6.23×10^{23}). Since it is a ratio, there are no dimensions (or units) for Avogadro's number.

Molar Mass and Percent Composition

The molar mass of a substance is the measure of the mass of one mole of the substance. For pure elements, the molar mass is also known as the atomic mass unit (amu) of the substance. For compounds, it can be calculated by adding the molar masses of each substance in the compound. For example, the molar mass of carbon is 12.01 g/mol, while the molar mass of water $(\mathrm{H_2O})$ requires finding the sum of the molar masses of the constituents:

$$\left(1.01 \times 2 = 2.02\frac{\mathrm{g}}{\mathrm{mol}}\text{ for hydrogen}\right) + \left(16.0\frac{\mathrm{g}}{\mathrm{mol}}\text{ for oxygen}\right) = 18.02\frac{\mathrm{g}}{\mathrm{mol}}$$

The percentage of a compound in a composition can be determined by taking the individual molar masses of each component divided by the total molar mass of the compound, multiplied by 100. Determining the percent composition of carbon dioxide $(\mathrm{CO_2})$ first requires the calculation of the molar mass of $\mathrm{CO_2}$.

$$\text{molar mass of carbon} = 12.01 \times 1 \text{ atom} = 12.01 \text{ g/mol}$$

$$\text{molar mass of oxygen} = 16.0 \times 2 \text{ atoms} = 32.0 \text{ g/mol}$$

$$\text{molar mass of CO2} = 12.01 \text{ g/mol} + 32.0 \text{ g/mol} = 44.01 \text{ g/mol}$$

Next, each individual mass is divided by the total mass and multiplied by 100 to get the percent composition of each component.

$$12.01/44.01 = (0.2729 \times 100) = 27.29\% \text{ carbon}$$

$$32.0/44.01 = (0.7271 \times 100) = 72.71\% \text{ oxygen}$$

(A quick check in the addition of the percentages should always yield 100%.)

Types of Organic Compounds and Naming Alkanes

Organic compounds can be classified into several families, which contain a specific type of bonding arrangement called functional groups. For example, compounds that contain $\mathrm{C-H}$ and $\mathrm{C-C}$ bonds belong to the family called alkanes. Compounds that contain a carbon atom bonded to a hydroxyl group (OH), for example, $\mathrm{C-OH}$ belong to the family called alcohols. Each family of compounds will exhibit different chemical and physical properties (alcohols generally have higher boiling points). Because of the significant number of organic compounds, chemists have adopted the naming convention of the International Union of Pure and Applied Chemistry (IUPAC) for each family to help identify compounds. Figure 1 displays a general family of organic compounds with the specific functional group and molecular formula. The first four families are hydrocarbon compounds that are composed of hydrogen and carbon, but each family will differ by the number of bonds that carbon can form. For example, alkanes only contain single $\mathrm{C-C}$ bonds, and alkynes will have carbon triple bonds, $\mathrm{C \equiv C}$. In Figure 1, within the general formula, the terms "R" and "X" refer to a carbon group and a halogen $(\mathrm{X = F, Cl, Br})$. The "Ar" term is a shorthand notation for "aromatic." The IUPAC and common names are given in the fourth and fifth rows. The common names of many compounds have their origins in the history and discovery of organic compounds (for example, urea) and tend to be a short, trivial name. However, there isn't a systematic naming convention for common names. The IUPAC method for naming organic compounds was adopted to name any organic compound systematically. Three general rules should be followed when applying the IUPAC method.

1) There is a base name that is used to indicate a parent chain (or ring) of carbon atoms within a given chemical structure.
2) A suffix, based on the functional group, is used. For instance, alkanes have the ending "ane," alkenes have the ending "ene," alkynes have the ending "yne," alcohols have the ending "ol," aldehydes have the ending "al," and ketones have the ending "one."
3) Substituent groups along the main chain are named.

	Family						
	Alkane	Alkene	Alkyne	Aromatic	Haloalkane	Alcohol	Ether
Functional group	C—H and C—C bonds	>C=C<	—C≡C—	Aromatic ring	—C—X:	—C—OH	—C—O—C—
General formula	RH	$RCH{=}CH_2$ $RCH{=}CHR$ $R_2C{=}CHR$ $R_2C{=}CR_2$	$RC{\equiv}CH$ $RC{\equiv}CR$	ArH	RX	ROH	ROR
Specific example	CH_3CH_3	$CH_2{=}CH_2$	$HC{\equiv}CH$	(benzene ring)	CH_3CH_2Cl	CH_3CH_2OH	CH_3OCH_3
IUPAC name	Ethane	Ethene	Ethyne	Benzene	Chloroethane	Ethanol	Methoxymethane
Common name	Ethane	Ethylene	Acetylene	Benzene	Ethyl chloride	Ethyl alcohol	Dimethyl ether

Family						
Amine	Aldehyde	Ketone	Carboxylic Acid	Ester	Amide	Nitrile
—C—N<	C(=O)—H	—C—C(=O)—C—	C(=O)—OH	C(=O)—O—C—	C(=O)—N<	—C≡N
RNH_2 R_2NH R_3N	RC(=O)H	RC(=O)R′	RC(=O)OH	RC(=O)OR′	$RC(=O)NH_2$ RC(=O)NHR′ RC(=O)NR′R″	RCN
CH_3NH_2	$CH_3C(=O)H$	$CH_3C(=O)CH_3$	$CH_3C(=O)OH$	$CH_3C(=O)OCH_3$	$CH_3C(=O)NH_2$	$CH_3C{\equiv}N$
Methanamine	Ethanal	Propanone	Ethanoic acid	Methyl ethanoate	Ethanamide	Ethanenitrile
Methylamine	Acetaldehyde	Acetone	Acetic acid	Methyl acetate	Acetamide	Acetonitrile

Figure 1. Families of organic compounds

Suppose we are given the following compounds belonging to the family called alkanes in Figure 1.

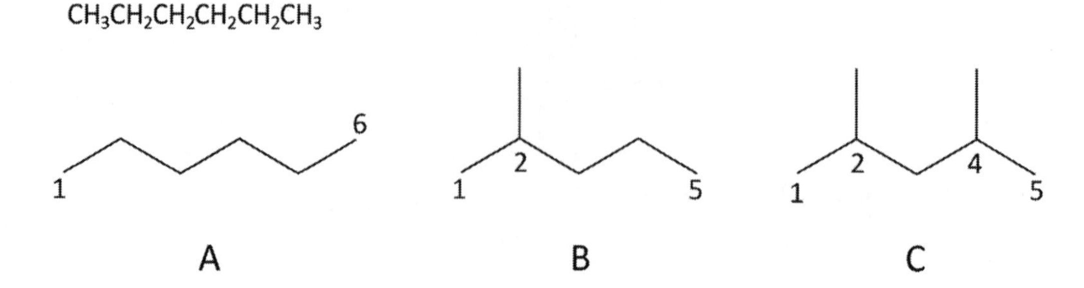

Figure 1. Stick structures of general alkanes

Structure A shows a general formula and a stick structure. The end of one stick corresponds to a carbon atom bonded to three hydrogen atoms, although hydrogen atoms are usually not shown in stick structures. The point where two sticks meet (corner) represents a carbon atom bonded to two hydrogen atoms. Stick structures are useful for representing larger molecules and to some degree the spatial orientation of atoms. The IUPAC method for naming alkane compounds consists of the rules shown in Table 1. Alkanes contain the suffix "ane" for each IUPAC name.

(1) Look for the longest continuous carbon chain and number it. Table 1 lists naming for alkanes from one to ten carbons.

Name	Number of carbon atoms	Name	Number of carbon atoms
Meth**ane**	1	hex**ane**	6
Eth**ane**	2	hept**ane**	7
Prop**ane**	3	oct**ane**	8
but**ane**	4	non**ane**	9
pent**ane**	5	dec**ane**	10

Table 1. Names of hydrocarbon chains with the alkane suffix "ane"

Structure A shown in the table above is a hydrocarbon that has six carbon atoms, and therefore it will be called hexane.

(2) Identify any groups connected to the chain and name them. Table 2 lists several groups and the associated names.

Name	Group	Name	Group
Methyl	$CH_3 -$	Butyl	$CH_3CH_2CH_2CH_2 -$
Ethyl	$CH_3CH_2 -$	Isobutyl	$(CH_3)_2CHCH_2 -$
Propyl	$CH_3CH_2CH_2 -$	Sec-butyl	$CH_3CH_2CH(CH_3) -$
Isopropyl	$(CH_3)_2CH -$	Tert-butyl	$(CH_3)_3 -$
Alkyl	$R -$		
Fluoro	$F -$	Bromo	$Br -$
Chloro	$Cl -$	Iodo	$I -$

Table 1. Names of hydrocarbon groups

(3) Starting at the end nearest a group or substituent, number the chain consecutively.

(4) For each group on the chain, assign a number and name. Groups closer to carbon 1 will be assigned the lower number.

(5) Put the name together in alphabetical order. Prefixes (for example, di, tri) are not considered when alphabetizing. For example, butyl comes before methyl. For halogens, bromo comes before chloro.

Structure B in Figure 2 has the longest chain, five carbon atoms, which corresponds to pentane. However, there is one substituent group that corresponds to a methyl group based on rule 2. Rule 3 says to give the substituent group the lowest possible number. Therefore, when numbering the longest chain, the methyl group will be assigned to carbon 2 (not carbon 4) and will be called "2-methyl." Based on rule 5, the names of the base or parent chain are combined with the name of the group in alphabetical order. Structure B in Figure 2 is called "2-methyl-pentane." In the same manner, structure C can be named accordingly and is called "2,4-dimethyl-pentane." Note that the prefix "di" is placed before the name of the group and that the base name follows last. Let's consider a few more structures below in Figure 3.

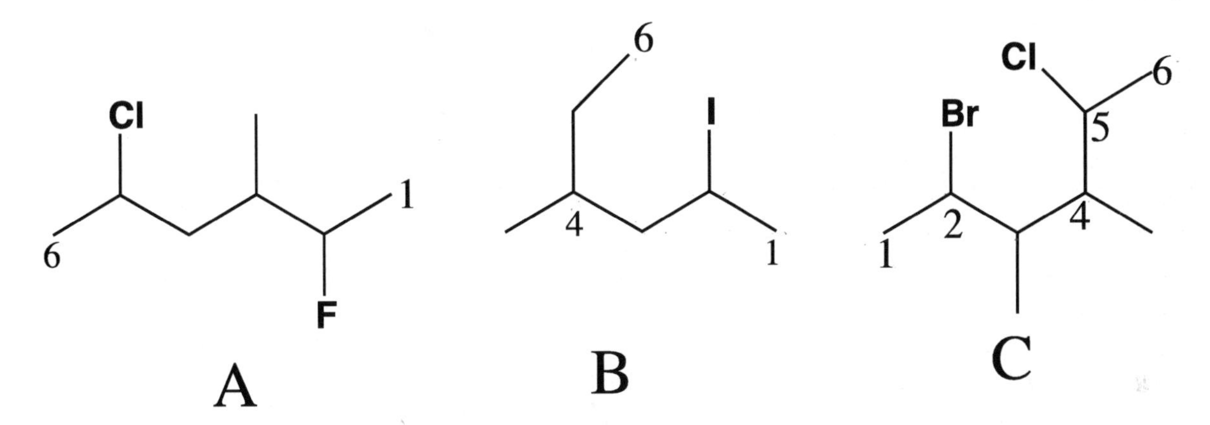

Figure 3. Alkanes containing halogens and side groups

In structure A, the longest chain contains six carbon atoms and will, therefore, have the base name of hexane. There are three side groups, which will have the names chloro (for chlorine, Cl), methyl, and fluoro (for fluorine, F). To number the groups, consider rule 3. In structure A, there are two groups relatively close to carbon 1. The fluoro group will be bonded to carbon 2 and called "2-fluoro." The methyl group will be called "3-methyl," and the chloro group is called "5-chloro." It would be incorrect to call the groups 2-chloro, 4-methyl, and 5-fluoro since these do not correspond to the lowest possible numbering. For example, when applying rule 5, the correct IUPAC name for structure A is called "5-chloro 2-fluoro 3-methylhexane" and not "2-chloro 5-fluoro 4-methylhexane." Similarly, structure B in Figure 3 is called 2-iodo 4-methylhexane. Structure C in Figure 3 is an interesting scenario because the halogens and methyl groups are spread evenly along the six-carbon parent chain called "hexane." There are two possible IUPAC names, which are "2-bromo 5-chloro 3,4-dimethylhexane" and "5-bromo 2-chloro 3,4-dimethylhexane." The compound name containing "2-bromo" would be correct since the numbering, which goes from small to large, is consistent with the alphabetization rule. Bromo comes first in the alphabet and therefore should have the lower number between the halogens.

Carbon Chains with Multiple Functional Groups

Functional groups substituted on hydrocarbon-like or alkane-like chains will follow the IUPAC rules with a suffix used to denote the appropriate group. Figure 4 shows examples of structures containing various types of functional groups that are shown in Figure 1. Structure A contains one hydroxyl or hydroxy group substituted on a six-carbon parent chain in addition to two methyl side groups (CH_3). The hydroxyl group will take priority over the methyl groups and should be assigned a lower number. The hydroxyl and the two methyl groups are found at the carbon two, four, and five atom positions concerning the parent chain. So it's expected that the IUPAC name may have the name such as 4,5-dimethyl 2-hydroxyl hexane. However, since this compound contains an alcohol, it is no longer a simple alkane, so the suffix "ane" must be replaced with "ol," giving the name 4,5-dimethyl-2-hexanol. The term "hydroxyl" is dropped since the suffix already indicates an alcohol-type compound. The IUPAC name may substitute "2-hexanol" for "hexan-2-ol," but both names are acceptable.

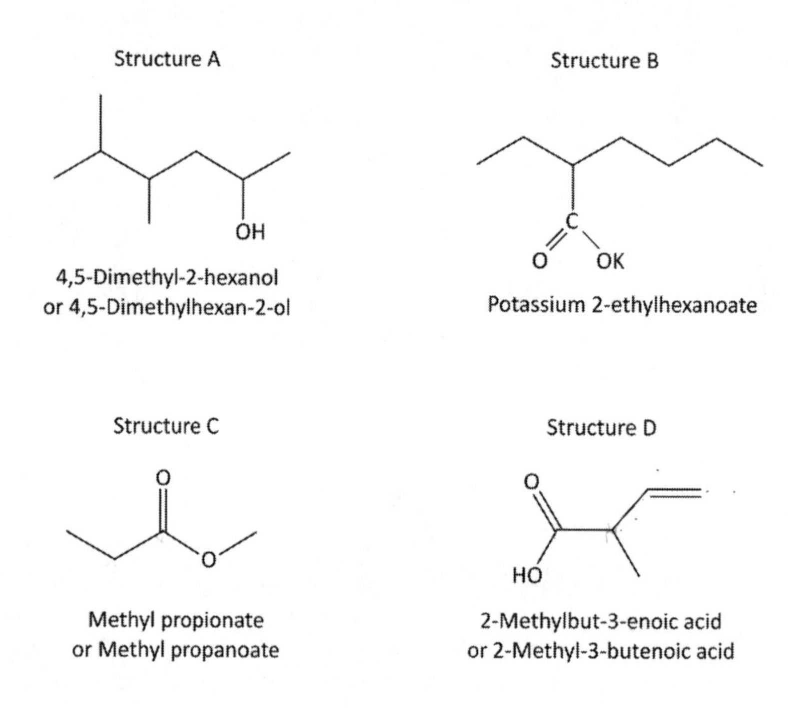

Figure 4. Naming structures with various functional groups

Structure B is an example of an alkane that contains a carboxylic acid functional group ($COOH$). However, the functional group exists in an unprotonated form as a carboxylate anion (COO^-), which is paired with a potassium cation (K^+). Instead of using "ic" in place of "ane" for the suffix, the term "oate," from carboxylate, is used. Importantly, when assigning an IUPAC name to carboxylic acids, look for the parent chain or longest continuous carbon chain that includes the acid group. In other words, the carbon atom from the functional group (COO^-) must be part of the parent chain. The numbering can increase to the left or right of the chain, whereby the carbon atom from the functional group is labeled as carbon atom one. The right side of the structure will be the longest, so the parent chain will contain six carbon atoms (hex). An ethyl group will be bonded to carbon atom two, so the IUPAC name should contain "2-ethyl." The IUPAC name may be called 2-ethyl hexanoate: hexan<u>e</u> is replaced with hexan<u>oate</u>. Since a potassium ion is shown in the structure, "potassium" must be placed in front of the IUPAC name, which is "potassium 2-ethylhexanoate." Because the carbon atom, which is from the functional group, is

carbon atom one, there is no numbering assigned (unlike, for example, 1-hexanoate). The compound is a potassium salt of 2-ethylhexanoic acid, which is the conjugate acid to the salt (contains $-\mathrm{COOH}$ instead of $-\mathrm{COOK}$).

Structure C contains an ester functional group ($\mathrm{R_1 - (CO) - O - R_2}$) and uses the same suffix group, "oate," as a carboxylate group. Ester groups include components of an alcohol ($\mathrm{H - O - R_2}$) and a carboxylic acid ($\mathrm{R_1 - (CO) - OH}$). Because a carbon atom is found in the functional group, the parent chain must include the functional group. The carbon atom from the functional group counts. The longest continuous chain consists of three carbon atoms and the name should consist of a variation of the term "propyl" or "propane." Since an ester group is present, the suffix "ane" in propane is replaced with "oate" to give propanoate. Since the functional group is attached to a methyl group ($\mathrm{R_2}$ is $\mathrm{CH_3}$), the name should include the term "methyl." Esters are named with the alkyl part first followed by the acid component (carboxylate). The IUPAC name is methyl propanoate or methyl propionate. The methyl group does not have to be assigned a number because it's directly connected to the functional group.

Structure D contains two functional groups, which include a carboxylic acid and an alkene. It's easy to mistake the structure for having three functional groups (alcohol, ketone, and an alkene). However, the hydroxyl group is bonded to a carbonyl group, which makes it a carboxylic acid. First, determine the parent chain that will include the carbon atom from the carboxylic acid. The longest continuous carbon chain consists of four carbon atoms. Therefore, the parent chain will be derived from butanoic acid: "e" from butane replaced with "oic," resulting in "butanoic." The carboxylic acid will have priority over the alkene in numbering, so the carbon atom in the acid group will be carbon atom one. The number of the alkene group will start at carbon atom three, so butanoic will be replaced with 3-butenoic. There is also a methyl side group located at carbon atom number two, which must be placed in front of the name. The correct IUPAC name is either 2-methyl-3-butenoic acid or 2-methylbut-3-enoic acid.

E and *Z* Isomers

In Figure 4, structure D shows an example of a structure in which the third carbon atom contains one substituent to the left of the double bond, $\mathrm{C_3 = C_4}$. When additional substituents are added to the left and right side of the double bond, the IUPAC naming scheme uses an "*E*" or "*Z*" to distinguish two structures with the same molecular formula. For example, in Figure 5, structure A shows a double bond at the third and fourth carbon, $\mathrm{C_3 = C_4}$, with a methyl group at the second carbon atom. The structure is similar to structure D in Figure 4 but contains a methyl group at carbon atom four, $\mathrm{C_3 = C_4 - CH_3}$. Using the IUPAC naming scheme for carboxylic acids would give 2-methyl-3-pentenoic acid. However, the name does not distinguish between structures A and B in Figure 5. In structure A, the methyl group is drawn above the double bond, whereas in structure B, it's shown below the double bond. Structures with the same connectivity but differ in the spatial arrangement are called stereoisomers. Structures A and B are called **diastereomers**, which are stereoisomers that are not mirror images of one another. The term "*Z*" is used to indicate a cis isomer and "*E*" to indicate a trans isomer. An isomer is trans or "*E*" if its substituents are on opposite sides of one another. In other words, in the illustrated structure one substituent is drawn above the double bond and another below. The isomer is cis or "*Z*" if its substituents are on the same side or below the double bond. In Figure 5, structure A, two dotted lines are drawn on both axes of the double bond to better distinguish a cis isomer from a trans isomer. There are two substituents, one in quadrant four and another in quadrant two. Quadrants two and four are opposite of one another, making the isomer trans. An "*E*" is placed in front of the IUPAC name. Structure B in Figure 5 is the same structure, but one of the substituents is now found in quadrant three. Since the substituents are located below the double bond in quadrants three and four, they are considered to be on the same side. A "*Z*" is placed in front of the IUPAC name.

Structure A

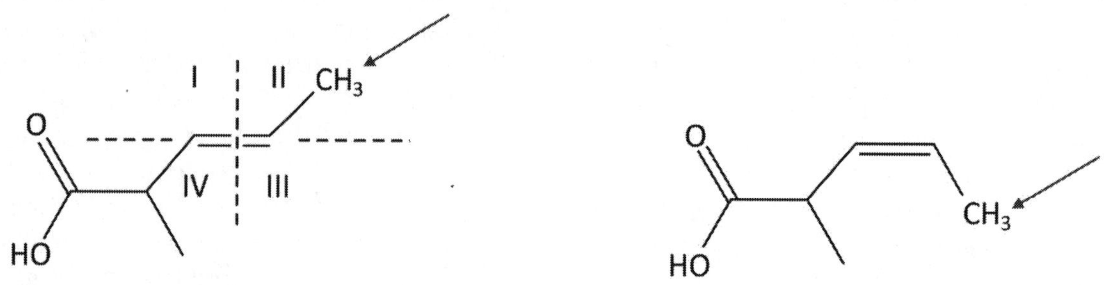

(*E*)-2-Methylpent-3-enoic acid
or (*E*)-2-Methyl-3-pentenoic acid

Structure B

(Z)-2-Methylpent-3-enoic acid
or (*Z*)-2-Methyl-3-pentenoic acid

Figure 5. Naming cis/trans stereoisomers

Aliphatic Rings

Cycloalkanes contain one or more rings of carbon atoms. The simplest class consists of single carbon rings that are unsubstituted. IUPAC names are given in Table 3.

Name	Molecular formula	Structural formula	Line formula
Cyclopropane	C_3H_6	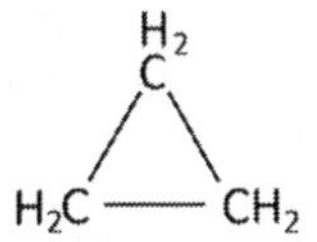 H_2C ring: CH_2–CH_2–CH_2	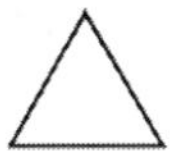 triangle
Cyclobutane	C_4H_8	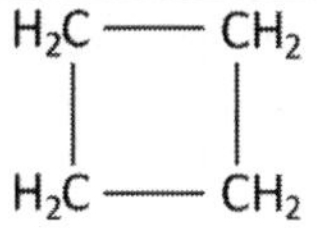 H_2C—CH_2, H_2C—CH_2	 square
Cyclopentane	C_5H_{10}	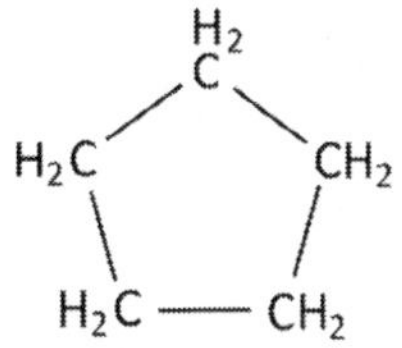 $(CH_2)_5$ ring	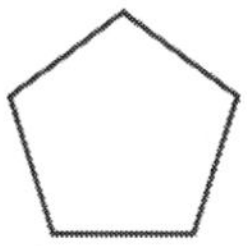 pentagon
Cyclohexane	C_6H_{12}	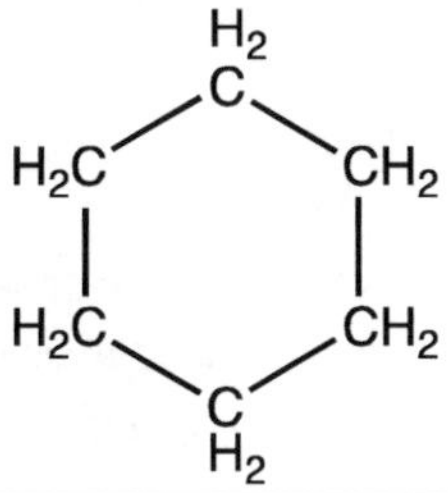 $(CH_2)_6$ ring	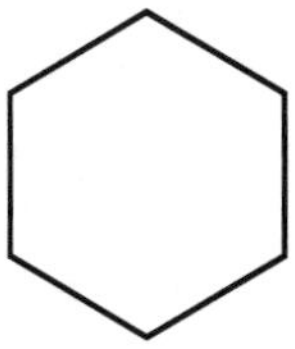 hexagon
Cycloheptane	C_7H_{14}	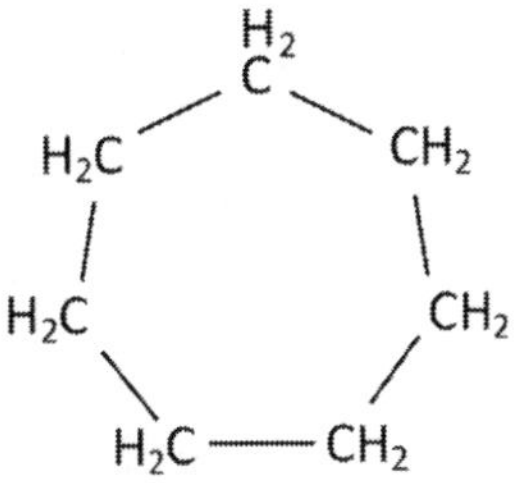 $(CH_2)_7$ ring	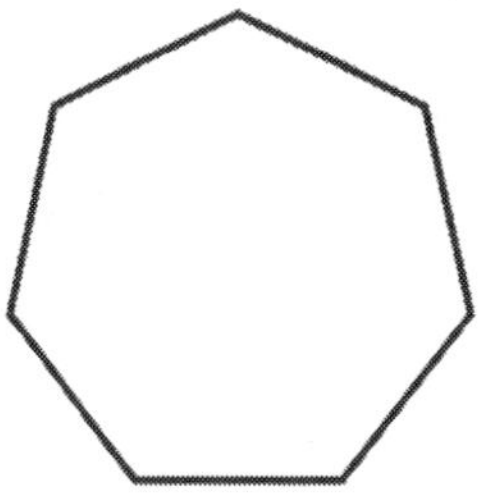 heptagon
Cycloalkane	C_nH_{2n}	$(CH_2)_n$	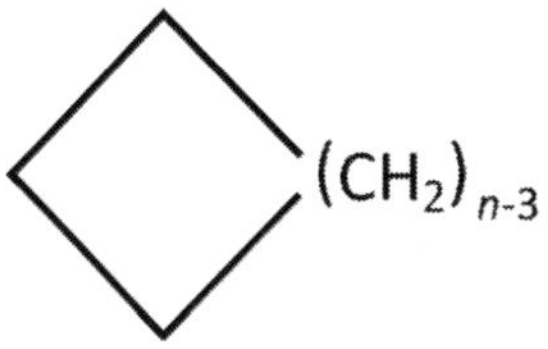 $(CH_2)_{n\text{-}3}$

Table 3. Simple Cycloalkanes

Substituted cycloalkanes have a naming convention similar to branched alkanes, but the primary difference is the numbering system, which starts at a substituted ring atom. In addition, the following aspects of the stereochemistry of cyclic compounds must be considered:

1. A location number for monosubstituted alkanes is not needed. The ring will give the root name with the substituent named as usual.

2. If the alkyl group bonded to the ring is larger, the ring can be named as a substituent.

3. If there are two substituents on the ring (for example, chlorine and fluorine), list in alphabetical order with the first substituent assigned to carbon atom one. Ring numbering for the remaining substituent must continue such that the second substituent has a lower location number.

4. When assigning the IUPAC name, all groups are listed in alphabetical order and each group is given a location number. Alcohols ($-\mathrm{OH}$) are given the highest priority with respect to carbon atom numbering and will have an "ol" ending. The prefixes di, tri, and tetra are used to designate groups of the same type but are not considered when alphabetizing. Figure 6 shows an example of a substituted cycloalkane.

HO Cl

H H

(1*S*,3*R*)-3-Chlorocyclohexanol

Figure 6. Substituted cycloalkane

The base ring contains six carbon atoms, which is called a cyclohexane. The two substituents are the hydroxyl group (ol) and a chlorine (chloro) atom. The alcohol group will have a higher priority and will be assigned to number one, while the chlorine atom will be assigned to number three. Both substituents are on the same side of the ring and will have a cis configuration. Therefore, the IUPAC name is cis-3-chlorocyclohexanol. If the hydroxyl group and chlorine atom were on opposite sides, then "trans" would be assigned to the IUPAC name. Alternatively, the stereochemistry of the compound at the stereogenic carbons can be given an IUPAC name using the Cahn-Ingold-Prelog rules.

Nomenclature of Benzene Derivatives

Benzene (C_6H_6) is an unusual compound with interesting properties (for example, carbon-carbon bonds have the same length). Benzene does not show the expected reactivity of a highly unsaturated compound, which is due to its structure resonance stabilizing effect, which makes the π (pi) electrons less reactive. Benzene is aromatic, which means that it has low hydrogen-to-carbon ratio. During the discovery of benzene and its derivatives, the compounds were found to have a characteristic fragrance. The nomenclature of substituted benzene rings is less systematic compared to alkanes and alkenes. Two systems are typically used in naming benzenes that have one substituent or are monosubstituted. In one system, some compounds have benzene as the parent name and the substituent as a prefix.

For example, Figure 7 shows some examples of combined names.

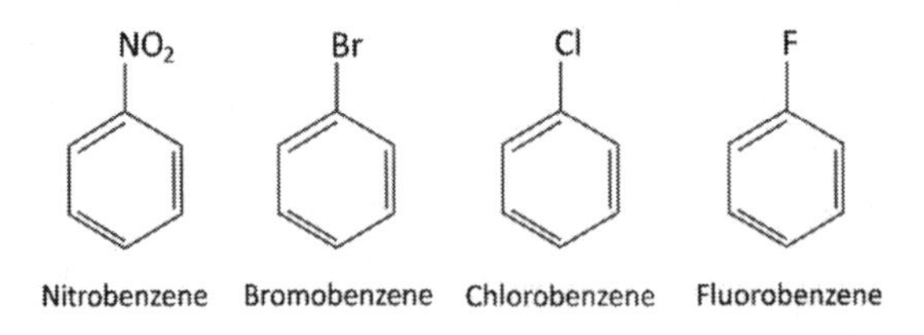

Figure 7. Combined names of some benzene compounds

In other types of compounds, the benzene ring and the substituent are used to form a new parent name. Toluene is another name for methylbenzene, aniline is the common name for aminobenzene, and phenol is called hydroxybenzene. Other compounds are listed below.

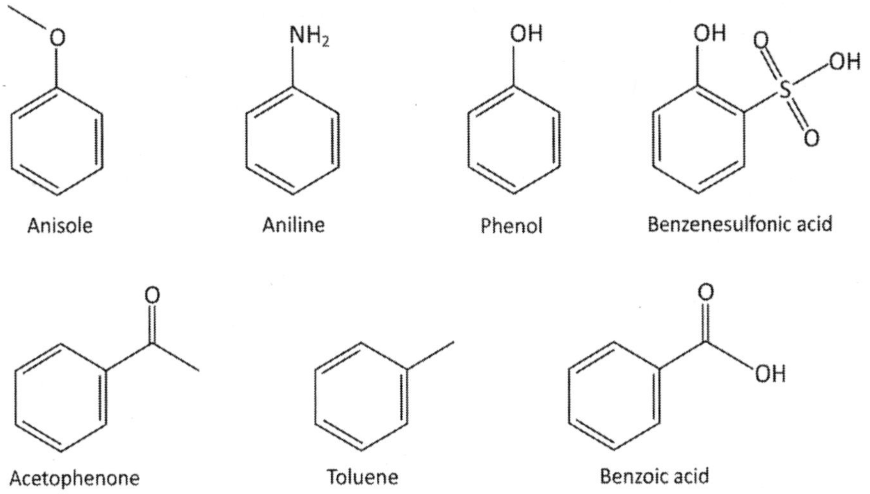

Anisole Aniline Phenol Benzenesulfonic acid

Acetophenone Toluene Benzoic acid

Figure 8. Singular names

Some typical substituents that include a benzene ring are phenyl (Ph) and benzyl (Bz). Phenyl refers to a benzene ring only $(C_6H_5 -)$, and benzyl refers to a benzene ring with a CH_2 group $(C_6H_5 - CH_2 -)$. The benzyl group is an alternate name for the phenylmethyl group. For instance, benzyl bromide is also called phenylmethyl bromide. The term "Ar" refers to any type of aromatic ring. Some benzene derivatives contain a saturated chain and a benzene ring. For example, butyl benzene is just $C_6H_5 - CH_2CH_2CH_2CH_3$ or $\mathrm{Ph} - CH_2CH_2CH_2CH_3$. Other examples include 2-phenyl-2-butene, which means that there is a benzene ring bonded to carbon atom two of the 2-butene. The compound 2-phenylhexane would have a benzene ring bonded to carbon atom two of a hexane chain.

When there are two substituents on a benzene ring, the relative position of each substituent is indicated by three prefixes: ortho (*o*-), meta (*m*-), and para (*p*-). Numbers can also be used to indicate the relative position of each group.

The difluorobenzenes and nitrobenzoic acids are shown in Figure 9.

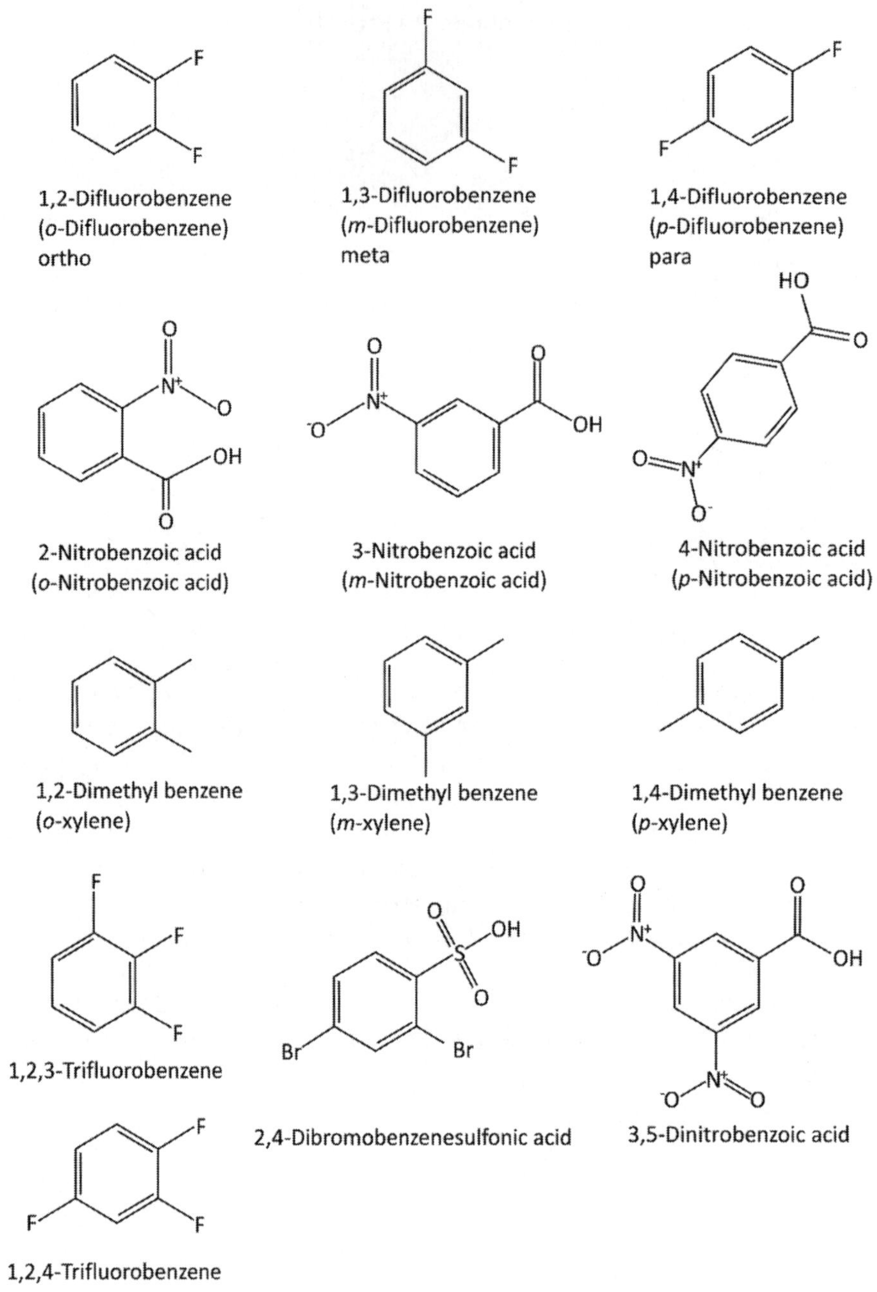

1,2-Difluorobenzene
(*o*-Difluorobenzene)
ortho

1,3-Difluorobenzene
(*m*-Difluorobenzene)
meta

1,4-Difluorobenzene
(*p*-Difluorobenzene)
para

2-Nitrobenzoic acid
(*o*-Nitrobenzoic acid)

3-Nitrobenzoic acid
(*m*-Nitrobenzoic acid)

4-Nitrobenzoic acid
(*p*-Nitrobenzoic acid)

1,2-Dimethyl benzene
(*o*-xylene)

1,3-Dimethyl benzene
(*m*-xylene)

1,4-Dimethyl benzene
(*p*-xylene)

1,2,3-Trifluorobenzene

2,4-Dibromobenzenesulfonic acid

3,5-Dinitrobenzoic acid

1,2,4-Trifluorobenzene

Figure 9. Derivatives of benzene

The dimethylbenzene derivatives are called xylenes, and each compound is distinguished by the use of o, m, and p. If there are more than two substituents on the phenyl or benzene ring, the positions will have to be indicated by numbers (not o, m, or p). The compounds 1,2,3-trifluorobenzene and 1,2,4-trifluorobenzene, shown in Figure 9 above, are some examples. The compounds are numbered with the lowest possible set of numbers with respect to the substituents. If more than two groups are present and if each is different, the substituents are listed in alphabetical order. If the substituent name is already part of the benzene ring (for example, benzoic acid), then that group will be assumed to start at

position one. For example, the compounds 3,5-dinitrobenzoic acid and 2,4-dibromobenzenesulfonic acid each have a parent name of benzoic acid and benzenesulfonic acid. In 3,5-dinitrobenzoic acid, the nitro groups are at the three and five positions with respect to the carboxylic acid group.

Structure, Hybridization, Resonance, Aromaticity

Lewis Structures

The Lewis dot diagram, named for Gilbert N. Lewis, shows the arrangement of the electrons in the outer shell and how these electrons can pair or bond with the outer shell electrons of other atoms when forming compounds. The diagram is created by writing the symbol of an element and then drawing dots to represent the outer shell of valence electrons around what would be an invisible square surrounding the symbol. The placement of the first two dots can vary; there are various schools of thinking on how to draw Lewis dot diagrams. In the given example, the first dot is placed on the top and the next dot is placed beside it, since it represents the pair of electrons in the 1s valence shell. The next dots (representing electrons) are placed on each side of the element symbol—right, bottom, left, right, bottom, left, etc.—until all the valence shell electrons are represented or the structure has eight dots (electrons), which means it is full.

Therefore, the first three electrons or dots that are placed on each remaining side correspond to valence electrons placed in the $2p_x$, $2p_y$, and $2p_z$ orbitals. Such a placement of electrons represents a low energy configuration and is consistent with Hund's rule. For example, consider the Lewis dot structure of nitrogen below.

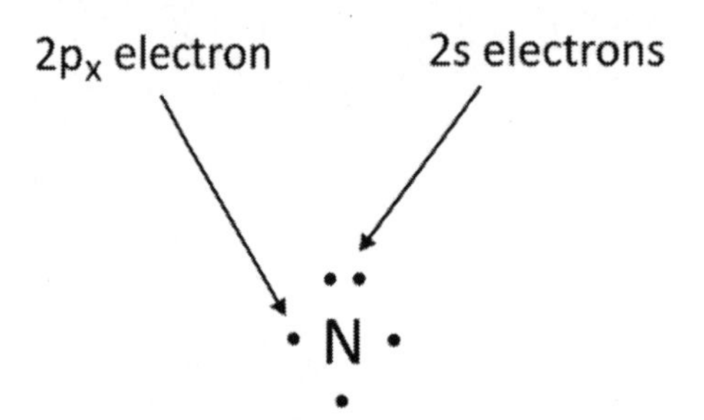

Figure 10. Lewis dot structure of nitrogen

The total number of valence electrons in nitrogen is equal to the number of dots shown and can be determined by looking at the group number of the atom. For instance, nitrogen belongs to group 5A and should have five dots placed around the atom. The Lewis method gives a more specific picture of compounds, how they are structured, and which electrons are available for bonding, sharing, and forming new compounds. For example, the compound sodium chloride is written separately, with sodium having one valence electron and chlorine having seven valence electrons. Then, combined with a total of eight electrons, it is written with two dots shared between the two elements.

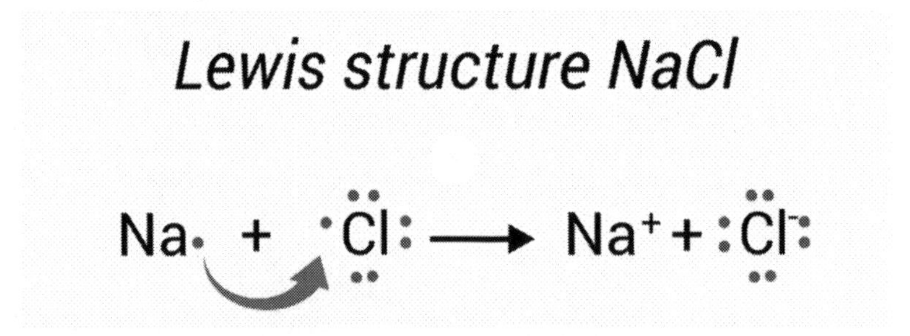

Figure 11. Lewis dot structure of sodium chloride

Lewis structures show all valence electrons and typically have an **octet** of electrons (a total of eight electrons). To determine the number of valence electrons in a compound, sum the valence electrons from each neutral atom. Then add an electron if the compound has a negative charge or subtract an electron if the compound has a positive charge. For example, the sodium atom belongs to group 1A and has one valence electron, represented by one dot. Chlorine belongs to group 7A and will have seven valence electrons. Therefore the total number of valence electrons is eight. Sodium chloride will be neutral in charge, so an electron does not need to be added or subtracted.

Using Formal Charges to Determine a Stable Lewis Structure

Formal charges (FCs) are hypothetical charges assigned to atoms within a molecule to determine the most stable Lewis structure, also called a Lewis electron-dot formula. A Lewis structure shows which valence electrons—called the **bonding electrons**—are shared between two atoms. The Lewis structure also shows the electrons that are not participating in chemical bonding; these are known as the **nonbonding electrons**. These nonbonding electrons reside on specific types of atoms; for example, nitrogen and oxygen typically contain nonbonding electrons. The equation below can be used to calculate the formal charge for an atom.

$$\text{Formal charge (FC) of an atom} = \#\text{ of valence e}^- - \left[\frac{1}{2}\#\text{ bonding e}^- + \#\text{nonbonding e}^-\right]$$

In the equation, the number of valence electrons always stays fixed for a chosen atom, which is determined from the group number in the periodic table. For instance, fluorine belongs to group 7A and contains seven valence electrons. Figure 12 shows a covalent structure of nitrogen and fluorine.

Lewis Symbols **Lewis Electron dot formula**

Nonbonding electrons

3 F + N ⟶ F N F
F

Bonding electrons

Figure 12. Lewis electron-dot formula for nitrogen trifluoride, NF_3

Each Lewis symbol for the specified atom will have a specific quantity of dots equal to the group number of that atom. The molecule is not charged, so the total number of electrons in the Lewis electron dot formula is 3×7 valence e^- F $+ 1 \times 5$ valence e^- N $= 26$ valence e^-. These dots should be placed around each atom such that the octet rule is satisfied. The formal charge for nitrogen and fluorine can be determined as follows:

$$\text{FC of nitrogen} = 5 - \left[\frac{1}{2}(6) + (2)\right] = 0$$

The number of valence, bonding, and nonbonding electrons in nitrogen is five, six, and two. Note that the number of electrons is used in the equation rather than the number of pairs of electrons. Each fluorine atom has the same bonding arrangement, so the formal charge only has to be calculated once. Fluorine has seven valence electrons, two bonding electrons, and six nonbonding electrons.

$$\text{FC of fluorine} = 7 - \left[\frac{1}{2}(2) + (6)\right] = 0$$

Suppose that you were not given a Lewis dot structure of a molecule but a list of different elements that make up a molecule, for example, two nitrogen atoms and one oxygen atom. To build the Lewis electron dot and structural formulas, consider the following general steps:

1. For chemical stability, take the least electronegative element and place it in the middle of a proposed skeletal structure. For example, for a compound with two nitrogen atoms and one oxygen atom, we would not put the oxygen in the middle of the structure.

$$\text{N} - \text{N} - \text{O (acceptable)} \qquad \text{N} - \text{O} - \text{N (not acceptable)}$$

2. Based on the skeletal structure, find the total number of electrons in a Lewis structure by first drawing the Lewis symbol for each atom. The number of required dots or electrons for each atomic symbol shown should be equal to the group number, which gives the number of valence electrons. Then sum each atom's valence electrons to get the total number of valence electrons in the molecule.

3. Use the skeletal structure and assign bonding and nonbonding electrons. When drawing the structural formula, you may use an em-dash (long dash) to represent the bonding electrons. Apply the octet rule and ensure that the structure has the correct number of valence electrons (count the dashes and nonbonding electrons). Some possible structures are listed in Figure 13.

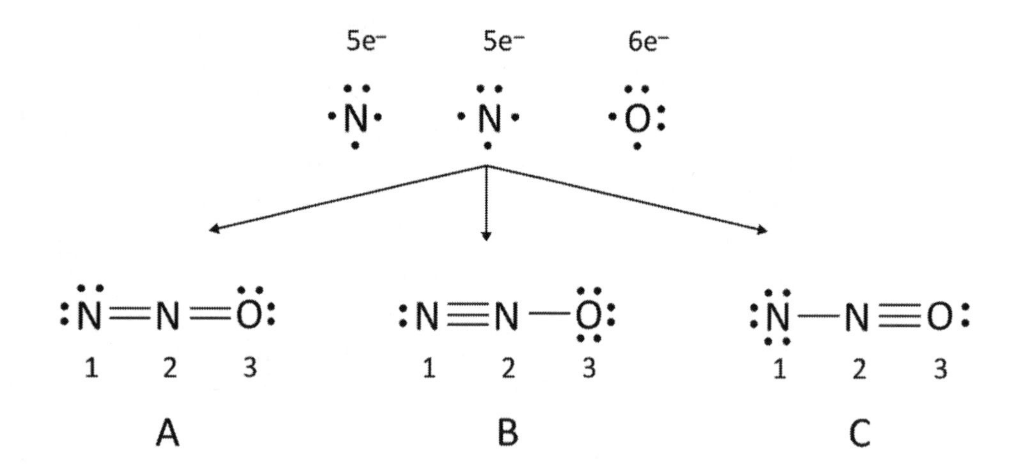

Figure 13. Possible structural formulas for the N − N − O compound

Each structural formula above shows a total of sixteen valence electrons, and each atom follows the octet rule. However, one of these structures is the lowest-energy Lewis structure.

4. To determine the most stable Lewis structure, find the formal charge for each atom in all possible structures. Atoms that have a small or zero formal charge are relatively more stable compared. For the most electronegative atoms, a negative formal charge is preferable over a positive formal charge.

The formal charges for the nitrogen and oxygen atoms, for each structure, are shown below.

Structure A

$$\text{Formal charge (FC) of N} - 1 = 5 - \left[\frac{1}{2}(4) + (4)\right] = -1$$

$$\text{Formal charge (FC) of N} - 2 = 5 - \left[\frac{1}{2}(8) + (0)\right] = +1$$

$$\text{Formal charge (FC) of O} - 3 = 6 - \left[\frac{1}{2}(4) + (4)\right] = 0$$

Structure B

$$\text{Formal charge (FC) of N} - 1 = 5 - \left[\frac{1}{2}(6) + (2)\right] = 0$$

$$\text{Formal charge (FC) of N} - 2 = 5 - \left[\frac{1}{2}(8) + (0)\right] = +1$$

$$\text{Formal charge (FC) of O} - 3 = 6 - \left[\frac{1}{2}(2) + (6)\right] = -1$$

Structure C

$$\text{Formal charge (FC) of N} - 1 = 5 - \left[\frac{1}{2}(2) + (6)\right] = -2$$

$$\text{Formal charge (FC) of N} - 2 = 5 - \left[\frac{1}{2}(8) + (0)\right] = +1$$

$$\text{Formal charge (FC) of O} - 3 = 6 - \left[\frac{1}{2}(6) + (2)\right] = +1$$

In Figure 13, each atom is labeled as 1, 2, or 3. For instance, structure A contains three atoms: an N (atom 1), an N (atom 2), and an O (atom 3). To find the formal charge for each atom, determine the number of valence, bonding, and nonbonding electrons. The valence electrons will always stay fixed and are equal to the group number for main group elements. Nitrogen (group VA) has five valence electrons, and oxygen (group 6A) has six valence electrons. In general, the most stable Lewis structure contains atoms that don't have a charge or atoms that have the smallest charge. In the Lewis structures of N_2O, the formal charge for the nitrogen and oxygen atoms change when going from single to multiple bonds. Structure B is preferable over structures A and C based on rule 4 since the oxygen atom in structure B bears a negative charge as opposed to a positive charge on nitrogen. Since oxygen is more electronegative, it will have a stronger electron pull and therefore will be partially more negatively charged.

Hybridization of Atomic Orbitals to Form Molecular Orbitals

In chemical bonding, two atomic orbitals from each atom will combine to form a low energy molecular orbital. Consider the combination of a hydrogen atomic orbital ($1s^2$) and an orbital belonging to the carbon atom, for example, methane, $CH_3 - H$. The carbon atom has the electron configuration of

$1s^22s^22p^2$, but the valence electrons are located in the 2s and 2p atomic orbitals. There are three 2p atomic orbitals and one 2s atomic orbital in carbon, which will combine to form a set of four hybrid atomic orbitals called sp^3 $(s + p + p + p)$. The hybridization allows the atomic orbitals of hydrogen and the hybrid orbitals of carbon to form four molecular orbitals oriented toward the corners of a tetrahedron, thereby minimizing repulsion. The angle between each molecular orbital in methane is about 109.5 degrees. The chemical bond or molecular orbital is called a sigma bond (sp^3–1s). Methane has four single bonds (sp^3–1s). Ethane (CH_3CH_3) contains seven sigma bonds or sp^3–1s type molecular orbitals. Figure 14 the different bond types of various hydrocarbons that result from the hybridization of carbons atomic orbitals. Each type of atomic orbital will overlap to a certain extent with another. As carbon forms more bonds, the hybridization will change, and the molecular geometry will be different.

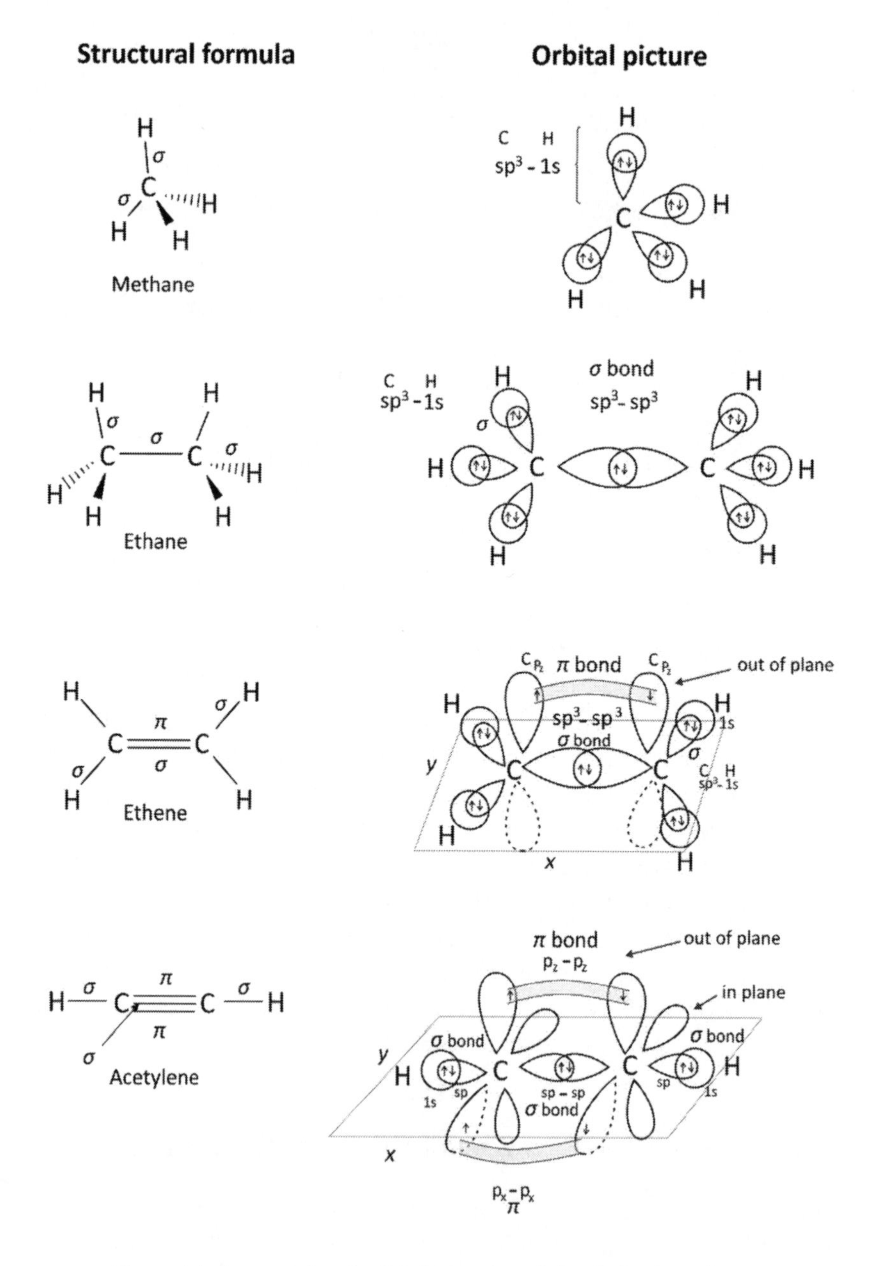

Figure 14. Structural and orbital pictures of simple hydrocarbons

An up and down arrow in the overlapping sections indicates two electrons with opposite spin. In the carbon atom, one 2s and two 2p atomic orbitals can also combine to form three sp^2 hybrid orbitals $(s + p + p)$ with one free 2p atomic orbital. Two carbon atoms, each with one sp^2 hybrid orbital, can combine to create an sp^2–sp^2 molecular orbital. The orbital picture of ethene shows that the combination of an sp^2 with a 1s or sp^2 atomic orbital will form a direct overlap. The chemical bond is also called a sigma bond since chemical bonding is direct. Each carbon atom in ethene will have a free 2p atomic orbital. The orbitals will combine into a 2p–2p molecular orbital called a pi bond, which is out-of-plane or perpendicular to the sigma bonds.

The carbon atoms in ethene, therefore, form a double bond. However, sigma bonds are stronger or require more energy to break compared to the weaker pi bond. For each carbon atom in ethene, the remaining two sp^2 atomic orbitals can combine with the 1s atomic orbitals of hydrogen, which form sp^2–1s molecular orbitals or single sigma bonds. All sigma bonds in ethene are in plane. The molecular geometry about the carbon atom will be trigonal planar with angles of 120° between each bond. The last type of hybridization in the carbon atom is called an "sp" hybridization and occurs when the carbon 2s and one 2p atomic orbital combine to form two sp atomic orbitals $(s + p)$.

In acetylene, both carbon atoms will form an sp–1s molecular orbital with hydrogen and an sp-sp molecular orbital with each other. Both molecular orbitals form direct overlaps and are also called sigma bonds. The resulting sp hybridization will also have two free 2p atomic orbitals, so two additional 2p–2p molecular orbitals or pi bonds can result. However, only one of the 2p–2p molecular orbitals will be in plane with the other sigma bonds, with the other 2p–2p molecular orbital out-of-plane. Therefore, the carbon atoms in acetylene form a triple bond, for example, two pi and one sigma bond). Acetylene has a linear molecular geometry about each carbon atom with angles of 180° between each sigma bond. Other atoms such as nitrogen and oxygen can adopt similar hybridizations. For example, ammonia, NH_3, can form sp^3 hybrid orbitals and form three sp^3–1s molecular orbitals or $N - H$ sigma bonds. The lone pair in nitrogen will occupy the remaining sp^3 orbital. The oxygen and carbon atom in formaldehyde (CH_2O) will both have sp^2 hybridization.

Resonance: Electron Delocalization

Depending on the molecule or ion, there may be multiple Lewis structures whereby each atom has an octet. For example, the charge on an atom can move from one atom to another. In other words, the bonding or nonbonding electrons may move around or delocalize from one atom to another within that same structure. For example, consider the following organic compound $(R - (CO) - C - (CO) - R)$ in

Figure 15, which shows the delocalization of electrons or **delocalized bonding** along the $O-C-C-C-O$ chain.

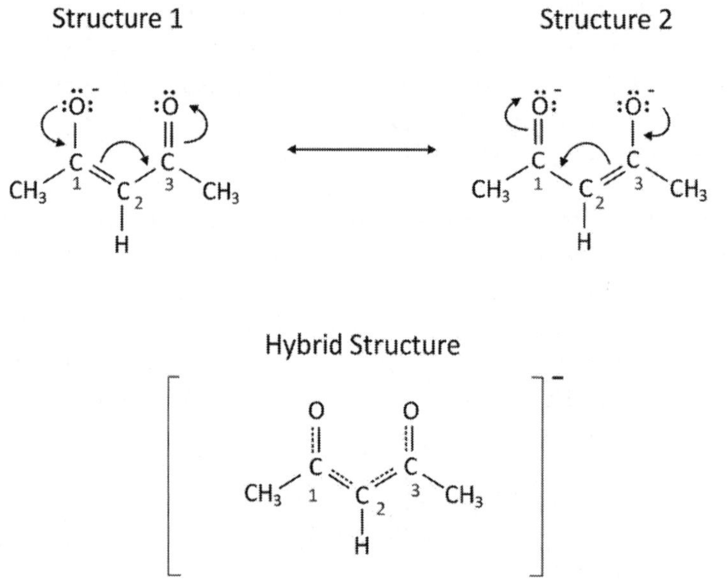

Structure 1

Structure 2

Hybrid Structure

Figure 15. Delocalization of electrons between the O-C-C-C-O atoms

The acid anhydride shown in Figure 15 has two possible structures. The curved double-headed arrows indicate the movement of a bonding pair that is equivalent to two electrons. The double-headed arrow connects the two possible structures or **resonance structures,** which are the possible Lewis dot-structures or structural formulas involved in delocalized bonding. For example, in the first structure, the lone pair of electrons from the O^- atom are transferred to carbon atom 1, forming a carbonyl double bond. Simultaneously, the pi bond or electron pair in the adjacent $C_1 = C_2$ bond moves to the single $C_2 - C_3$ bond, which becomes a $C_2 = C_3$ bond (structure 2). Lastly, a bonding electron pair in carbon atom 3's carboxy bond moves to the oxygen atom as a nonbonding pair, $C_3 - O^-$. Electron delocalization will occur again in a concerted but reverse fashion. The actual structure is a composite of both resonance structures, which are just theoretical descriptions that show one possible electronic structure of a molecule. Resonance structures are not the actual molecular structures but exist as one **hybrid** or **true structure**, which is a fusion or combination of all possible resonance structures.

Aromaticity

Molecules tend to be more stable if they exist as cyclic rings (for example, cyclohexane), contain a planar geometry, or have a continuous π (pi) system where electron delocalization can occur. In particular, aromatic compounds tend to have pi-electron delocalization within a ring system, making them unusually stable. The term "aromatic" was used traditionally to describe the fragrances of certain natural substances such as vanilla beans or cinnamon bark. Vanillin is an aromatic organic compound, $(C_8H_8O_3)$, extracted from vanilla beans, that contains a phenolic ring with an aldehyde, ether, and hydroxyl functional group.

Aromatic compounds tend to have double bonds, a low hydrogen-to-carbon ratio, and more chemical stability compared to alkenes. The stability can be attributed to the π system whereby electron

delocalization can occur. For a compound to be considered aromatic, the following factors must be satisfied.

(1). The molecule must contain a cycle of sp^2 hybridized atoms (for example, C, N). Recall that the overlapping of two "p" orbitals, parallel to one another, makes up the pi bond or pi molecular orbital. A cycle or pi array means there will be several pi molecular orbitals in a conjugated fashion (for example, $C-C=C-C=C-$).
(2). The number of electrons in the π array within the molecule will be equal to $4n+2$, where n is zero or some integer ($n = 0, 1, 2, 3...$). This rule is referred to as **Hückel's rule**. Benzene contains 6 π electrons and is aromatic since $4n+2=6$ or $4(1)+2=6$ when $n=1$.

Aromatic systems may be ions such as carbocations or carbanions, which contain a positive or negative charge on one of the carbon atoms. The ring system does not have to be a six-membered ring (hexagon), but can be a five or even three-membered ring. Figure 16 shows several examples of compounds that follow the aromaticity rules.

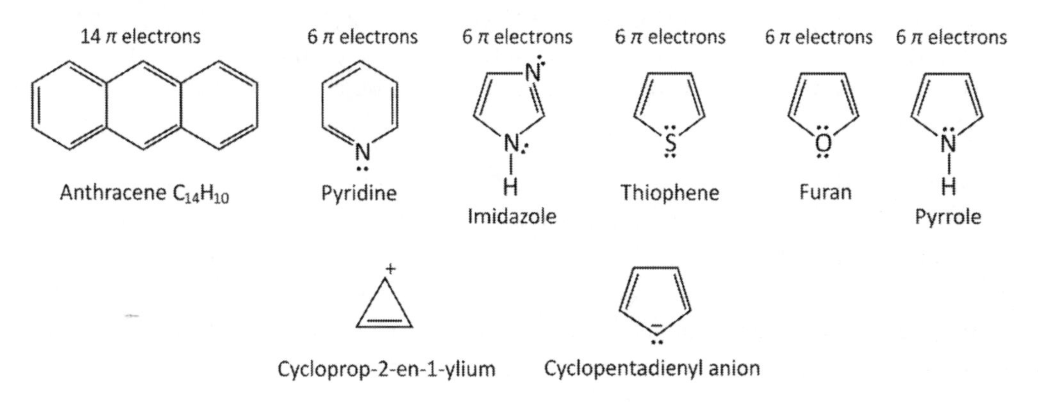

Figure 16. Examples of heterocyclic aromatic compounds

Anthracene is a compound that contains three fused hexagonal rings with a total of 14 π electrons. Based on Hückel's rule, $4n+2=14$, so $n=3$ since $4(3)+2=14$, which makes anthracene aromatic. Some heterocyclic aromatic compounds may have lone pairs on the heteroatoms, which may or may not contribute to the π electrons system. For instance, pyridine is similar to benzene and has 6 π electrons but with one nitrogen atom, $4n+2=6, n=1$. The one-electron pair in pyridine is not involved or part of the π electron system. However, the nitrogen atom in pyridine may bond to hydrogen without disrupting the π system. Some of the five-membered heterocyclic rings (containing N, S, and O) may have lone pairs that are part of the π system. Imidazole includes two nitrogen atoms that each have a lone pair of electrons. The lone pair found on the nitrogen bonded to hydrogen will contribute to the π system, but the lone pair on the other nitrogen atom will not. Therefore, imidazole will be aromatic since it has 6 π electrons: $4n+2=6, n=1$. Most five-membered rings shown in Figure 16 tend to have a 6 π electron system, which may be created by the donation of a lone pair from one atom. Even though pyridine contains a lone pair from the nitrogen atom, the electron pairs do not need to be donated since a 6 π electron system already exists. In pyridine, one of the 2p atomic orbitals from nitrogen is combined with a 2p atomic orbital from the adjacent carbon atom, forming a π molecular orbital.

In contrast, imidazole contains one sp^3 hybridized carbon atom and an sp^2 hybridized atom (like pyridine). If the sp^3 nitrogen atom rehybridizes as an sp^2 hybridized nitrogen atom, the 2p orbital carrying the lone pair can then combine with a neighboring 2p carbon orbital to form a π molecular orbital. Atoms containing lone pairs can rehybridize from sp^3 to sp^2 such that a new π bond can form, which provides more stability to the ring structure. For example, thiophene contains a sulfur atom that has two lone pairs in which one lone pair will contribute to the π system providing a total of 6 π electrons. Furan like thiophene will also have a 6 π electron since one lone pair from oxygen is donated to the π system. Pyrrole has a 6 π system and a contains a nitrogen atom that gives its lone pair to the aromatic π conjugated system, like imidazole. Pyrrole is aromatic since $4n + 2 = 6$ where $n = 1$.

In Figure 16, cycloprop-2-en-1-ylium (cyclopropene cation) and cyclopentadienyl anion are examples of a carbocation and a carbanion. The three-ring structure is a 2 π electron system ($4n + 2 = 2$, where $n = 0$) and contains one positive charge on an sp^2 hybridized carbon atom. In other words, there is a 2p orbital from the positively charged carbon atom that can accept an electron pair. The resonance structure can be written three different ways, whereby the positively charged carbon will be opposite of the π bond.

The carbanion contains a lone pair within a 2p orbital on a negatively charged sp^2 hybridized carbon atom. The carbon atom can form a π molecular orbital by bonding to an adjacent 2p carbon orbital, thereby donating its lone pair to the π system. As electron delocalization occurs, another carbon atom will accept a lone pair and become negatively charged. The carbanion is a 6 π electron system since $4n + 2 = 6$, where $n = 1$.

Some compounds contain a conjugated ring system but are antiaromatic, whereby the π system contains pi electrons ($n = 1,2,3...$). Antiaromatic compounds tend to be less stable or more reactive. The cylcopropene or cyclopropenyl anion, a carbanion, is an example of an antiaromatic compound. Each carbon atom in the cyclopropenyl anion is sp^2 hybridized, but there are 4 π electrons ($4n = 4, n = 1$), which makes it antiaromatic. The carbon atom bears a negative charge and holds the lone pair electron in the 2p orbital, which contributes to the π system. Figure 17 shows some examples of other antiaromatic compounds.

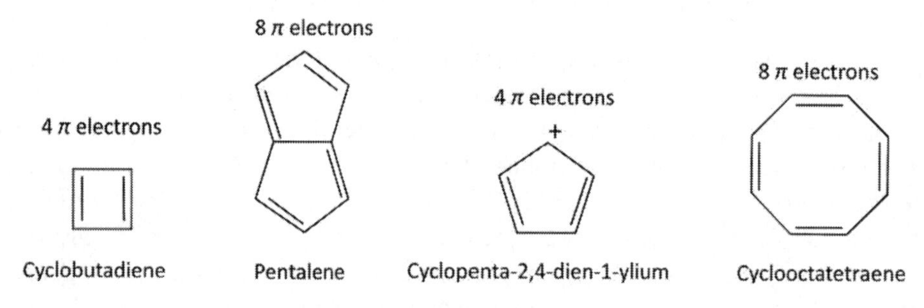

Figure 17. Antiaromatic compounds that follow the $4n$ rule

Compounds that do not follow the aromatic $(4n + 2)$ or antiaromatic $(4n)$ criteria are considered nonaromatic. Cyclopropene, shown in Figure 18, is nonaromatic because it contains one sp^3 hybridized carbon atom that cannot form a π bond. Nonaromatic compounds are not planar or flat since the sp^3 hybridized carbon is tetrahedral with respect to its bonded atoms.

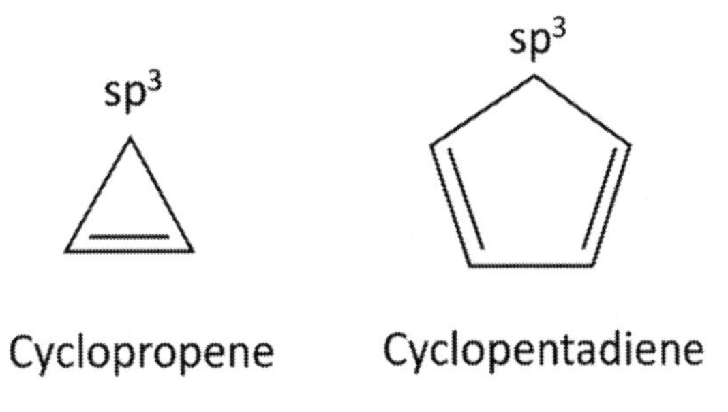

Figure 18. Nonaromatic compounds

Acids and Bases

Acid-Base Reactions

Understanding the acidic and basic properties of organic compounds, with various functional groups, is essential to understanding how an organic reaction occurs. Adding an acid or base (hydrochloric acid (HCl), pyridine, etc.) to a solution will change the proton/hydronium (H^+) or hydroxide (OH^-) ion concentration in the solution. In general, an **acid** can be described as a substance that increases the concentration of H^+ ions when it is dissolved in water. A **base** is a substance that increases the concentration of OH^- ions when it is dissolved in water. An important definition of an acid or base comes from the Brønsted-Lowry and Lewis theories.

A Brønsted-Lowry acid is a species that donates or loses a proton, and a **Brønsted-Lowry base** is a species that will accept a proton. The addition of HCl or hydrogen chloride gas to water creates an acidic solution. HCl is a strong acid that acts as a Brønsted-Lowry acid because it donates its proton to a water molecule. Water is the Brønsted-Lowry base that removes the proton from HCl. The reaction is shown in Figure 19 below.

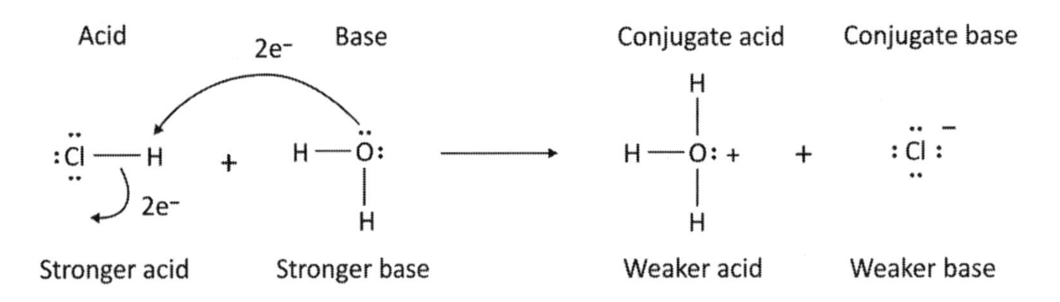

Figure 19. Acid-base reaction

Hydronium ion (H_3O^+) is the **conjugate acid** or molecule that forms when a base (e.g., water) accepts a proton. The chloride ion is the **conjugate base** or species that results when the acid (e.g., HCl) loses its proton. Water is typically present in acid-base reactions or aqueous solutions and can act as a base to form its conjugate acid (H_3O^+). Alternatively, water may act as an acid to form its conjugate base, hydroxide ion (OH^-). A **Lewis acid** is defined as an electron-pair acceptor, and a **Lewis base** is an electron-pair donor. The Lewis theory is a broader definition of acids and bases and includes all Brønsted-Lowry reactions. For example, consider the reaction of ammonia and aluminum chloride in Figure 20 below.

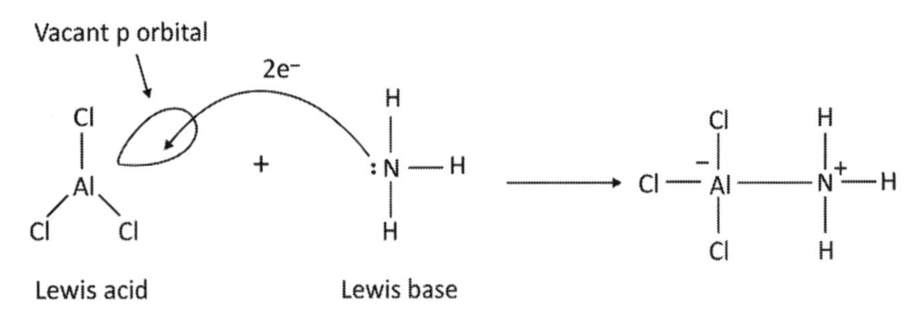

Figure 20. Lewis acid-base reaction

Ammonia acts as a Lewis base because it donates its electron pair to the Lewis acid, aluminum chloride. The reactivity of two compounds results from the attraction of two oppositely charged species. Ammonia contains a lone pair of electrons that is electron-rich (polarized slightly negative, $\delta -$), and aluminum chloride contains an electron-deficient region (polarized slightly positive, $\delta +$) that will be attracted to the lone electron pair on nitrogen. The differences in electron densities or polarization will result in a reaction where the nonbonding electron pair of ammonia attacks the aluminum atom, filling its valence p shell. Aluminum will carry a formal negative charge, and the nitrogen atom will have a formal positive charge.

Heterolysis in Carbon Bonds: Carbanions and Carbocations

Heterolysis refers to unsymmetrical bond breaking in a carbon bond, which will result in an electron pair that will move to one of the atoms that make up the chemical bond (e.g., $\mathrm{R - C_1 - C_2 - R'}$). One of the carbon atoms ($\mathrm{C_1}$ or $\mathrm{C_2}$) will form a short-lived and highly reactive intermediate ion called a *carbanion* or a *carbocation*. **Carbanions** will form when the two electrons reside on the carbon atom, making it negatively charged (e.g., $\mathrm{R - C_1{:}^-}$). **Carbocations** will form when the two shared electrons move to the other atom (e.g., $\mathrm{R' - C_2{}^+}$), resulting in an ion with a positive charge at the carbon atom.

$$\mathrm{R - C_1 - C_2 - R'} \xrightarrow{2e^-} \mathrm{R - C_1{:}^-} + \mathrm{{}^+C_2 - R'}$$

Unsymmetrical bond breaking — Carbanion — Carbocation

Figure 21. Heterolytic bond breakage

Carbocations are Lewis acids and are electron because they have six electrons in their valence shell. Carbocations are electron-seeking reagents called **electrophiles** and will react to attain a stable valence shell. Protons ($\mathrm{H^+}$) are examples of Lewis acids and electrophiles. In contrast, carbanions are **nucleophiles** or Lewis bases because they will seek a positive center or proton, which will allow their electron pair to be donated, thereby neutralizing the negative charge. In an acid-base reaction, curved arrows are used to show the direction of electron flow. The curved arrow starts at the covalent bond or lone electron pair (high electron density area) and points to the area that is electron-deficient (positive charge). A half-arrow indicates the transfer of one electron.

The pH Scale

The term **pH** refers to the power or potential of hydrogen atoms and is used as a scale for a substance's acidity. In chemistry, pH represents the hydrogen ion concentration (written as $[\mathrm{H^+}]$) in an aqueous, or watery, solution. The hydrogen ion concentration, $[\mathrm{H^+}]$, is measured in moles of $\mathrm{H^+}$ per liter of solution.

The **pH scale** is a logarithmic scale used to quantify how acidic or basic a substance is. The pH for a solution is the negative logarithm of its hydrogen ion concentration: $\mathrm{pH} = -\log[\mathrm{H}^+]$. A one-unit change in pH correlates with a ten-fold change in the hydrogen ion concentration. The pH scale typically ranges from zero to 14, although it is possible to have pH values outside of this range. Pure water has a pH of 7, which is considered **neutral**. Any values of pH that are less than 7 are considered **acidic**, while pH values greater than 7 are considered **basic**, or **alkaline**.

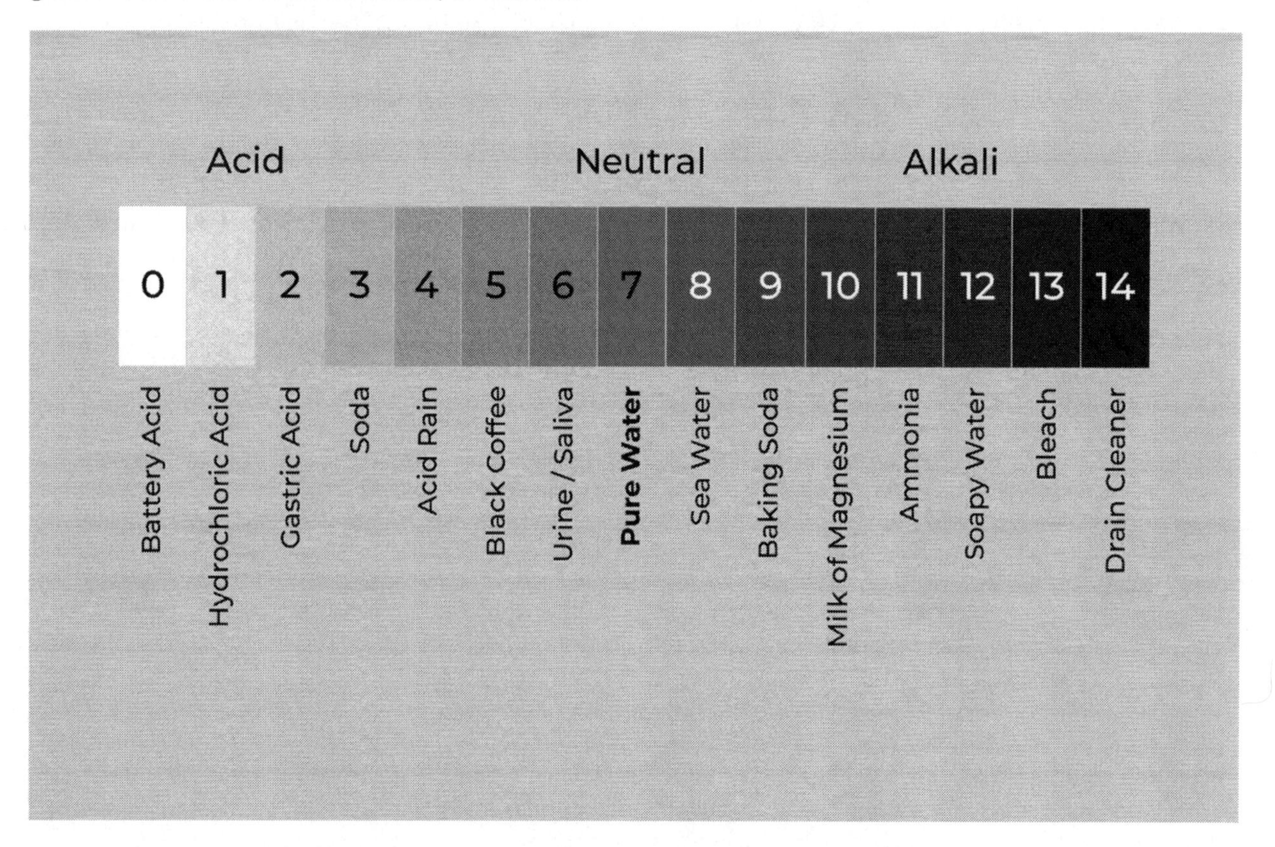

Figure 22. The pH scale showing pH values of common substances

An aqueous acid or base will have a certain pH, which is based on its hydronium or hydroxide concentration in water or some organic solvent, such as diethyl ether (Et_2O), tetrahydrofuran (THF), and dimethylformamide (DMF).

The pH of a solution will change the bonding structure of compound and the conformation of proteins in a biological system. For instance, suppose an amino acid (alanine [Ala]) was dissolved in a solution with a pH of 13. Which of the structures (A-D) in Figure 23 below would be the predominate species?

A

$H_2N—CH(CH_3)—C(=O)—O^-$

B

$H_3N^+—CH(CH_3)—C(=O)—O^-$

C

$H_3N^+—CH(CH_3)—C(=O)—OH$

D

$H_2N—CH(CH_3)—C(=O)—OH$

Figure 23. pH and chemical structure

The carboxylic acid $(-\mathrm{COOH})$ and amino group $(\mathrm{R}-\mathrm{NH_2})$ are the two main functional groups on the amino acid. The carboxylic acid group exists in equilibrium between a protonated and unprotonated form: $-\mathrm{COOH}$ and $-\mathrm{COO^-}$. Similarly, the amino group can have two forms: $-\mathrm{NH_3}^+$ and $-\mathrm{NH_2}$. If the solution is acidic with a $\mathrm{pH} < 7$, the hydronium concentration will be relatively greater than the hydroxide ion concentration $([\mathrm{H^+}] > [\mathrm{OH^-}])$. Consequently, the carboxylic acid and amino groups will be protonated due to the relatively high concentration of $\mathrm{H^+}$, which would react with the carboxylate or amino group. On the other hand, if the $\mathrm{pH} > 7$, then $[\mathrm{OH^-}] > [\mathrm{H^+}]$, and the acid and amino group will exist in an unprotonated form because $\mathrm{OH^-}$ removes a proton from each functional group. Structure A would be the correct choice because both functional groups are deprotonated, indicating that this species would be most present in a basic solution.

Predicting Acid-Base Strength: K_a and $\mathrm{p}K_\mathrm{a}$

Acids and bases are characterized as strong, weak, or somewhere in between. Strong acids and bases completely or almost completely ionize in an aqueous solution. The chemical reaction is driven completely forward (→), to the right side of the equation, where the acidic or basic ions are formed. Weak acids and bases do not completely disassociate in an aqueous solution. They only partially ionize, and the solution becomes a mixture of the acid or base, water, and the acidic or basic ions. For the dissociation of an acid (HA) in an aqueous solution, the equilibrium constant (K_{eq}) and **acidity constant** can be (K_a) expressed as:

$$HA(aq) + H_2O(l) \rightleftarrows A^-(aq) + H_3O^+(aq)$$

$$K_a = K_{eq}[H_2O] = \frac{[A^-][H_3O^+]}{[HA]}$$

The term A is the unprotonated molecule of HA. The expression will apply mainly to weak acids that partially dissociate or ionize in water. For example, acetic acid is a weak acid and has the following acidity constant expression:

$$CH_3COOH(aq) + H_2O(l) \rightleftarrows CH_3COO^-(aq) + H_3O^+(aq)$$

$$K_a = \frac{[CH_3COO^-][H_3O^+]}{[CH_3COOH]}$$

The larger the value of K_a, the stronger the acid, and the smaller the value of K_a, the weaker the acid. Strong acids will typically have values of K_a greater than 10, which means that the acid, for the most part, will completely dissociate in water. The negative logarithm of K_a or pK_a ($pK_a = -\log(K_a)$) is also used to relate acid strength. There is an inverse relationship between the magnitude of pK_a and its strength. For instance, the stronger the acid, the smaller the value of pK_a. Table 1 lists acids with their associated pK_a values and conjugate bases. Carboxylic acids typically have pK_a values between 3 and 5, and alcohols have values between 15 and 18.

Strongest Acid	Acid	pK_a	Conjugate Base	Weakest Base
↑	$HSbF_6$	< -12	SbF_6^-	↓
	HI	-10	I^-	
	H_2SO_4	-9	HSO_4^-	
	HBr	-9	Br^-	
	HCl	-7	Cl^-	
	$C_6H_5-SO_3H$	-6.5	$C_6H_5-SO_3^-$	
	$(CH_3)_2O^+H$	-3.8	$(CH_3)_2O$	
	$(CH_3)_2C=O^+H$	-2.9	$(CH_3)_2C=O$	
	$CH_3O^+H_2$	-2.5	CH_3OH	
	H_3O^+	-1.74	H_2O	
	HNO_3	-1.4	NO_3^-	
	CF_3CO_2H	0.18	$CF_3CO_2^-$	
	HF	3.2	F^-	
	H_2CO_3	3.7	HCO_3^-	
	CH_3COOH	4.75	CH_3COO^-	
	$CH_3COC\mathbf{H_2}COCH_3$	9.0	$CH_3COC^-\mathbf{H}COCH_3$	
	NH_4^+	9.2	NH_3	
	C_6H_5-OH	9.9	$C_6H_5-O^-$	
	HCO_3^-	10.2	CO_3^{2-}	
	$CH_3NH_3^+$	10.6	CH_3NH_2	
	H_2O	15.7	OH^-	
	CH_3CH_2-OH	16	$CH_3CH_2-O^-$	
	$(CH_3)_3COH$	18	$(CH_3)_3CO^-$	
	CH_3COCH_3	19.2	$CH_3COCH_2^-$	
	$HC\equiv CH$	25	$HC\equiv C^-$	
	H_2	35	H^-	
	NH_3	38	NH_2^-	
	$CH_2=CH_2$	44	$CH_2=CH^-$	
Weakest acid	CH_3CH_3	50	$CH_3CH_2^-$	Strongest base

Table 4. Acid strength and conjugate bases

Table 4 shows a relationship between the strength of an acid and its conjugate base. In general, the stronger the acid, the weaker the conjugate base. The stronger the base, the larger the pK_a of the conjugate acid and the weaker the conjugate acid. Acid-base reactions favor the formation of the weaker acid and weaker base, which is determined by the equilibrium position. Chemical reactions under equilibrium control will favor the most thermodynamically stable or lowest energy (potential energy) species. To predict a chemical reaction, determine the stronger acid and base, which will both react to form the weaker acid and base. For example, the reaction of aniline ($C_6H_5-NH_2$, $pK_a = 4.87$) with hydronium ion (H_3O^+, $pK_a = -1.74$) will proceed primarily in one direction ($\rightarrow$) toward the weaker acid ($C_6H_5-NH_3{}^+$, $pK_a = 11.2$) and weaker base, water (H_2O, $pK_a = 15.7$).

Chemical Structure and Acidity Relationship: Inductive Effects, Resonance, and Hybridization

Periodic Trends

The strength of a chemical bond to hydrogen within a compound in a vertical column of the periodic table will have a dominating effect. For instance, hydrogen halides will increase in acidity going down a vertical column:

$$\Rightarrow \text{increasing acidity}$$

$$\mathrm{H-F}\ (\mathrm{p}K_\mathrm{a} = 3.2) < \mathrm{H-Cl}\ (\mathrm{p}K_\mathrm{a} = -7) < \mathrm{H-Br}\ (\mathrm{p}K_\mathrm{a} = -9) < \mathrm{H-I}\ (\mathrm{p}K_\mathrm{a} = -10)$$

The strongest acid is $\mathrm{H-I}$ because the valence shell is farther away from the nucleus of the atom, which decreases the effective nuclear charge or pull. The conjugate bases are all very weak, and the basicity decreases as follows:

$$\Leftarrow \text{increasing basicity}$$

$$\mathrm{F^-} > \mathrm{Cl^-} > \mathrm{Br^-} > \mathrm{I^-}$$

The fluoride ion is the strongest conjugate base. Other trends in other vertical columns can be seen for group 6 elements that contain hydrogen:

$$\Rightarrow \text{increasing acidity}$$

$$\mathrm{H_2O} < \mathrm{H_2S} < \mathrm{H_2Se}$$

The strongest acid is $\mathrm{H_2Se}$ and contains the weakest bond, $\mathrm{Se-H}$. For the conjugate bases:

$$\Leftarrow \text{increasing basicity}$$

$$\mathrm{OH^-} > \mathrm{SH^-} > \mathrm{SeH^-}$$

For compounds in a horizontal row, the acidity will increase, going from left to right on the periodic table. The dominant factor is electronegativity, which will affect acidity by changing the polarity of the bond to the proton and the relative stability of the conjugate base anion. Both effects can be seen when looking at the acidities of some first-row element hydrides.

$$\Rightarrow \text{increasing acidity}$$

$$\mathrm{H_3}\overset{\delta-}{\overset{\frown}{\mathrm{C}}} - \overset{\delta+}{\overset{\frown}{\mathrm{H}}} < \mathrm{H_2}\overset{\delta-}{\overset{\frown}{\mathrm{N}}} - \overset{\delta+}{\overset{\frown}{\mathrm{H}}} < \mathrm{H}\overset{\delta-}{\overset{\frown}{\mathrm{O}}} - \overset{\delta+}{\overset{\frown}{\mathrm{H}}} < \overset{\delta-}{\overset{\frown}{\mathrm{F}}} - \overset{\delta+}{\overset{\frown}{\mathrm{H}}}$$

Fluorine is the most electronegative element; therefore, the $\mathrm{H-F}$ bond will have the greatest polarization. The hydrogen atom will dissociate more easily compared to the other hydrides. The conjugate base, the fluoride ion ($\mathrm{F^-}$), will be the weakest and will accommodate the negative charge more readily than the hydroxide ion ($\mathrm{OH^-}$), the amide ion ($\mathrm{H_2N^-}$), and the methanide ion ($\mathrm{CH_3}^-$). The methanide ion is the least stable anion because carbon is the least electronegative element, making it the strongest base, followed by the amide ion.

Induction and Resonance

Electronic induction (electronegativity) and resonance (electron delocalization) are the two main factors that will influence molecular stability. Inductive effects will be due to electron-withdrawing substituents on an acid or base. Stronger acids will contain more electron-withdrawing atoms compared to weaker acids. To determine which species is strong or weak, examine the substituents for possible induction and resonance effects.

A: $F_2HC-CH_2-C(=O)-OH$

3,3-Difluoropropanoic acid

B: $F-CH(F)-C(=O)-OH$

C: $Cl-CH(Cl)-C(=O)-OH$

D: $H-CH(H)-C(=O)-OH$

Acetic acid
$pK_a = 4.76$

Figure 24. Induction effects

In Figure 23, structure B will be the strongest acid because it contains fluorine, the most electronegative element. The electron-attracting nature of fluorine will create a pull, or electron-withdrawing, effect called an **inductive effect** through the bonds of the molecule. The closer an atom is to fluorine, the greater the pull. Structure D will be the weakest acid because the fluorine groups are replaced with hydrogens. The weaker the acid, the larger the pK_a. The order of acid strength is B > C > A > D. Structure A also has two halogens, but the inductive effect decreases with distance.

Electron delocalization describes how, shown by arrows, which can result in two or more Lewis or **resonance structures** that each represent one bonding arrangement. The greater the number of resonance structures, the greater the stability of that molecule. Comparing the resonance between two acids for each reactant and product will help determine which compound is the stronger acid. The reaction with the stronger acid will have products that are more thermodynamically stable ($-\Delta G^{\circ}$, standard Gibbs free energy) with respect to the reactants. The direction of reaction will proceed from the stronger acid or base to the weaker conjugate acid or base.

Consider the structures below with different substituents on the aromatic ring (Figure 25). Which of these compounds is the strongest base? First, write out the reaction of each compound with an acid to see how resonance stabilization plays a role in the base and formed conjugate acid. A strong base favors the formation of the products.

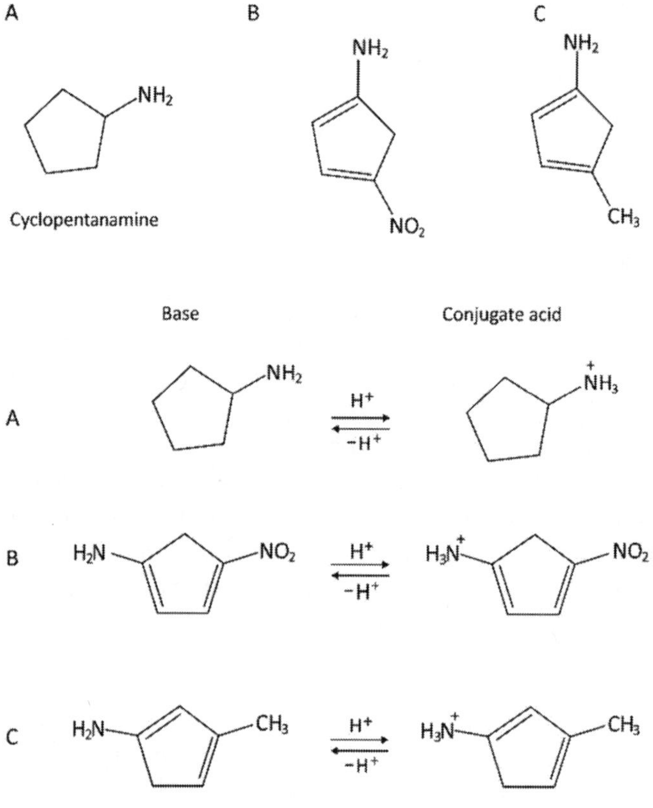

Figure 25. Resonance in bases

Structure A is aliphatic, and the lone pair on the nitrogen cannot delocalize or resonance stabilize. The base forms or reactants of structures B and C can be resonance stabilized, which makes them weaker bases compared to structure A.

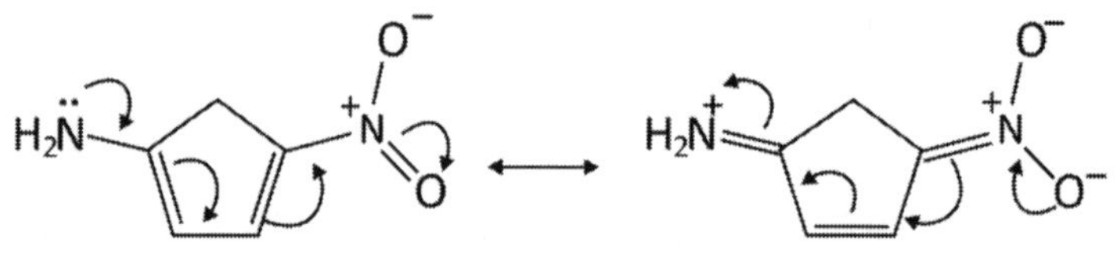

Figure 26. Resonance stabilization of 4-nitro-1,3-cyclopentadien-1-amine (Figure 25 structure B)

Structure B has more possible resonance structures due to the nitro group, meaning that the base form of structure B is more stable than structure C. In other words, structure B is a weaker base than C and is less likely to proceed to the products (protonated amine, NH_3^+). The order of the strongest to the weakest base is A > C > B.

Now consider the reaction of anilinium and methylammonium ion in water as shown in Figure 27 below. Which compound is the stronger acid?

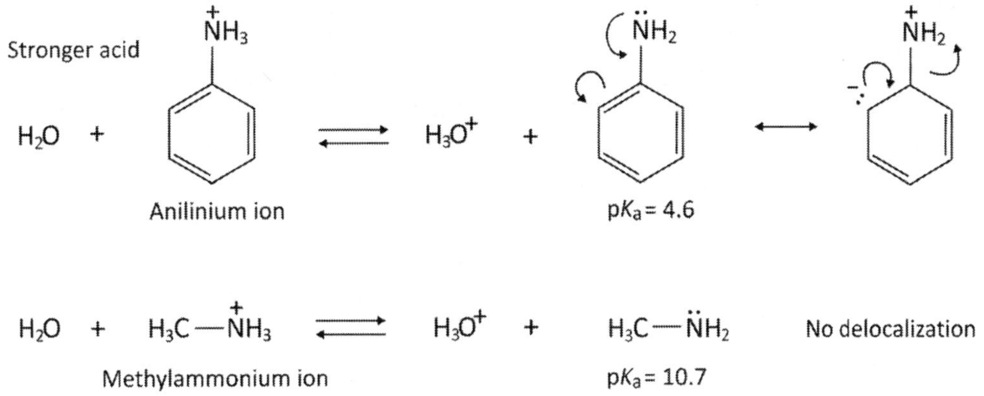

Figure 27. Resonance in acids

Anilinium ion is a stronger acid because its product is resonance stabilized. In contrast, methylammonium ion is a weaker acid because its conjugate base ($CH_3 - NH_2$) can't delocalize or form a resonance-stabilized structure, thereby making the product less relatively stable. Other functional groups on the molecule can also contribute to more Lewis structures due to induction and resonance. Both resonance and induction can play a role, as shown for the benzoic compounds in Figure 28. Which compound is the weakest acid? Each benzene ring contains a carboxylic acid group in addition to another substituent that may be electron withdrawing or donating.

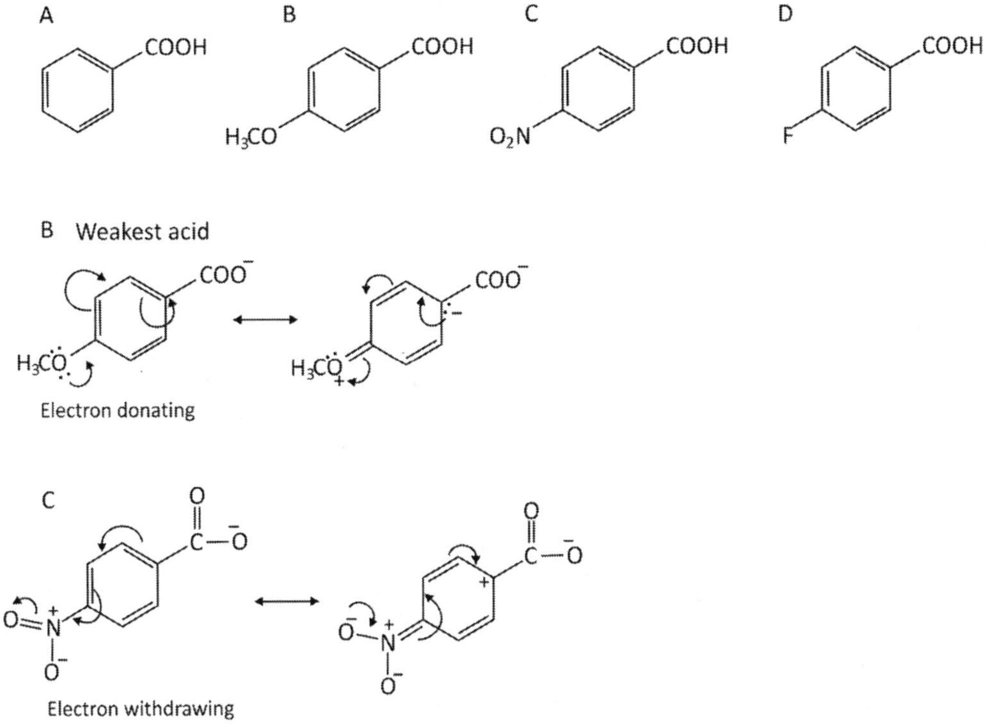

Figure 28. Induction and resonance in acids

Structure A can be used as a reference. Electron-withdrawing groups (nitro group) will draw the electron density away from the ring, and electron-donating groups (methoxy group) will push the electron density toward the ring. Electron-withdrawing substituents will make the hydrogen, on the carboxylic acid group, more acidic and therefore a stronger acid. Both the nitro and halogen groups are relatively more electronegative compared to the methoxy group. The nitro group will also be stabilized by resonance. The nitrogen atom is polarized slightly positive because it is bonded to two more electronegative atoms. Choices C and D are stronger acids than choice A (benzoic acid) because they contain electron-withdrawing groups. Electron-donating groups will have the opposite effect and make the hydrogen less acidic, which means the compound will become a weaker acid. Choice B includes an electron-donating methoxy group, which can resonance stabilize such that there is a lone electron pair on the benzene ring. However, this resonance structure will be unstable because there is a positive charge on the methoxy oxygen atom and a negative charge on the ring close to the negatively charged unprotonated carboxylic acid. The weakest possible acid must be choice B because the unprotonated form is the least stable.

In some cases, induction and resonance will compete with one another. For example, aniline $(\mathrm{Ph} - \mathrm{NH_2})$ can be substituted with various groups that may be electron donating or electron withdrawing, which will have an impact on the hydrogen atoms bonded to nitrogen ($-\mathrm{NH_2}$, Figure 29).

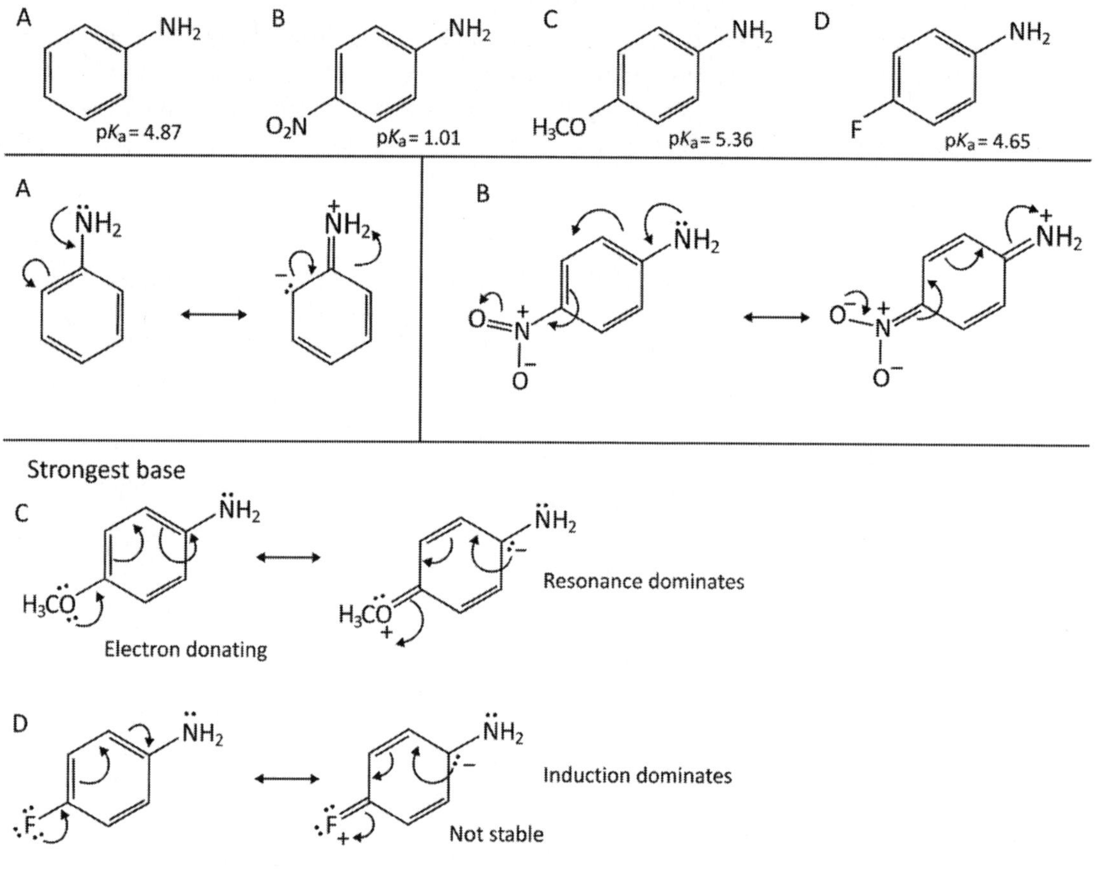

Figure 29. Induction and resonance competition in bases

Inductive and resonance effects must be considered again to identify the strong and weak bases. Aniline (A) can undergo resonance stabilization only when its amino group is unprotonated. When protonated, the nitrogen atom cannot form an $N = C$ double bond, making aniline or the reactant resonance stabilized. The addition of an electron-withdrawing group can provide more stabilization to structure A with respect to the protonated form. The nitro group on nitroaniline, structure B, will result in resonance stabilization, but the hydrogens on the amino group (NH_2) become more acidic, thereby making it a weaker base compared to aniline. The methoxy (structure C) and halogen groups (structure D) are electron withdrawing. However, they can also push the electron density to the ring due to resonance stabilization.

From an inductive point of view, methoxyaniline (C) and fluoroaniline (D) should be weaker bases than aniline. However, from a resonance point of view, both would be stronger bases than aniline. Which factor is more dominant: resonance or induction? Fluoroaniline (D) is less likely to form a double bond given that it is more electronegative than the oxygen atom found within the methoxy group of methoxyaniline. Therefore, the resonance contribution of the fluorine group will be minor, and induction will be a significant factor. Fluoroaniline is a weaker base than aniline. The opposite is seen in methoxyaniline (C). The resonance structure of methoxyaniline will result in the electron density shifting to the ring (the oxygen atom has a positive charge) more so than aniline, and induction will play a minor role. Therefore, methoxyaniline is a stronger base than aniline. Choice C is the strongest base. Note that the greater the pK_a, the stronger the base.

Hybridization Effect

Hydrocarbons, such as alkenes, can be acidic or contain acidic hydrogens. Alkenes contain double bonds, which have greater electron density compared to a single carbon-carbon bond. The protons of ethyne ($HC \equiv CH$, $pK_a = 25$) will be more acidic than ethene ($H_2C = CH_2$, $pK_a = 44$), which is more acidic than ethane ($H_3C - CH_3$, $pK_a = 50$). The removal of a proton on a carbon atom will form a carbanion, and the strength of an acid will depend on the stability of the carbanion. In carbon, the 2s orbital has lower energy compared to a 2p orbital because the electrons in the 2s orbital are closer, on average, to the nucleus. Hybrid orbitals with greater s character are more stable. Therefore, a carbon with greater s character in its hybrid orbitals will result in lower energy and greater stability to the lone electron pair on the carbanion. The order of stability for a carbanion increases with greater s character, e.g., $sp > sp^2 > sp^3$. An sp hybrid orbital contains $\frac{1}{2}$ s and $\frac{1}{2}$ p character (e.g., $HC \equiv C:^-$). An sp^2 hybrid orbital contains $\frac{1}{3}$ s and $\frac{2}{3}$ p character (e.g., $H_2C = CH^-$). For an sp^3 hybrid orbital on a carbanion ($H_3C - CH_2^-$), there is $\frac{1}{4}$ s and $\frac{3}{4}$ p character. The sp carbon atoms found in the ethyne molecule will be more electronegative compared to the hybrid orbitals found in ethene and ethane. Polarization of the C-H bond is greatest in ethyne, which will cause it to donate its proton more readily than ethene and ethane. The ethynide ion ($HC \equiv C:^-$) will be the weakest base because its carbon atom can stabilize the negative charge more readily. Consider the compound in Figure 30 below.

$$H_2C{=}C(H^a)-CH_2-CH_2(H^b)-C{\equiv}C-H^c$$

Figure 30. Acidic hydrogens based on hybridization

The most acidic hydrogen is found at point c because the hydrogen atom is bonded to an sp hybridized carbon. Removal of the hydrogen at point c would give the most stable carbanion. The least acidic hydrogen is found at point b, which is bonded to an sp^3 carbon atom. Removal of the proton gives a carbanion with the lone electron pairs in the sp^3 hybrid orbital but is the least stable due to the smaller s character.

Hybridization is not the only factor that contributes to the acidity or stability of a carbanion. The ability of the carbanion to undergo delocalization or resonance stabilization will increase the stability of the carbanion. To determine which hydrogen atom is the most acidic, remove the hydrogen and draw out the possible resonance structures. The more delocalization or resonance structures that can be drawn, the more stable the carbanion is, thereby making that specific hydrogen more acidic.

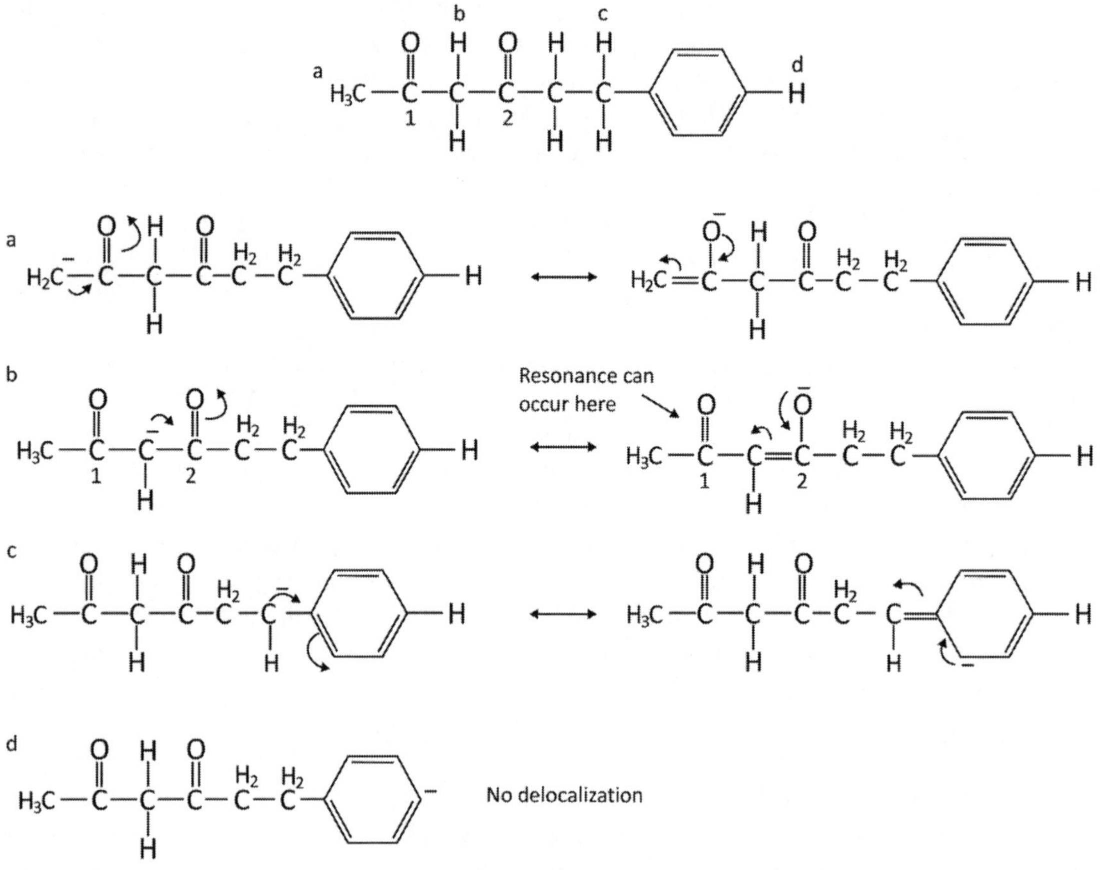

Resonance can occur here

No delocalization

Figure 31. Hybridization and resonance

In Figure 31 above, four hydrogens are indicated by letters a-d. Removal of hydrogen at each letter gives the associated structures, also labeled a-d. The negative sign represents a lone pair (: , not shown) or carbanion. The carbanions are sp^3, sp^3, sp^3, and sp^2 hybridized for structures a-d. Choice c is more acidic than d, which cannot form a resonance-stabilized structure because the lone pair is perpendicular to the benzene ring (no interaction). Choices a and b will have resonance structures that are more stable than c because they have the negative charge placed on the oxygen atom, which is more stable than a negative charge on a benzene ring. The resonance structure of choice b is more stable compared to a because it has a resonance structure within the $(CO) - C - (CO)$ bonding network (position 2). There is another resonance structure (labeled at position 1) at the other carbonyl carbon. Therefore, the most acidic

hydrogen is associated with choice b because its carbanion forms the most and more stable resonance structures.

Inductive effects and hybridization also contribute to acid strength. Consider the ionization reactions in Figure 32 below and determine the strongest acid.

A B C D

$(CH_3)_2CH{-}\overset{+}{O}H_2$ $\quad (H_3C)_2C{=}\overset{+}{O}{-}H \quad (CH_3)_2CH{-}\overset{+}{N}H_3 \quad (CF_3)(CH_3)CH{-}\overset{+}{N}H_3$

Acid Conjugate base Acid Conjugate base

A
$$(CH_3)_2CH{-}\overset{+}{O}H_2 \underset{H^+}{\overset{-H^+}{\rightleftharpoons}} (CH_3)_2CH{-}OH$$

B
$$(H_3C)_2C{=}\overset{+}{O}{-}H \underset{H^+}{\overset{-H^+}{\rightleftharpoons}} (H_3C)_2C{=}\overset{+}{O}$$

C
$$(CH_3)_2CH{-}\overset{+}{N}H_3 \underset{H^+}{\overset{-H^+}{\rightleftharpoons}} (CH_3)_2CH{-}NH_2$$

D
$$(CF_3)(CH_3)CH{-}\overset{+}{N}H_3 \underset{H^+}{\overset{-H^+}{\rightleftharpoons}} (CF_3)(CH_3)CH{-}NH_2$$

Figure 32. Hybridization and induction

Structures A and B, which have positive charges on the oxygen atom, are more acidic than structures C and D. Nitrogen is less electronegative than oxygen; therefore, a positive charge on a nitrogen atom is more stable. Between C and D, choice D is a stronger acid due to the inductive effect of the fluorine atoms. Between A and B, choice B is more acidic because its conjugate base is sp^2 hybridized (oxygen atom) and has $\frac{1}{3}$ s character, making it more acidic because the product is stabilized. The conjugate base of choice A is sp^3 hybridized (oxygen atom) and has $\frac{1}{4}$ s character. The order from the strongest to the weakest acid is B > A > D > C.

Stereoisomerism

Isomers

Compounds that have the same molecular formula are called **isomers.** When the same group of atoms bond or connect in different ways, the compounds are called **constitutional isomers.** Figure 33 shows the constitutional isomers of C_5H_{10} hydrocarbons.

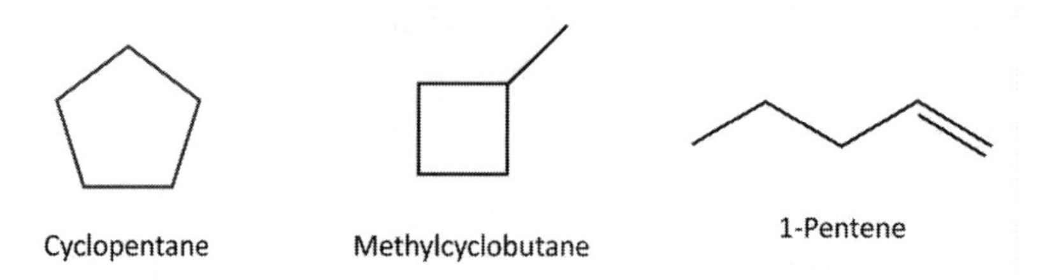

Figure 33. Constitutional isomers

Each isomer shown in the figure contains 15 atoms but each isomer's atoms are connected in different ways and each will a have different IUPAC name. Another possible isomer of C_5H_{10} is $CH_3CH_2 - C = C - CH_3$, which would be called 2-pentene based on the IUPAC rules. However, as discussed in the naming of isomers in the nomenclature section of this document, the molecule will have two possible structures, as shown in Figure 34.

H_3C—CH_2 ... CH_3

(*E*)-2-Pentene

H_3C—CH_2 ... CH_3

(*Z*)-2-Pentene

Figure 34. Cis (*Z*) and trans (*E*) isomers

E-2-pentene and *Z*-2-pentene are also called trans-2-pentene and cis-2-pentene using the IUPAC rules. Both isomers are **stereoisomers**, which are isomers that have the same bond connectivity but differ in how the atoms are arranged in space. Recall the meaning of "cis" and "trans." The trans isomer (*E*) will contain substituents that are opposites of each other. One substituent is above the double bond in the chemical structure and the other substituent is below the double bond, or vice versa. The cis isomer (*Z*) contains substituents that are both above and below the double bond, as shown in Figure 34.

Conformational Isomers

Isomers may also assume different types of geometries that can occur by the rotation around a sigma bond resulting in a change in the three-dimensional shape of the molecule. **Conformations** describe how molecules undergo a change in shape by the rotation or twisting around a single bond. Consider the hydrocarbon called butane (C_4H_{10} or $CH_3 - CH_2 - CH_2 - CH_3$), which can rotate around the central

$C_2 - C_3$ sigma bond, giving a variety of different conformations. Figure 35 shows several conformations of butane and the change in potential energy associated with each conformational structure.

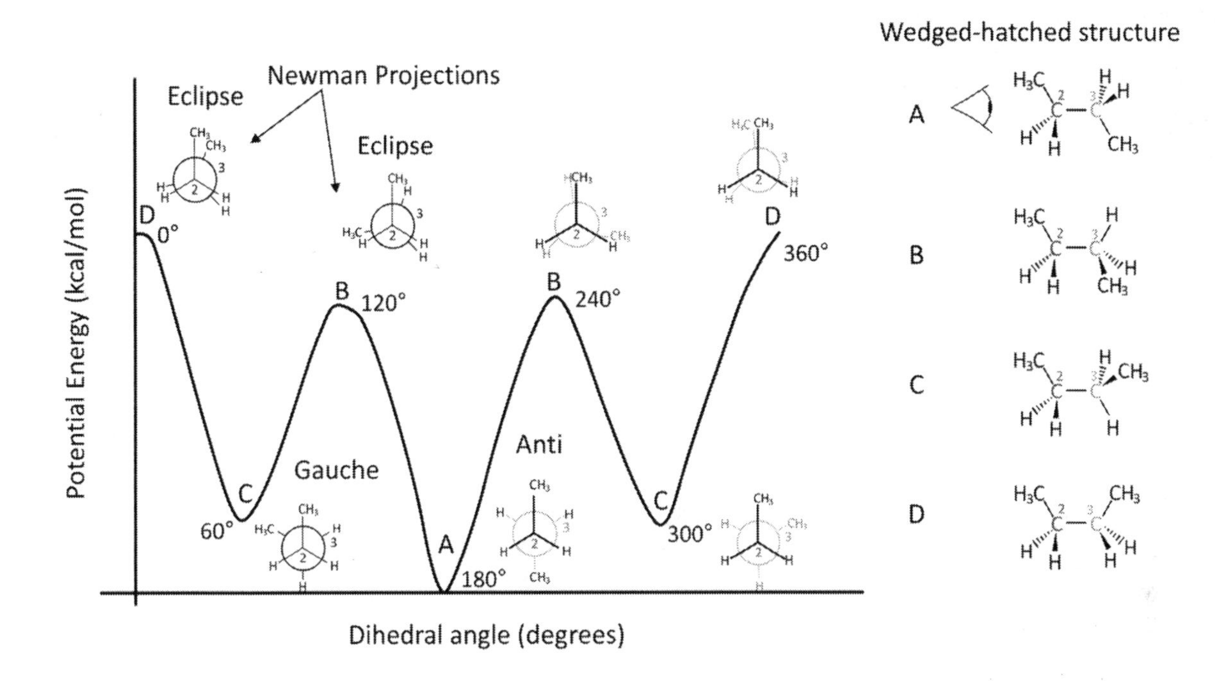

Figure 35. Conformations of *n*-butane and the associated energies

The right-hand side of the graph shows four wedged-hashed conformations of butane (structures A through D). The wedged-hashed structures partially indicate the geometry about carbon atoms 2 and 3. Recall that bold wedges indicate that the atoms are pointed toward the viewer, and the hashed wedges refer to bonds pointed away from the viewer. Each structure is associated with a specific energy, as indicated in the potential energy surface graph. The energy plot illustrates the change in conformational energy with respect to the rotation around the C2 − C3 bond. Structure A is called the anti conformation since the methyl groups are oriented furthest away from one another, thereby minimizing steric interaction. As a result, the anti-conformer is energetically the most stable conformer and has the lowest potential energy. **Newman projections** are useful in alkane stereochemistry since they allow one to see the conformation of a molecule from front to back. Black lines or dots represent the front atoms or proximal atoms. A circle which connects the remaining atoms represents the distal or back atoms. Figure 35 shows a lateral eye point of view to indicate how the molecule is visualized from one side, which is then used to draw a Newman projection.

Rotation around the carbon 2 to carbon 3 bond will change the conformation and relative energy of butane. In the anti conformation, the dihedral angle of separation between the methyl groups shown in the Newman projection is 180°. If the proximal atoms were kept fixed and if a rotation of 60 °around the C2 − C3 in a counterclockwise or clockwise fashion were applied, butane would obtain an eclipsed conformation. Two lower-energy eclipsed conformations are shown in the energy diagram and are found at dihedral angles of 120 and 240°. An eclipsed conformation means that the proximal and distal atoms line up with one another. The eclipsed conformations are expected to have higher energy because the proximal and distal atoms are closer to one another, which increases the interaction or potential energy. Starting at an angle of 240°, if the C2 − C3 bond were rotated 60° counterclockwise,

the proximal and distal atoms would no longer be eclipsed but would attain a lower-energy gauche conformation. Like the anti conformation, the gauche conformation will correspond to a minimum on the potential energy surface since the interaction energy (electron repulsion, etc.) is minimized. The gauche conformer is higher in energy by about 0.9 kcal/mol with respect to the anti conformer, which is due to the crowding or additional steric strain of the methyl groups. However, if the angle is rotated another 60° counterclockwise, butane will have a high energy eclipsed conformation where the methyl groups are closest to one another. Both high energy eclipse structures at dihedral angles of 0 and 360 °, shown in the potential energy surface, are equivalent in energy and geometry.

Stereoisomers: Enantiomers and Diastereomers

Enantiomers are one class of stereoisomers that are mirror images of one another but not superimposable. Figure 36 illustrates the meaning of nonsuperimposable images.

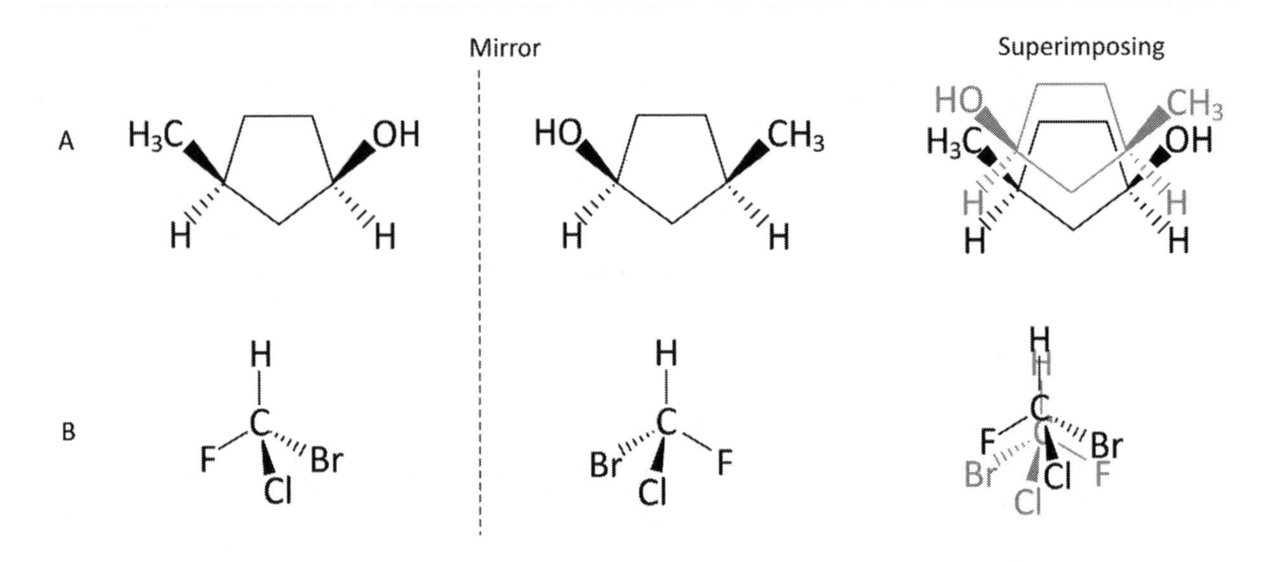

Figure 36. Enantiomers

The left side of Figure 36 represents two real structures with their mirror images on the right side. The figure also illustrates the superposition of the actual and the mirror structure on top of one another. However, the structures are not superimposable and are, therefore, different structures. Enantiomers contain a single mirror image pair that is optically active and can rotate plane-polarized light. The enantiomers have the same physical properties, but the two enantiomers rotate plane-polarized light in opposite directions. If the two enantiomers are present in equal concentrations, a phenomenon called a **racemic mixture** or **racemate**, the mixture is optically inactive. **Diastereomers** are stereoisomers that do not have mirror images and are nonsuperimposable.

Some examples of diastereomers are shown in Figure 37.

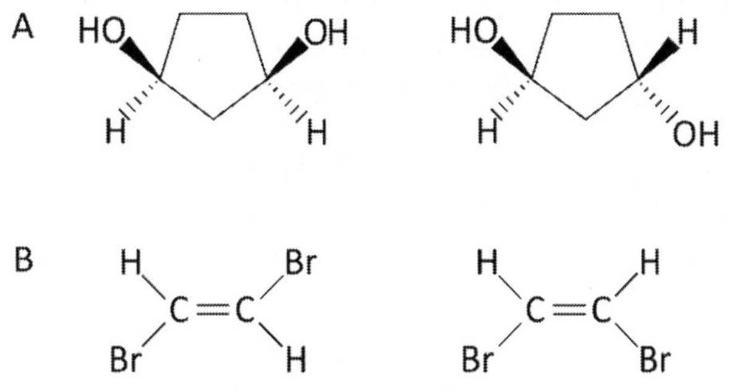

Figure 37. Diastereomers

Figure 37 shows a concept map that describes the classifications of the various stereoisomers that were discussed. The gauche and anti-conformations of butane are conformers of one another and belong to a class of diastereomers.

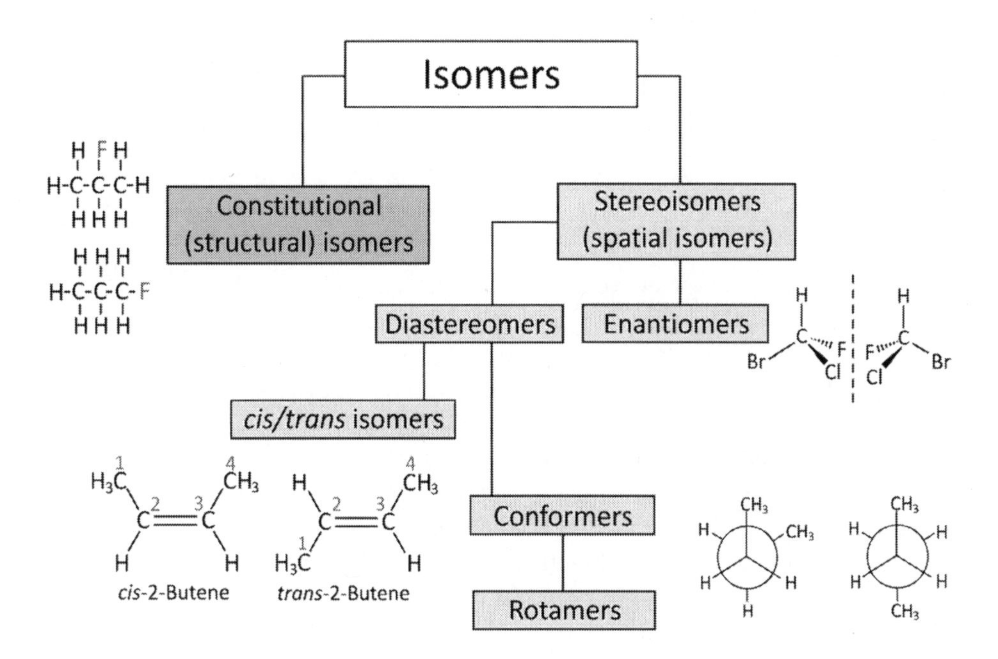

Figure 38. Isomer classification

However, the butane conformers with dihedral angles of 120° and 240 °, which correspond to the lower-energy eclipsed conformers, can be considered conformational enantiomers. They are mirror images to one another but not superimposable. Similarly, the gauche conformers of butane are also conformational enantiomers. The gauche, eclipsed, and anti conformations of butane are **rotamers** to one another since they differ by rotation around the sigma $C_2 - C_3$ bond.

Chirality

Any molecule or object can be classified as chiral or achiral. Molecules that have **chirality** are said to have "handedness" or be "handed." A chiral molecule is nonsuperimposable, meaning it is not identical to its mirror image. For example, your left hand is "handed," meaning that its mirror image (your right hand) cannot be superimposed on it. Some other cases of objects that have handedness are hockey sticks, shoes, and pairs of scissors. A chiral object or molecule and its mirror images are enantiomers. One enantiomer may be called left-handed and the other right-handed. Amino acids are classified as left-handed, and most natural sugars are considered right-handed.

Molecules that are superimposable on their mirror images are not "handed" and are called **achiral.** Some examples of achiral objects include a baseball bat, a pen, and a round ball. Figure 39 shows 2-propanol and its mirror image. The two structures are superimposable and, therefore, achiral.

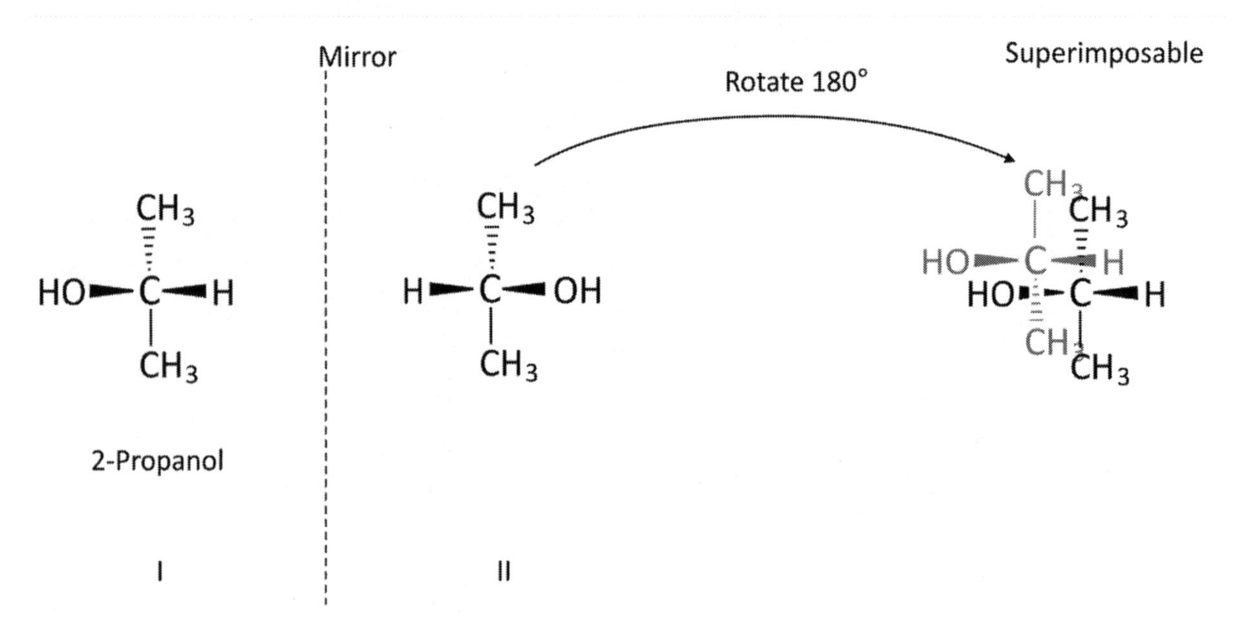

Figure 39. 2-propanol (I) and its mirror image (II)

One way to test whether a molecule is chiral is to determine whether there is a plane of symmetry. Some objects have a **symmetry element**, which is described as a point or line drawn along an object. Rotation around the point, or reflection around the line, leaves the object indistinguishable from the original orientation of that object. Achiral objects may have a reflective symmetry element. Chiral objects may have a rotational symmetry element but not a reflective element.

Asymmetry refers to the absence of any symmetry element (rotational and reflective), and **dissymmetry** refers to the lack of reflective symmetry elements in an object. Therefore, all asymmetric and dissymmetric molecules or objects are chiral. Figure 40 shows a structure of (*E*)-1,2-dibromoethene (I) and its mirror image (II).

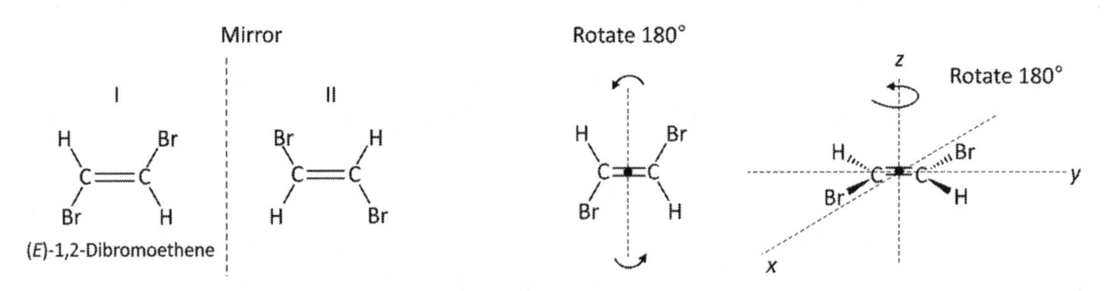

Figure 40. Chirality and rotational symmetry

The molecule shown in Figure 40 (I and II) is a trans isomer. Rotating the molecule's mirror image by 180° around the z-axis would make the mirror image superimposable on the molecule. A mirror plane or **plane of symmetry** is an imaginary plane that bisects an object or molecule such that each half of the object are mirror images. (*E*)-1,2-dibromoethene has a plane of symmetry along the x-y plane, and a point of symmetry where rotation around the z-axis (called C_2 for 180° rotation) makes it indistinguishable from the molecule's original position. The molecule is achiral since it has a plane of symmetry.

Molecules that don't possess planes of symmetry, asymmetric, tend to be chiral. For example, carbon atoms that are bonded to four different substituents or groups are called **asymmetric carbons** since they lose all symmetry. A pair of enantiomers each contain one tetrahedral atom with four different groups bonded to it. In Figure 36, structure B, the tetrahedral carbon atom is bonded to a hydrogen, fluorine, bromine, and chlorine atom. The carbon atom is a **stereocenter** or atom that contains substituents whereby interchanging any two groups will create a stereoisomer (for example, when the Br and F atoms are interchanged). Not all stereocenters are tetrahedral. The carbon atoms found in (*E*)-1,2-dibromoethene are trigonal planar stereocenters. Interchanging the groups at any one carbon atom will produce a diastereomer (Figure 37, structure B, Br and H can be interchanged). Stereocenters generally imply a tetrahedral stereocenter, which may be a stereogenic carbon, a carbon that is a stereocenter. 2-butanol contains four different groups, and it is nonsuperimposable on its mirror image. Interchanging two groups within 2-butanol that are bonded to the stereogenic carbon will produce its enantiomer or mirror image. As shown in Figure 41, 2-butanol is chiral since it has a left- and right-handed version of the molecule.

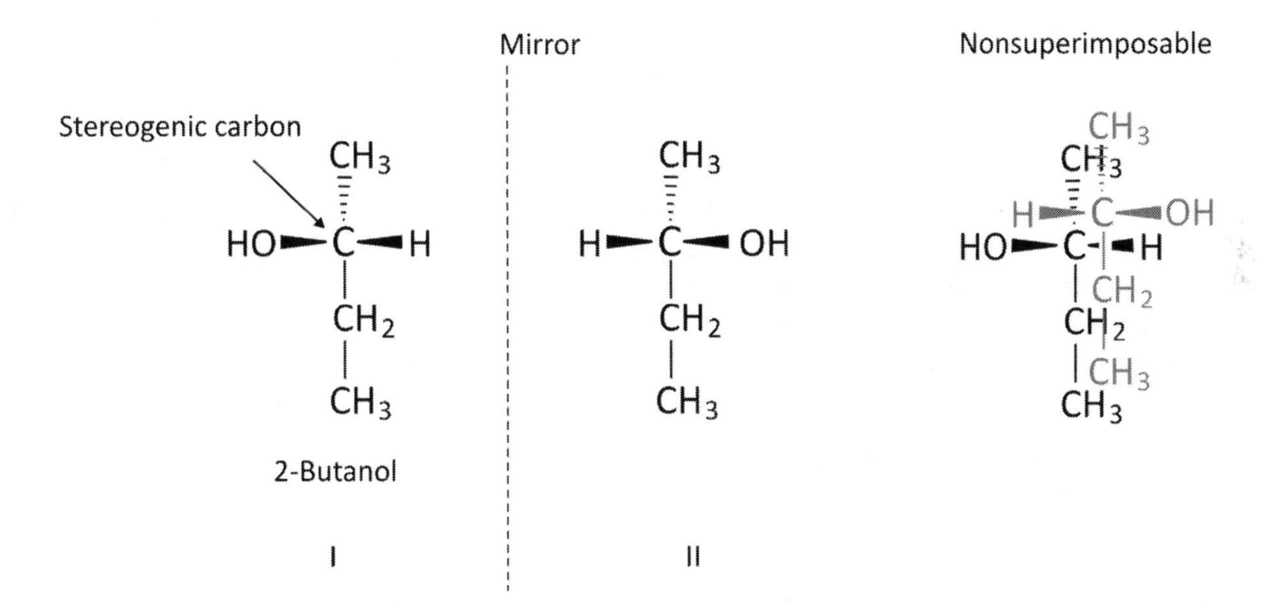

Figure 41. The 2-butanol enantiomers are nonsuperimposable

The Cahn-Ingold-Prelog Rules: The *R-S* Convention for Stereoisomers

The enantiomers of 2-butanol, shown in Figure 41 have the same name and must be distinguished by a distinct name. Within the IUPAC system, the scientists R. Cahn, C. Ingold, and V. Prelog developed an *R-S* nomenclature system, which was used to name each enantiomer that contained tetrahedral stereogenic carbons. The naming convention is also applied to alkenes that include several substituent groups. Each group is assigned a priority based on the atomic number of the atoms closest to the stereogenic carbon or around a $C = C$ bond. Based on the *R-S* system, one enantiomer of 2-butanol will be called (*R*)-2-butanol, and the other enantiomer would be designated (*S*)-2-butanol. The term "*R*" stands for rectus, Latin for right, and "*S*" stands for sinister, meaning left. The (*R*) and (*S*) convention follows a few basic rules as outlined below.

(1). For each group bonded to the stereogenic carbon, a priority letter (a, b, c, d) is assigned based on the atomic number (Z). The group with the highest atomic number will be given a priority of "a," and the group with the lowest priority will be assigned a "d." For instance, if these rules are applied to 2-butanol (structure I, Figure 41), then the following structure of 2-butanol would have the following groups labeled accordingly (Figure 42).

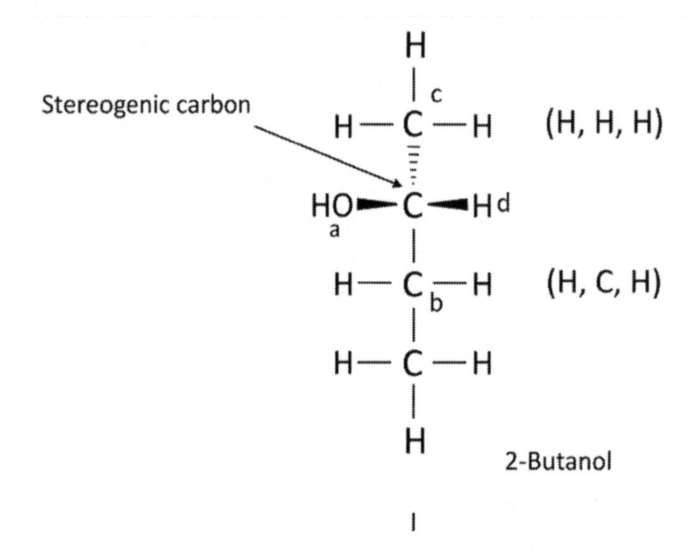

Figure 42. Assigning priority groups

The stereogenic carbon is bonded to a hydroxyl group, a hydrogen atom, a methyl group, and an ethyl group. The oxygen atom in the hydroxyl group is directly bonded to the stereogenic carbon and will have the highest priority group (a) since oxygen has the highest atomic number ($Z = 8$). Hydrogen will have the lowest priority number (d) since it has the lowest atomic number ($Z = 1$). Because the stereogenic carbon is bonded to two carbon atoms, another set of rules has been created.

(2). When a stereogenic carbon is bonded to two similar atoms with the same atomic number, the priority is determined by the next set of atoms within each group. In other words, a priority is assigned at the first point of change along the chain. For instance, the carbon atom in the methyl group is bonded to three other hydrogen atoms, and each has an atomic number of one. In contrast, the carbon atom from the ethyl group, which is directly bonded to the stereogenic carbon, is bonded to two hydrogen atoms and to the other carbon atom in the ethyl chain. The highest atomic number in this bonding set is six. Therefore, the ethyl group will have a higher priority (b) compared to the methyl group (c).

(3). To determine whether an (*R*) or (*S*) is assigned to the molecule (for example, 2-butanol), direct the lowest priority group (d) away from you, as shown in Figure 43.

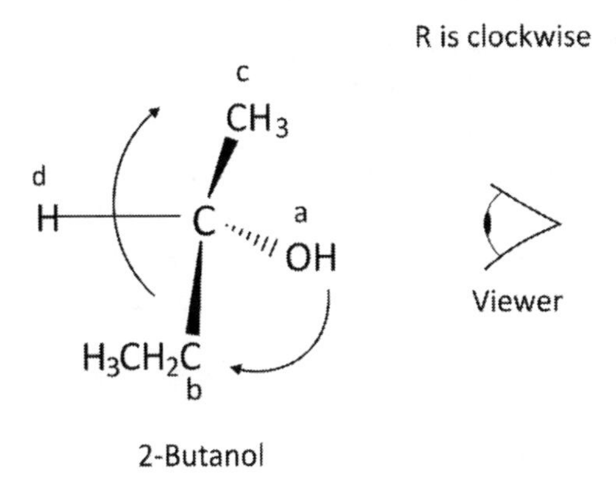

Figure 43. (*R*)-2-butanol

Trace the path in a circular motion, from highest to lowest priority (a to c). The direction is clockwise, which is indicated by the arrows in the figure. The enantiomer is designated (*R*) for a clockwise motion. If the motion followed a counterclockwise direction, then the enantiomer would be designated (*S*). In Figure 41, structure I is (*R*)-2-butanol and structure II is (*S*)-2-butanol.

(4). For stereogenic carbons bonded to atoms within a group, which may contain double or triple bonds, the priority is assigned as if those atoms were doubled or tripled. Figure 44 illustrates the concept with some examples.

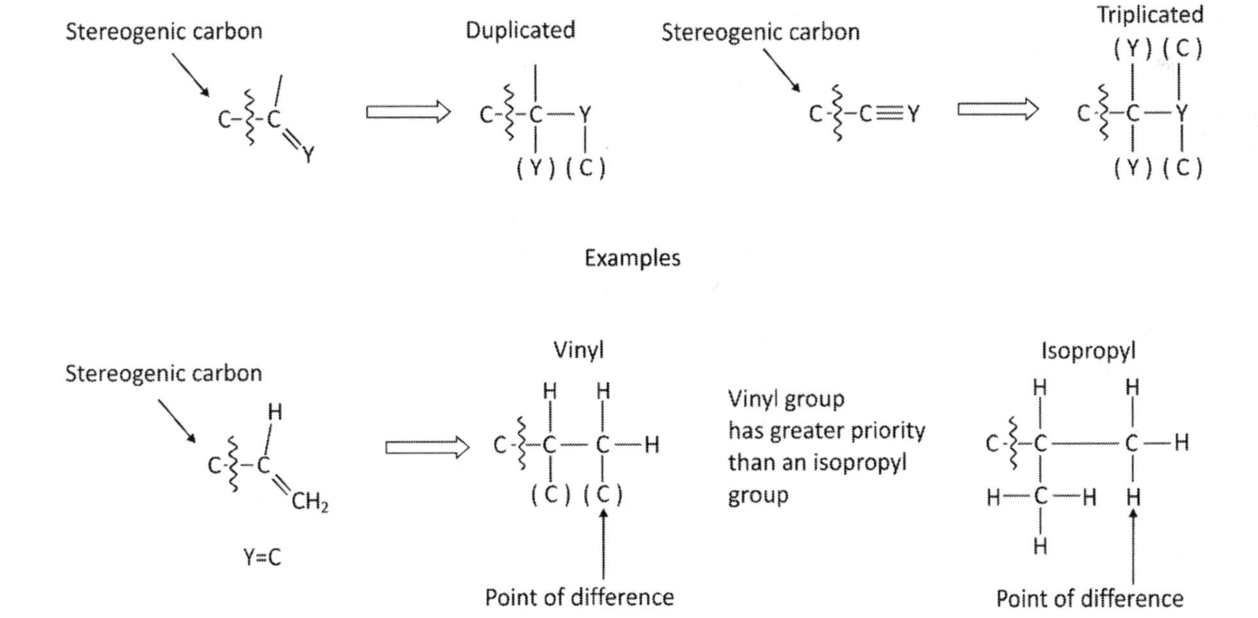

Figure 44. Duplication and triplication scheme for priority assignments

The symbols that are enclosed in parentheses are either duplicated or triplicated. For example, the $C = Y$ bond is converted to a single bond, and two additional $C - Y$ or $Y - C$ bonds are created. In the example shown in Figure 44, the vinyl group $(CH = CH_2)$ is redrawn with two additional $C - C$ bonds. The vinyl group would have higher priority than an isopropyl group $-CH(CH_3)_2$ since there is a point of difference between the second set of atoms in the vinyl group (carbon bonded to H, H, C). For the first set of atoms in the vinyl group, carbon is bonded to a hydrogen and two carbon atoms (carbon bonded to H, C, C). Similarly, in the isopropyl group, the first set of atoms bonded to carbon is H, C, C. The point of difference is found at the second set of atoms. Along either branch (the methyl groups) in the isopropyl group, carbon is bonded to three hydrogen atoms (H, H, H). Therefore the vinyl group (carbon bonded to H, H, C) has higher priority than the isopropyl group (carbon bonded to H, H, H).

The Cahn-Ingold-Prelog rules are also applied when designating a configuration around a $C = C$ double bond. For example, in Figure 45, some alkenes may have multiple substituents bonded to the carbon atoms of the $C = C$ double bond.

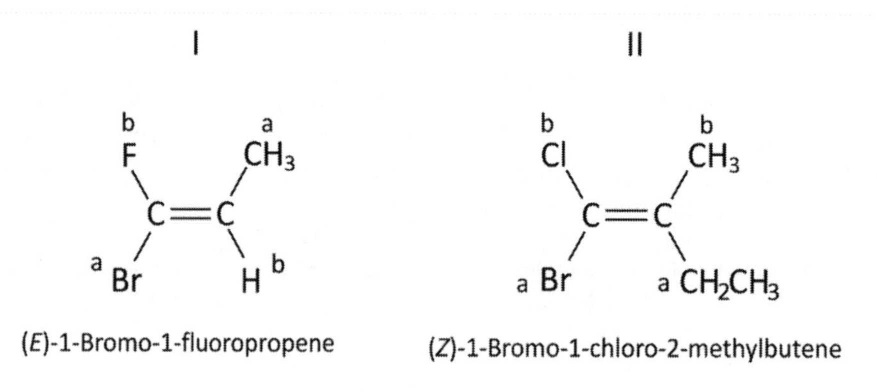

Figure 45. Alkenes with four substituent groups

For structures I and II, cis (*Z*) or trans (*E*) isomers, priorities between two substituents on each of the double-bonded carbon atoms are given. In structure I, one of the double-bonded carbon atoms is bonded to a fluorine atom and a bromine atom. Since the atomic number of bromine is greater than fluorine, a higher priority will be given to bromine (labeled "a" in Figure 45). The second double-bonded carbon atom is connected to a methyl group and a hydrogen atom. The carbon atom within the methyl group will have a higher priority compared to the hydrogen atom (labeled "a" in Figure 45). Note that priorities are only assigned to groups that are not stereocenters. Structure I will have the highest priority groups that are opposite of one another, as shown in Figure 45. In contrast, structure II will have the highest priority groups on the same side or beneath the $C = C$ double bond with respect to the above structure.

Meso compounds or meso isomers are a set of stereoisomers that contain two stereogenic centers (chiral centers). The compounds are constitutionally symmetrical and contain a point of symmetry or an internal mirror plane.

Meso compounds such as tartaric acid are achiral and are superimposable, as shown in Figure 46.

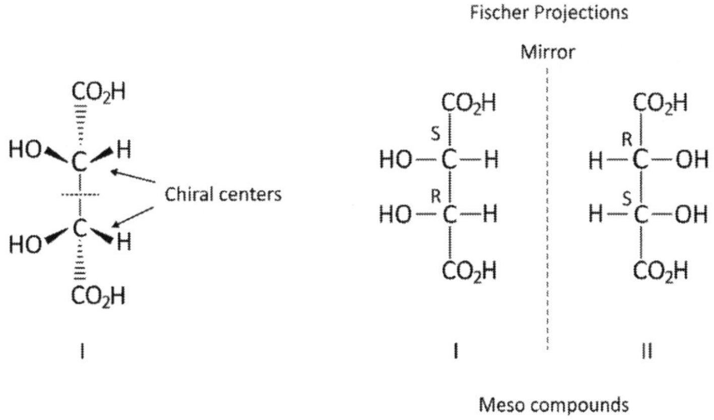

Figure 46. Tartaric acid

The Fischer projection of structure I, (2*S*,3*R*) tartaric acid, is shown in addition to its mirror image (2*R*,3*S*), tartaric acid. Reflecting the meso compound, structure I, through a mirror image, will give the same stereochemistry; for example, if structure II is rotated by 180°. Therefore, the two isomers, structures I and II, are equivalent to one another, making the entire molecule achiral. The compound is achiral, but the two stereocenters are chiral. Meso compounds are similar to 50:50 racemic mixtures (two optically active compounds), in that neither will rotate light within a polarimeter.

Conformations of Cyclohexane Rings

Conformations generally refer to different stereochemical representations for a given molecule, which can interconvert to other representations by rotation around a single bond. For example, *n*-butane has several conformations, such as anti, gauche, and eclipse. Rotation at the $C2 = C3$ would break the π bond, which would give a different representation. In contrast, the term configuration refers to different stereoisomers, which can only interconvert by breaking and forming bonds. *E*-1,2-dibromoethene can only convert to *Z*-1,2-dibromoethene if the π bond, between the $C = C$, breaks. Ring structures such as cyclohexane (C_6H_{12}) can have several conformations, which involves twisting of the hexagonal ring. Rotation at the sigma bonds is limited in the ring structure. The cyclohexane ring will form a twisted structure as some of the carbon-carbon bonds move out-of-plane with respect to the ring. Cyclohexane will adopt non-planar conformations such as the "boat," "twist-boat," and chair conformation. Figure 47 shows a potential energy surface for each conformation.

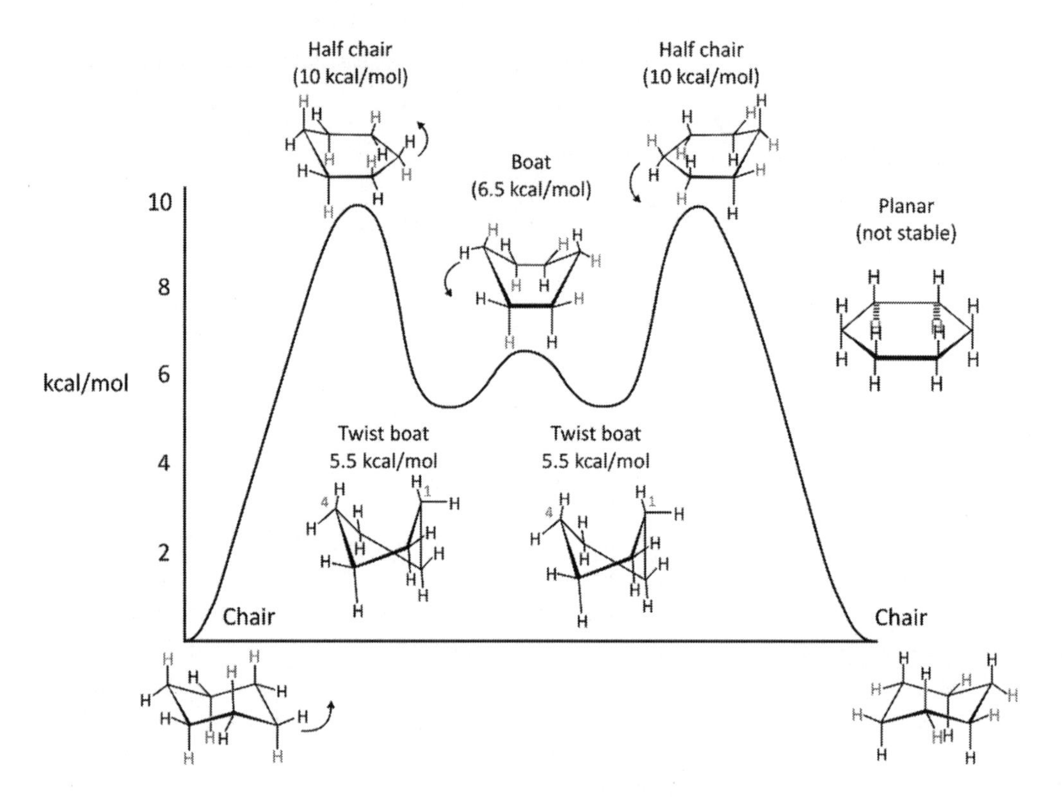

Figure 47. Conformations of cyclohexane

The **planar structure** of cyclohexane is unstable since it has a C-C-C angle of 120° (greater than 109.5° from a tetrahedral angle), resulting in ring strain. Since the carbon and hydrogen atoms are on the same plane, there will be a certain amount of eclipsing strain. The **boat conformer** has two eclipsed bonds $(\mathrm{C}-\mathrm{H})$ at the base. There is also steric crowding or hindrance from two hydrogen atoms at the bow and stern of the boat. Twisting the boat gives a **twist-boat** conformer, which relieves some of the steric hindrances, but there will still be some angle (ring), eclipsing, and steric strain. The most stable structure is the **chair conformer**, which results from lifting one carbon above the ring plane and placing another below the ring plane. The chair conformer contains minimal steric strain but no angle strain or eclipsing strain. For the chair conformation of cyclohexane, twelve hydrogens lie along two different axes. Six of the hydrogen atoms or $\mathrm{C}-\mathrm{H}$ bonds lie in an **equatorial** position or near the periphery of the carbon ring. The other six hydrogen atoms or $\mathrm{C}-\mathrm{H}$ bonds are pointed above and below the ring and are called the **axial** hydrogens since they are aligned parallel to the ring axis. Figure 48 displays the axial and equatorial hydrogens.

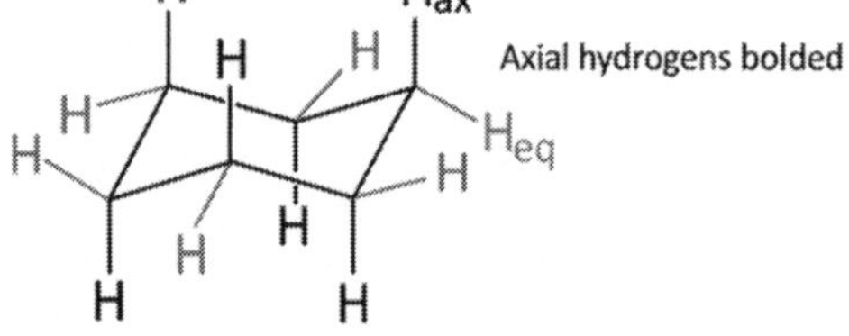

Figure 48. Chair conformation showing the axial (ax) and equatorial (eq) hydrogens

Bulky substituents, in place of hydrogen, found in the axial position, will be subject to more significant steric crowding compared substituents in an equatorial position. Substituted cyclohexanes containing bulky groups will tend to adopt conformations that place the groups at the equatorial position. Steric hindrance is minimized at the equatorial position, which makes these structures more stable. Cyclohexane can form different conformers and even stabilize through interconversion. For example, a chair conformer with six hydrogen atoms in an axial position can convert to a chair conformer where those axial hydrogens move to an equatorial position.

Nucleophilic Substitutions and Eliminations

Nucleophilic Substitution Reactions

In a **nucleophilic substitution reaction**, an electron-rich species called a **nucleophile** attacks a partially electron-deficient carbon atom, for example, alkyl halide $R - X$ $(X = Cl, Br)$. The electronegative halogen (X) polarizes the C-X bond, making it more likely to be attacked. The nucleophile acts as a Lewis base and contains an electron pair that can be donated to the partially positive carbon atom (δ+), which is bonded to an electronegative atom that is partially negative (δ-). The result of the reaction is a displaced electronegative atom, called the "leaving group." A new bond between the nucleophile and the carbon atom ($R - X$, X an electronegative atom) also forms. The reaction can be summarized as follows.

$$\ddot{Nu}^{-} + \overset{\delta^{+}}{R}—\overset{\delta^{-}}{X} \longrightarrow R—Nu + \ddot{X}^{-}$$

Figure 49. Nucleophilic substitution reaction

Each arrow represents the transfer of two electrons. The example shown below is the displacement of chlorine from methyl chloride by a hydroxide ion.

$$:\ddot{O}H^{-} + CH_3—\ddot{Cl}: \longrightarrow H\ddot{O}—CH_3 + :\ddot{Cl}:^{-}$$

Figure 50. Nucleophilic attack on methyl chloride by a hydroxide ion

The alkyl halide, CH_3Cl, is the **substrate**, and the nucleophile is the hydroxide ion, which contains the electron pair that is donated to the partially positive carbon. The substitution reaction replaces the chlorine atom with a chloride ion, which acts as the leaving group. The carbon-halogen bond undergoes heterolysis bond cleavage, and the lone pair from the nucleophile forms a new covalent bond with the carbon atom. The nucleophile can be a negative ion or neutral molecule that contains at least one lone electron pair. Hydroxide ions and water can act as nucleophiles and react with alkyl halides $(R - X)$ to produce alcohols. For a substrate to be reactive, it must have a good leaving group, which must be a relatively stable ion (for example, Cl^{-}, Br^{-}) or a weak basic molecule (for example, H_2O).

If the carbon-halogen bond breaks as a new bond between the nucleophile (for example, OH^{-}) and the carbon atom forms, this would be described as a one-step mechanism. A two-step mechanism would describe the breaking of the $C - X$ bond and formation of $Nu - C$ bond in two separate steps.

The Substitution Nucleophilic Biomolecular Reaction (S_N2): Rates and Stereochemistry

The rate of reaction between methyl chloride and hydroxide ion can be represented with the following rate equation.

$$\text{Rate} = k[CH_3Cl][OH^-]$$

The reaction occurs in one step and is first order for both the alkyl halide and the nucleophile, but the reaction is second order overall. The reaction is bimolecular since both methyl chloride, and the hydroxide ion must collide. Therefore the reaction is called an S_N2 reaction, which stands for "substitution, nucleophilic, bimolecular." The mechanism is described as a "backside attack," meaning that the nucleophile will approach the partially positive carbon atom from the back or in a direction opposite of the side of the leaving group. The Hughes-Ingold mechanism for an S_N2 reaction is described as a one-step mechanism. There is one reaction barrier whereby the reaction results in the formation of a **transition state**, or an unstable arrangement of atoms, at the highest energy point along the barrier. There are no reaction intermediates. In the transition state, the nucleophile and leaving group are partially bonded to the carbon atom. The reaction mechanism is shown in Figure 51.

A

Bromomethane — Transition state — Methanol

B

(*S*)-2-Bromopentane — Transition state — (*R*)-2-Pentanol

Figure 51. Mechanism and stereochemistry of an S_N2 reaction

In reaction A, the partially charged carbon atom on bromomethane or methyl bromide initially maintains a tetrahedral bonding geometry. However, when the hydroxide ion nucleophile attacks the carbon atom to form a partial bond, the configuration of the carbon atom changes and is inverted or turned inside out. This mechanism is similar to an umbrella turning inside out in a strong wind. However, inversion cannot be distinguished experimentally since one form of the methyl bromide is the same as its inverted form. For example, methyl bromide is achiral since its mirror image is superimposable on the actual structure of methyl bromide.

In contrast, 2-bromopentane contains a stereogenic carbon with four different groups. In reaction B, (*S*)-2-bromopentane is an enantiomer, and its mirror image is (*R*)-2-bromopentane. When the hydroxide ion attacks (*S*)-2-bromopentane from the backside, a configuration inversion can be detected experimentally. A **polarimeter** is a device used to measure changes of plane-polarized light on compounds that are optically active. Devices such as a polarimeter can be used to detect a stereochemical inversion.

The hydroxide ion will bond on the opposite side of the structure from where bromine is replaced (Figure 51), resulting in a stereochemical inversion that can be detected. In other words, for S_N2 reactions involving a stereocenter, S_N2 reactions will result in a configurational inversion. For a given pair of enantiomers, one compound will rotate plane-polarized light in a clockwise direction, which is called dextrorotatory (+, positive rotation in degrees). The other compound or enantiomer will rotate plane-polarized light in a clockwise manner (−, negative rotation in degrees). There is no correlation between the (*S*) and (*R*) designations or configurations of enantiomers and the direction of rotation for plane-polarized light.

The Substitution Nucleophilic Unimolecular Reaction (S_N1): Rates and Stereochemistry

S_N2 reactions generally involve reactions of a nucleophile (for example, OH^-) and a substrate containing a methyl ($CH_3 - X$), primary ($(CH_3)CH_2 - X$), or secondary ($(CH_3)_2CH - X$) carbon bonded to an electronegative atom. Tertiary carbons bonded to an electronegative atom (for example, tert-butyl chloride, ($(CH_3)_3C - Cl$) will undergo a different type of reaction mechanism and will have different reaction kinetics. This can be attributed to the stability of a tertiary carbocation, which has greater stability than a secondary carbocation:

$$3° \, ((CH_3)_3C^+) > 2° \, ((CH_3)_2CH^+) > 1° \left(CH_3CH_2{}^+\right) > \text{methyl} \, (CH_3{}^+)$$

A system that is charged is stabilized when that charge can be dispersed or delocalized around more carbon atoms. In other words, alkyl groups are more likely to release electrons or shift the electron density to a positive charge compared to hydrogen atoms. Alkyl groups take on part of the positive charge and stabilize the carbocation. As a result, tertiary compounds will undergo a substitution, nucleophilic, unimolecular, or **S_N1 reaction** when attacked by a nucleophile. For example, tert-butyl chloride ($(CH_3)_3C - Cl$) will react with the hydroxide ion when mixed with water and acetone to form tert-butyl alcohol ($(CH_3)_3C - OH$). However, the rate of reaction is independent of the nucleophile or hydroxide ion concentration and dependent on the substrate or tert-butyl chloride. The S_N1 reaction is first order overall.

$$\text{Rate} = k[(CH_3)_3CCl)]$$

The S_N1 reaction is a multistep reaction that has a slow or **rate-determining step**. The rate constant for the first step ((k_1) will be relatively small compared to the second ((k_2) and third steps ($k_1 \ll k_2$ or k_3). Since the rate constants for the second and third steps are greater, these steps will take place faster. The reaction of tert-butyl chloride with water involves three steps and has two distinct intermediates, as shown in Figure 52.

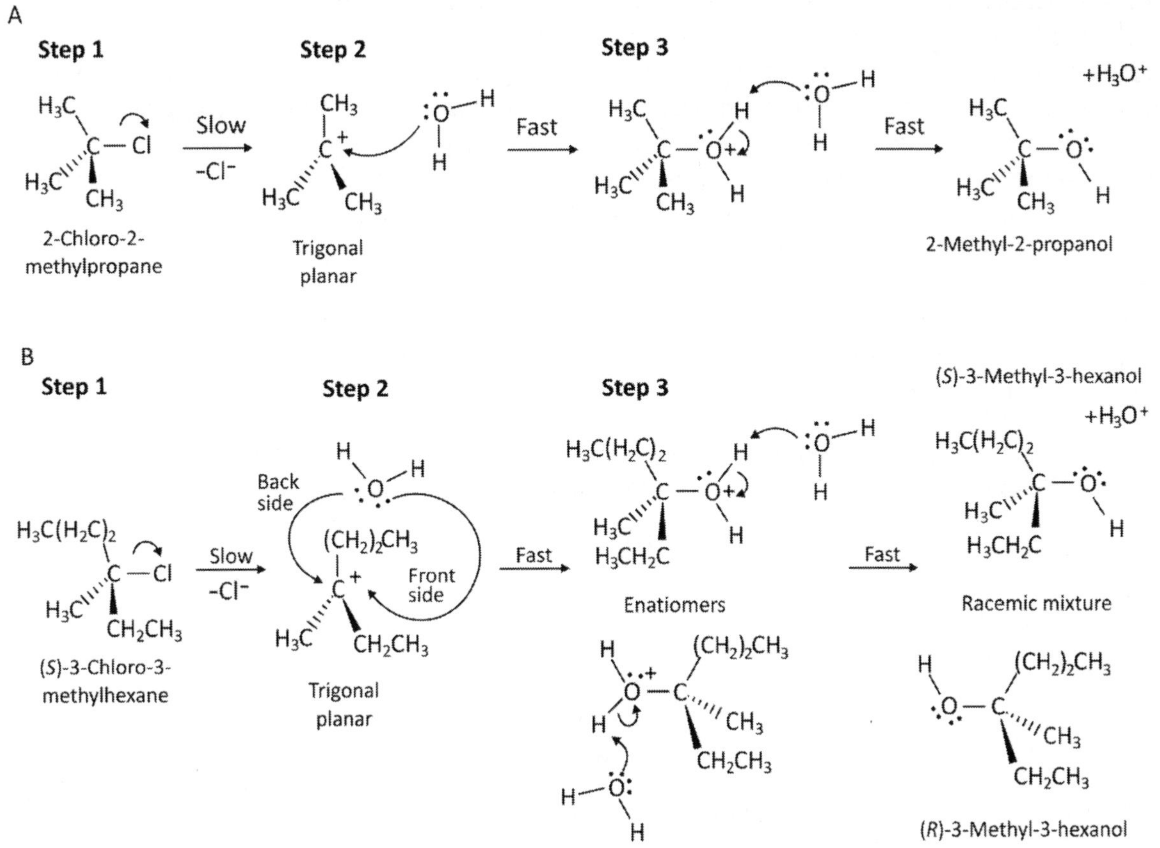

Figure 52. The S_N1 reaction (A) and its stereochemistry (B)

Reactions A and B, shown in Figure 52, are examples of **solvolysis**, which is an S_N1 reaction of an alkyl halide with two water molecules. The solvent, water, is the nucleophile and is also called a **hydrolysis** reaction. Both reactions are three-step mechanisms that have three reaction barriers or three transition state structures in addition to two reaction intermediates. In reaction A, the chlorine atom cleaves with an electron pair, aided by the polar solvent (water), which produces a tertiary carbocation (3°) and a chloride ion. In step 2, water acts as a Lewis base and gives an electron pair to the carbocation, which produces a tert-butyloxonium ion. A second water molecule then acts as a Bronsted base and accepts a proton from the protonated tert-butyl alcohol, which forms 2-methyl-2-propanol.

Regarding the stereochemistry of reaction A, water could attack the carbocation either from the front or the back. However, the stereochemistry of the compound will not change. In reaction B, the initial compound contains a stereogenic carbon atom, for example, (*S*)-3-chloro-3-methylhexane, which can produce a racemic mixture when undergoing hydrolysis. In the second step, the water molecule can attack the achiral carbocation from the front or the back, which will produce enantiomers of 3-methyl-3-hexanol in equivalent amounts. One of the compounds will be optically active, and the other compound will be optically inactive. However, racemization will occur when a reaction results in a chiral compound changing to an achiral intermediate. The mixture will be optically inactive.

The E2 Reaction

Alkyl halides can undergo elimination reactions whereby parts of the molecule are removed from adjacent atoms, which results in the formation of multiple bonds. **Dehydrohalogenation** reactions are some examples of elimination reactions that form alkenes and involves the removal of HX from adjacent atoms within an alkyl halide. Relatively strong bases (compared to water) such as sodium ethoxide (CH_3CH_2ONa), sodium alkoxide ($R - ONa$), sodium hydroxide ($NaOH$), and potassium tert-butoxide ($(CH_3)_3CK$), can be used. The base helps remove parts of the hydrogen halide (HX) from the haloalkane to produce an alkene. As the base attacks the alkyl halide, a leaving group is produced. The alpha (α) carbon atom is the carbon atom that is bonded to the halogen atom substituent. The beta (β) carbon atom is the carbon atom that is adjacent or bonded to the alpha carbon atom. The beta hydrogen atom is the atom bonded to the beta carbon atom.

Elimination bimolecular or E2 reactions have a rate equation that is first order for the base and alkyl halide and is second order overall. The E2 reaction mechanism is shown in Figure 53.

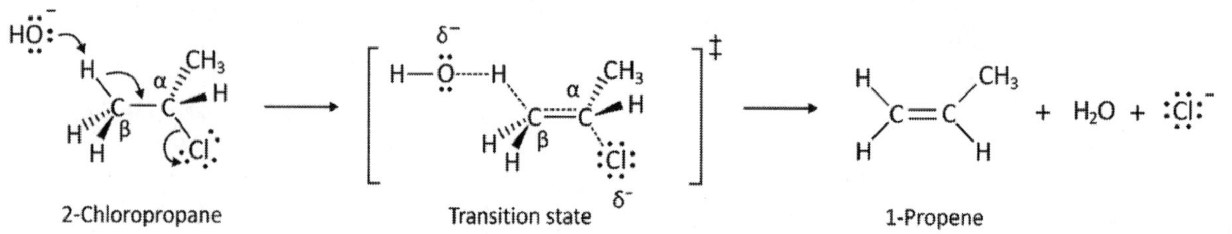

2-Chloropropane → Transition state → 1-Propene + H_2O + $:\ddot{Cl}:^-$

Figure 53. E2 reaction mechanism

The hydroxide ion begins to remove a proton from the β carbon by using one of its lone pairs to form a bond (shown by the dotted line). Simultaneously, the electron pair from the β carbon-hydrogen bond starts to move in between the carbon-carbon bond to form a π bond (dotted line between the α and β carbons). The chlorine atom begins to leave the α carbon with an electron pair from the carbon-chlorine bond. The reaction occurs in step and has one transition state structure and one reaction barrier. Notice at the transition state that there are two partial bonds between the oxygen atom and the β hydrogen atom and between the α carbon and chlorine. The $C_\alpha - C_\beta$ bond shows the formation of a partial π bond. The byproduct shown in Figure 53 is 1-propene, which contains the fully formed double bond. The geometry of the α and β carbons is now trigonal planar. The remaining products are water and a chloride ion.

The E1 Reaction

The unimolecular elimination reaction or E1 can occur with tertiary alkyl halides (for example, tert-butyl chloride) when treated with 80% ethanol (25 °C). The byproduct is typically an alkene. However, alcohol or ether substitution (S_N1) byproducts can also form. When tert-butyl chloride reacts with 80% ethanol at 25 °C it produces 17% 2-methylpropene and 83% tert-butyl alcohol and tert-butyl ethyl ether. Substitution or elimination mechanisms will depend on the fast step. The nucleophile (for example, solvent) will either attack the positive carbon atom or 3° carbocation (tert-butyl cation) via S_N1 or at the β hydrogen atom by a E1 route. The mechanism for the E1 reaction occurs in two steps, as shown in Figure 54.

Step 1 **Step 2**

2-Chloro-2-methylpropane — Slow, $-Cl^-$ → Trigonal planar — Slow, $-Cl^-$ → H_3O^+ + 2-Methyl-1-propene

Figure 54. E1 mechanism

The polar solvent (ethanol) will promote the removal of the chlorine atom, which will leave with an electron pair taken from the $C - Cl$ bond, forming a chloride ion. Recall that the slow step produces a stable 3° carbocation. Both ions are solvated or stabilized by the water molecules. In step 2, a water molecule removes or attacks a β hydrogen atom with its electron pair. At the same time, the electrons from the β carbon and hydrogen bond move in between the $C_\alpha - C_\beta$ to form a double bond, thereby producing an alkene and a hydronium ion.

Substitution and Elimination Reactions

There is a competition between substitution and elimination reactions. If the substrate is a primary halide ($CH_3CH_2 - X$) and the base is an ethoxide ion, a substitution reaction (S_N2) will be favored over elimination (E1). In the SN2 mechanism, the base can approach the partially positive carbon (or carbon connected to the leaving group) easily. For secondary halides, elimination (E2) is favored over substitution (S_N2) due to steric hindrance. In other words, for steric reasons, it's easier for the β hydrogen atom to be removed as opposed to the nucleophile or base attacking the partially positive carbon directly. Furthermore, for steric reasons, an S_N2 reaction cannot occur for tertiary (3°) halides, and elimination will be highly favored and more so at higher temperatures. However, S_N1 reactions can still take place at a 3° halides but to a lesser extent compared to E2 reactions. For example, consider the following reaction:

$$CH_3CH_2^- + (CH_3)_3C - Br \xrightarrow{\text{ethanol, } 25\,°C} \overbrace{(CH_3)_3C - O - CH_2CH_3}^{9\%\ S_N1} + \overbrace{CH_2 = C(CH_3)_2}^{91\%\ E2}$$

At higher temperatures, the previous reaction will favor E1 and E2 mechanisms. Elimination reactions are also favored if a strong sterically hindered base attacks the alkyl halide (for example, tert-butoxide). Elimination reactions are also favored when using strong, slightly polarizable bases (for example, amide ion NH_2^- or CH_3O^-). Alkoxide ions (hindered) favor E2 mechanisms. S_N2 reactions are favorable with weakly basic ions (for example, Cl^-, $CH_3CO_2^-$) or weakly basic and highly polarizable ions (for example, Br^-, I^-).

E1 mechanisms are favored if the substrates form stable carbocations (3° halides) and if weak nucleophiles or bases in polar solvents are utilized. SN1 tends to be more favorable over E1 reactions at low temperatures, but 3° halides tend to undergo eliminations more easily. E1 is favored at higher temperatures over S_N1. A general summary for all reaction types is given in Table 5.

Methyl Carbon	Primary, 1° Carbon	Primary, 2° Carbon	Primary, 3° Carbon
Bimolecular reactions			S_N1, E1, or E2
S_N2	S_N2, E2 with a strong hindered base such as $(CH_3)_3CO^-$	S_N2 with weak bases such as I^-, CN^-, RCO_2^-. E2 with strong bases such as RO^-	S_N1/E1 with hydrolysis. S_N1 is favorable at low temperatures. E2 with strong bases such as RO^-

Table 5. Summary of substitution and elimination reactions

Electrophilic Additions

Hydrogen Halide Addition to Alkenes

Carbon-carbon double bonds ($C = C$, alkene) and triple bonds ($C \equiv C$, alkyne) contain one and two π bonds, which can dissociate so that electrons can delocalize within a specific compound. The electron-rich double bonds act as a nucleophile whereby the π electrons are donated to an **electrophile**, which is an electron-deficient or electron-seeking species. Electrophiles accept electron pairs. Similar to how bases donate their lone pair electrons in a substitution or elimination reaction to a substrate, the π electrons in double or triple carbon bond can attack an electrophile. Protons (H^+) found in aqueous solutions, bromine, Lewis acids (for example, BF_3 and $AlCl_3$), and metal ions (Ag^+, Hg^{2+}, Pt^{2+}) are examples of electrophiles. Hydrogen halides (HX) contain a partially positive and negative end and can react with alkenes in two steps by donating a proton to the π bond. The electrophile (E) will bond to one of the carbon atoms, which gives two of its π electrons to form a σ bond with a carbon atom. The general reaction mechanism is illustrated in Figure 55.

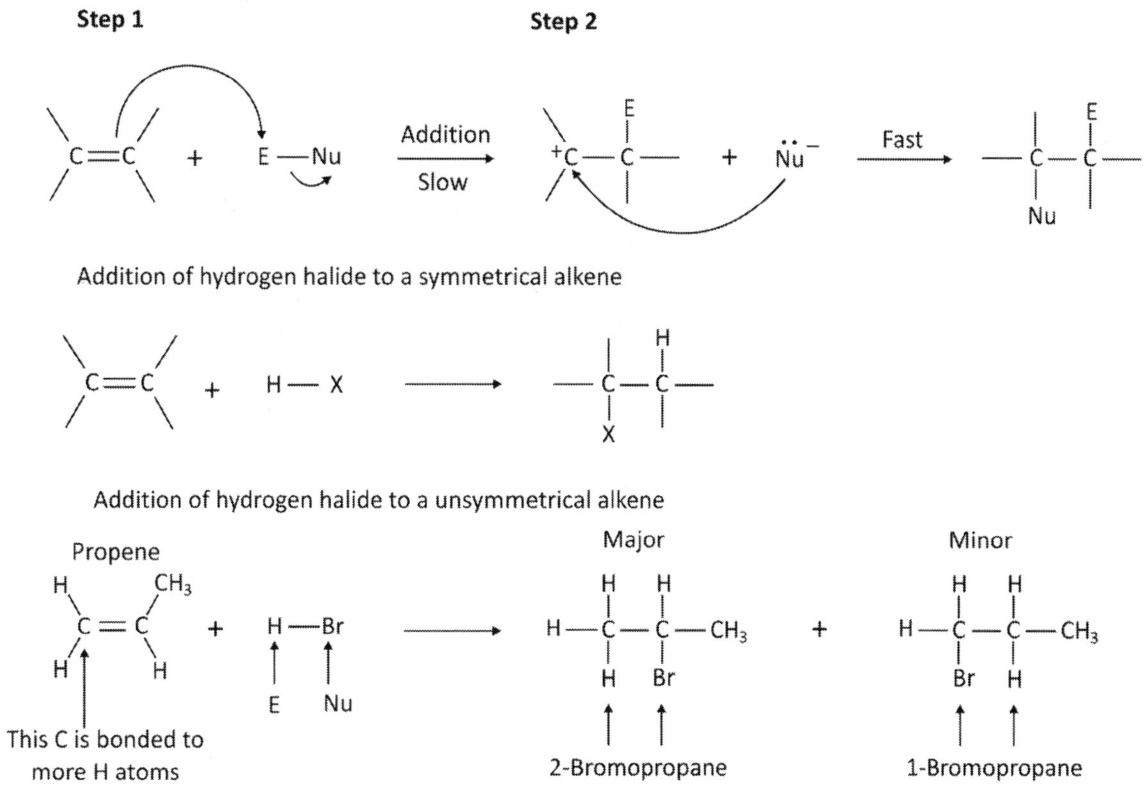

Step 1 | Step 2

Addition (Slow) | Fast

Addition of hydrogen halide to a symmetrical alkene

Addition of hydrogen halide to a unsymmetrical alkene

Propene + H—Br (E, Nu) → Major: 2-Bromopropane + Minor: 1-Bromopropane

This C is bonded to more H atoms

Figure 55. Mechanism for an addition reaction

The term "E" refers to the partially positive atom or electrophile, and "Nu" refers to the nucleophile or partially negative atom. In the addition reaction shown above, a π bond ($C = C$) and one σ bond ($E - Nu$) are converted into two σ bonds ($C - Nu$, $C - E$). In the first step, which is a slow or rate-determining step, the alkene acts as a nucleophile and donates its electrons to the electrophile to form a

$C-E$ bond. In the second step, there is a vacant p orbital at the highly reactive carbocation or electrophile, which reacts or is attacked quickly by the nucleophile (Lewis base). Hydrogen halides can be added to alkenes and contain electrophilic (H) and nucleophilic parts (X). The order of reactivity of hydrogen halides is $HI > HBr > HCl > HF$.

Markovnikov's Rule

Addition of a hydrogen halide to an unsymmetrical alkene can result in a major product and a minor product, unlike one symmetrical alkene that produces one product. In the addition of HBr to propene, 2-bromopropane is the major product, and 1-bromopropane is the minor product. According to Markovnikov's rule, when a hydrogen halide (HX) is added to an unsymmetrical alkene, the electrophilic hydrogen atom is attached to the carbon atom, in $C=C$, that is bonded to more hydrogen atoms (Figure 55). The Markovnikov addition is attributed to the carbocation's stability in the first step. For example, in the formation of 2-bromopropane, the carbocation formed in the first step is a secondary 2° carbocation (remove Br from 2-bromopropane and add + charge to C). The carbocation precursor that is converted to 1-bromopropane is a primary $1°$ carbocation. Secondary cations are more stable or form faster than primary cations, which results in 2-bromopropane being the primary product. Specifically, the first transition state structure in the two-step mechanism that resembles a 2° carbocation has a lower free energy of activation compared to the transition state structure resembling a $1°$ cation. The major product, 2-bromopropane, is the kinetic product because it forms faster.

Markovnikov additions are **regioselective** because the addition reactions don't give two or more constitutional isomers (for example, 2-bromopropane and 1-bromopropane) in equal amounts but produce one predominant product. There are exceptions to Markovnikov's rule, which occur when the addition reaction (HBr + alkene) is mixed with a peroxide $(R-OO-R)$. The major product (2-bromopropane) now becomes the minor product, and the minor product (1-bromopropane) becomes the major product. The anti-Markovnikov addition only occurs with HBr and peroxide, and not with other hydrogen halides. Hydrogen halide addition to an alkene is also called ionic addition.

Stereochemistry of Ionic Addition

The carbocation that is formed in the first step can be achiral, which means that the halide ion can attack the trigonal planar cation from above or below to give two different isomers. For example, 1-butene can react with HX to give a racemate composed of (*S*)-2-halobutane and (*R*)-2-halobutane.

Oxymercuration-Demercuration: Formation of Alcohols from Alkenes

In a multistep process, alcohols can be produced by alkenes through a useful laboratory method called oxymercuration-demercuration. The first part of the reaction, called oxymercuration, takes place by combining an alkene with mercuric acetate $(Hg(OAc)_2 \rightleftarrows Hg^{+}OAc + OAc^{-})$ in a mixture of tetrahydrofuran (THF) and water. In a second reaction called **demercuration**, the hydroxyalkyl mercury

compound is reduced with sodium borohydride ($NaBH_4$), to form the alcohol. Figure 56 shows the reaction mechanism below for an unsymmetrical alkene.

Step 1: 3,3-Dimethyl-1-butene + $\overset{+}{H}gOAc$

Step 2: Mercury-bridged carbocation

Step 3

Step 4: Hydroxyalkyl mercury compound $+H_3O^+$ — OH^-, $NaBH_4$ →

Step 3: 3,3-Dimethyl-2-butanol

Figure 56. Oxymercuration and demercuration

The first three reaction steps correspond to oxymercuration. Mercuric acetate dissociates to an electrophilic HgOAc⁺ ion, which accepts an electron pair from the $C = C$ of 3,3-dimethyl-1-butene (step 1). A mercury-bridged carbocation forms and the positive charge is shared between the 2° carbon atom and mercury. Notice that the $C - HgOAc$ bond forms on the carbon atom with the most hydrogens indicating regioselectivity, which is in accord with Markovnikov's rule. In step 2, a lone pair from a water molecule attacks the partially positive carbon atom. In step 3, another water molecule then attacks one of the hydrogen atoms bonded to oxygen, which results in the formation of an alcohol. The mercury compound undergoes demercuration in step 4 by reacting with a hydroxyl ion and $NaBH_4$. A hydrogen atom from $NaBH_4$ attaches to the carbon atom, initially the $C = C$, that initially had the higher number of carbon-hydrogen bonds (indicated by arrows in step 4).

Acid-Catalyzed Hydration and Alkoxylation: Alkenes to Alcohols and Ethers

Water can be added to an alkene (hydration) in the presence of an acid such as sulfuric or phosphoric acid. Acid-catalyzed hydration is regioselective and will follow Markovnikov's rule, and it typically does not yield primary ° alcohols. One exception is the addition of reaction of ethylene with water and phosphoric acid at 300 °C to produce ethanol. The acid-catalyzed hydration for an alkene can be described in three steps, with the first step being rate-determining or slow, as shown in Figure 57.

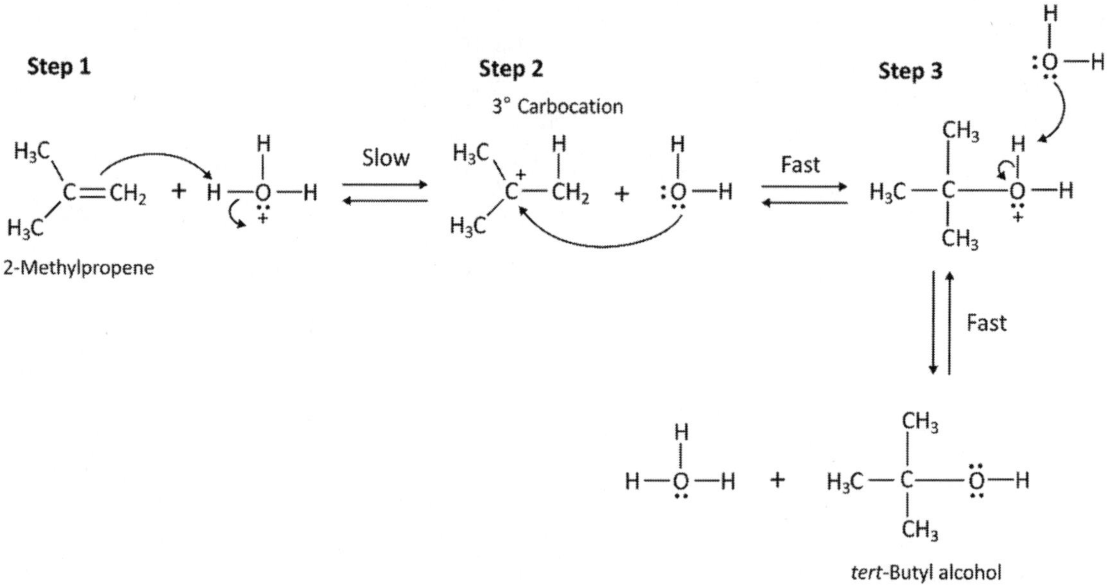

Step 1 — 2-Methylpropene + H_3O^+ (Slow) → Step 2 — 3° Carbocation + H_2O (Fast) → Step 3 — protonated alcohol + H_2O (Fast) → H_3O^+ + *tert*-Butyl alcohol

Figure 57. Reaction mechanism for acid-catalyzed hydration

2-methylpropene will follow a Markovnikov addition with the proton going to the carbon that has more hydrogens, which forms the 3° carbocation (step 1). A diluted acid, the source of the hydronium ion, is typically used to keep the concentration of the water high. The carbocation then reacts with water to form a protonated alcohol (step 2). Another water molecule (step 3) then removes a proton from the protonated alcohol to give the tert-butyl alcohol and hydronium ion. The preparation of alcohols through alkene hydration has some limitations in the laboratory. Because a carbocation forms in the slow step, it can rearrange to a more stable carbocation and form a different product. For example, the acid-catalyzed hydration reaction of 3,3-dimethyl-1-butene is expected to form a 2 °carbocation (see Figure 58) and produce 3,3-dimethyl-2-butanol. However, the issue with acid catalyzation is that the 2°

carbocation can rearrange to a 3° carbocation, which leads to a different product called 2,3-dimethyl-2-butanol (Figure 58).

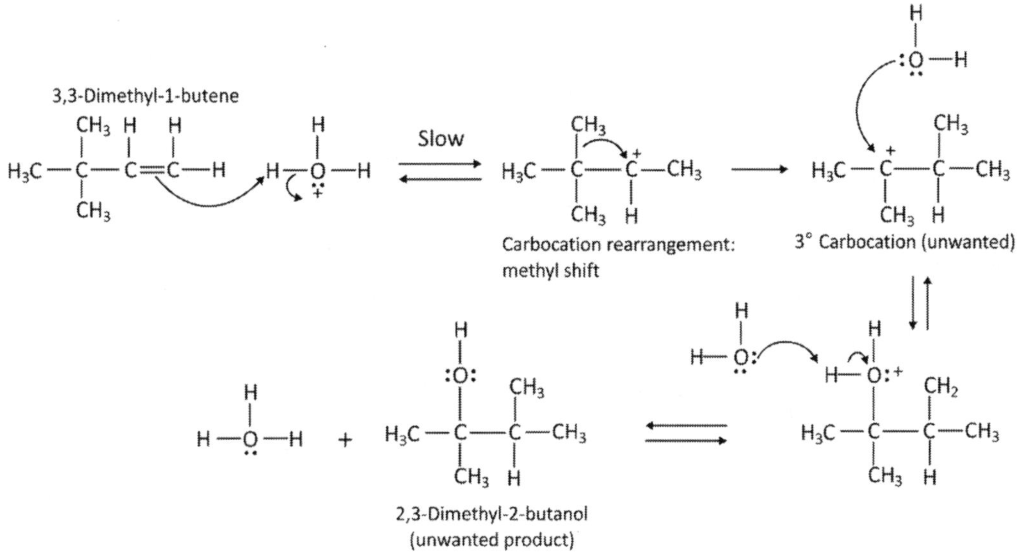

3,3-Dimethyl-1-butene

Slow

Carbocation rearrangement: methyl shift

3° Carbocation (unwanted)

2,3-Dimethyl-2-butanol (unwanted product)

Figure 58. Carbocation rearrangement

Rearrangement reactions due to carbocation rearrangements have limited the use of alkene hydrations in the laboratory. Consequently, chemists developed novel reaction methods such as oxymercuration-demercuration and hydroboration-oxidation. Both methods can avoid rearrangements.

Acid-catalyzed alkoxylation of an alkene forms an ether (ROR) instead of an alcohol (ROH). Acid-catalyzed alkoxylation is similar to acid-catalyzed hydration except that an alcohol (ROH) reagent is used in place of water. The reaction can lead to two products: (1) a major product from Markovnikov addition and (2) a minor product from anti-Markovnikov addition. The lone pair from the oxygen atom, from the alcohol group (instead of water), attacks the carbocation, which forms an oxonium ion. In the third step, another alcohol (ROH) deprotonates the oxonium ion to form an ether. Figure 59 shows an example of the acid-catalyzed alkoxylation of 2,3-dihydrofuran.

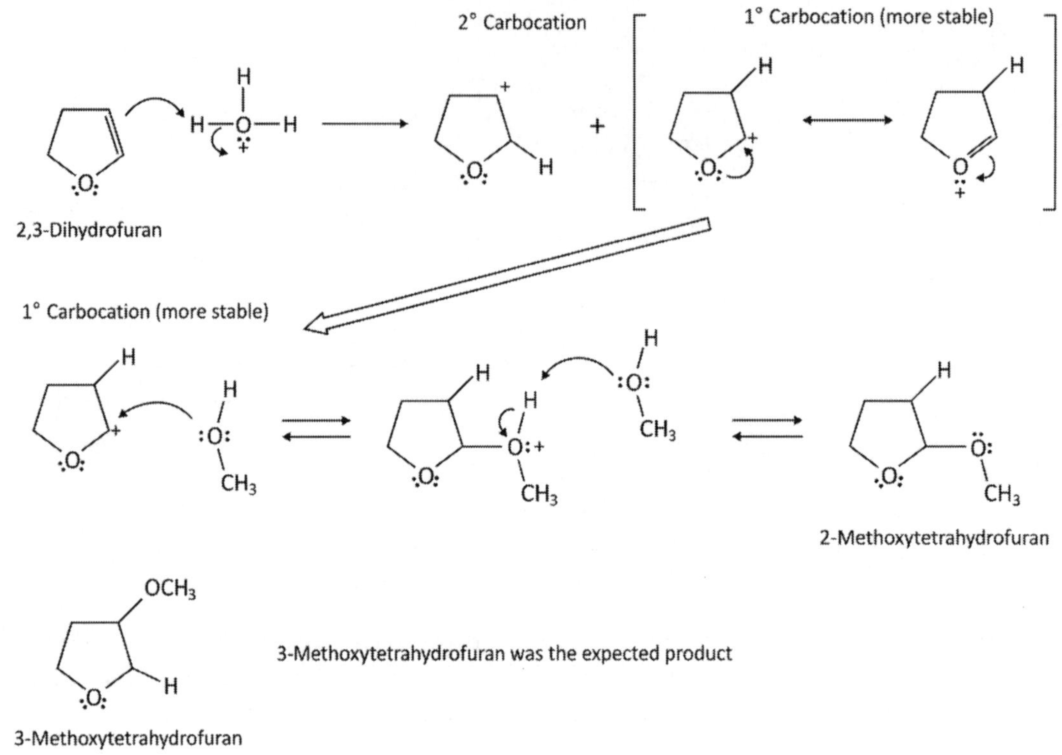

2° Carbocation

1° Carbocation (more stable)

2,3-Dihydrofuran

1° Carbocation (more stable)

2-Methoxytetrahydrofuran

3-Methoxytetrahydrofuran was the expected product

3-Methoxytetrahydrofuran

Figure 59. Acid-catalyzed alkoxylation

The 2° carbocation becomes the minor precursor as opposed to the major precursor, which is a 1° carbocation. The major precursor or the 1° carbocation is a more stable carbocation since it can undergo resonance delocalization. The oxygen atom can donate an electron pair to the 1° carbocation, thereby lowering the energy of the structure. As a result, the alcohol group (for example, methanol) attacks at the 1° carbocation to form 2-methoxy tetrahydrofuran. 3-methoxytetrahydrofuran, the minor product, would have been the expected product if the alcohol primarily attacked the 2° carbocation.

Hydroboration-Oxidation: Forming Alcohols from Alkenes

A hydroxyl group can also be added to an alkene by using diborane or tetrahydrofuran/ borane (BH_3). However, the addition of water is not direct, and two major reaction steps typically follow. In the first reaction step, borane is added to the $C = C$ bond, which is a process called **hydroboration**. In the second step, oxidation and hydrolysis of the organo-borane intermediate are carried out with hydrogen

peroxide (H_2O_2) and sodium hydroxide ($NaOH$), which converts the compound to an alcohol and a borate ion (or boric acid).

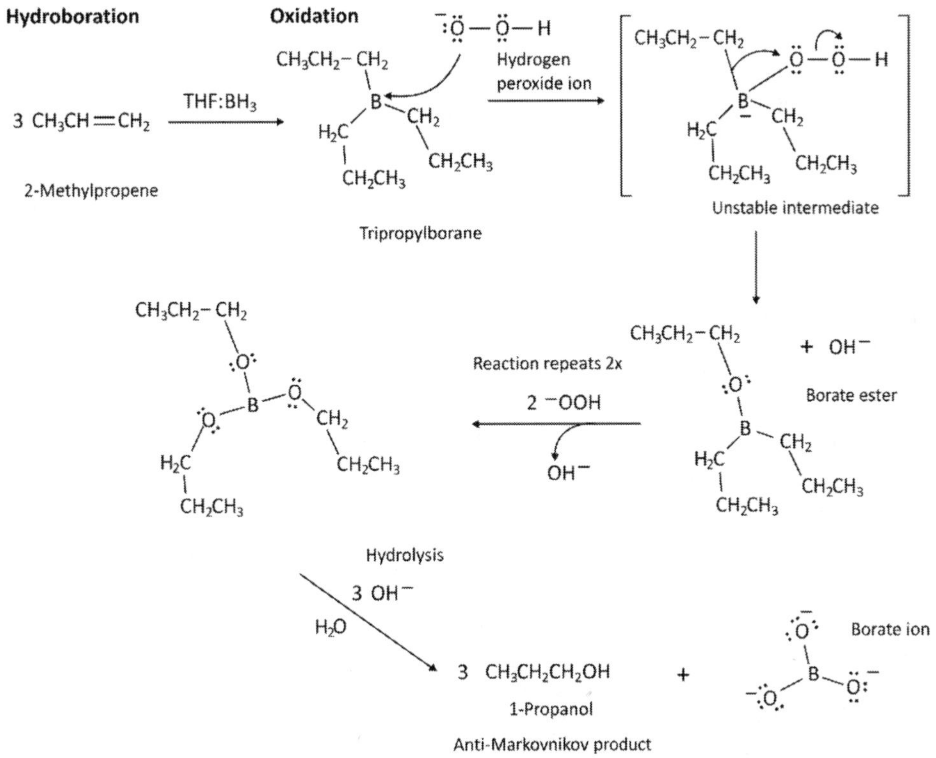

Figure 60. Hydroboration and oxidation

In the oxidation process shown in Figure 60, boron accepts an electron pair from the hydroperoxide ion (OOH^-). The unstable intermediate then converts to the borate ester by transferring one of its alkyl groups to an adjacent oxygen atom, which allows the hydroxide ion to leave. The reaction repeats twice more to form a trialkyl borate ester, which then undergoes basic hydrolysis to produce a borate ion and three alcohol molecules. Hydroboration reactions are regioselective and primarily give an anti-Markovnikov product, which cannot be obtained by acid-catalyzed hydration or oxymercuration-demercuration. The oxidation step retains the stereochemical configuration, and the hydroxyl group changes place with the boron atom. The first two steps then are a "syn" addition of the hydrogen and hydroxyl group. For example, consider the hydroboration-oxidation of 1-methylcylocpentene in Figure 61.

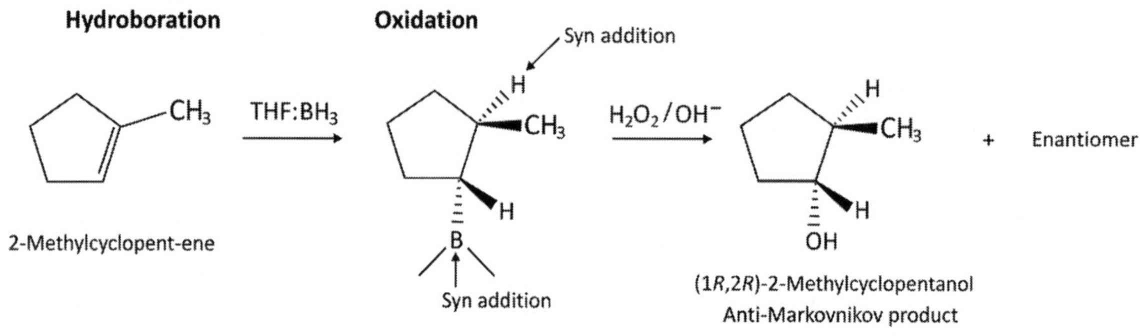

Hydroboration **Oxidation**

2-Methylcyclopent-ene $\xrightarrow{THF:BH_3}$ (Syn addition) $\xrightarrow{H_2O_2/OH^-}$ (1*R*,2*R*)-2-Methylcyclopentanol + Enantiomer

Anti-Markovnikov product

Figure 61. Stereochemistry of hydroboration-oxidation

The second step replaces the boron atom with the hydroxyl group with retention of the stereochemical configuration. The product is trans with respect to the hydroxyl and methyl groups. Note that trans-2-methylcyclopentanol is the anti-Markovnikov product. Acid catalyzation would produce a 3° carbocation and place the hydroxyl group at the carbon atom bonded to the methyl group (the Markovnikov product).

Reaction of Alkenes with Carbenes

Carbenes are neutral divalent ("divalent" means two bonds) carbon compounds that can react with a high degree of stereospecificity and can be used in the preparation of three-membered rings. The simplest carbene is methylene, $:CH_2$, and it can react with alkenes by addition to the $C = C$ to form a cyclopropane. Dihalocarbenes, $:CX_2$, are other types of carbenes and include compounds such as dichlorocarbene, $:CCl_2$. The reaction of $:CCl_2$ with an alkene is stereospecific. For example, if the alkyl groups (R) of the alkene are cis (or trans), they will be cis (trans) in the product (Figure 62, reaction B).

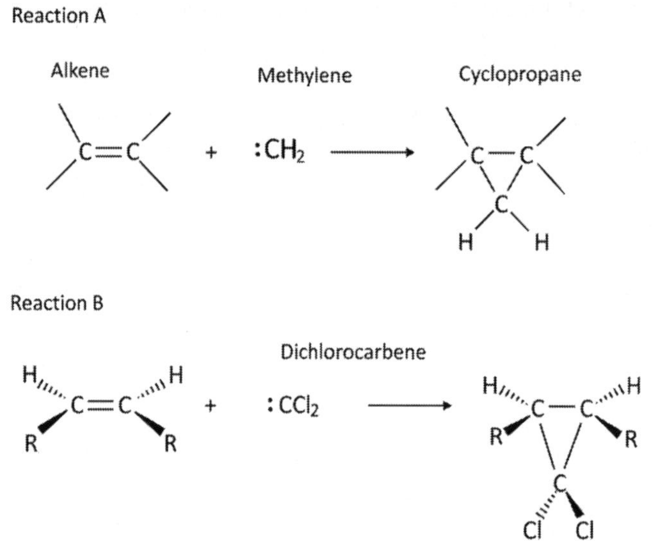

Reaction A

Alkene + Methylene ($:CH_2$) $\longrightarrow$ Cyclopropane

Reaction B

Alkene + Dichlorocarbene ($:CCl_2$) $\longrightarrow$ product

Figure 62. Reaction of carbenes

The dichlorocarbene can be generated by reacting a base, such as potassium tert-butoxide, with chloroform, which produces dichlorocarbene. Derivatives of cyclopropane can then be synthesized by mixing dichlorocarbene with an alkene. The reaction of cyclohexene with chloroform/*tert*-butoxide produces a bicyclic compound (Figure 63).

Step 1

$$(CH_3)_3C-\ddot{O}:^- K^+ + H:CCl_3 \rightleftharpoons (CH_3)_3C-\ddot{O}H + {}^-:CCl_3 + K^+ \xrightarrow{\text{Slow}} :CCl_2 + :\ddot{Cl}:^-$$

Dichlorocarbene

Step 2

Cyclohexene + $:CCl_2$ → (1*R*,6*S*)-7,7-Dichlorobicyclo[4.1.0]heptane (59%)

Figure 63. Generation and reaction of dichlorocarbene with cyclohexene

Halogen Addition to Alkenes

Chlorine (Cl_2) and bromine (Br_2) gas can react with alkenes at a low temperature or at room temperature in non-nucleophile solvents (for example, CCl_4) to give vicinal dihalides. The addition of the halogen, in particular, is an ionic mechanism where "anti" addition occurs; for example, each halogen is trans to one another. The mechanism is an ionic mechanism and is shown below.

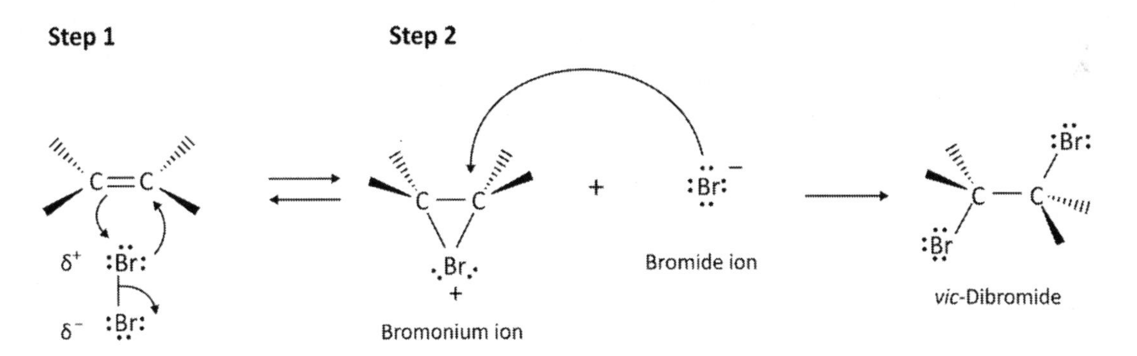

Figure 64. Mechanism for bromine addition to an alkene

As an alkene approaches, the bromine molecule becomes polarized (London dispersion forces) such that the bromine atom furthest from the alkene is polarized partially negative. The bromine closer to the alkene is polarized partially positive. The $Br - Br$ bond weakens and breaks heterolytically. The positive bromine atom is transferred to the alkene with six of its valence shell electrons, and a bromide ion departs. The positive bromine atom in the formed bromonium ion is bonded to two carbon atoms with one pair of electrons from the π bond and another pair from the bromine atom. In the second step, a bromide ion nucleophile attacks the backside of a carbon atom via an S_N2 reaction, which opens the ring and forms a *vic*-dibromide. The addition of bromine (or a halogen) is a stereospecific reaction and is an example of an **anti-addition**. The bromonium ion can form from above or below the C = C bond. Figure 65 shows some cases of an alkene or a specific stereoisomer that reacts to give a different stereoisomer.

Cyclopentene

Br_2

bromonium ion

Inversion of configuration

Trans enatiomers

(1*R*,2*R*)-1,2-Dibromocyclopentane

(1*S*,2*S*)-1,2-Dibromocyclopentane

cis-2-Butene

bromonium ion (achiral)

(2*R*,3*R*)-2,3-Dibromobutane (chiral)

(2*S*,3*S*)-2,3-Dibromobutane (chiral)

trans-2-Butene

bromonium ion (chiral)

(2*R*,3*S*)-2,3-Dibromobutane (meso)

(2*R*,3*S*)-2,3-Dibromobutane (meso)

Figure 65. The stereochemistry of halogen addition to alkenes

Nucleophilic Addition at Carbonyl Groups

Nucleophilic Addition to Carbonyl Groups in Ketones and Aldehydes

Carbonyl groups contain a carbon atom double-bonded to an oxygen atom ($C = O$) and can be found in functional groups such as ketones, aldehydes, carboxylic acids, ethers, and amides (see Figure 1). The carbonyl group is polar since the carbon atom is polarized partially positive and the more electronegative oxygen atom is polarized partially negative. The carbon atom will be electron-deficient (electrophilic). The trigonal planar arrangement of groups around the carbonyl carbon will make it susceptible to attack by a nucleophile from above or below its plane. The carbonyl oxygen atom will be vulnerable to acid catalysis due to its partially negative charge.

In the first step, if a strong nucleophile "Nu" (for example, the reagent) attacks the carbon atom, an electron pair will be donated to the carbon atom to form a σ bond. Simultaneously, the π bond between the carbon and oxygen will break, and the electrons will move to the oxygen atom to become a lone pair. The carbon atom initially has an sp^2 hybridization and is trigonal planar around the carbon atom. However, after the nucleophilic attack, the carbon atom will become sp^3 hybridized and will have a tetrahedral geometry around the carbon atom. The tetrahedral intermediate is also called an alkoxide ion. In the second step, the negatively charged oxygen is strongly basic and will remove a proton from an acid or $H - Nu$. In protic environments (solvents with $N - H$ or $O - H$ bonds, for example, water is polar protic), the alkoxide intermediate will be protonated to become an alcohol type product. Figure 66 shows the mechanism for nucleophilic addition to the $C = O$ within an aldehyde or ketone.

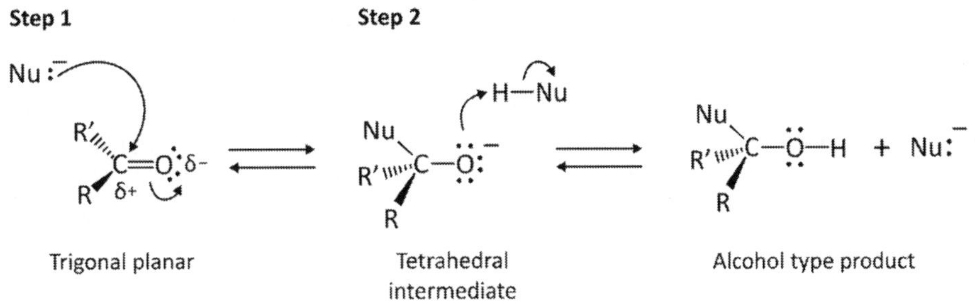

Step 1

Step 2

Trigonal planar

Tetrahedral intermediate

Alcohol type product

Figure 66. Nucleophilic addition to the carbonyl group

The carbonyl compound may be a ketone (R' and R are C) or an aldehyde (R' or R is H). Nucleophilic attacks are more likely if a strong acid (H^+) is used to protonate the carbonyl group. The nucleophile may also be weak. If a proton or Lewis Acid donates its proton to the electron pair of the carbonyl oxygen atom, the oxygen atom will become positively charged and will produce an **oxonium cation**. Resonance can occur, and the carbon-oxygen π bond will dissociate and localized as a nonbonding pair on the oxygen atom, thereby forming a carbocation. Delocalization will cause the carbon atom to obtain a positive-partial charge, thus making it more electrophilic or highly reactive and susceptible to attack by a nucleophile. In step 2, the oxonium cation accepts an electron pair from the nucleophile, and the base removes a proton from the positively charged nucleophile. The addition product is formed along with the regeneration of the acid. Figure 67 shows the mechanism for acid-catalyzed nucleophilic addition.

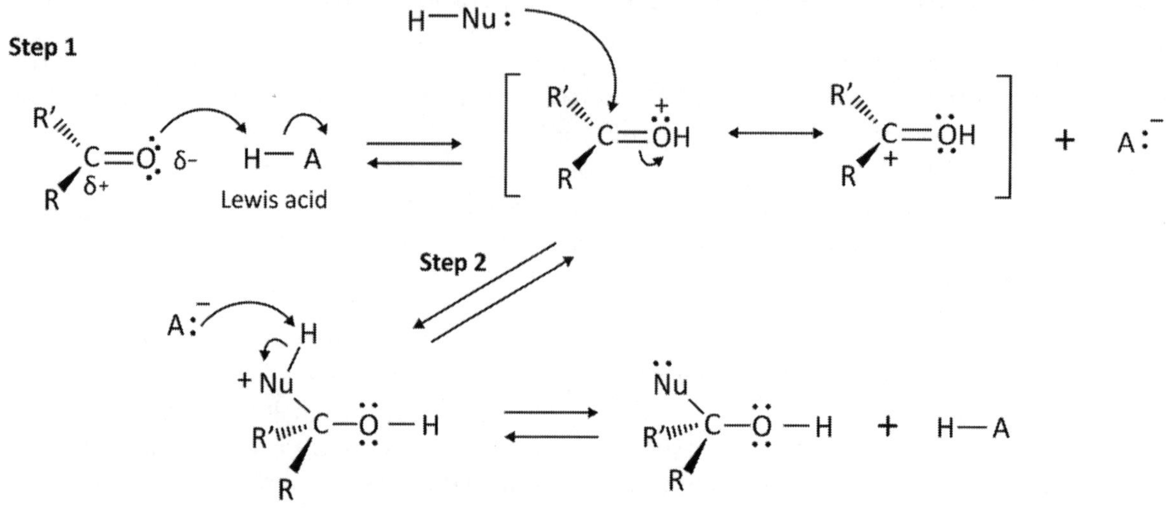

Figure 67. Acid-catalyzed nucleophilic addition

Reversibility of Nucleophilic Addition Reactions: Electronic and Steric Factors

Addition reactions to carbonyl groups are reversible (for example, alcohol product to carbonyl) unlike electrophilic addition to $C = O$ bonds and nucleophilic substitution of saturated hydrocarbons. Reversibility is more likely if the nucleophile is a weak base and an excellent leaving group. In other words, there will be an equilibrium between the addition product (for example, alcohol) and the carbonyl group. Electronic factors and steric hinderance will determine the ease of nucleophilic attack and the direction of equilibrium. For example, electron releasing or withdrawing groups directly bonded to the carbonyl carbon will either stabilize or destabilize the carbonyl compound. If the substituent is electron releasing or donating (for example, CH_3), then the slightly positive polarized charge on the carbonyl carbon will lessen, thereby making it more stable. The equilibrium will shift more toward the left. The carbonyl carbon is less susceptible to attack by a nucleophile.

In contrast, if the substituent bonded to the carbonyl carbon is electron-withdrawing (for example, $-CF_3$ or $-CCl_3$ groups), then the partially positive polarized charge on the carbonyl carbon will increase or become more positive. The carbon atom will be more electrophilic, which will increase the probability of the carbon atom undergoing nucleophilic attack. The carbonyl carbon is destabilized, and the equilibrium will shift to the right or toward the addition product.

Aldehydes $(R - (CO) - H)$ will be more reactive than ketones in regard to electronic factors. Aldehydes contain one alkyl group which is electron releasing and will stabilize or partially neutralize the polarized positive charge on the carbonyl carbon. In contrast, ketones $(R - (CO) - R)$ will have two alkyl or electron releasing groups that will stabilize the carbonyl carbon atom to a greater extent. The carbonyl carbon atom becomes less positive, which means that equilibrium constant for the formation of the tetrahedral product is smaller and less favorable. Therefore, a nucleophilic attack is less likely to occur.

Figure 68 shows four different structures that each contain a carbonyl group. The nucleophilic addition of compound B will exist as a hydrate to a much greater extent than the other compounds. The reason is due to steric and electronic factors.

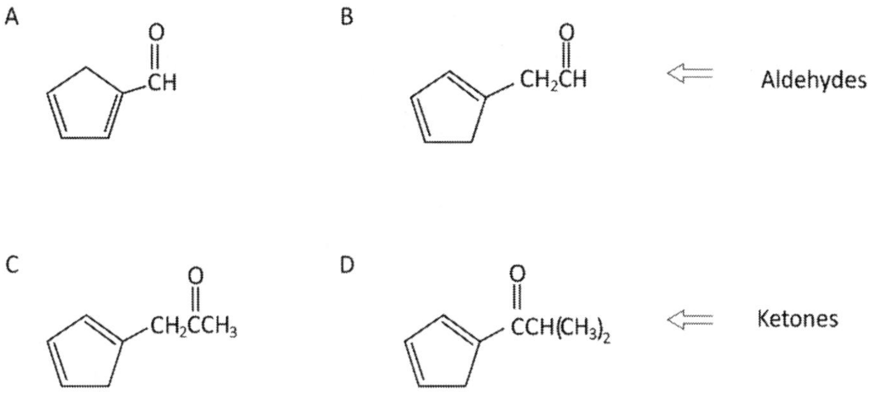

A: CH (O) B: CH_2CH (O) ⇐ Aldehydes

C: CH_2CCH_3 (O) D: $CCH(CH_3)_2$ (O) ⇐ Ketones

Figure 68. Steric and electronic contributions in addition reactions

Compounds A and B are both aldehydes $\left(\mathrm{R-(CO-H)}\right)$, while compounds C and D are ketones. If a nucleophile such as water attacks the carbonyl carbon atom at any of the shown compounds, a tetrahedral intermediate will form. The reaction process is reversible. The ketones have two electron releasing groups, which must come closer as the tetrahedral intermediate forms ($\mathrm{C-C-C}$ bond angles changes from about 120° to 109.5°). There will be greater steric repulsion in the ketones (alkyl to alkyl) compare to aldehydes (alkyl to hydrogen), so there will be less ketone product at equilibrium. Choices C and D are more stable or less reactive than choices A and B. Compound A will be more stable than B since its conjugated ($\mathrm{C=C-(C=O)-H}$), which makes compound B the most reactive and most likely to undergo addition.

Nucleophilic Addition to Derivatives of Ammonia

Aldehydes and ketones can react with primary amines ($\mathrm{R-NH_2}$) or derivatives of ammonia ($\mathrm{Y-NH_2}$), which can act as nucleophiles by attacking the carbonyl carbon and forming a tetrahedral intermediate. The intermediate will result in the formation of water and a carbon-nitrogen double bond called an **imine**, $\mathrm{C=N}$. Formation of an imine linkage is important in biochemical or visual processes, for example, photochemistry of vision. These addition reactions are catalyzed by an acid and will form a mixture of (*E*) and (*Z*) isomers. Reactions with primary amines occur fastest at a pH between 4 and 5 but slow otherwise. Figure 69 shows the mechanism for imine formation.

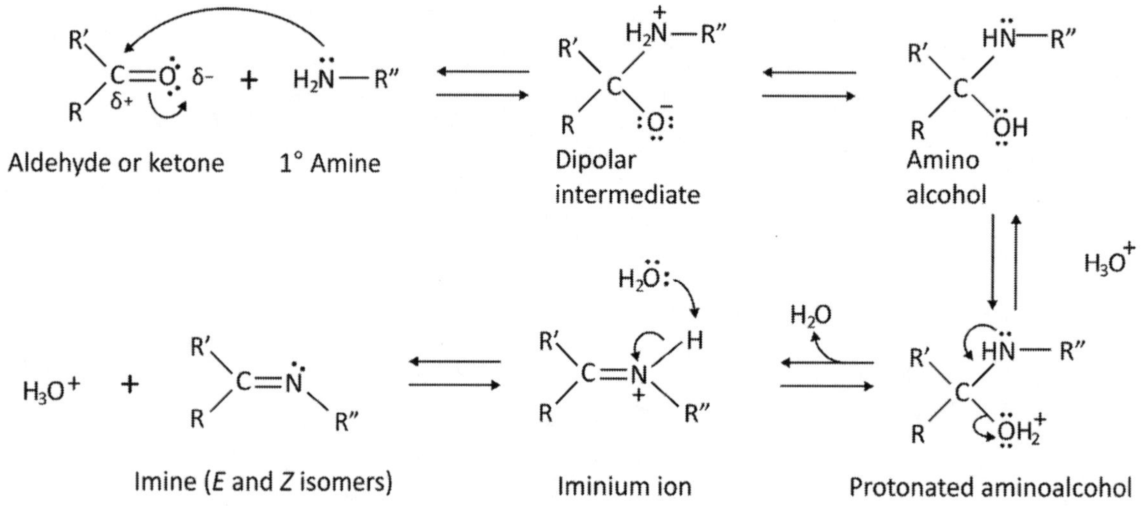

Aldehyde or ketone | 1° Amine | Dipolar intermediate | Amino alcohol | H_3O^+ | Protonated aminoalcohol | H_2O | Iminium ion | H_3O^+ + Imine (*E* and *Z* isomers)

Figure 69. The formation of an imine through addition

The nonbonding pair from the amine is donated to the carbon carbonyl group, which forms the tetrahedral dipolar intermediate. Intermolecular proton transfer at the nitrogen to oxygen atom occurs, which creates an amino alcohol. The alcohol is protonated at the oxygen atom. The vital step occurs when the protonated amino-alcohol loses a water molecule to become an iminium ion. Protonation of the alcohol group allows the acid to create a good leaving group (OH_2^+). A water molecule removes a proton from the nitrogen atom to form an imine and hydronium ion. Decreasing the pH (higher H^+ concentration) slows the reaction since protonation of the amine decreases the concentration of the nucleophile or amine required in the first step.

Consequently, the concentration of the protonated amino-alcohol becomes lower. Secondary amines can react with aldehydes or ketones, which will lose water, and result in the formation an **enamine**. Addition products such as amines and enamines can be converted back to a carbonyl compound by the addition of water (hydrolysis) with aqueous acid.

Acid-Catalyzed Acetal Formation: Addition of Alcohols

Mixing an aldehyde with an alcohol will slowly form a compound called a **hemiacetal or hemiketals** (carbonyl carbon bonded to OR and OH). An equilibrium will exist between the carbonyl compound and the product. Hemiacetals are typically unstable but more stable as a five or six-membered ring. The nucleophilic addition can be catalyzed with an acid or base in alcohol. An **acetal or ketal** is a compound that has two $-OR$ groups attached to the carbonyl carbon atom. The formation of an acetal compound can be catalyzed with an acid first to form the hemiacetal. The hydroxyl group is then removed from the hemiacetal, by acid-catalyzed elimination, forming a second addition to the alcohol, which involves the loss of a proton.

Figure 70 shows a reaction mechanism for acid-catalyzed acetal synthesis.

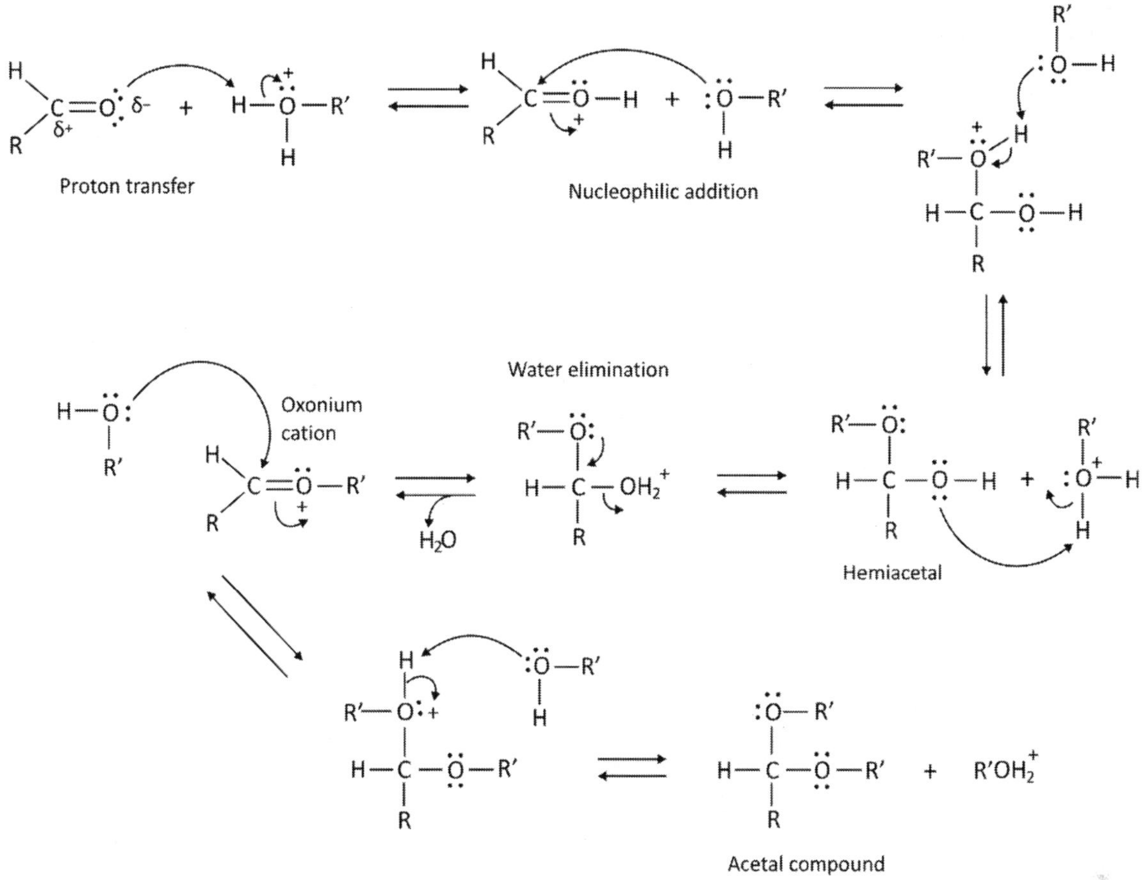

Proton transfer

Nucleophilic addition

Water elimination

Oxonium cation

Hemiacetal

Acetal compound

Figure 70. Acid-catalyzed hemiacetal and acetal formation

An acid such as hydrochloric acid (gaseous HCl or concentrated sulfuric acid, H_2SO_4) protonates the alcohol. The carbonyl oxygen atom from the aldehyde (or ketone) then reacts with the protonated alcohol by removing a proton. An addition reaction occurs when an alcohol attacks the carbonyl carbon atom. Another alcohol molecule then removes a proton from the positive oxygen, which produces a hemiacetal. The hydroxyl group of the hemiacetal compound is then protonated, which leads to water elimination, followed by the formation of a reactive oxonium cation. A second alcohol then attacks the carbonyl carbon from the ion, which is followed by proton removal and formation of the acetal. Formation of the acetal compound is reversible and can occur through acid-catalyzed hydrolysis, which favors the formation of the aldehyde.

The formation of acetals from ketones is not favored with simple alcohols and gaseous HCl, but cyclic acetal formation can occur with excess 1,2-diol and small amounts of acid. The reaction is also reversible by acid-catalyzed hydrolysis. In a basic solution, the acetals are stable and act as protecting groups. Acetal groups can protect ketone or aldehyde groups from any unwanted reactions. For example, suppose a compound contained a ketone and an ester group. If you wanted to convert the ester group to an alcohol, first convert the ketone to a cyclic acetal group by treating with an alcohol or acid. Then

reduce the ester group in basic solution to convert it to an alcohol. Finally, hydrolyze the acetal group to convert it back to a ketone.

1,2 and 1,4 Additions to α,β-unsaturated Aldehydes and Ketones

Carbonyl groups found in aldehydes and ketones that are not saturated at the α or β carbons can undergo 1,2 or 1,4-additions with a nucleophile. Figure 71 shows an example of the α or β carbon atoms in an aldehyde and ketone.

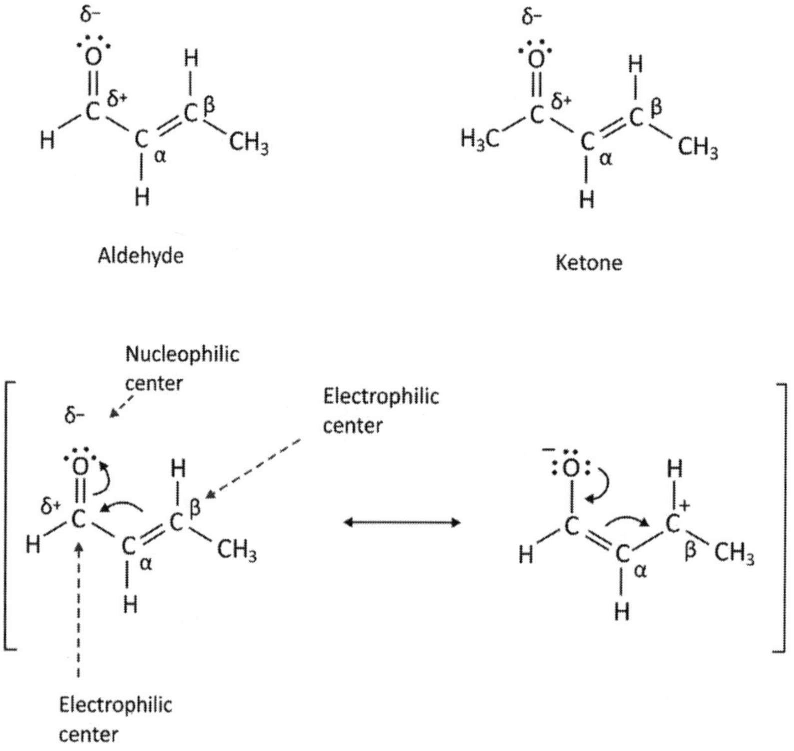

Aldehyde

Ketone

Nucleophilic center

Electrophilic center

Electrophilic center

Figure 71. α and β positions of unsaturated aldehydes and ketones

If a nucleophile attacks the carbonyl carbon, the addition is a 1,2 nucleophilic addition. 1,2-addition reactions can occur with strong and basic nucleophiles such as Grignard (for example, RMgX) or organolithium reagents (RLi). Some examples of aldehydes or ketones reacting with these reagents are

shown in Figure 72. 1,2-additions are the kinetically favored product. Reagents such as $LiAlH_4$, CH3MgBr, and $(C_6H_5)_3PCH_2$ are strong basic nucleophiles, which will give a 1,2-addition product.

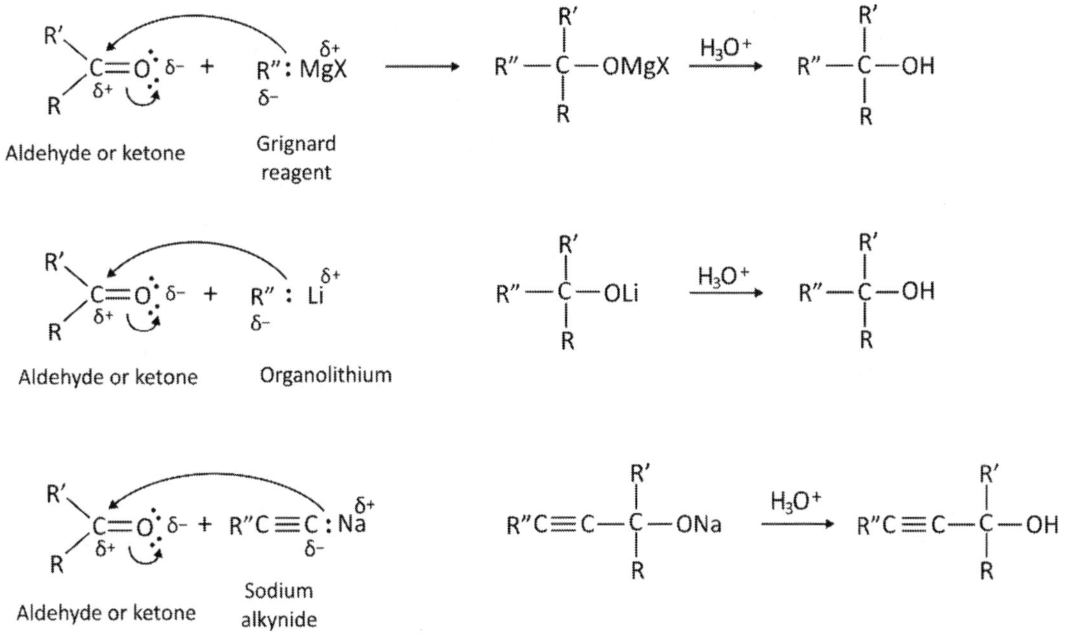

R'R C=O (δ+ C, δ− O) + R″: MgX (δ− R″, δ+ MgX) ⟶ R″—C(R')(R)—OMgX $\xrightarrow{H_3O^+}$ R″—C(R')(R)—OH

Aldehyde or ketone, Grignard reagent

R'R C=O (δ+ C, δ− O) + R″ : Li (δ− R″, δ+ Li) ⟶ R″—C(R')(R)—OLi $\xrightarrow{H_3O^+}$ R″—C(R')(R)—OH

Aldehyde or ketone, Organolithium

R'R C=O (δ+ C, δ− O) + R″C≡C : Na (δ− C, δ+ Na) ⟶ R″C≡C—C(R')(R)—ONa $\xrightarrow{H_3O^+}$ R″C≡C—C(R')(R)—OH

Aldehyde or ketone, Sodium alkynide

Figure 72. Reformatsky reaction: addition of organometallic reagents

If the nucleophile attacks the β carbon atom, then the reaction is a 1,4-nucleophilic addition (or conjugate addition). In contrast, 1,4-additions will occur with weakly basic nucleophiles such or organocuprates (for example, R_2CuLi), amines, and the cyanide ion. The mechanism for 1,4 addition occurs in two steps, as shown in Figure 73.

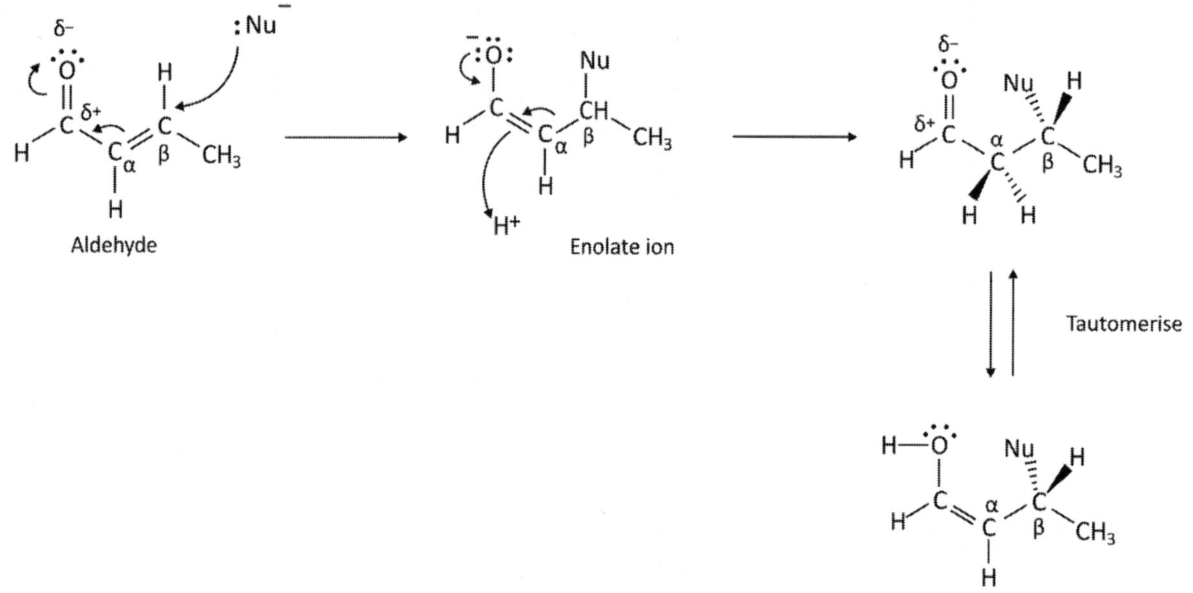

Figure 73. Mechanism of 1,4 addition

In the first step, the nucleophile will attack the β carbon atom and form a bond. Simultaneously, the $C_\alpha = C_\beta$ π bond breaks, which delocalizes to create a new bond with the carbonyl carbon and the α carbon atom. The π electrons from the $C = O$ bond also delocalize to the carbonyl oxygen atom. The intermediate is an enolate ion. The third lone pair of electrons from the oxygen atom then delocalizes back to the $C - O$ bond. At the same time, the π electrons between the carbonyl carbon and α carbon atom move to form a σ bond between a proton and the α carbon. The proton may be provided from the nucleophile (for example, HCN). The 1,4 addition is the thermodynamically favored product and can undergo tautomerization. Weak bases or their salts (for example, HCN and NaCN) are weak nucleophiles that will give a 1,4-addition product.

The Wittig Reaction

Aldehydes and ketones can react with phosphorus ylides to produce a triphenylphosphine oxide and an alkene. The reaction is called a Wittig reaction and can result in a mixture of (*E*) and (*Z*) isomers. One advantage in a Wittig reaction is that there is no ambiguity regarding the location of the double bond in the product (unlike E1 reactions). The reaction occurs by nucleophilic substitution. Triphenylphosphine is an example of a good nucleophile and weak base and can react readily with 1° and 2° alkyl halides via

S_N2 to produce the phosphorus ylide (phosphorene). The general reaction mechanism is shown in Figure 74.

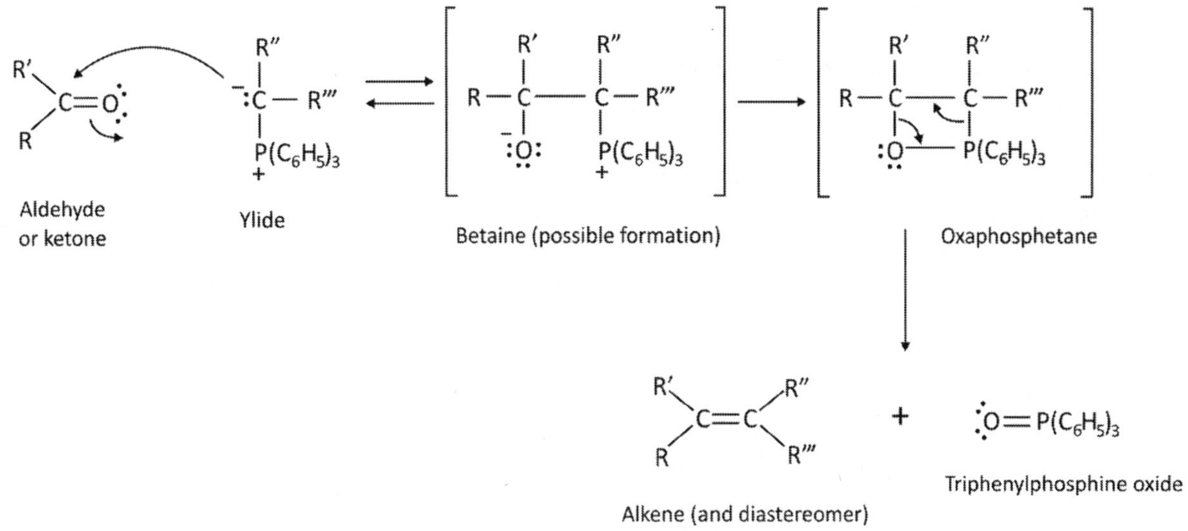

Aldehyde or ketone

Ylide

Betaine (possible formation)

Oxaphosphetane

Alkene (and diastereomer)

Triphenylphosphine oxide

Figure 74. Wittig reaction

Nucleophilic Substitution at Carbonyl Groups

Nucleophilic Acyl Substitution Reactions

Nucleophilic acyl substitution reactions can take place for carboxylic acids and their derivatives, which include esters, amides, anhydrides, and acyl halides. Recall that the carbonyl group is partially polarized at the carbon atom, and partially polarized negative at the oxygen atom. Therefore, the carbonyl carbon is electrophilic and can undergo nucleophilic attack to form a tetrahedral intermediate. Nucleophilic acyl substitution takes place by a **nucleophilic addition-elimination mechanism**. Like nucleophilic addition for ketones and aldehydes, the first step in both reaction types will have nucleophilic addition at the carbon carbonyl atom. However, the two reaction types will differ after nucleophilic addition. For nucleophilic addition to ketones/aldehydes, the tetrahedral intermediate will accept a proton to produce a stable addition product. For acyl substitution, the tetrahedral intermediate will **eliminate** a leaving group $L:^-$, while simultaneously converting the $C - O$ single bond to a $C = O$ double bond, thereby forming a substitution product (the nucleophile). Therefore, the nucleophile is being substituted for the leaving group with retention of the carbonyl group, which is unlike other types of carbonyl chemistry that were previously discussed. For a ketone or aldehyde to undergo acyl substitution, the tetrahedral intermediate would have to produce an alkanide ion ($R:^-$) or hydride ion ($H:^-$). However, both these ions are very strong bases, and therefore very poor leaving groups, so these types of reactions occur rarely. Acyl substitutions commonly occur in living organisms, for example, Acetyl-coenzyme A can act as an acyl transfer agent. The general reaction mechanism for nucleophilic acyl substitution is shown in Figure 75.

Figure 75. Nucleophilic acyl substitution

Acyl compounds can react readily because they typically have a good leaving group (for example, Cl ion is a good leaving group and a weak base). The addition of an acid can further catalyze a nucleophilic acyl substitution reaction, which will increase the electrophilic character of the carbonyl carbon atom. The leaving groups can also be protonated to make them better leaving groups, thereby increasing the tendency of dissociation of the $C - L$ bond.

The order of increasing reactivity for acid derivatives in nucleophilic acyl substitution is acyl chloride > acid anhydride > ester > amide. Understanding the basicity of the leaving groups can provide the general order of reactivity. In acyl chloride compounds, the chloride ion is a weak conjugate base of a strong acid (for example, HCl). The leaving group for the acid anhydride is a carboxylic acid or carboxylate ion ($-COO:^-$), which is a stronger base than the chloride ion (its conjugate acid would be weaker than

HCl). The leaving group for esters is an alcohol or water. For amides, it is ammonia or an amine; amines are one of the strongest bases and therefore are the least reactive.

Preparation and Reactions of Acyl Chlorides

Special inorganic acid chloride reagents such as phosphorus pentachloride (PCl_5), phosphorus trichloride (PCl_3), and thionyl chloride ($SOCl_2$) are often reacted with carboxylic acids ($R-(CO)-H$) to prepare an acyl chloride ($R-(CO)-Cl$). The reactions of the inorganic reagents with the carboxylic acid occur by nucleophilic addition-elimination. The mechanism of the reaction (Figure 76) begins with a nucleophilic attack from the oxygen atom of the hydroxyl group to the sulfur atom. The result leads to dissociation of the chloride ion to produce a protonated acyl chlorosulfite (or chlorophosphite/chlorophosphate). The chloride ion then attacks the carbonyl carbon, and through a series of subsequent reactions, the acyl chloride is produced along with additional leaving groups.

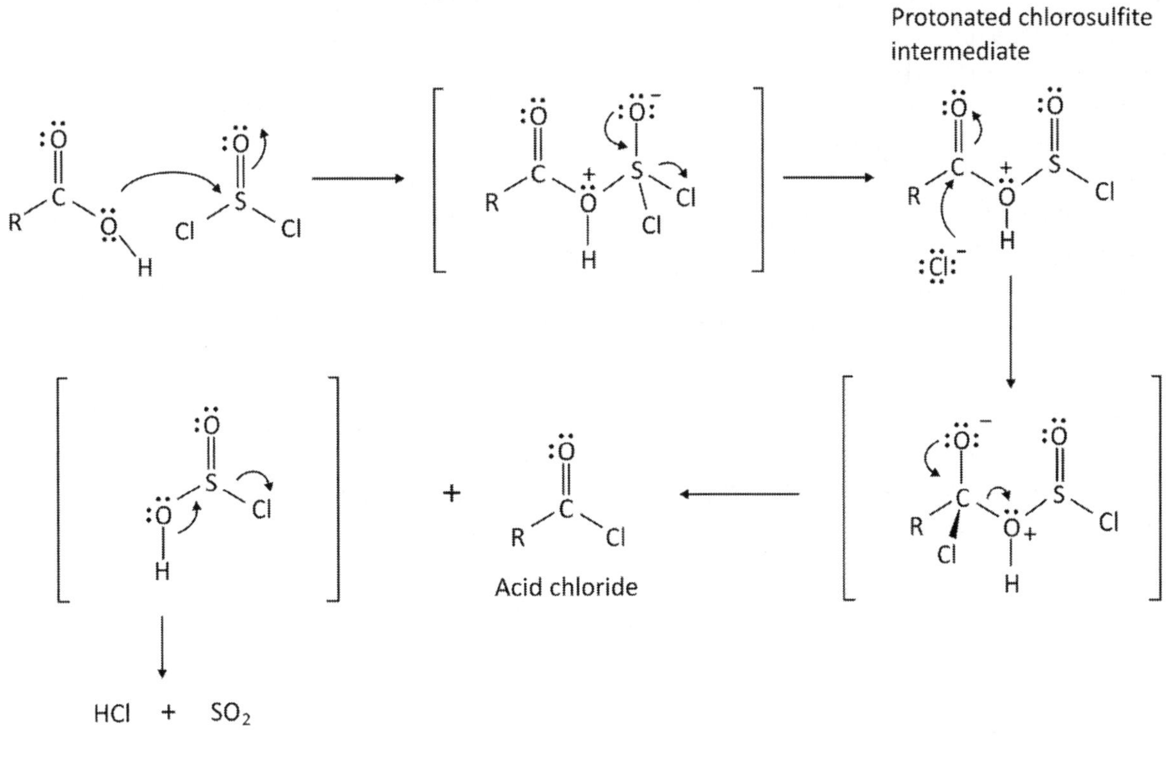

Protonated chlorosulfite intermediate

Acid chloride

HCl + SO_2

Figure 76. Formation of acyl chlorides with thionyl chloride

Acyl chlorides can react with water or more rapidly with an aqueous base. However, these reactions will be converted to the original carboxylic acid or salt, as shown in Figure 77. The reaction of an acyl chloride with water or a base is typically not carried out since they are used, instead, to prepare less reactive acyl compounds such as anhydrides, esters, and amides. Generally, less reactive acyl compounds can be produced from more reactive ones; for example, anhydrides can react with alcohol and ammonia to produce an ester and an amide.

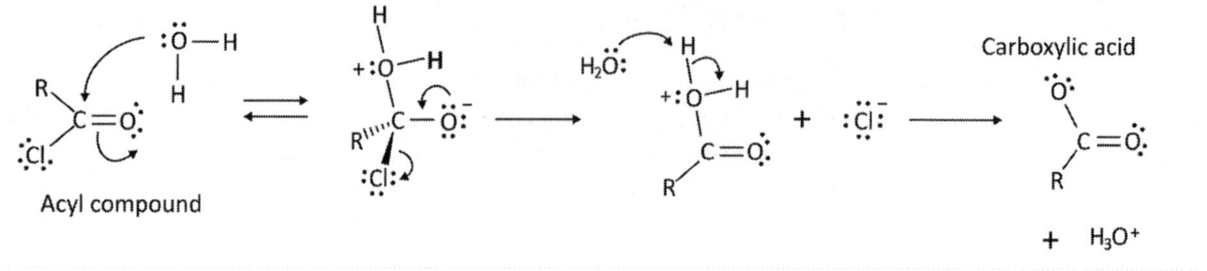

Figure 77. Reaction of acyl compound with water (nucleophile)

An acyl chloride $(\mathrm{R-(CO)-Cl})$ can react with a carboxylic acid $(\mathrm{R'-(CO)-OH})$ or carboxylate $(\mathrm{R'-(CO)-O^{-}Na^{+}})$ in the presence of pyridine to form an anhydride $(\mathrm{R-(CO)-O-(CO)-R'})$. The carboxylate anion will act as a nucleophile, which will result in nucleophilic substitution at the acyl carbon. The reaction of the acyl chloride $(\mathrm{R-(CO)-Cl})$ with a primary alcohol $(\mathrm{R'-OH})$ in pyridine/base will produce an ester $(\mathrm{R-(CO)-OR'})$. Acyl chlorides can be converted to an amide$(\mathrm{R-(CO)-NH_2})$, a N-substituted amide $(\mathrm{R-(CO)-NHR'})$, and $\mathrm{N,N}$ disubstituted amides $(\mathrm{R-(CO)-NR'R''})$ in the presence of excess ammonia $(\mathrm{NH_3})$, a primary amine $(\mathrm{R'NH_2})$, and a secondary amine $(\mathrm{R'R''NH_2})$. Conversion of an acyl chloride to a ketone can be carried by either mixing it with benzene $(\mathrm{C_6H_6})$ and aluminum chloride $(\mathrm{AlCl_3})$ to produce $(\mathrm{C_6H_6-(C=O)-R'})$ or with a organometallic reagent $(\mathrm{R_2'CuLi})$ to produce $(\mathrm{R-(C=O)-R'})$. Acyl chlorides can also be reduced with $\mathrm{LiAlH(OC(CH_3)_3)_3}$ in (1) diethyl ether $(\mathrm{Et_2O})$ and (2) water to produce $(\mathrm{R-(CO)-H})$.

Reactions of Acid Anhydrides

A carboxylic acid anhydride can undergo hydrolysis or react with water or a base, such that it produces carboxylate molecular or anion. The leaving group is a weak base and a good leaving group. Figure 78 shows a general reaction.

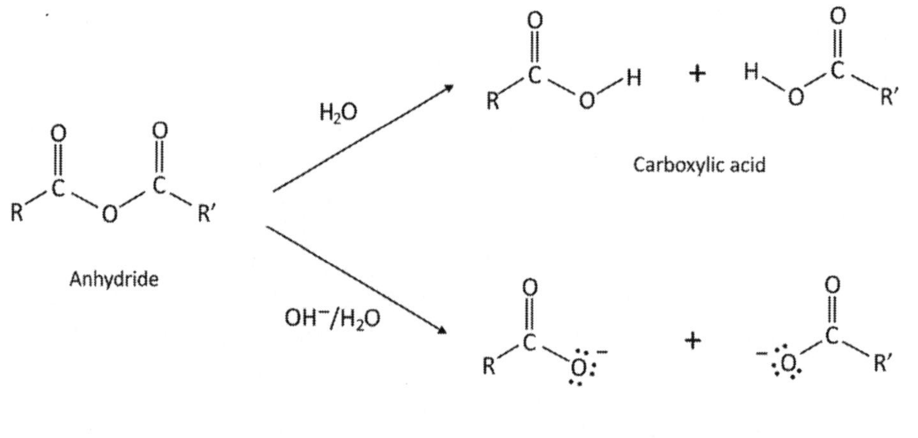

Figure 78. Reaction of acid anhydrides with water or an aqueous base

Reactions of Esters

Esters $(R - (CO) - O - R')$ will undergo nucleophilic acyl substitution by base-promoted hydrolysis or **saponification**. Refluxing an ester with water and sodium hydroxide (aqueous sodium hydroxide) will produce an alcohol molecule and the sodium salt of the ester. The leaving group is an alkoxide ion $(RO:^{-})$, which is a weak base and a good leaving group. Saponification is basically an irreversible reaction, and the carboxylate ion will be unreactive in nucleophilic substitution due to the negative charge. The general reaction mechanism for nucleophilic acyl substitution is shown in Figure 79.

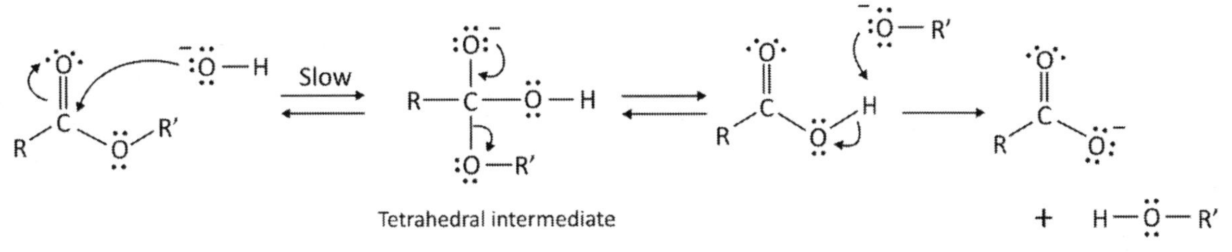

Figure 79. Saponification of an Ester

The first step is slow; the hydroxide ion attacks the carbonyl carbon to form a tetrahedral intermediate, which then produces the leaving group or alkoxide ion. Due to the strong basic conditions, a proton will be removed immediately from the carbonyl compound or carboxylic acid by the leaving group, which leads to the final products: an alcohol and sodium carboxylate.

Addition of electron-withdrawing or donating groups at R or R' will change the reactivity of the ester. For example, suppose three molecules containing varying groups of R and R' are given as follows: Ester molecule 1: $R = CF_3$, $R' = CH_3$, ester molecule 2: $R = CH_3$, $R' = CH_3$, ester molecule 3: $R = CH_3$, $R' = C(CH3)3$. Ester molecule 1 will be the most reactive since the three fluorine atoms are electron-withdrawing, which makes the carbonyl carbon atom the most polarized-positively charged. Ester molecule 3 contains three alkyl groups making it the least reactive since the carbonyl carbon will have a relatively smaller polarized-positive charge.

Saponification of the carboxylic ester of a chiral alcohol will occur with retention of configuration. For example, consider the hydrolysis of the compound in Figure 80. The labeled oxygen atom (O^{18}) bonded to the carbonyl carbon atom will remain with the alkoxide ion or leaving group. The configuration at the stereogenic carbon, on the leaving group, will stay the same.

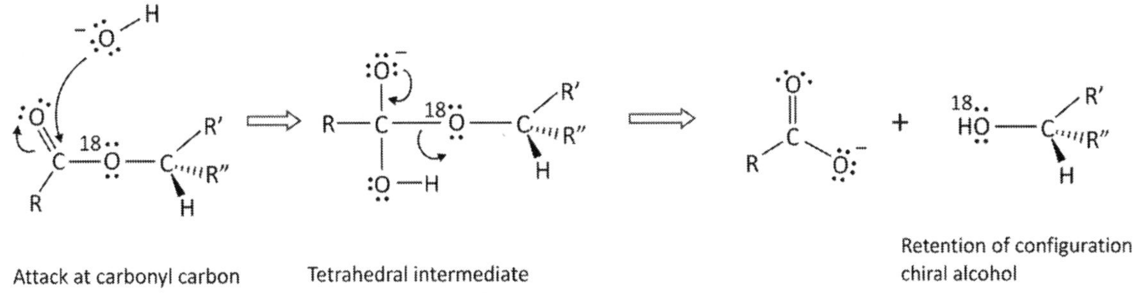

Attack at carbonyl carbon

Tetrahedral intermediate

Retention of configuration chiral alcohol

Figure 80. Saponification results in retention of configuration

Esters can also undergo acid-catalyzed nucleophilic substitution (Figure 81) by protonation of the carbonyl oxygen atom. The carbonyl carbon atom will be more electrophilic and will undergo attack by a water molecule. Therefore, the tetrahedral intermediate will have a protonated carbonyl oxygen atom, with a water molecule attached to the carbonyl carbon. The general reaction mechanism is shown in Figure 81.

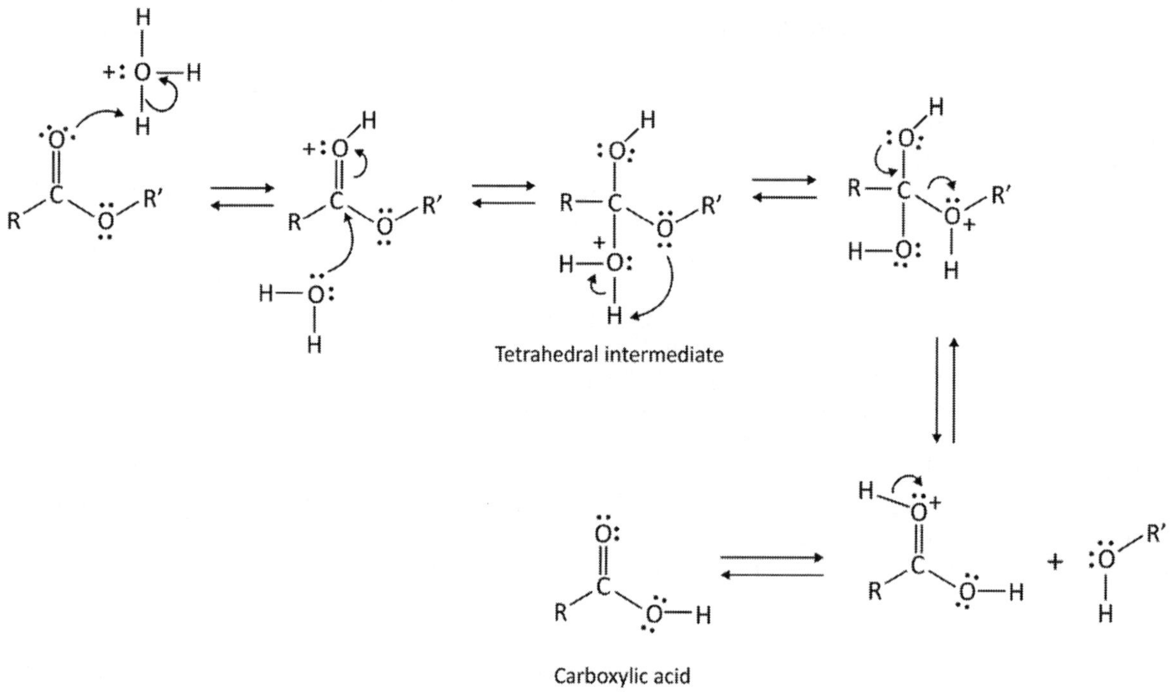

Tetrahedral intermediate

Carboxylic acid

Figure 81. Acid-catalyzed nucleophilic substitution of an ester

Esters $(R-(CO)-O-R')$ can react with other bases such as an alkoxide (for example, $R''O'^{-}$ or potassium ethoxide, $CH_3CH_2O^-K^+$) or a solution of boiling alcohol (for example, $R''O'H$ or ethanol (CH_3CH_2OH)). The reaction, called **transesterification,** will produce an ester with an alkyl chain $(R-(CO)-O'R'')$ provided by the alkoxide or alcohol. The equilibrium shifts to the right toward the lower boiling alcohol $(R'O-H)$ that is produced, which will distill more readily. The transesterification mechanism is similar to acid-catalyzed ester hydrolysis or esterification. The transesterification reaction of methyl acrylate and butyl alcohol will react in aqueous acid to produce butyl acrylate (94%) and methanol.

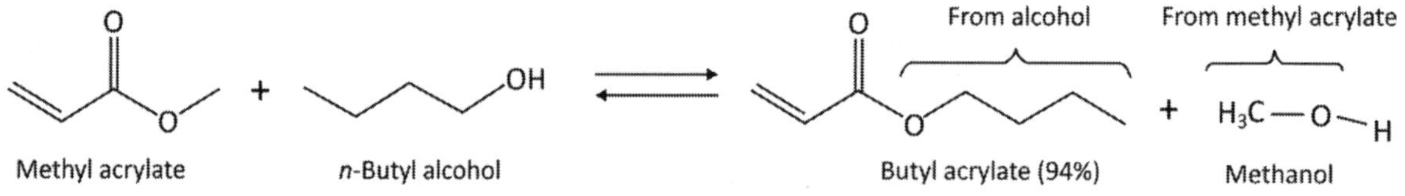

Methyl acrylate + *n*-Butyl alcohol ⇌ Butyl acrylate (94%) + Methanol

From alcohol — From methyl acrylate

Figure 82. Transesterification

Esters can react with two molar equivalents of a Grignard reagent (for example, $R{:}\,MgX$) to produce a tertiary (3°) alcohol. A bonding electron pair from the Grignard reagent acts as a nucleophile and attacks

the carbonyl carbon atom of the ester, which causes the π electrons from the carbonyl $C = O$ bond to delocalize to the oxygen atom. The nonbonding electrons found on the same oxygen atom then bond to the metal halide (MgX). However, the initial product that is formed is unstable and the σ electrons in the $O - MgX$ delocalize. Dissociation follows which results in the formation of the π bond in the carbonyl $C = O$ bond.

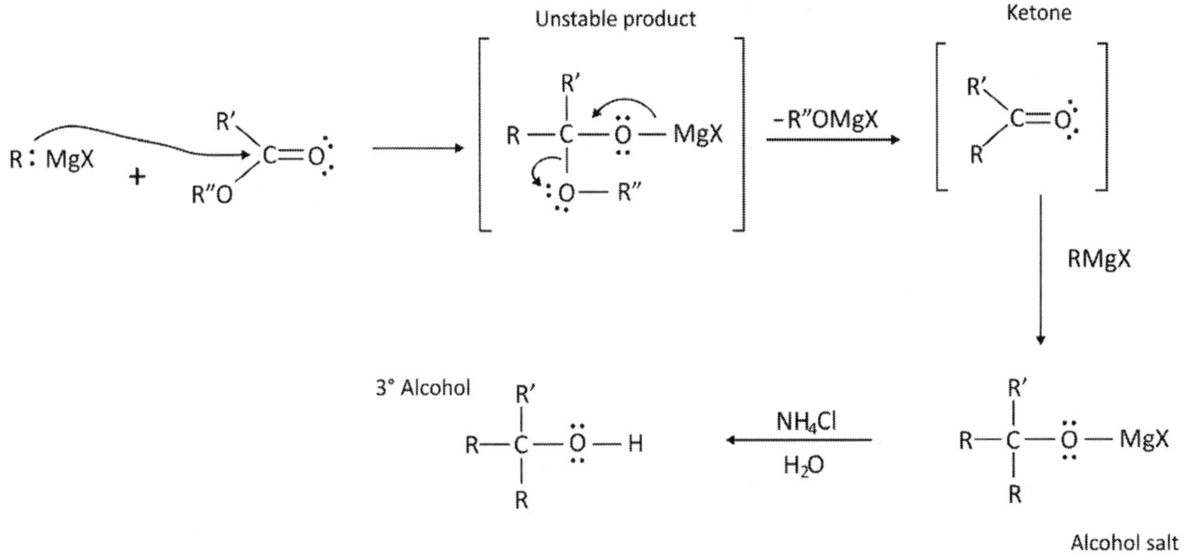

Unstable product
Ketone
-R″OMgX
RMgX
3° Alcohol
NH_4Cl
H_2O
Alcohol salt

Figure 83. Ester reaction with Grignard reagents

A ketone $(R' - (CO) - R)$ and magnesium alkoxide $(OR'' - MgX)$ compound is formed. The ketone will react with one molar equivalent of $R{:}\,MgX$ to produce an alcohol salt $(R_2R' - C - OMgX)$. In the next step, the alcohol salt will react with an aqueous acid or acidic salt (for example, NH_4Cl/H_2O), a process called hydrolysis, to produce a tertiary alcohol. The final alcohol contains two of the same alkyl groups that both belong to the alkyl portion of the Grignard reagent (R) and another from the ester group (R'). Less reactive organometallic reagents such as R_2CuLi only react with acyl halide $(R - (CO) - X)$ and not with the produced ketone.

Reactions of Amides

Amides will undergo acyl substitution by basic hydrolysis with aqueous sodium hydroxide and will regenerate the base (for example, $HO{:}^-$) and produce an amine or ammonia molecule. The generated leaving groups are weak bases such as ammonia. The reaction mechanism for basic hydrolysis is shown in Figure 84.

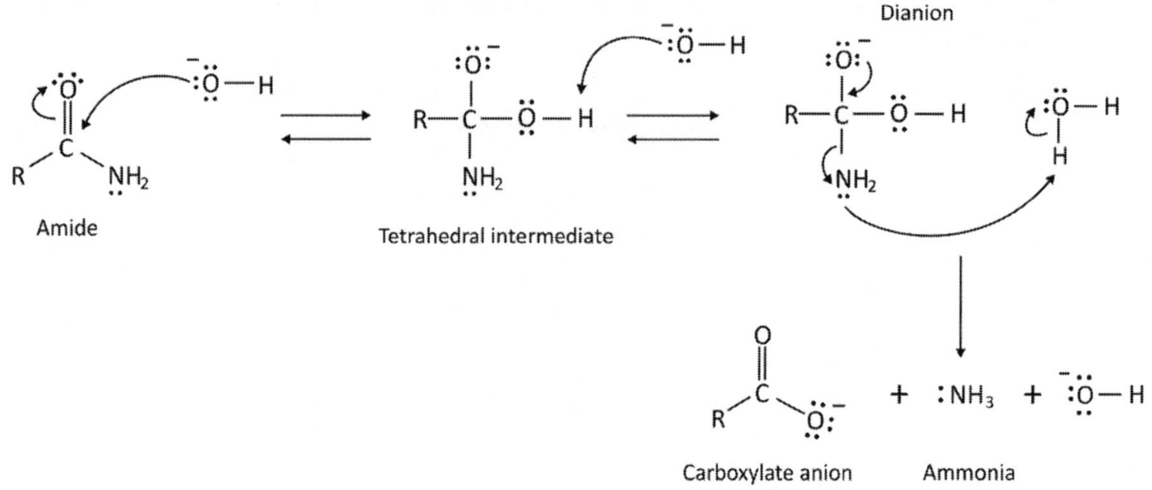

Amide

Tetrahedral intermediate

Dianion

Carboxylate anion

Ammonia

Figure 84. Basic hydrolysis-acyl substitution of an amide

In the first step, the hydroxide ion will attack the carbonyl or acyl carbon of the amide, which will then form a tetrahedral intermediate. Another hydroxide ion will use its nonbonding electron pair from the oxygen atom to remove a proton from the hydroxyl group. In a synchronized step, the dianion (two oxygen atoms with a negative charge) will lose an ammonia molecule (or an amine). Note that a proton is transferred from water.

N-substituted and N, N-disubstituted amides will also undergo acidic hydrolysis when heated with aqueous acid. The hydrolysis of amides is generally slower compared to esters and typically requires forcing (heat) conditions.

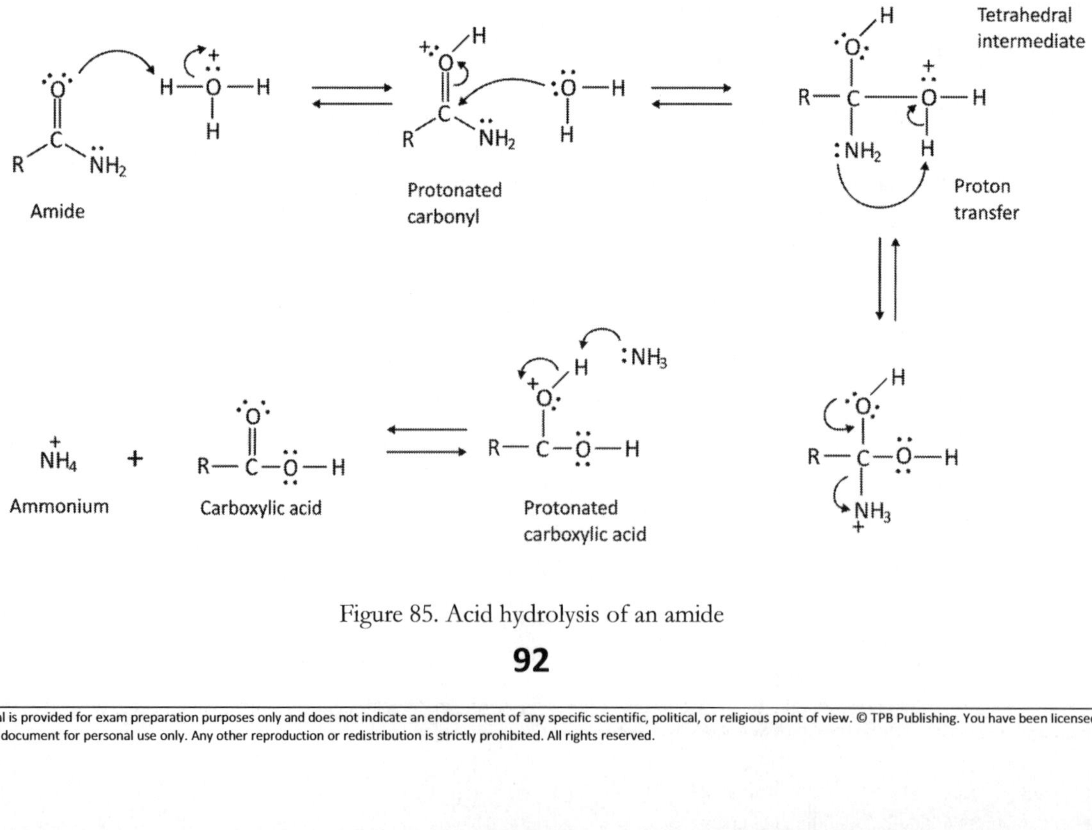

Amide

Protonated carbonyl

Tetrahedral intermediate

Proton transfer

Ammonium

Carboxylic acid

Protonated carboxylic acid

Figure 85. Acid hydrolysis of an amide

In the first step of the reaction mechanism (Figure 85), the carbonyl oxygen atom attacks or accepts a proton from the hydronium ion, which was produced by the acid. A water molecule acts as a base and attacks the protonated carbonyl oxygen atom, which results in the formation of a tetrahedral intermediate. Intramolecular proton transfer from the oxygen atom $(-OH_2^{\ +})$ to the nitrogen atom occurs, which results in the formation of ammonia (leaving group) and a protonated carboxylic acid. The nonbonding electron pair on the nitrogen atom, from ammonia, removes a proton from the protonated carboxylic acid, which produces a carboxylic acid and an ammonium molecule.

Reducing Carbonyl Compounds to Form Alcohols

Carbonyl compounds such as carboxylic acids, esters, aldehydes, and ketones can be transformed into primary and secondary alcohols. Powerful reducing agents such as lithium aluminum hydride (LAH) can reduce a carboxylic acid, ester, and an aldehyde to a primary alcohol. A ketone will be reduced to a secondary alcohol (Figure 86).

$$R-C(=O)-O-H \text{ (Carboxylic acid)} \xrightarrow{\text{LAH}} R-CH_2-O-H \text{ (1° Alcohol)}$$

$$R-C(=O)-O-R' \text{ (Ester)} \xrightarrow{\text{LAH}} R-CH_2-O-H \text{ (1° Alcohol)} + R'OH$$

$$R-C(=O)-R' \text{ (Ketone)} \xrightarrow{\text{NaBH}_4 \text{ or LAH}} R-CH(OH)-R' \text{ (2° Alcohol)}$$

$$R-C(=O)-H \text{ (Ketone)} \xrightarrow{\text{NaBH}_4 \text{ or LAH}} R-CH_2-O-H \text{ (1° Alcohol)}$$

Figure 86. Reduction of carbonyl compounds

Carboxylic acids can be treated with LAH in diethyl ether (Et_2O) followed by treatment in aqueous sulfuric acid $((H_2O)/(H_2SO_4))$ to produce a primary alcohol in high yields. Esters can be reduced to a primary alcohol under high-pressure (5,000 psi) hydrogenation with H_2 gas and $CuO \cdot CuCr_2O_4$ at 175 °C at the industrial scale. Alternatively, esters can be reduced with LAH/Et_2O and H_2O/H_2SO_4 at the lab scale.

Aldehydes and ketones can be reduced with reagents such as H_2/Pt (metal catalyst), sodium in alcohol, or with LAH. However, sodium borohydride $(NaBH_4/H_2O)$, a less powerful reducing agent, is commonly used to reduce aldehydes and ketones only. Both LAH and $NaBH_4$ enable the transfer of a hydride ion (H^-) from the metal, which acts as a nucleophile and attacks at the carbonyl carbon. The tetrahedral intermediate is an alkoxide ion that donates a nonbonding electron pair from the oxygen atom to the proton on a water molecule, which produces the alcohol (Figure 87).

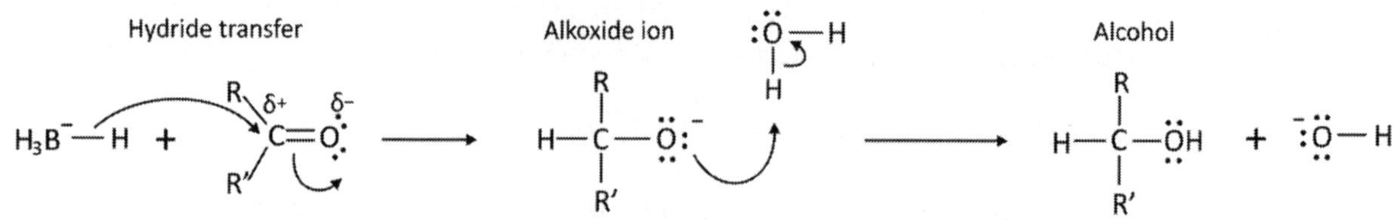

Figure 87. Hydride transfer mechanism for aldehydes/ketones

The ease of reduction increases from carboxylic acids (carboxylates) to esters, ketones, and aldehydes. LAH is typically mixed with anhydrous reagents (for example, anhydrous ether) in a separate step to avoid a violent reaction with water (for example, $LaAlH_4/Et_2O$ and then H_2O/H_2SO_4).

Enols and Enolate Ion Reactions

The Acidity of α Hydrogens in Carbonyl Compounds

Aldehyde and ketones have been shown to undergo nucleophilic addition at the carbonyl carbon of the carbonyl group. Hydrogen atoms bonded to carbon atoms that are adjacent to the carbonyl group have high acidity and are referred to as the α **hydrogen**. The hydrogens on an sp^3 α **carbon**, for a carbonyl compound, can be at least 30 orders of magnitude more acidic than a hydrogen atom bonded to an sp^3 carbon atom within a hydrocarbon (no carbonyl group). The pK_a for an α hydrogen ranges between 19 and 20 compared to 40–50 for β hydrogens. In other words, the α hydrogen is more likely to dissociate since the carbonyl group has a strong electron-withdrawing character. Loss of the α hydrogen creates an anion that is stabilized by resonance. Carbonyl compounds containing at least one α hydrogen will be in equilibrium with respect to their tautomers, as shown in Figure 99.

The negative charge on the anion, by removal of the α hydrogen, creates a resonance-stabilized anion called an **enolate anion**. For example, the negatively charged anion can have two resonance structures that interconvert to keto form and an enol form. In resonance structure A, there is a negative charge on the carbon, and in structure B the negative charge is now on the oxygen atom, which can form the enol form by accepting an α-hydrogen to the carbonyl oxygen atom. Resonance structure B is better able to accommodate the negative charge.

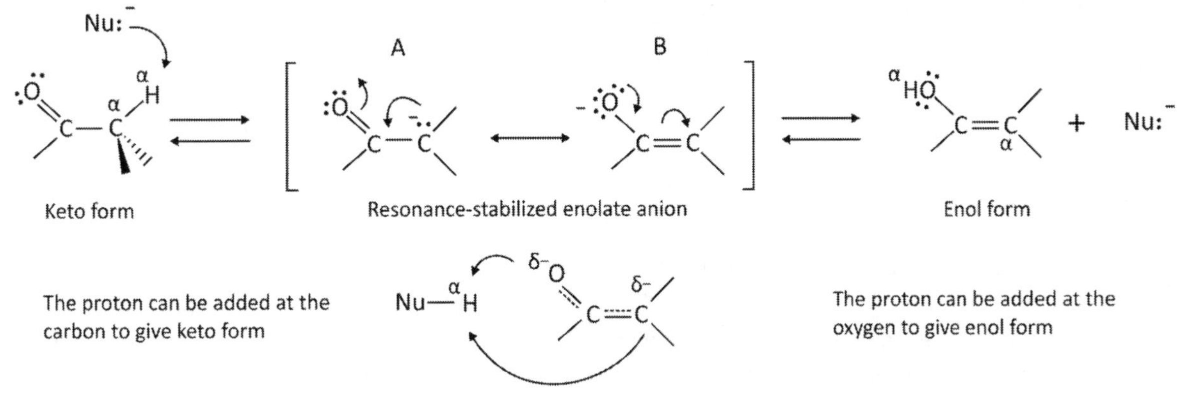

Figure 88. The enolate anion and its tautomers

Enol and Keto Tautomers

The enolate ion can exist in equilibrium between an enol form and a keto form and is called a tautomer. A **tautomer** is a compound (for example, enolate ion) that can exist as two or more isomers in equilibrium, and can rapidly interchange to another isomer by the migration of one atom to another (for example, intramolecular proton transfer). The interconversion between the constitutional isomers, for example, the keto and the enol, is called **tautomerization.** The enolate ion can accept a proton at the carbonyl oxygen atom, which produces an enol, or it can take a proton at the α carbon to form the initial carbonyl compound.

For simple monocarbonyl compounds (for example, acetone and acetaldehyde), the amount of enol tautomer will be relatively negligible since the carbon-oxygen π bond has greater bond strength. For compounds that have two carbonyl groups separated by a $-CH_2-$ group, a β-dicarbonyl ($R-(C=O)-C-(C=O)-R$) compound, the enol concentration at equilibrium is much greater. Many carbonyl compounds favor the keto form, and the β-dicarbonyls prefer the enol tautomer due to hydrogen bonding and conjugation. β-dicarbonyls will be acidic since its conjugate base is highly stable.

Reactions of Enols and Enolate Anions

Interconversion between each tautomer can be increased in the presence of an acid or base. Racemization can take place in the presence of an acid or base, for a carbonyl compound, if the α carbon is stereogenic. The enol that is formed is achiral and can revert to the original carbonyl compound (ketone or aldehyde) to produce equal amounts of its enantiomers. The carbonyl carbon in aldehydes and ketones contain two modes of reactivity. For instance, the carbonyl carbon can undergo addition reactions in the presence of an acid, which will result in a nucleophile attacking the carbonyl carbon. The acid-catalyzed nucleophilic addition was discussed previously (Figure 67) and is shown for a keto-enol in Figure 89.

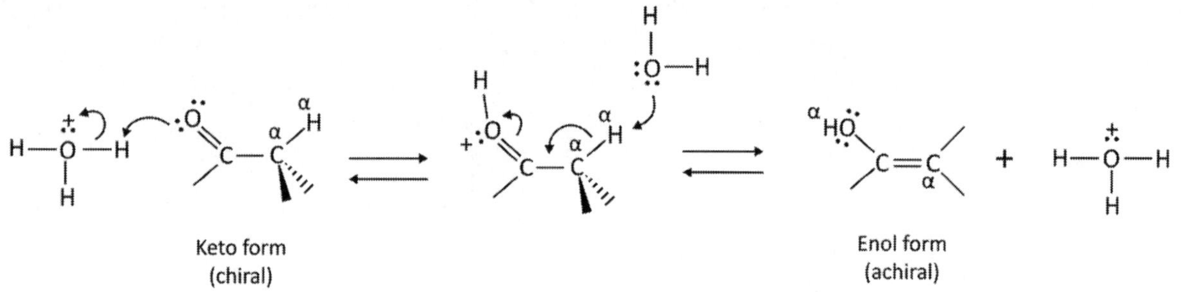

Keto form
(chiral)

Enol form
(achiral)

Figure 89. Acid-catalyzed enolization mechanism

In a second scenario, the α carbon can be deprotonated by a base to form an α carbon anion or enolate ion. The structure can undergo resonance, which results in a structure where the α carbon forms a double bond with the carbonyl carbon. The π electrons between the carbonyl carbon and the oxygen atom are transferred as a nonbonding pair to the oxygen atom. The enolate ion, which contains the negatively charged carbonyl oxygen atom, can now act as a nucleophile (Figure 90).

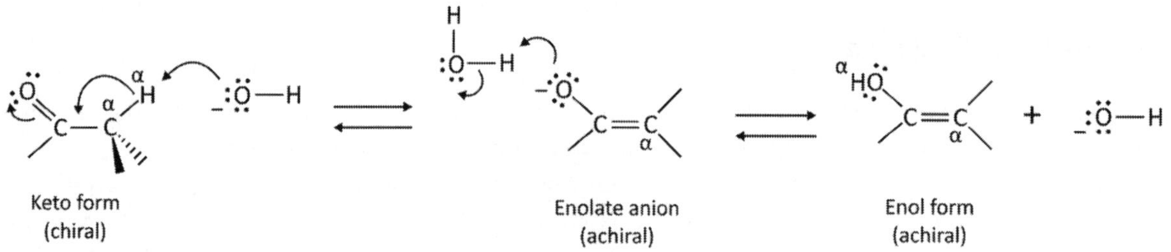

Keto form
(chiral)

Enolate anion
(achiral)

Enol form
(achiral)

Figure 90. Base-catalyzed enolization mechanism

Alkoxide ions ($RO:^-$), which act as bases, can convert the keto-enol tautomers or carbonyl compounds to an enolate ion. Strong bases such as sodium hydride, LDA, and $((CH_3)_2CH)_2N^-Li^+$ can be used to produce an enolate.

α Halogenation of Ketones and Aldehydes

Ketones and aldehydes with an α hydrogen can readily undergo a substitution reaction with a halogen at the α carbon. The reaction rate will increase in the presence of an acid or base and is independent of the halogen concentration. In an acid or base medium, the formation of the enolate anion or enol occurs slowly, before the halogen is substituted.

Halogenation of ketones is base promoted and takes place initially with the slow formation of an enolate ion or enol. Base promoted means the base or nucleophile is not regenerated, and base catalyzed means that the base is regenerated within the reaction mechanism. The base or nucleophile will first remove the α hydrogen, resulting in slow formation of the enolate anion. Once the enolate anion is formed, interconversion to an enol occurs. In the second step, the enolate carbanion (deprotonated α carbon) will attack or react quickly with the halogen (Figure 91).

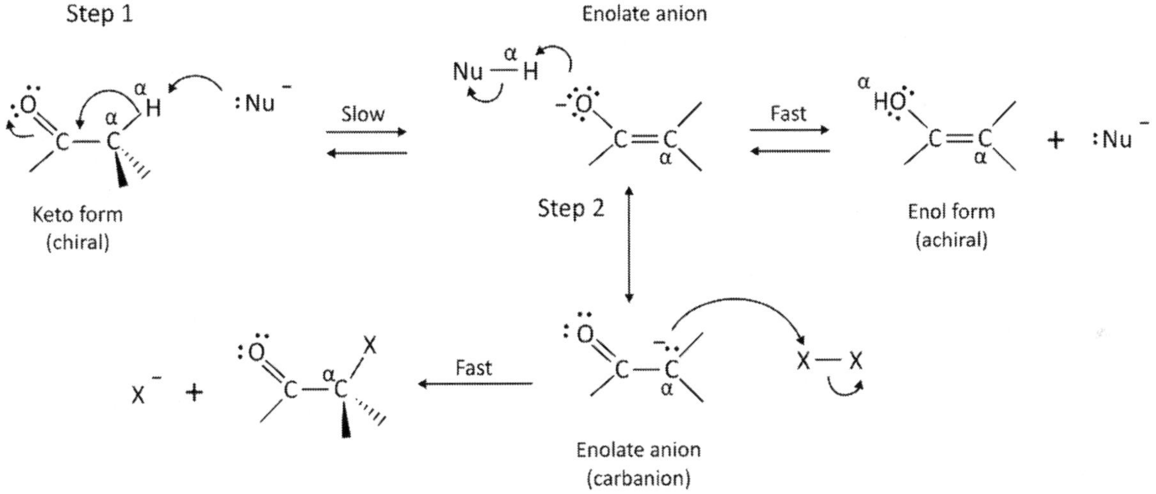

Figure 91. Base promoted halogenation of aldehydes/ketones

Acids, on the other hand, can catalyze the halogenation of ketones. In the first step, the carbonyl oxygen atom readily donates its nonbonding pair to a hydrogen atom from the acid. The conjugate base of the acid then removes the α hydrogen, which slowly forms the enol along with the regenerated acid. In the second step, the π electrons from the carbon-carbon double bond readily attack the halogen, thereby creating the substituted product. The halide ion then donates its nonbonding pair to hydrogen on the protonated carbonyl oxygen atom, which forms a halogenated carbonyl compound.

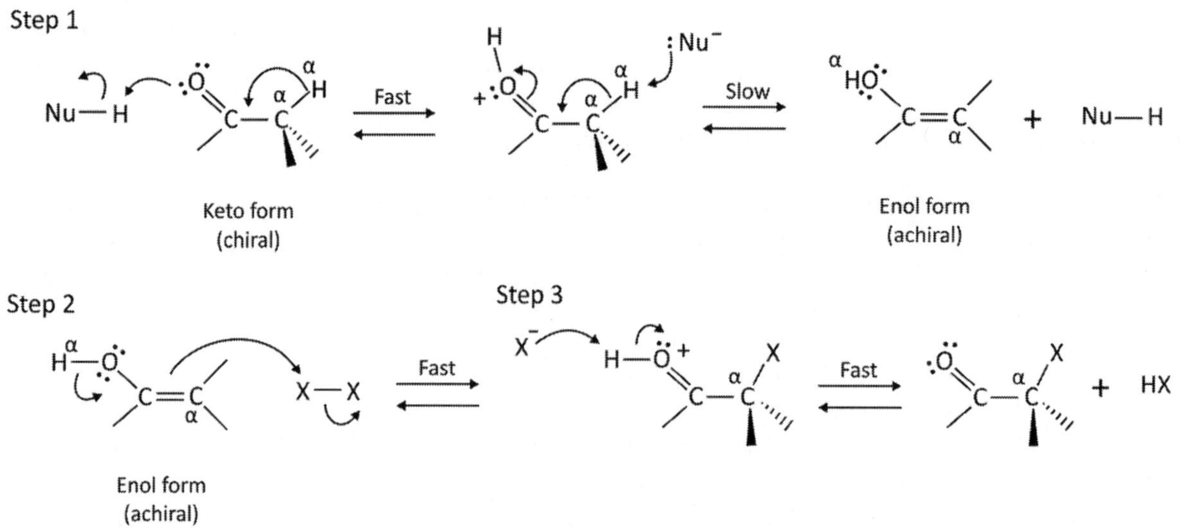
Step 1
Nu—H
Fast
Slow
:Nu⁻
Nu—H
Keto form
(chiral)
Enol form
(achiral)
Step 2
Step 3
X—X
Fast
Fast
HX
Enol form
(achiral)

Figure 92. Acid-catalyzed halogenation of aldehydes/ketones

Multiple halogenations can take place for a methyl ketone in the presence of a base, since adding the first halogen makes the remaining α hydrogens more acidic (Figure 93).

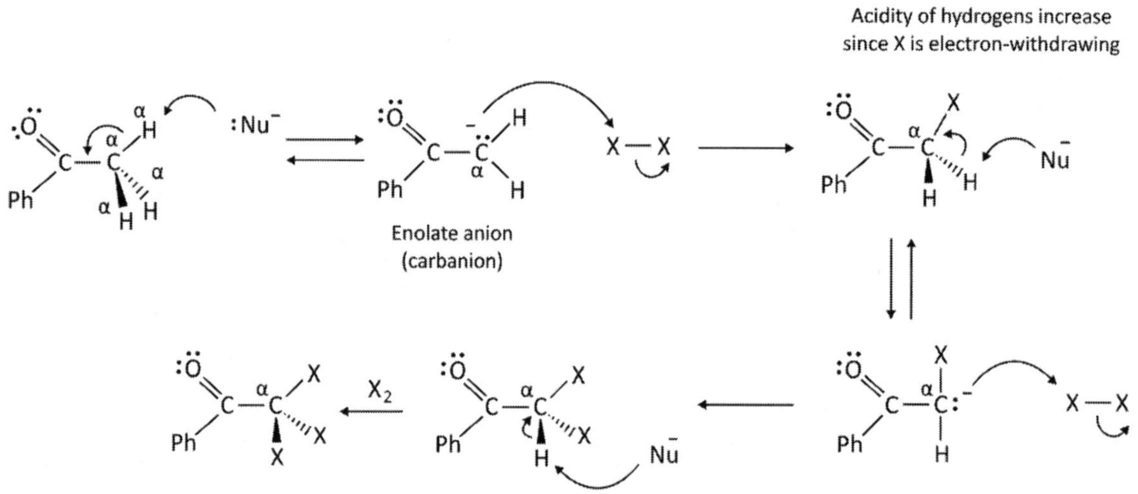
Acidity of hydrogens increase
since X is electron-withdrawing
:Nu⁻
Ph
X—X
Enolate anion
(carbanion)
X_2

Figure 93. The haloform reaction

The reaction can occur in aqueous sodium hydroxide or base, where the hydroxide ion can first attack one of the α hydrogens. The enolate anion or carbanion can then attack a halogen to form the first substituted halogenated carbonyl compound. Following this step, the hydroxide ion can then attack another α hydrogen, which results in the formation of the enolate anion or carbanion. The reaction repeats; the carbanion attacks the halogen to produce a disubstituted halogenated carbonyl compound. The haloform reaction will continue a third time or until all the α hydrogens are removed.

The Aldol Reaction

In the aldol reaction, an enolate anion can undergo an addition reaction and can combine with an aldehyde or ketone. An **aldol addition reaction** (aldol condensation if the α, β-unsaturated carbonyl compound is formed) can occur by a nucleophilic addition mechanism if the nucleophilic carbonyl group attacks another carbonyl compound. For example, two molecules of acetaldehyde can combine in aqueous sodium hydroxide, near room temperature, to produce 3-hydroxybutanal which is both an ald̲ehyde and alcoho̲l or **an aldol**. A **dimerization** occurs, which means that two similar molecules, for example, two carbonyl compound such as the aldehyde an enol, are combined during the reaction. The mechanism of aldol base–catalyzed addition is shown in Figure 94.

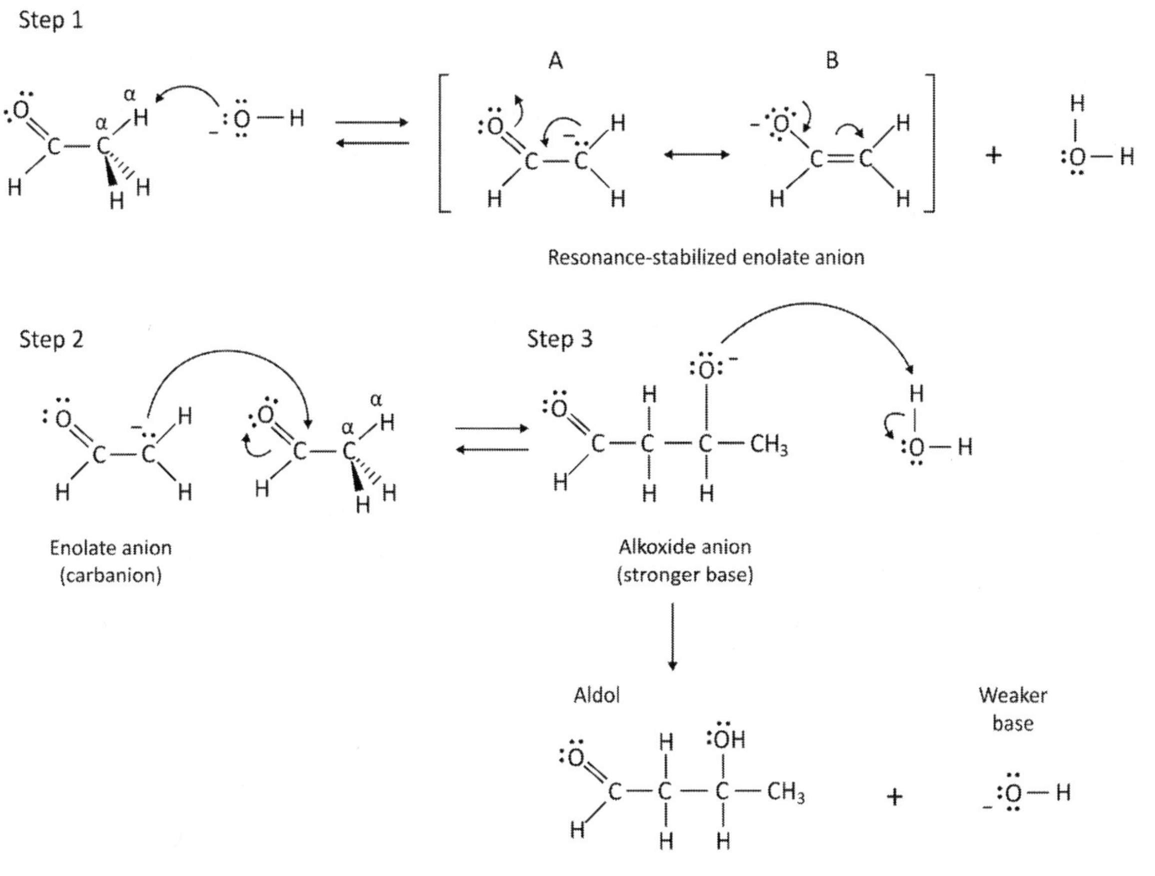

Step 1

A B

Resonance-stabilized enolate anion

Step 2

Step 3

Enolate anion (carbanion)

Alkoxide anion (stronger base)

Aldol

Weaker base

Figure 94. Aldol addition with a base

In the first step of an aldol addition, the hydroxide ion attacks an α hydrogen on the α carbon, which forms a α carbanion or the resonance stabilized enolate anion, and a molecule of water. The α carbanion then attacks the carbonyl carbon on the second molecule of acetaldehyde to produce an alkoxide anion. A nonbonding electron pair from an oxygen atom on the anion acts as a strong base or nucleophile by attacking a proton on a water molecule. An aldol is produced along with a molecule of hydroxide ion, the weaker base. However, dehydration of the aldol can happen readily in some aldol additions. In an **aldol condensation reaction**, an aldol addition occurs followed by intermolecular elimination of a water or alcohol molecule (Figure 95).

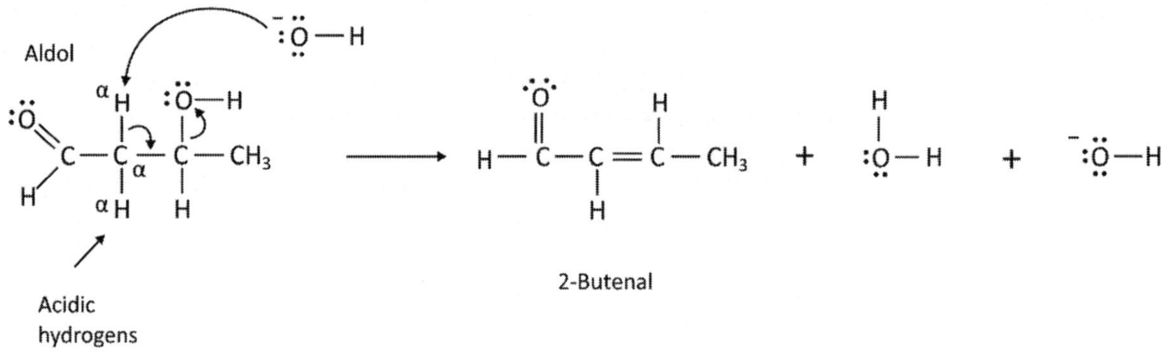

Figure 95. Aldol condensation or dehydration of the aldol addition product

Ketones may also undergo aldol additions with a base, but the equilibrium toward the right is promoted by removing the product as it forms. Note that for reasons having to do with steric and electronic factors, aldehydes containing the negatively charged oxygen atom will be more reactive than ketones. For example, two acetone molecules can undergo an aldol addition with a base, and the aldol can be separated through a special apparatus. However, the reaction is reversible, and a retro-aldol reaction can occur if the aldol is heated with a strong base, for example, the aldol will decompose back to two acetone molecules. Instead of a base, ketones can undergo acid-catalyzed aldol condensations (Figure 96).

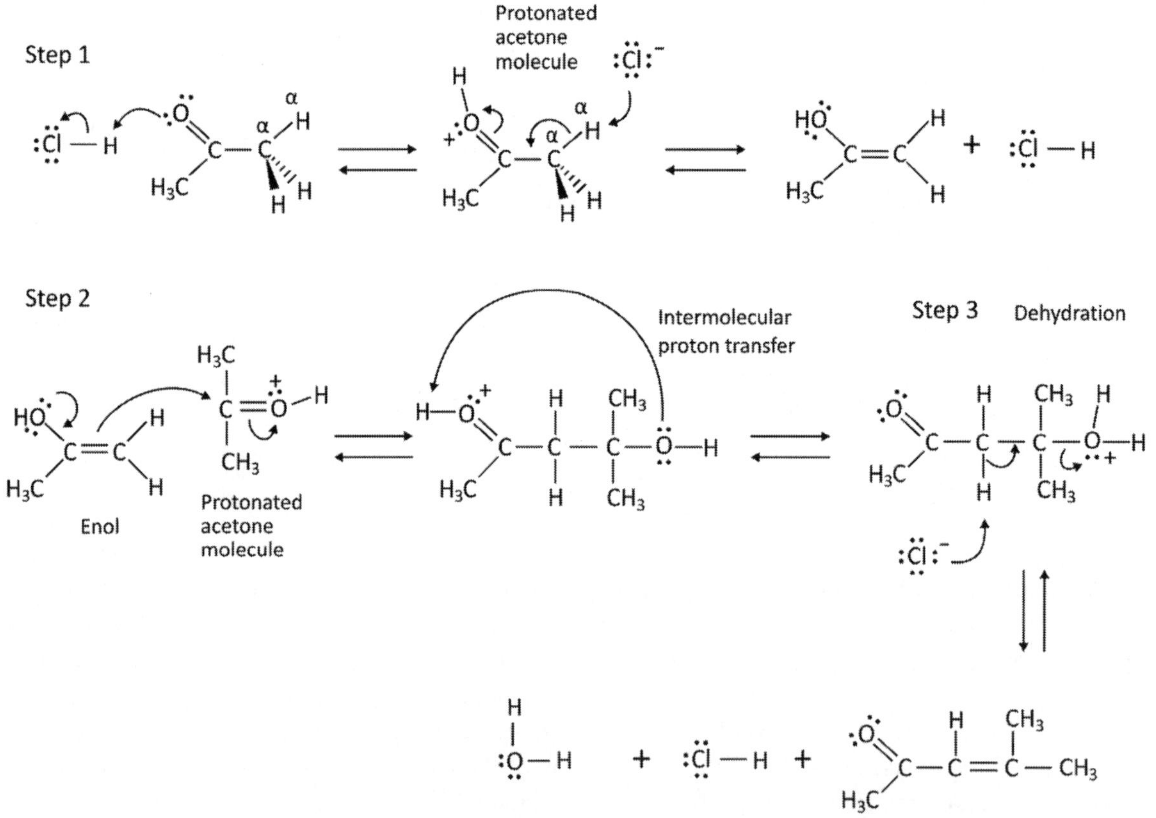

Figure 96. Acid-catalyzed aldol condensation

In the first step, the carbonyl oxygen atom on acetone donates its nonbonding pair to the proton of the hydrochloric acid. The chloride ion then attacks an α hydrogen, which results in regeneration of the acid and formation of the enol. In the second step, the π electrons from the carbonyl carbon and α carbon attack the carbonyl carbon of another protonated acetone molecule. Intramolecular proton transfer occurs, which transfers a proton from the positively charged oxygen atom to the oxygen atom from the hydroxyl group. In the last step, dehydration occurs when a chloride ion attacks an α hydrogen, which results in the formation of the aldol, the acid, and a molecule of water.

Claisen-Condensation Reactions

β-dicarbonyl compounds are useful reagents in the synthesis of many organic compounds. For instance, the α hydrogens between the carbonyl groups in β-dicarbonyl compounds, such as β-keto esters, are highly acidic and can react with an alkoxide base to form an enolate, which can then undergo acylation. β-keto esters are more acidic than esters since the enolate anions are more stabilized by resonance.

The β-dicarbonyl system

A β-keto ester

Alkoxide base

OR^-

+ HOR

pK_a = 9-11
Acidic hydrogen

Figure 97. β-dicarbonyl compounds and stabilization

β-dicarbonyl compounds can be prepared by Claisen condensation. In a **Claisen condensation reaction**, a carbonyl compound such as an ester (for example, ethyl acetate) can react with a nucleophile or base such as sodium ethoxide to produce an acetoacetic ester carbanion. Ethyl and methyl esters are typical ester reactants. For instance, methyl esters are reacted with sodium methoxide, and ethyl esters are reacted with sodium ethoxide. An alkoxide that has a similar alkyl group to that of the ester is used to avoid transesterification.

Similar to an aldol condensation, the α carbon of one ester molecule and the carbonyl group of the other ester will combine to form the carbanion. One ester loses an α hydrogen, and the other loses an ethoxide ion. During the reaction, an alcohol group can be removed by nucleophilic substitution at the α-carbon atom. In the first step, an ethoxide anion removes an α hydrogen from an ester to form an enolate ion or carbanion that is stabilized by resonance (Figure 98).

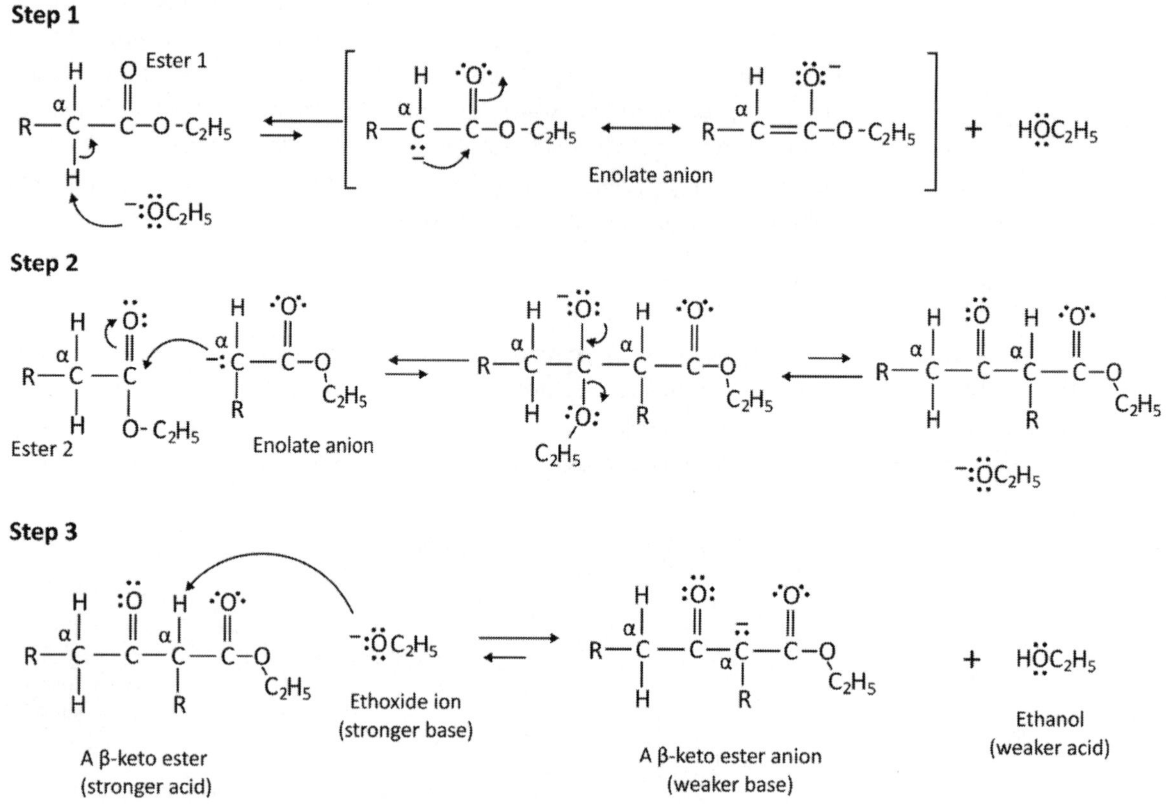

Step 1

Ester 1

Enolate anion

$+ \; HOC_2H_5$

$^-:OC_2H_5$

Step 2

Ester 2

Enolate anion

$^-:OC_2H_5$

Step 3

$^-:OC_2H_5$

Ethoxide ion
(stronger base)

A β-keto ester
(stronger acid)

A β-keto ester anion
(weaker base)

$+ \; HOC_2H_5$

Ethanol
(weaker acid)

Figure 98. Claisen condensation

In the second step, the carbanion attacks the carbonyl carbon on the second ester, which produces a β-keto ester and an ethoxide ion in small amounts (equilibrium is mostly to the left). Unlike the aldol reaction where nucleophilic attack leads to addition, the Claisen condensation reaction will result in addition-elimination. However, in the third step, ethoxide acts as a strong base and attacks a β-hydrogen on the β-keto ester. The equilibrium is favorable and proceeds to the right. Distilling the ethanol that is formed will push the equilibrium further to the right (Le Chatelier's principle). Note that the reaction proceeds in the direction toward the weaker base (β-keto ester anion) and the weaker acid (ethanol). In the last step (Figure 99), an acid is added to the β-keto ester anion, which results in rapid protonation of the carbanion and production of the β-keto ester that is in equilibrium with its enol and keto form.

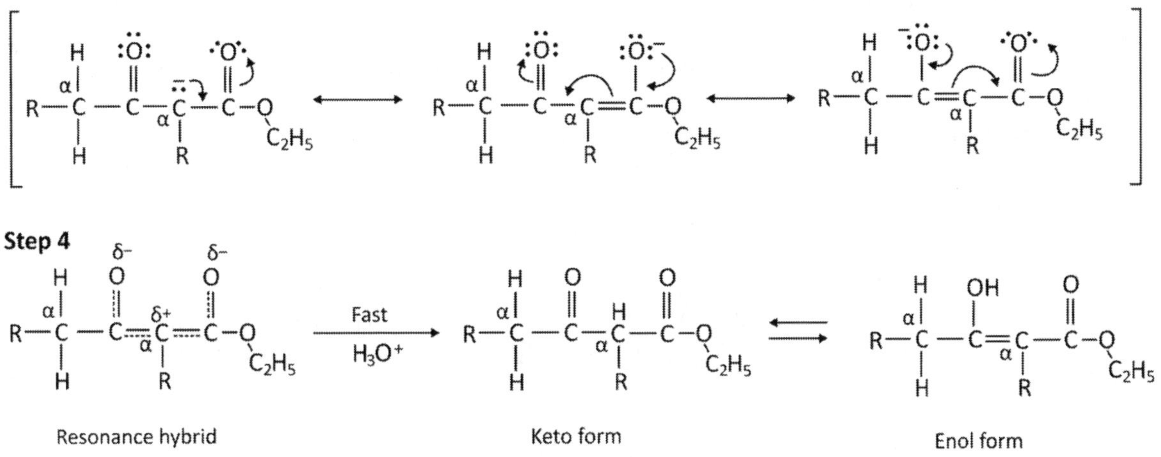

Resonance hybrid Keto form Enol form

Figure 99. Claisen condensation: addition

Claisen condensations with sodium ethoxide will not occur for esters that have an α-hydrogen since an acidic hydrogen will be absent in step 3 of the reaction mechanism, thereby keeping the reaction from proceeding forward.

Cross Aldol and Condensation Reactions

Carbonyl containing compounds such as aldehydes, ketones, esters, and β-dicarbonyls can undergo Claisen or aldol types reactions. For reactions that include various functional groups with carbonyl groups, the product of the reaction can be determined as follows.

1). Determine which compound has the most acidic α-hydrogen, and then write the formula that represents or shows the anion or nucleophilic form (for example, enolate ion or structure showing the negatively charged carbonyl oxygen atom). For example, consider the three different hydrogens shown in Figure 100.

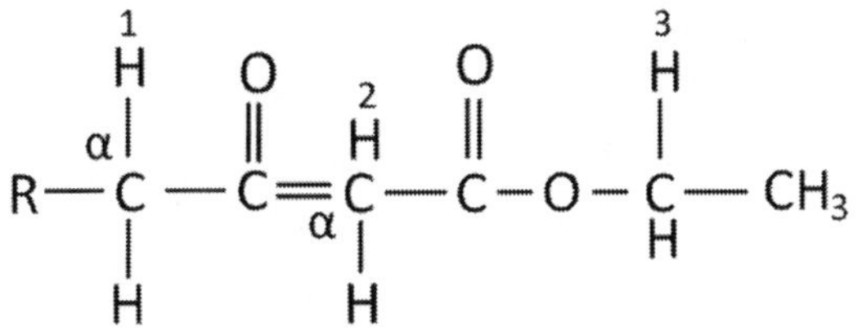

Figure 100. Acidic hydrogens

The acidity of each hydrogen will depend on how stable the conjugate bases are when a proton is removed. When hydrogen is removed from carbon atom 1, the conjugate base can have three resonance structures. However, when hydrogen is removed from carbon atom 2, there are three resonance structures for that conjugate base (see Claisen condensation addition), which indicates that the proton removed from atom 2 is more acidic than the one attached to carbon atom 1. The hydrogen at carbon atom 3 is the least acidic, and its removal will give conjugate base that does not have any resonance structures.

2). Write the formula showing a nucleophilic attack on the other carbonyl compound, which may occur by either an addition-elimination or through a substitution reaction. Enols may also act as nucleophiles if the other reactant is strongly electrophilic, for example, protonated carbonyl groups or halogens.

In a **crossed aldol reaction**, two different carbonyl compounds, both with α-hydrogens, can react in aqueous sodium hydroxide to give a mixture of products. The reaction of propanol and acetaldehyde can provide at least four reaction products. Crossed aldol reactions with sodium hydroxide base are more practical if only one of the reactants has an α-hydrogen. The reaction of benzaldehyde and propanol with sodium hydroxide at 10 °C produces an enolate of propanol, which reacts with the reactant that has no α-hydrogen (benzaldehyde). The product then undergoes dehydration to produce 2-methyl-3-phenyl-2-propenal. Dehydration is more likely if the final product has an extended conjugated system.

In a crossed **Claisen condensation reaction**, one ester molecule containing an α-hydrogen can react with different ester molecule that contains no α-hydrogens to produce a β-keto ester. The ester without the α-hydrogen will not form an enolate ion, nor will it undergo self-condensation. For instance, ethyl benzoate (no α-hydrogen) can undergo a condensation reaction with ethyl benzoylacetate, with sodium ethoxide and a hydronium ion, to produce ethyl benzoylacetate. The use of a very strong base such as sodium triphenylmethanide ($Na^{+}{:}^{-}\,C(C_6H_5)_3$) in diethyl ether can convert an ester without an α-hydrogen to an enolate ion in a quantitative yield, which can then be acylated by treating with an acyl chloride. When an aldehyde is reacted with a ketone in the presence of a sodium hydroxide base, the aldol reaction is called a **Claisen-Schmidt reaction**. Self-condensation does not occur to a great extent compared to the aldol condensation of two different aldehydes (Figure 101).

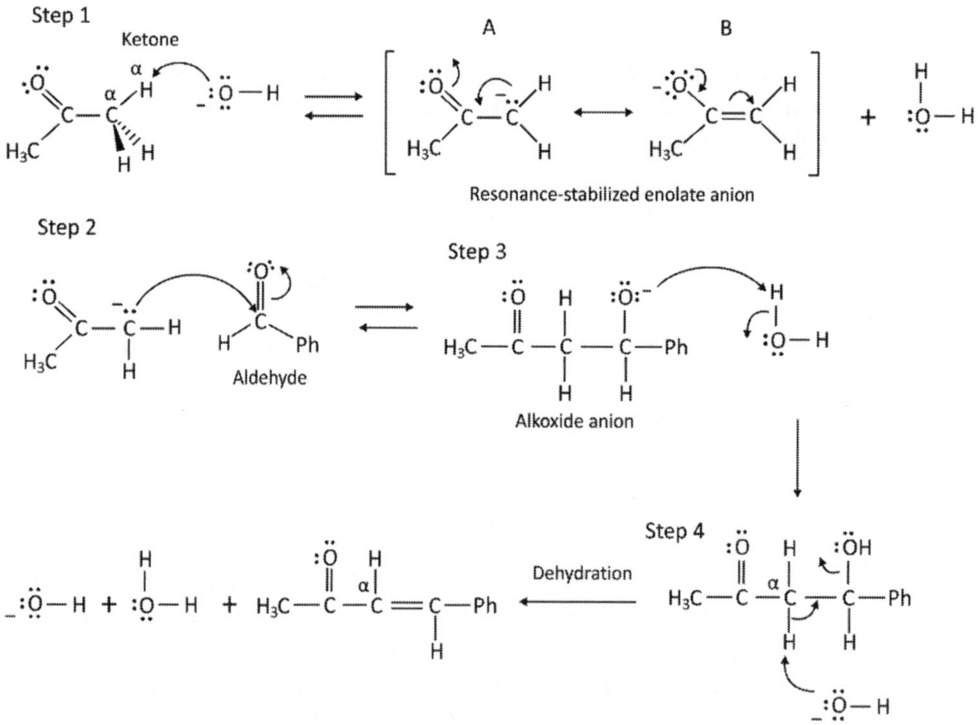

Figure 101. Claisen-Schmidt reaction (ketone + aldehyde)

Nitriles ($R - C \equiv N$) and nitroalkanes ($R - NO_2$) may undergo similar Claisen or aldol type reactions. The α-hydrogens nitrile compounds are acidic, but less than ketones or aldehydes. Acetonitrile (CH_3CN) has a pK_a of 25, which will allow the nitrile to undergo an aldol condensation. The reaction of benzaldehyde with phenylacetonitrile in sodium ethoxide and ethanol is one example. The α-hydrogens in nitroalkanes are much more acidic than aldehydes, ketones, and nitriles and have a pK_a of 10, which is due to the strong electron-withdrawing nature of the nitro group and its resonance stabilization. A nitroalkane with an α-hydrogen can undergo base-catalyzed reactions with ketones and aldehydes similar to aldol condensations, for example, the reaction of nitromethane and benzaldehyde in sodium hydroxide (Figure 102).

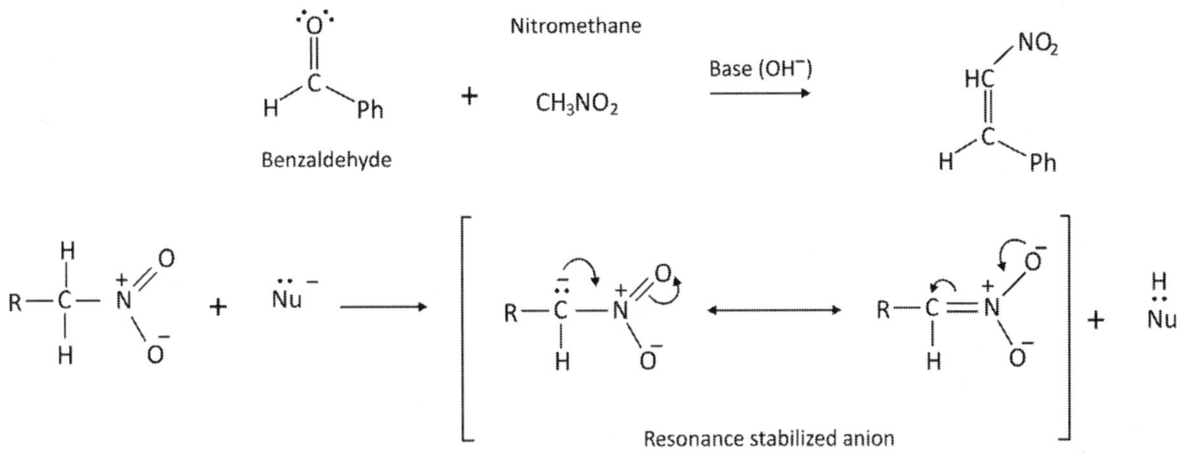

Figure 102. Nitroalkane condensation and resonance stabilized anion

Lithium Enolates: Regioselective Formation and Aldol Reactions

The strength of the base will determine the extent of formation of the enolate anion. The equilibrium of a reaction will shift toward the weaker base and acid. In other words, for the reaction to shift right, the enolate anion must be a weaker base than the aqueous base used (for example, NaOH) to carry out the reaction. Otherwise, the reaction will shift to the left. For instance, the reaction of NaOH and acetone will have an equilibrium that lies mostly to the left since the enolate ion formed is a stronger base than NaOH. However, the reaction can be shifted right if a very strong base such as lithium diisopropylamide, $(i - C_3H_7)_2N^-Li^+$ (or LDA), is added to acetone since its stronger than the enolate ion.

Unsymmetrical ketones can react with a base to form two possible enolates. The enolate that is mainly formed will depend on the base and conditions. The **thermodynamic enolate** is the more stable enolate anion that is more highly substituted at the carbon-carbon double bond. The thermodynamically more stable enolate that is primarily present at equilibrium is produced with a relatively weak base in a protic solvent (for example, solvents that have a labile proton such as water, alcohols, and ammonia). The **kinetic enolate** is the rate or kinetically controlled enolate with fewer substituents at the double bond. The kinetic enolate typically forms faster since the removal of hydrogen, needed to make the anion, is less sterically hindered. Strong sterically hindered bases such as LDA can be used to favor the kinetic enolate, and readily remove the α hydrogen from the less hindered and less substituted α carbon of the ketone. Solvents such as 1,2-dimethoxyethane (aprotic, $CH_3OCH_2CH_2OCH_3$) or DME are often used (Figure 103).

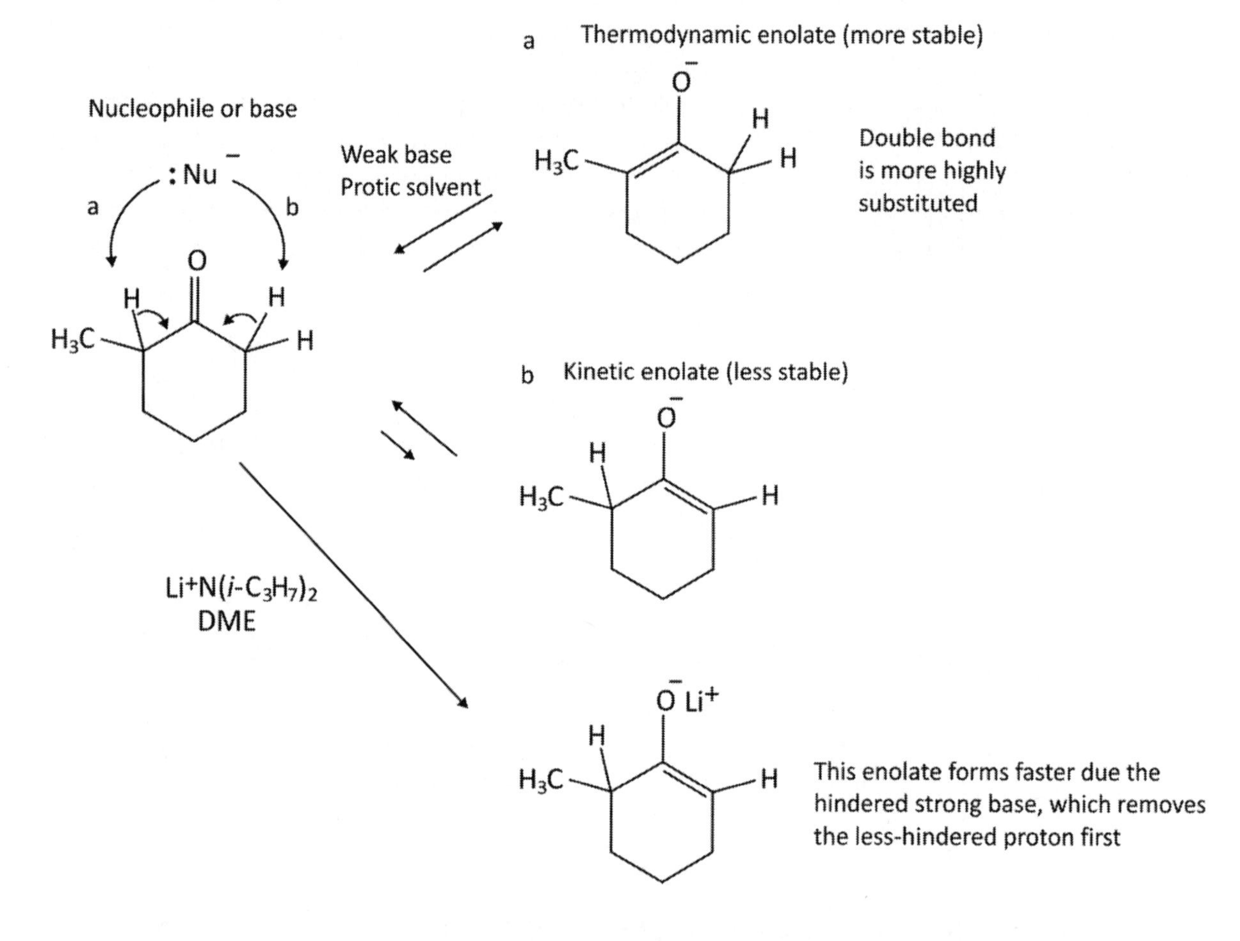

Figure 103. Formation of enolate anions: regioselectivity and thermodynamic/kinetic products

In a **directed cross aldol reaction**, a ketone can be added to LDA to produce an enolate, followed by the addition of an aldehyde to produce the aldol. When the ketone is unsymmetrical, regioselectivity can occur, thereby producing a kinetic enolate (Figure 104).

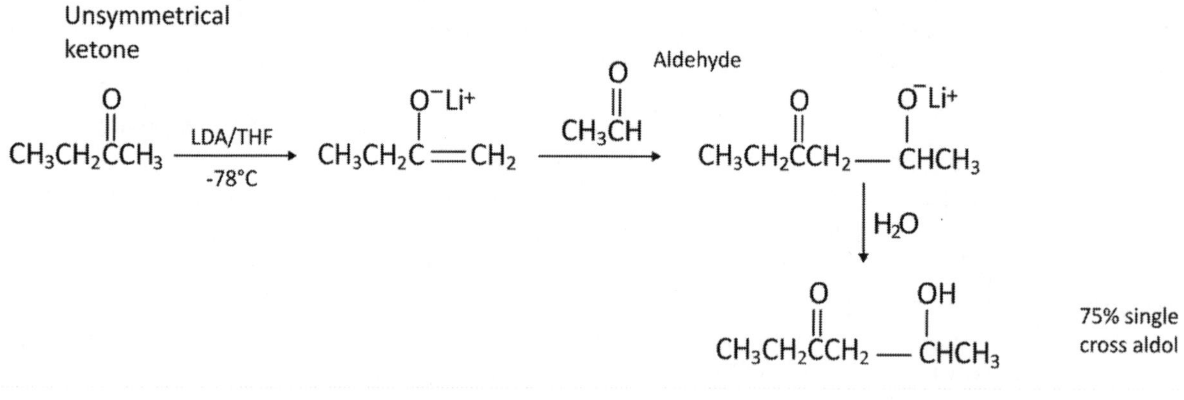

Unsymmetrical ketone

$$CH_3CH_2C(=O)CH_3 \xrightarrow[-78°C]{LDA/THF} CH_3CH_2C(O^-Li^+){=}CH_2 \xrightarrow{CH_3CH(=O)\ \text{(Aldehyde)}} CH_3CH_2C(=O)CH_2—CH(O^-Li^+)CH_3$$

$$\xrightarrow{H_2O} CH_3CH_2C(=O)CH_2—CH(OH)CH_3$$

75% single cross aldol

Figure 104. Aldol reaction of an unsymmetrical ketone with LDA: kinetic enolate

On the other hand, if an aldol (Claisen-Schmidt) reaction were carried out with hydroxide ions in a protic solvent, then a mixture of the kinetic and thermodynamic enolate would be produced from the ketone.

Lithium enolates formed using the base LDA are very useful for the alkylation of ketones in a regioselective manner. 2-methylcyclohexanone can be methylated by first forming the kinetic enolate, followed by treatment of methyl iodide (Figure 105).

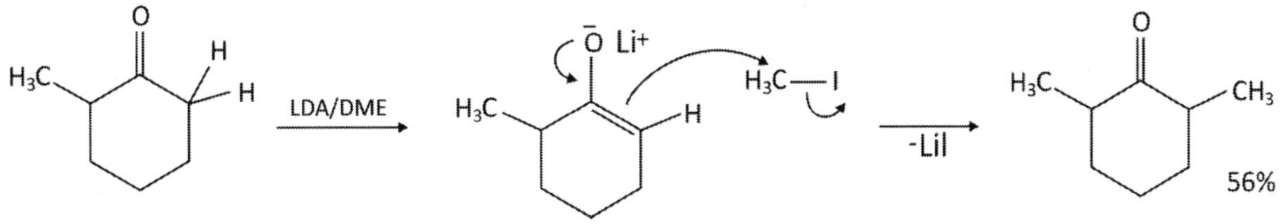

Figure 105. Alkylation of a lithium enolate followed by a reaction with methyl iodide

The reactions are S_N2 reactions and will occur when 1°- alkyl, benzylic, and allylic halides are used. Elimination will take place if the halide is °2 or °3.

Electrophilic and Nucleophilic Aromatic Substitution

Electrophilic Aromatic Substitution

Arenes are aromatic hydrocarbon rings (for example, benzene) that commonly undergo electrophilic substitution. Arenes can be designated by ArH, where the H refers to the hydrogen atom that is substituted or removed. If a hydrogen atom is removed, the compound becomes an **aryl group**, designated by Ar. Benzenoid arenes can react with electrophilic reagents by a general substitution. The reason benzene can undergo electrophilic attack is due to its exposed π electrons that delocalize within the ring. A substitution reaction on benzene initially breaks the sextet of π electrons. However, after the electrophilic substitution reaction, the sextet is regenerated. Through the use of a reagent (for example, aluminum chloride), an electrophile (E) is produced and acts as a Lewis acid. Specifically, the electrophile undergoes a nucleophilic attack and accepts an electron pair from the aromatic π electrons. The general reaction mechanism is shown in Figure 106.

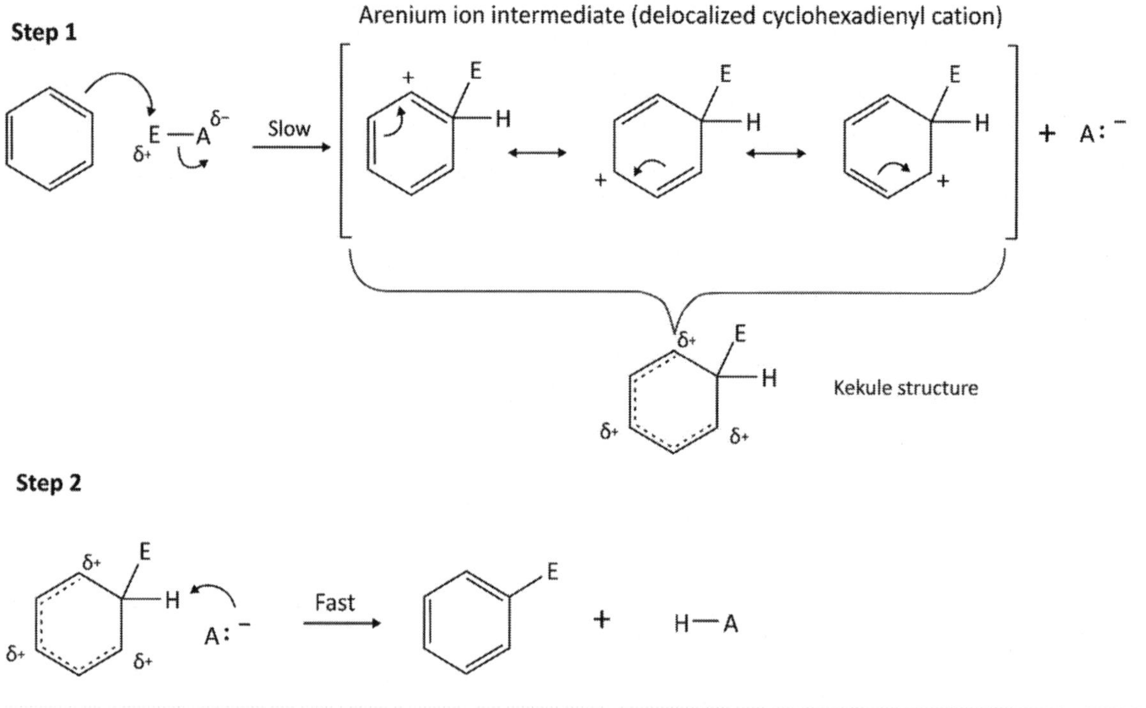

Figure 106. Reaction mechanism for electrophilic aromatic substitution

The electrophile attacks the π system of benzene to form an intermediate called an **arenium ion**. The nonaromatic carbocation or cyclohexadienyl cation that is generated is missing a proton but eventually forms an aromatic ring containing the electrophile. In the first rate-determining step, the electrophile forms a sigma (σ) bond by taking two electrons from the six-electron π system of benzene. The carbon atom that forms a σ bond to E becomes sp^3 hybridized and loses its p orbital. Only five carbon atoms will be sp^2 hybridized, and each contains a p orbital. The four π electrons will delocalize only in these p orbitals. Therefore, in **electrophilic aromatic substitution**, the electrophile substitutes for a hydrogen atom on the aromatic ring. The rate-limiting step in the reaction is the addition of the electrophile to the aromatic ring.

Electrophilic aromatic substitutions can provide a direct way of substituting different groups onto the aromatic ring. The five general types of substitution are halogenation (X_2 with $FeX_3, X = Cl, Br$), nitration ($HONO_2$ and H_2SO_4), sulfonation (SO_3 and H_2SO_4), Friedel-Crafts alkylation (RCl, $AlCl_3$), and Friedel-Crafts acylation ($R-(CO)-Cl$, $AlCl_3$). Figure 107 shows the five types of electrophilic aromatic substitutions.

X
Halogenation
X_2, FeX_3 (X=Cl, Br)
NO_2
Nitration
HNO_3
H_2SO_4
SO_3
SO_3H
H_2SO_4
Sulfonation
RCl, $AlCl_3$
R
RCOCl, $AlCl_3$
O
Friedel-Crafts alkylation
R
Friedel-Crafts acylation

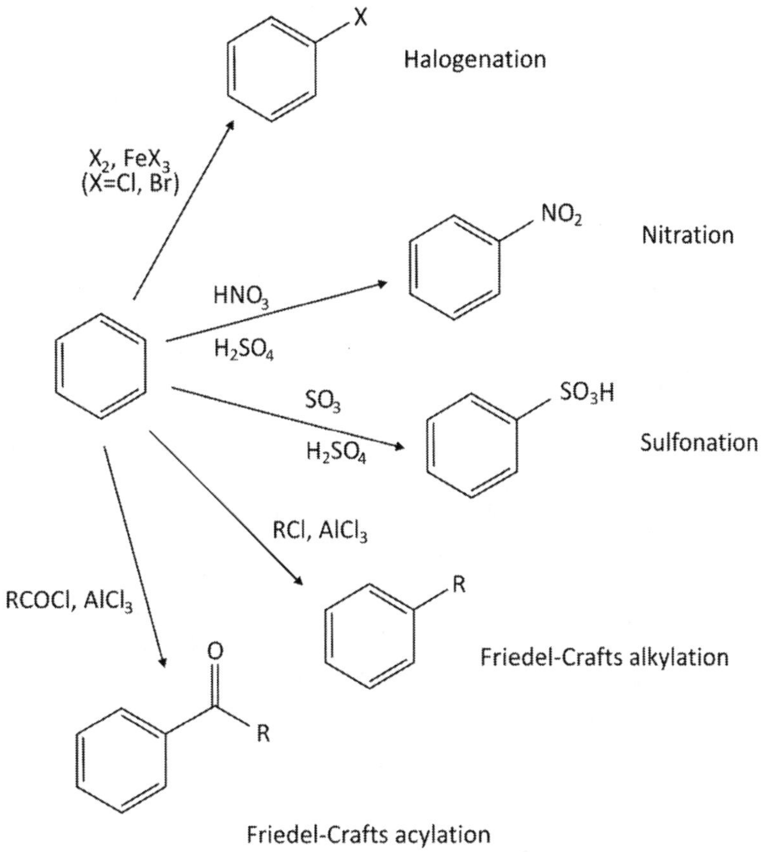

Figure 107. Types of electrophilic aromatic substitutions

Halogenation

The addition of a halogen such as chlorine or bromine onto benzene does not occur unless a Lewis acid is present in the reaction mixture. Lewis acids include anhydrous $FeCl_3$, $FeBr_3$, and $AlCl_3$. Consider the reaction of a benzene ring with a halogen gas (for example, Br_2) and an iron compound ($FeBr_3$). The general reaction mechanism is shown below.

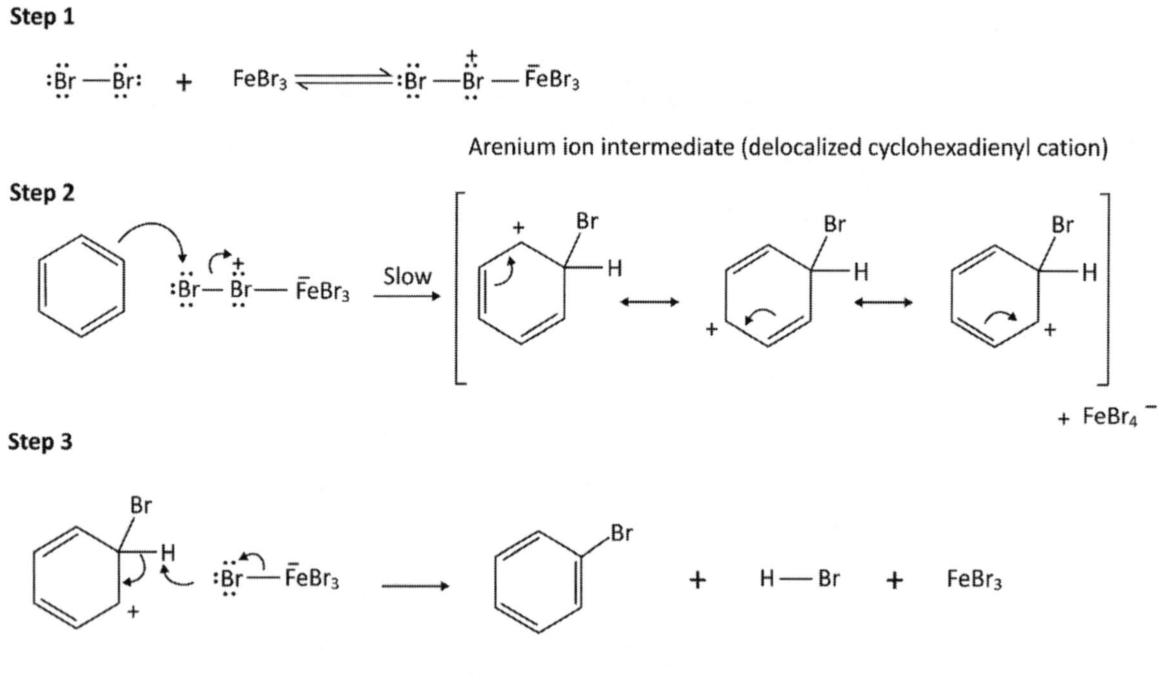

Step 1

:Br—Br: + $FeBr_3$ ⇌ :Br—$\overset{+}{Br}$—$\overset{-}{Fe}Br_3$

Arenium ion intermediate (delocalized cyclohexadienyl cation)

Step 2

:Br—Br—$\overset{-}{Fe}Br_3$ Slow → [Br, H ⟷ Br, H ⟷ Br, H] + $FeBr_4^-$

Step 3

Br, H :Br—$\overset{-}{Fe}Br_3$ → Br + H—Br + $FeBr_3$

Figure 108. Electrophilic aromatic bromination

The reaction indicates that one of the hydrogen atoms on benzene is replaced with a halogen atom (for example, Br). The reaction is a substitution reaction. In step 1, bromine reacts with the compound $FeBr_3$ to form a complex. The compound $FeBr_3$ acts as a Lewis acid and can direct the halogen gas (for example, Br_2) to form a complex, which will serve as the source of the electrophile, Br^+ . Note that the formed complex shows an incomplete octet for one of the Br^+ atoms, thereby making a strong electrophile. In step 2, the complex then dissociates to form $FeBr_4^-$ and a positively charged bromine ion. The Br^+ cation is attacked by the aromatic ring and accepts an electron pair to form a cyclohexadienyl or arenium cation. As the substitution product is formed in step 3, $FeBr_4^-$ acts as a nucleophile and removes a hydrogen atom/proton located at the site of the leaving group, thereby forming bromobenzene (75%). Hydrogen bromide is produced, and the catalyst $FeBr_3$ is regenerated.

The chlorination of benzene at 25 °C with ferric chloride ($FeCl_3$) is similar, and the catalyst helps with the production and transfer of the Cl^+ ion to the arenium ring, which eventually forms chlorobenzene (90%). Fluorination of benzene is more difficult, and special conditions are needed. Iodine is unreactive with benzene, so different conditions are required (for example, nitric acid HNO_3) to produce Iodobenzene.

Nitration Reactions of Benzene

The reaction of hot (50–55 °C), concentrated nitric acid with benzene produces nitrobenzene (85%). The rate of reaction can be increased by mixing concentrated sulfuric acid (stronger acid, $pK_a = -9$) and

nitric acid ($pK_a = -1.4$). The concentration of the electrophile (NO_2^+) is increased with the acid mixture, which allows the reaction to occur much faster. The mechanism is shown below.

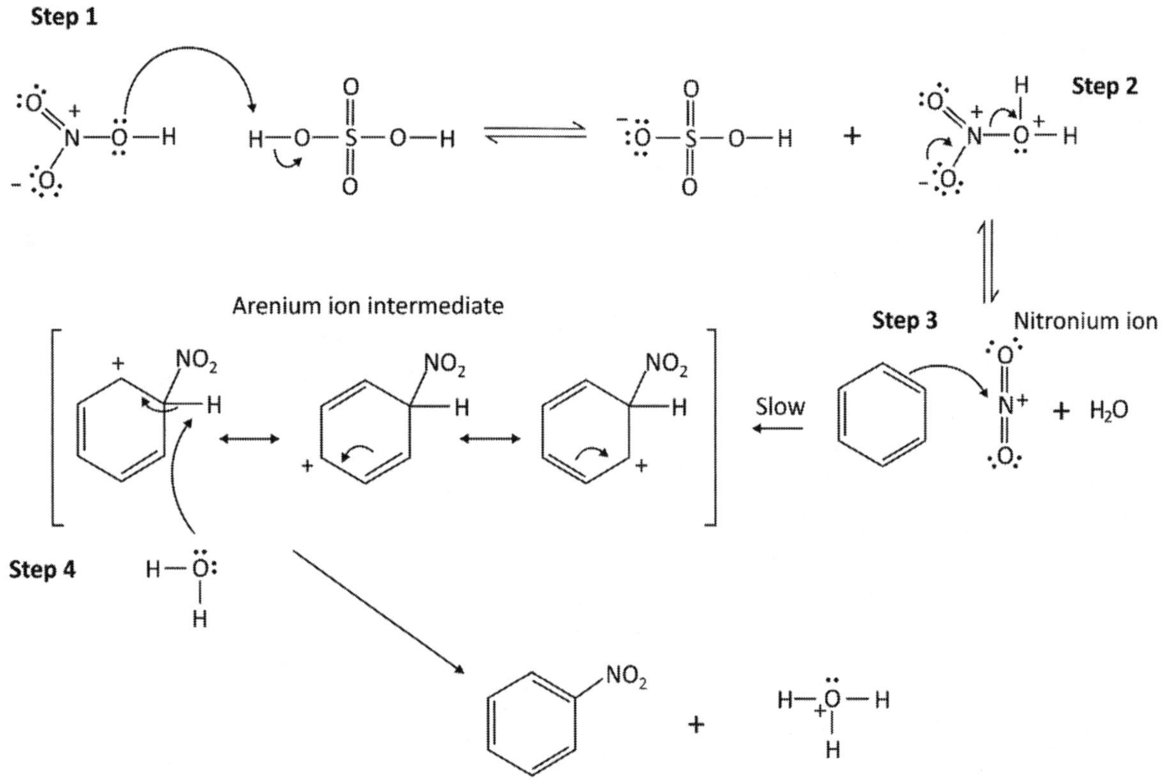

Step 1

Step 2

Arenium ion intermediate

Step 3

Nitronium ion

Slow

Step 4

Figure 109. Mechanism for the nitration of benzene

In the first step, nitric acid accepts a proton from sulfuric acid. In the second step, the protonated nitric acid dissociates into a water molecule and a nitronium ion. In the third step, the electrophilic nitronium ion reacts with benzene to produce a resonance-stabilized arenium ion. In step 4, a water molecule acts as a Lewis base and attacks or removes a proton from the arenium ion. The final products are nitrobenzene and hydronium ion.

Sulfonation Reactions of Benzene

When fuming sulfuric acid at room temperature (25 °C) is reacted with benzene, benzenesulfonic acid is produced. Fuming sulfuric will breaks down into sulfur trioxide. The electrophile, sulfur trioxide, reacts directly with benzene, as shown in the reaction mechanism below.

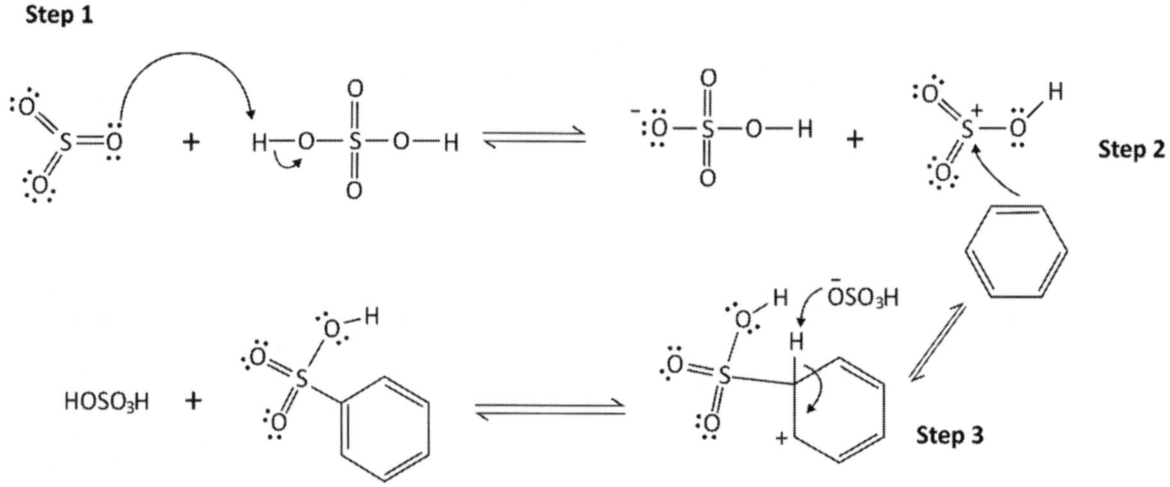

Step 1

Step 2

Step 3

Figure 110. Sulfonation of benzene mechanism

In the first step, sulfuric acid breaks down and exists in equilibrium with a mixture of sulfur trioxide, hydronium ion, and hydrogen sulfate ion. In the second step, the π electrons on benzene attack the sulfur atom on the protonated sulfur trioxide, which slowly produces the arenium ion and other resonance structures. In step three, the hydrogen sulfate ion removes a proton that is attached to the aromatic carbon atom bonded to the sulfur atom. The reaction occurs quickly and produces benzenesulfonic acid (56%). Note that all steps in the reaction are in equilibrium, and that the position of equilibrium can be influenced by changing the conditions. For instance, to reverse the reaction to the left, steam can be passed with a mixture of dilute sulfuric acid, which leads to desulfonation or the production of benzene. Distilling benzene out of solution moves the equilibrium further to the left.

Friedel-Crafts Alkylation

A Friedel-Crafts alkylation is useful for the preparation of alkylbenzenes $(\mathrm{Ar}-\mathrm{R})$. The general reaction involves the reagent compounds $\mathrm{R}-\mathrm{X}$ (in this example, the halogen is chlorine) and a Lewis acid (in this

case, $AlCl_3$), which react with benzene to produce $Ar - R$ and HX. The mechanism of the reaction is shown below.

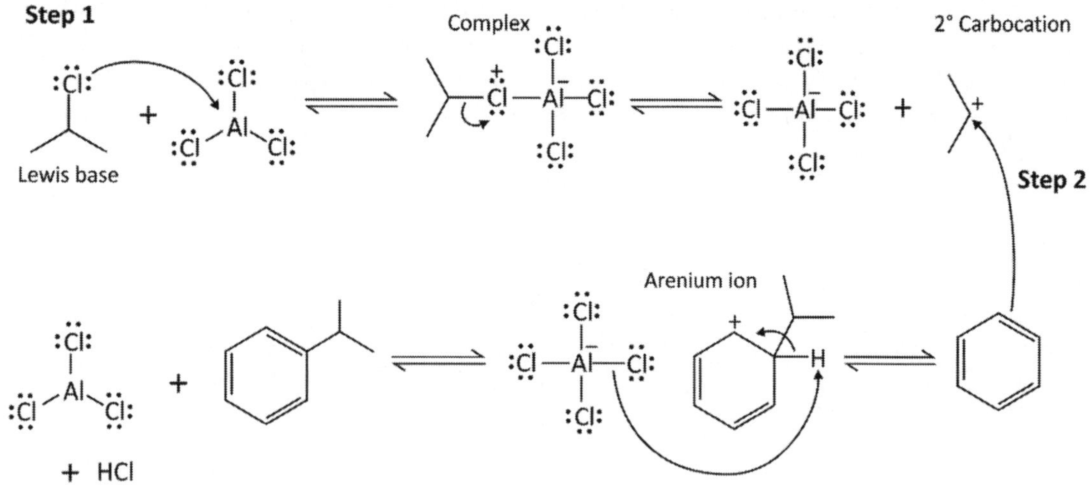

Figure 111. Mechanism for a Friedel-Crafts alkylation

Isopropyl chloride, a secondary 2° halide, represents the compound $R - X$, which acts as nucleophile or Lewis base by attacking $AlCl_3$, the Lewis acid. In the first step, an intermediate Lewis acid-base complex is formed, which then dissociates to form $AlCl_4^-$ and a secondary 2° carbocation. In the second step, the π electrons of benzene attack the electrophilic carbocation forming the arenium ion and other resonance structures. In the final step, a chlorine atom from $AlCl_4^-$ dissociates while simultaneously removing a proton from the arenium ion. Isopropylbenzene and hydrochloric acid are produced, and aluminum chloride is regenerated.

Reactions with primary 1° halides do not result in the formation of a carbocation but they do form a complex with aluminum chloride. The complex becomes a strong electrophile. The carbon atom bonded to the halogen will be polarized slightly positive.

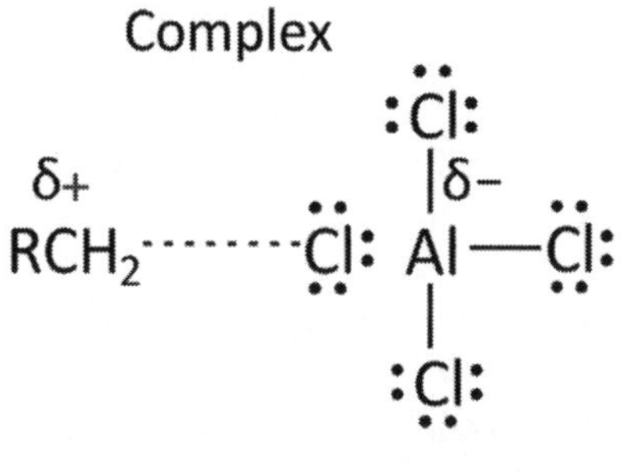

Figure 112. Electrophile complex

The positive alkyl group is then (electrophile) transferred to the benzene ring. In a Friedel-Crafts alkylation, other reagents such as HF/propene (0 °C), HF/cyclohexene (0 °C), and BF_3/Cyclohexanol (60 °C) can react with benzene to form a carbocation or carbocation-like intermediate, followed by the formation of the alkylbenzene [for example, Isopropylbenzene (84%), cyclohexylbenzene (62%), and cyclohexylbenzene(56%)].

Friedel-Crafts Acylation

A Friedel-Crafts acylation is useful for the preparation of acylbenzenes $(\mathrm{Ar} - (\mathrm{C} = \mathrm{O}) - \mathrm{R})$ and involves the transfer of an acyl group onto an aromatic ring. The acyl group is designated by $-(\mathrm{C} = \mathrm{O}) - \mathrm{R}$. The acetyl $(\mathrm{CH_3} - (\mathrm{C} = \mathrm{O}) -)$ and benzoyl $(\mathrm{Ar} - (\mathrm{C} = \mathrm{O}) -)$ groups are two common acyl groups. The reaction requires treating an acyl halide with an aromatic ring using a Lewis acid such as aluminum chloride. The first two steps of the reaction mechanism in a Friedel-Crafts acylation involve the formation of an acylium ion.

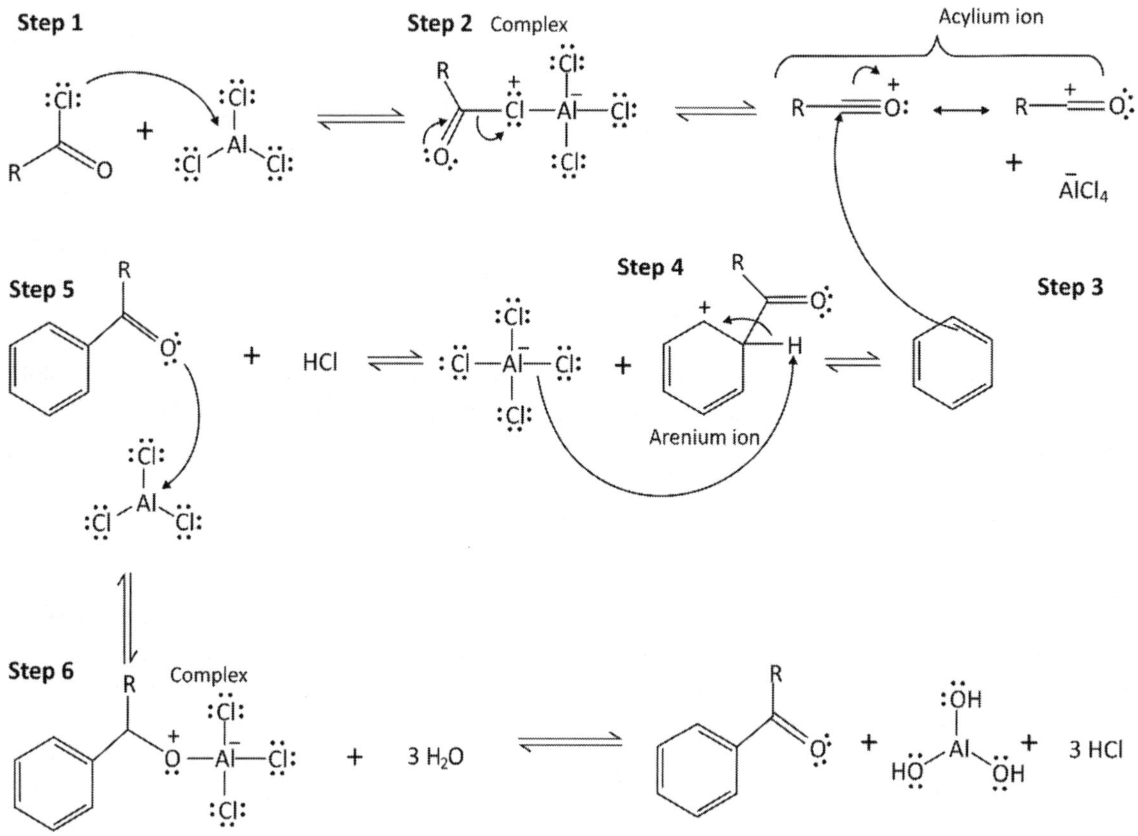

Figure 113. Mechanism of a Friedel-Crafts acylation

In the first step, the acyl halide acts as a Lewis base and reacts with aluminum chloride to form a complex. The C-Cl bond dissociates to form an acylium ion (resonance hybrid) and $\mathrm{AlCl_4}^-$. Acylium ion acts as the electrophile when it reacts with the benzene ring and creates an arenium ion. In step four, a hydrogen atom is removed from the arenium ion by $\mathrm{AlCl_4}^-$. The resulting compound creates a ketone and hydrochloric acid. The Lewis acid, aluminum chloride, is regenerated in the process but reacts with the benzoyl group in step 5 to form a complex. However, when the complex is treated with water in step 6, the ketone is freed and aluminum hydroxide is produced.

Restrictions of Friedel-Crafts Alkylations and Acylation Reactions

Carbocations produced from alcohols, alkenes, or alkyl halides can usually rearrange themselves into a more stable carbocation (3° > 2° > 1°). The major product that is formed is typically the one with the more stable carbocation. Friedel-Crafts reactions usually give poor yields if strong electron-withdrawing groups are on the benzene or aromatic ring. These groups may include $\mathrm{Ar-NO_2}$, $\mathrm{Ar-N(CH_3)_3}$, $\mathrm{Ar-COOH}$, $\mathrm{Ar-(CO)-R}$, $\mathrm{Ar-CF_3}$, $\mathrm{Ar-SO_3H}$, and $\mathrm{Ar-NH_2}$ ($\mathrm{Ar-NHR}$ and $\mathrm{-NR_2}$). The reason electron-withdrawing groups reduce the reaction yield is that the ring is rendered less reactive since the electron density on the ring lessens or becomes deficient. Electron-withdrawing groups are meta-directing groups that make an aromatic ring electron-deficient such that a Friedel-Crafts reaction will not occur. For instance, when the compound $\mathrm{Ar-NH_2}$ reacts with aluminum chloride and the alkyl/acyl group, no reaction occurs. Instead, a complex between the amino group and aluminum chloride forms.

When vinylic halides (for example, $\mathrm{-C=C-Cl}$) or aryl halides (for example, $\mathrm{Ar-Cl}$) react with benzene and aluminum chloride, no Friedel-Crafts reactions occur. This is attributed to the stability of the carbocation, which cannot readily form. When an aromatic ring reacts with isopropyl alcohol (and $\mathrm{BF_3}$), multiple alkylations or polyalkylations can take place on the same aromatic ring. Since alkyl groups are electron-releasing groups, when one alkyl group is introduced on the ring, it allows the ring to undergo further substitution (for example, at the para position). In contrast, a Friedel-Crafts polyacylation is unlikely to occur, and instead, only monoacylation takes place. Since the acyl group $\mathrm{(R-(CO)-)}$ is electron-withdrawing, when it forms a complex with aluminum chloride in the final step, the group becomes more electron-withdrawing. As a result, additional substitution is less likely to occur.

Electron-Donating and Electron-Withdrawing Substituent Groups: Orientation and Reactivity

When substituted aromatic rings are under electrophilic attack, the groups attached to the ring affect the site of attack (for example, ortho, meta, para positions) and the reaction rate. Therefore, in electrophilic aromatic substitutions, the substituent groups affect orientation and reactivity.

Activating groups are groups present on benzene that make it more reactive than benzene itself. **Deactivating groups** are groups present on benzene that make it less reactive than benzene. If the aromatic ring already contains a group (for example, a nitro or halide group), the added electrophile has three possible locations, with respect to the group, to substitute or attach. These activating and deactivating groups can be divided into two classes, which called ortho-para directors and meta directors. **Ortho-para directors** are groups that direct an incoming group to the ortho and para positions on the benzene ring. **Meta directors** are groups that direct the incoming electrophile to the meta position on the ring.

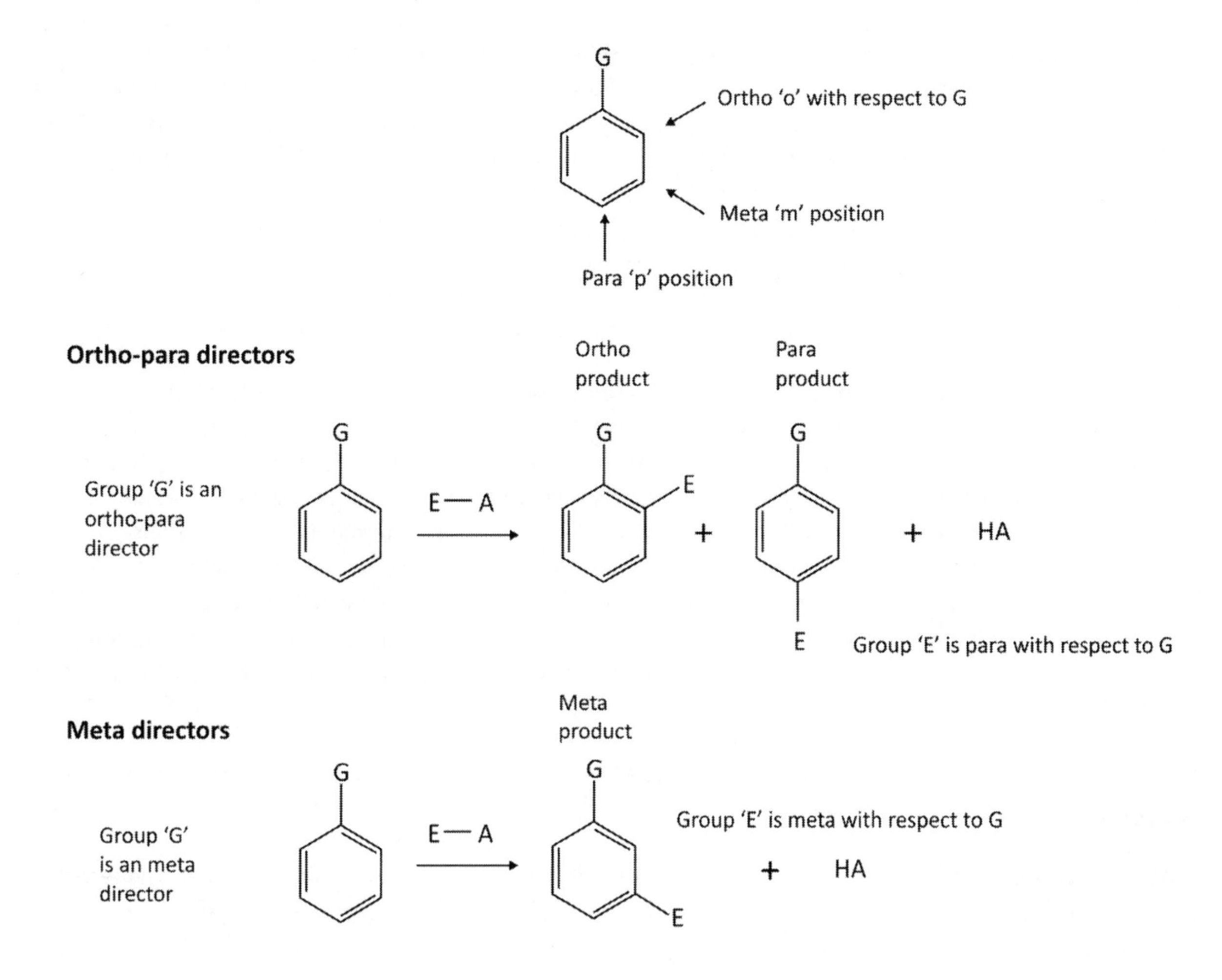

Figure 114. Ortho-para and meta directors

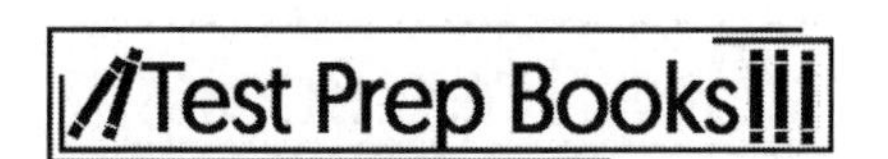

The table below lists several ortho-para and meta directing groups.

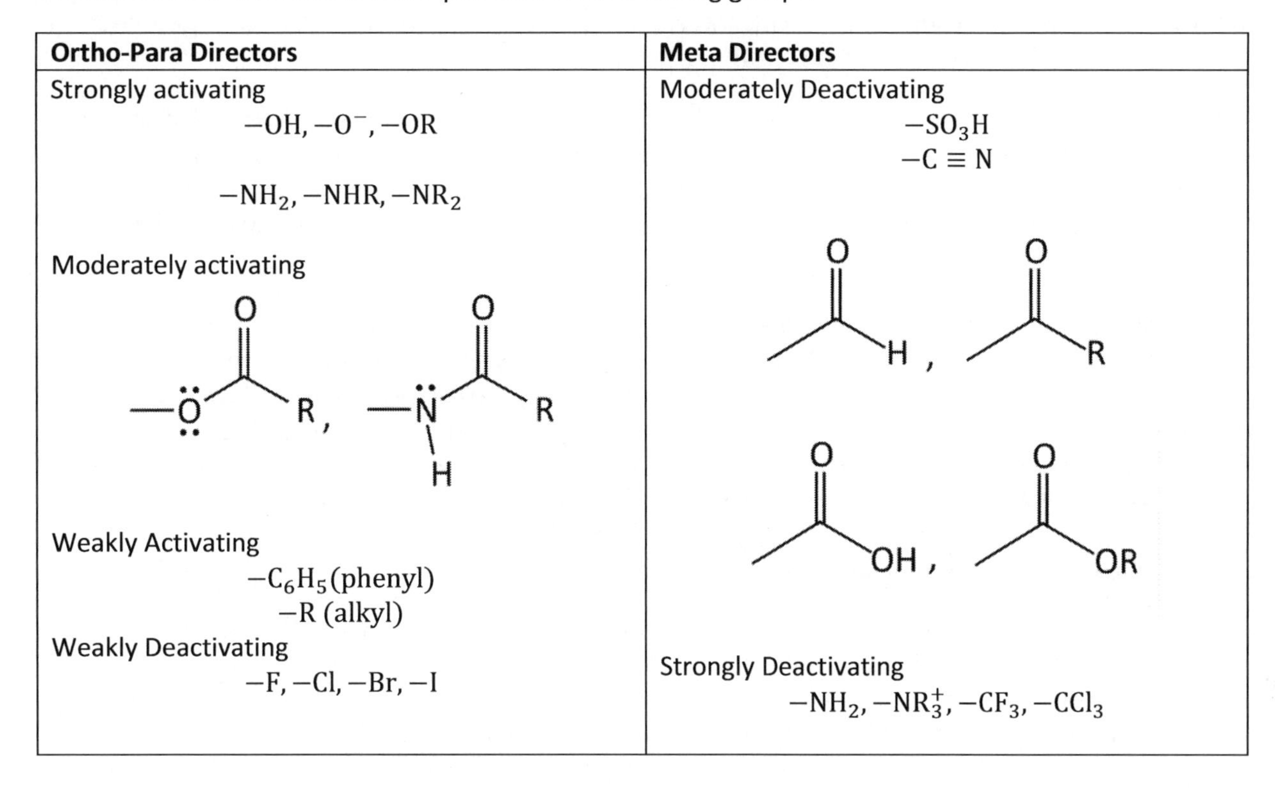

Ortho-Para Directors	Meta Directors
Strongly activating $-OH, -O^-, -OR$ $-NH_2, -NHR, -NR_2$	Moderately Deactivating $-SO_3H$ $-C \equiv N$
Moderately activating $-\ddot{O}-C(=O)-R$, $-\ddot{N}(H)-C(=O)-R$	$-C(=O)-H$, $-C(=O)-R$ $-C(=O)-OH$, $-C(=O)-OR$
Weakly Activating $-C_6H_5$(phenyl) $-R$ (alkyl) Weakly Deactivating $-F, -Cl, -Br, -I$	Strongly Deactivating $-NH_2, -NR_3^+, -CF_3, -CCl_3$

Table 6. Substituent types in electrophilic aromatic substitution

Activating Groups (Electron-Donating) are Ortho-Para Directors

Toluene is a benzene ring bonded to a methyl group $(Ar - CH_3)$ and is more reactive than benzene by itself. Therefore, the methyl group is the activating group and an ortho-para director. In the electrophilic-substitution nitration reaction of toluene (with nitric acid and sulfuric acid), o-nitrotoluene (59%), p-nitrotoluene (37%), and m-nitrotoluene (4%) are produced. Notice that only 4% of the products contain the nitro group in the meta position. Other examples of strong activating groups that are ortho-para directors include the methoxyl group $(CH_3O -)$, the acetamido group $(CH_3CONH -)$, the hydroxyl group $(-OH)$, and the amino group $(-NH_2)$.

Deactivating Groups (Electron-Withdrawing) are Meta Directors

Nitrobenzene contains a nitro group (NO_2) substituted on a benzene ring, and it is less reactive than benzene itself. The nitro group is a meta director. When nitrobenzene is nitrated with nitric and sulfuric acid, 93% of the electrophilic substitution occurs at the meta position. Other deactivating groups and meta directors include the trifluoromethyl $(-CF_3)$, the sulfo $(-SO_3H)$, and the carboxyl group $(-CO_2H)$. Benzene substituted with halogen groups (for example, chloro and bromo) is less reactive than a benzene compound. The chloro and bromo groups are weak deactivating groups but are ortho-para directors.

Inductive and Resonance Effects on Electrophilic Aromatic Substitution

Depending on the group type (for example $-CH_3$) that is attached to the ring, the group can change the reactivity of the aromatic ring. Therefore, the group type determines where the electrophile attacks on the ring. Electron-donating groups (for example, CH_3, NH_2) and electron-withdrawing groups (for example, NO_2) change the electron density of the ring by inductive and resonance effects. Resonance has a larger influence on the electron density than induction.

Inductive effects result when a substituent brings about an electrostatic interaction from a polarized bond, which can result in a positive charge developing either at the ring or at the substituent. For example, if the substituent is electronegative, then the benzene ring will be at the positive end with respect to the dipole. An electrophilic attack is unlikely since it would lead to an increase in positive charge on the ring.

Resonance effects describe how a substituent group may decrease or increase the resonance stabilization of the intermediate arenium ion. For example, the arenium ion can form several resonance-stabilized structures. However, the presence of a substituent group can favor one of those resonance structures over the other. In addition, if the substituent group contains a lone bonding electron pair, the arenium ion will further stabilize and form a fourth resonance structure. Some substituents with lone pairs include the following, ranging from the most to least electron-donating:

(most electron-donating) $-NH_2, -NR_2 > -OH, -OR > -X$ (least electron-donating)

Whether a group is electron-withdrawing or electron-donating determines where the electrophile is added with respect to the group. For example, an electron-withdrawing group reduces the electron density at the ortho and para positions to a greater extent than at the meta position. The greater electron density at the meta position means that that position (meta carbon) will attack the electrophile. In contrast, electron-donating groups increase the electron density more at the ortho and para positions than at the meta position, such that electrophiles attach at those two positions. If a group contains an atom with nonbonded electrons (for example, lone pairs in NH_2, OCH_3) next to the aromatic ring, the electron density increases. Electron-donating groups are **activating** groups that increase the electron density of the ring. Resonance or electron delocalization will occur from the activating group to the ring, thereby increasing the aromatic ring activity. Ortho-para directors, such as methoxybenzene and aminobenzene, can undergo resonance such that the resonance structures contain a carbanion at the ortho or para position. Specifically, the arenium ion resonance structures for aniline (aminobenzene) undergoing electrophilic aromatic substitution indicate why the ortho and para

positions are predominant. Ortho and para attacks lead to relatively stable resonance structures that contribute to the hybrids. These resonance contributors are not seen in a meta attack.

Ortho attack

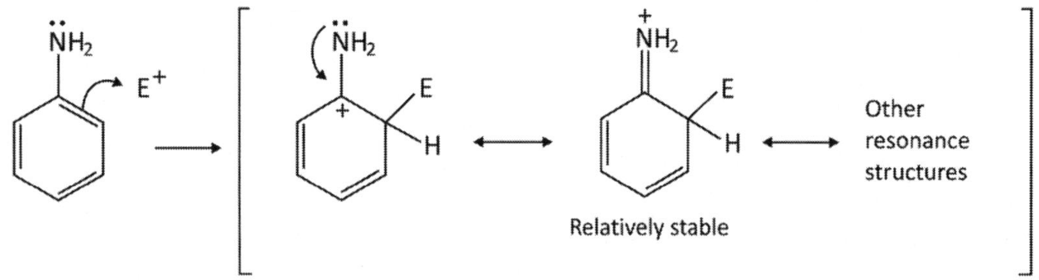

NH_2 E^+ NH_2 E H $\overset{+}{N}H_2$ E H Other resonance structures

Relatively stable

Para attack

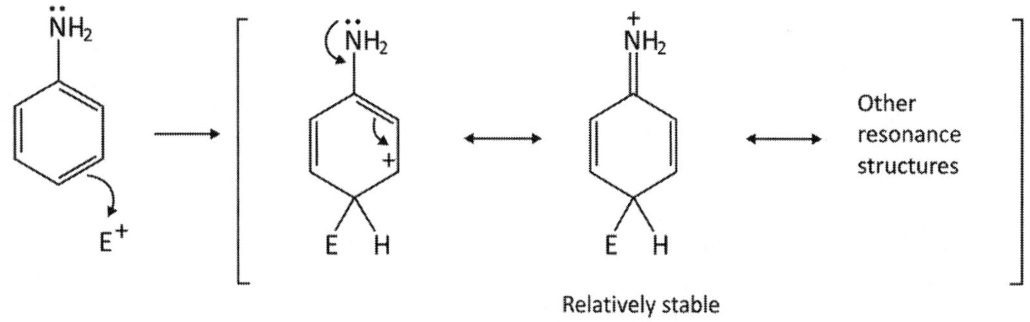

NH_2 E^+ NH_2 E H $\overset{+}{N}H_2$ E H Other resonance structures

Relatively stable

Figure 115. Stability of ortho and para resonance structures

Electron-withdrawing groups, such as benzoic acid (for example, $Ar - COOH$) or nitrobenzene, can contain several electronegative atoms bonded (single or double) to an atom (the carbon atom in $Ar - C - OOH$) connected to the benzene ring. The electron density of the ring will decrease as the withdrawing group forms a resonance structure with a negative charge on the electronegative atom. Electron-withdrawing groups act as a **deactivating group** since they decrease the electron density of the ring by induction or resonance. Therefore, aromatic rings with electron-withdrawing groups are less reactive than a benzene ring. Electron-withdrawing groups are considered meta directors because the ortho and para attacks lead to unstable arenium resonance structures.

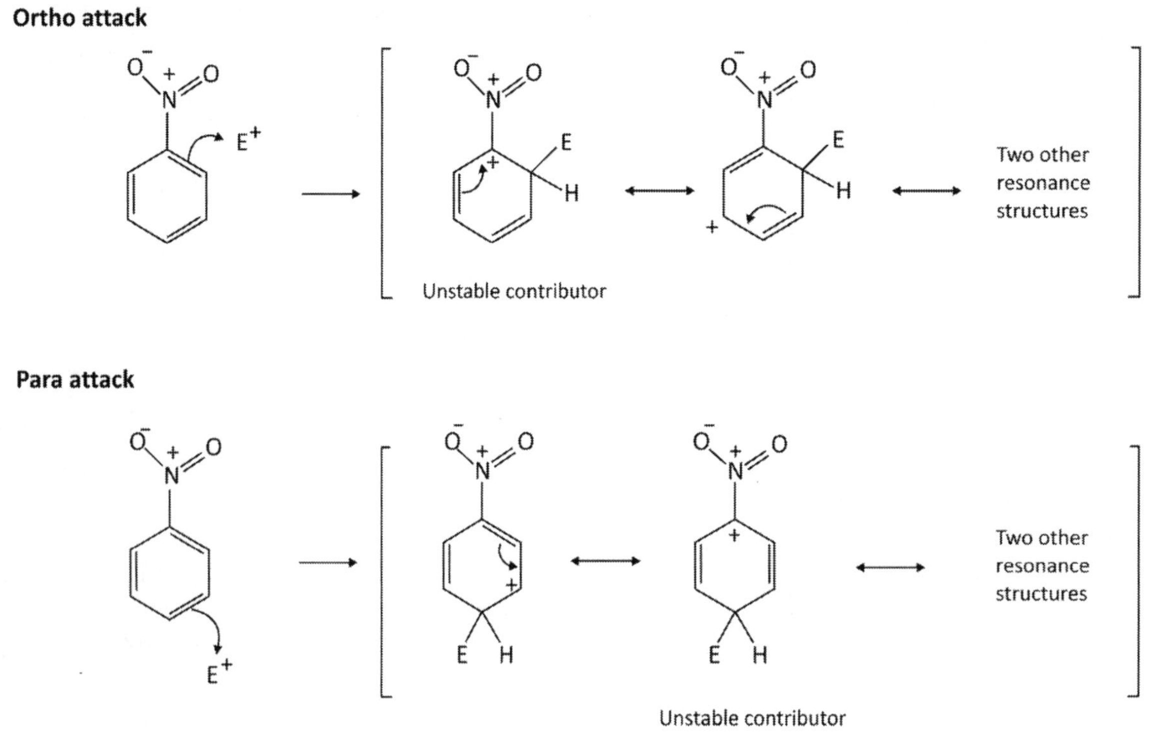

Ortho attack

Unstable contributor

Two other resonance structures

Para attack

Two other resonance structures

Unstable contributor

Figure 116. Instability of ortho and para resonance structures for deactivating groups

The carboxyl group $(-COOH)$ is a deactivating group and will pull electrons toward the carbonyl oxygen atom through resonance. The acetoxy group $(-O-(O=C)-CH_3)$ is a weak activating group since electrons on the oxygen atom can delocalize to the carbonyl group. The acetoxy group will donate electrons to the aromatic ring to form a carbanion. The halogen atom contains various electron pairs making it a possible activating group through resonance. However, halogen atoms can be strongly electronegative. The halogen atoms (for example, chlorine) are larger than oxygen and carbon; therefore, the halogen atom will contribute fewer electrons to the ring with respect to the acetoxy group. From an inductive point of view, chlorine (halogen) is more electronegative than hydrogen, thereby reducing the electron density of the aromatic ring.

Nucleophilic Aromatic Substitution

Aromatic rings can undergo nucleophilic aromatic substitution (S_NAr) by two pathways: addition-elimination and elimination-addition. These aromatic systems have one or more electron-withdrawing groups (for example, NO_2), which are ortho or para to the substituted group (Figure 117). One of the groups is a good leaving group (for example Cl). The greater the number of electron-withdrawing groups on the aromatic ring, the more electrophilic the ring. Therefore, the reactivity toward the nucleophile also increases.

Addition-Elimination: S_NAr Mechanism

If an aromatic compound contains a strong electron-withdrawing group in addition to an electron-leaving group, it can undergo **nucleophilic aromatic substitution** (S_N2) by addition-elimination. In an **addition-elimination reaction** mechanism, the aromatic ring acts as a Lewis acid and accepts an electron pair from a nucleophile (Figure 117, $NaOH/H_2O$ reagents and heat). An anionic intermediate initially forms. However, the reaction typically occurs when the aromatic ring contains a strong electron-withdrawing group such as a nitro group (NO_2). If the nitro group is not present, the reaction does not occur. The nitro group stabilizes the formed anion (anionic intermediate) by resonance. After the formation of the anion through addition, a specific leaving group can be eliminated. The reaction mechanism is shown below.

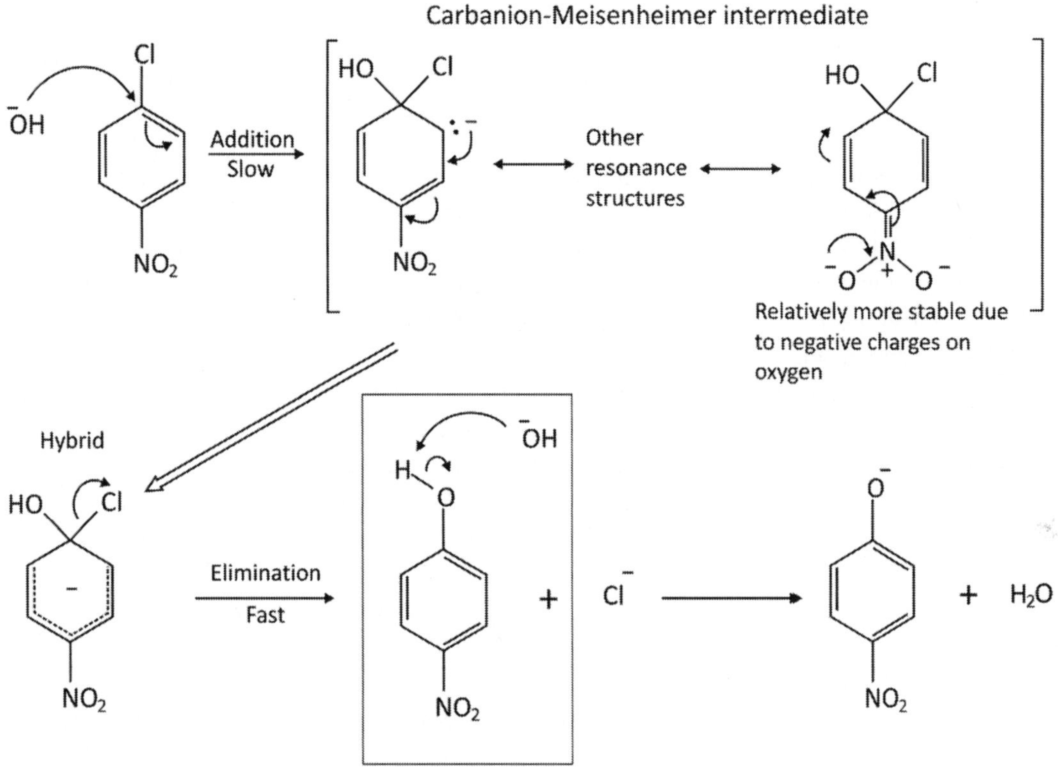

Figure 117. Nucleophilic aromatic substitution by addition-elimination

A nucleophile (OH^-) adds to a site on the ring that contains a good leaving group (Cl). Good leaving groups include halides $F > Cl > Br > I$. Hydrides ($H{:}^-$) are poor leaving groups, so the nucleophile substitutes near a group that contains the better leaving group.

Elimination Addition: S_NAr Mechanisms

In an **elimination-addition reaction** mechanism, a strong nucleophilic base (for example, NH_2^- or OH^-) initiates an elimination and forms a highly reactive benzyne compound. The reactive compound then undergoes a nucleophilic addition mechanism. An example of the elimination-addition reaction is shown below for the reaction of bromobenzene and amide ion.

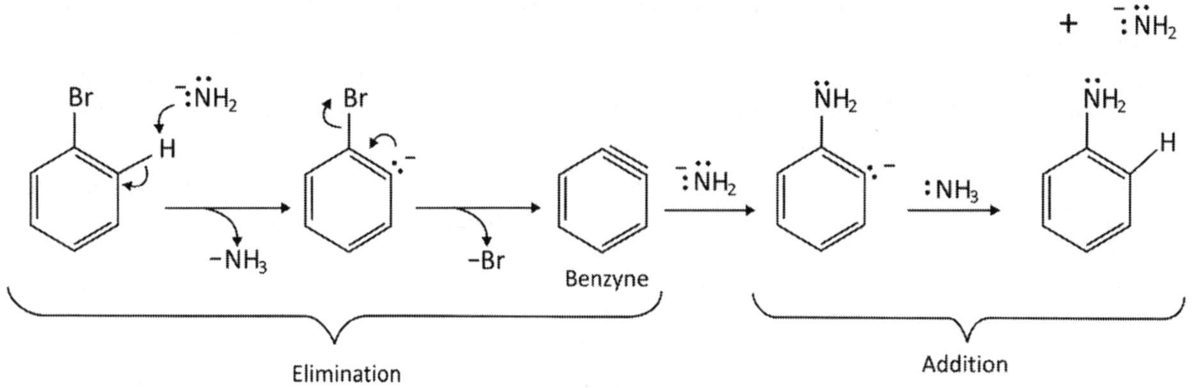

Figure 118. Benzyne S_N2 elimination addition mechanism

After the amide ion abstracts a proton, a negative charge forms at the ortho carbon and is stabilized by the inductive effects from bromine. A bromide ion is removed, and an unstable and reactive benzyne compound is formed. The reaction of benzyne and the amide base results in a two-step addition that produces aniline. Elimination-addition reactions generally require at least one ortho hydrogen, a strong nucleophilic base (for example, amide ion NH_2^-), a relatively good leaving group (for example, Br, F). Such highly forcing conditions for an elimination-addition make it less common than an addition-elimination mechanism. In an addition-elimination, the nucleophile can attach to the site containing the leaving group. However, in an elimination-addition aromatic reaction, the nucleophile can connect at the site bearing the ortho hydrogen or at the site attached to the leaving group.

Free Radical Substitutions and Additions

Free radicals or radicals are species that contain an unpaired electron. Species such as $CH_3\cdot$ and $Br\cdot$ are examples of free radicals. A single dot is placed after the species to indicate that it has one electron. Since these species don't contain a full octet of electrons, these radicals are electron-deficient and highly reactive. Radicals have no formal charge and are electrically neutral. Ionic species that have a formal charge must undergo substitution nucleophilic reactions and elimination reactions (for example, S_N2 and E2) in the presence of a solvent. However, free radicals don't require a solvent to undergo an organic reaction. Dichlorofluoromethane (CCl_2F_2) is a compound that was once commonly found in refrigerants (Freon-12) and aerosol sprays. A free radical reaction can take place between ozone (O_3) and CCl_2F_2 in the gas phase. Consequently, several countries have banned the use of CCl_2F_2 due to its damaging effect on the Earth's ozone layer.

Free-radical reactions can occur in one of two ways: through a substitution or an addition reaction mechanism. For example, a hydrocarbon such as methane can undergo halogenation with chlorine through a free-radical substitution reaction mechanism. The general reaction mechanism is shown below.

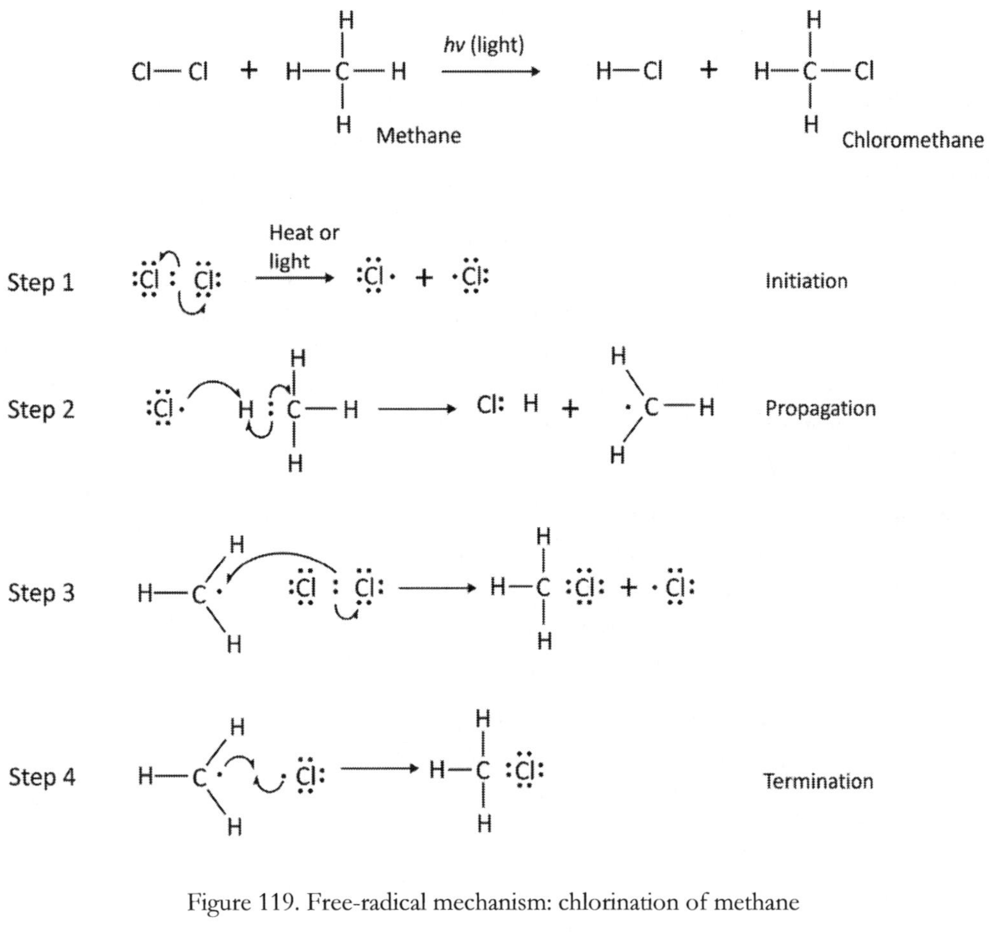

$$Cl{-}Cl + CH_4 \text{ (Methane)} \xrightarrow{hv\text{ (light)}} H{-}Cl + CH_3Cl \text{ (Chloromethane)}$$

Step 1 (Initiation): $:\ddot{Cl}:\ddot{Cl}: \xrightarrow{\text{Heat or light}} :\ddot{Cl}\cdot + \cdot\ddot{Cl}:$

Step 2 (Propagation): $:\ddot{Cl}\cdot + H:CH_3 \longrightarrow Cl:H + \cdot CH_3$

Step 3: $H_3C\cdot + :\ddot{Cl}:\ddot{Cl}: \longrightarrow H_3C:\ddot{Cl}: + \cdot\ddot{Cl}:$

Step 4 (Termination): $H_3C\cdot + \cdot\ddot{Cl}: \longrightarrow H_3C:\ddot{Cl}:$

Figure 119. Free-radical mechanism: chlorination of methane

Radical reactions can occur in the gas or solution phase. Radical reactions can be initiated by ultraviolet light (designated as *hv*), heat (> 100 °C), and chemically with a radical initiator (AIBN) and peroxides (RO-OR). All radical substitution and addition reactions are chain reactions that occur in steps. The three general reaction steps are called **initiation**, **propagation**, and **termination**. The initiation step leads to the generation of radicals. Propagation is the second step. It involves the reaction of a radical and a stable molecule to produce a new radical molecule. Radicals are regenerated in the propagation step. The created radical reacts with another stable molecule to generate another radical, and so on. In the final step, termination, the reaction stops when all the remaining radicals have reacted with one another.

Figure 119 shows the general steps involved in each reaction process. Methane and chlorine react in the presence of ultraviolet light. Chlorine gas absorbs a specific wavelength of light and dissociates. The reaction can also occur in the dark if the reaction mixture is heated to a temperature greater than 100 °C. In the first step, chlorine gas dissociates homolytically under the influence of light or heat. Each chlorine atom takes one bonding electron. Note that a single "barbed" arrow indicates the movement or attack of an electron. The first step produces two highly reactive chlorine atoms. In a second step, called hydrogen abstraction, a chlorine atom abstracts hydrogen from methane. A molecule of hydrogen chloride (HCl) and a methyl radical are created. Chain propagation is completed in the third step, when halogen abstraction occurs. This step involves a methyl radical abstracting a chlorine atom from chlorine gas. The third step generates a chlorine atom and a molecule of chloromethane.

Most importantly, notice that the chlorine radical can participate in the second step repeatedly. Step 3 can be repeated and will occur thousands of times. Therefore, steps 2 and 3 lead to what is called a **chain reaction** in which each step creates a reactive intermediate that allows the next cycle to occur. In the final step, a chlorine and methyl radical are coupled. The reaction eventually depletes the pool of reactive intermediates and terminates the chain reaction. Figure 119 shows one possible scenario of chain termination. However, two methyl radicals can also be coupled to produce an ethane molecule. Two chlorine radicals may also be combined to produce chlorine gas. Other halogenated products such as $\mathrm{CH_2Cl_2}$, $\mathrm{CHCl_3}$, and $\mathrm{CCl_4}$ can be produced through side reactions in the free-radical mechanism. For example, in the propagation step, a chlorine radical can react with chloromethane $(\mathrm{CHCl_3})$ to produce HCl and a chloromethyl radical. The produced radical then reacts with chlorine gas to generate dichloromethane and a chlorine radical. These steps are repeated such that dichloromethane is produced continuously by a chain reaction.

The energy required to generate a radical depends on the stability of the radical. For instance, the most stable radicals form rapidly and require the least amount of light or heat energy. For organic radicals, the stability of the radical increases as the carbon atom bearing the unpaired electron becomes more substituted. Benzylic and allylic radicals (Figure 120) are generally the most stable radicals since they can stabilize through resonance. The order of stability in organic radicals is:

$$\text{benzylic/allylic} > 3^\circ > 2^\circ > 1^\circ\ \text{alkyl} > \text{methyl} > \text{aryl/vinylic}$$

Therefore, breaking a tertiary C — H bond requires the least amount of energy, and breaking an aryl C — H bond requires the greatest amount of energy.

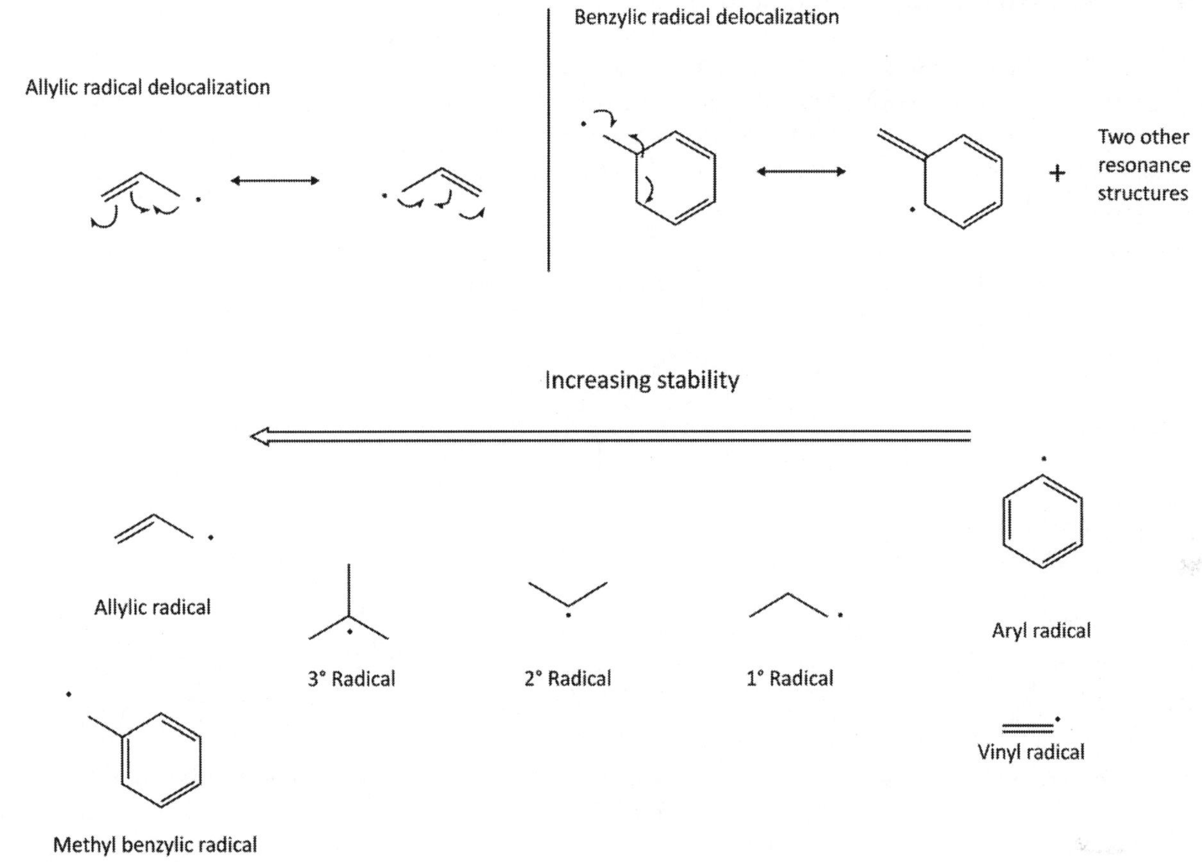

Figure 120. Resonance in allylic radicals

Alkanes that contain more carbon atoms react with halogens through the same chain reaction mechanism. Specifically, chlorination of alkanes containing more than two carbon atoms gives a mixture of isomeric and highly chlorinated compounds. Chlorination does not occur selectively. For instance, the chlorination of propane produces 1-chloropropane (45%) and 2-chloropropane (55%).There is a connection between the reactivity of distinct hydrogen atoms and the type of hydrogen atom (3°, 2°, and 1°) that is replaced. Primary hydrogen atoms are the least reactive (giving a 1° radical), and the tertiary hydrogen atoms in an alkane are the most reactive (giving a 3° radical).

Fluorine is less selective than chlorine since the energy of activation for the removal of a hydrogen atom by fluorine is low. Reactions of fluorine with an alkane occur equally at 1°, 2°, and 3° hydrogens, and the distribution of products are primarily the same.

Bromine Selectivity

Bromine is less reactive than chlorine and is more selective at the site of attack. Bromine can distinguish the different types of hydrogen atoms on the alkane. Bromine undergoes a selective substitution at the site where the most stable radical intermediate is formed. For example, the bromination of 2-

methylpropane produces a product that is 99% 2-bromo-2-methylpropane with trace amounts of 1-bromo-2-methylpropane. Bromination occurs at the 2° radical.

Stereochemistry of Radical Reactions

Achiral molecules (for example, pentane) that undergo halogenation produce a compound that contains a single tetrahedral carbon with a chiral center. The reaction products are a racemic mixture. The chlorination of pentane produces (±)-2-chloropentane in addition to highly chlorinated achiral products such as 1-chloropentane and 3-chloropentane. The reaction mechanism below indicates how a racemic form is obtained.

C2 carbon
C2 carbon
Cl·
Enantiomer 1
Enantiomer 2
CH_3
$Cl\cdot + Cl—C$
H
$CH_2CH_2CH_3$
Cl_2
CH_3
C
H
$CH_2CH_2CH_3$
Cl_2
H_3C
H
C—Cl + Cl·
$H_3CH_2CH_2C$
(*S*)-2-Chloropentane (50%)
Trigonal planar radical
(*R*)-2-Chloropentane (50%)

Figure 121. The stereochemistry of chlorination of pentane

A hydrogen atom removed at the second carbon atom (from either side) produces a 2° alkyl radical that has a trigonal planar geometry. Note that the hydrogens removed at the second carbon atom (C2) of pentane are **enantiotopic,** meaning enantiomers are formed after a radical attack at the C2 hydrogens. The radical can react with chlorine gas from either side of the molecule. The radical is achiral, and chlorination at either side has an equal probability. Two enantiomers are produced in equal amounts (racemic): (*S*)-2-chloropentane (50%) and (*R*)-2-chloropentane (50%).

A second chiral center can be created when a chiral product such as (*S*)-2-chloropentane) undergoes chlorination at C3. The hydrogens at the C3 site are **diastereotopic** or without symmetry. A chiral trigonal planar radical is created when a hydrogen atom is removed at the C3 site. The radical then reacts with chlorine on either side with different probabilities to produce a pair of chiral diastereomers: (2*S*,3*S*)-2,3-dichloropentane, and (2*S*,3*R*)-2,3-dichloropentane. Each product is optically active, and its mixture would also be optically active since the diastereomers are not produced in equal amounts. Each diastereomer has different physical properties and can be separated by fractional distillation or gas chromatography.

Allylic Substitution Reactions

Allylic groups contain groups or atoms bonded to an sp^3-hybridized carbon next to an alkene ($C = C$). The figure below shows several arrows that point to atoms that are allylic. The chlorine atom below is bonded at an allylic position.

Allylic position

Cl

Figure 122. Allylic atoms and positions

Allylic hydrogens are generally considered the most reactive in a radical substitution reaction. The dissociation energy of a carbon-hydrogen bond in the following compounds decreases in energy in the following order with the formation of a radical: ethene (vinyl radical) > propane (1° and 2° radical) > isobutane (3° radical) > propene (allyl radical). The formation of allylic radicals is the most stable since there are more contributing resonance structures. Halogen bonding or substitution can occur at either end of an allylic radical. However, if the allylic radical is unsymmetrical, then constitutional isomers are produced. Allylic halides can be produced by substituting the allylic hydrogens. For instance, the chlorination or bromination of propene at high temperatures and low concentrations of the halogen results in an **allylic substitution**.

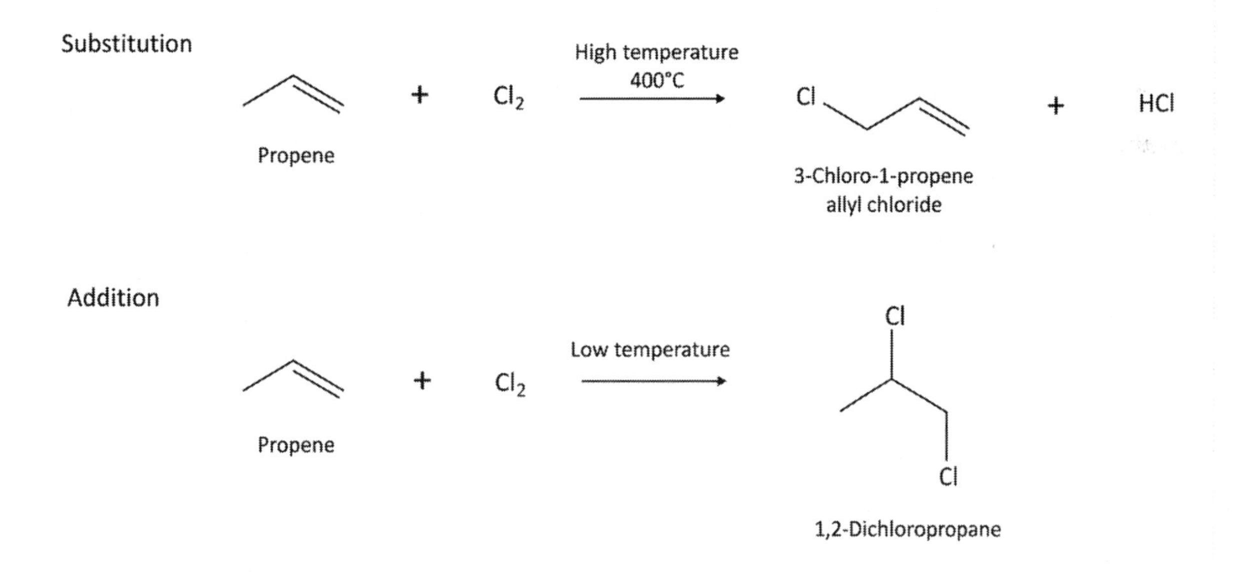

Figure 123. Allylic substitution and addition

However, at lower temperatures, the chlorination (or bromination) results in an addition reaction. The reaction mechanism for allylic substitution is the same as the alkane halogenation shown earlier. For example, in the chlorination of propene, chain initiation involves the homolytic cleavage of chlorine gas to produce two chlorine radicals. In the first propagation step, the chlorine radical abstracts an allylic hydrogen to create an allylic radical and hydrogen chloride. In the second propagation step, a chlorine gas molecule reacts with the allylic radical to produce an allyl chloride (3-chloro-1-propene, Figure 124) and a chlorine radical. The chain reaction continues until termination.

Different reaction conditions are required for the bromination of propene. When propene is treated with N-bromosuccinimide (NBS) and light or peroxide, an allyl bromide is created. The reaction is initiated when a bromine radical attacks an allylic hydrogen within propene. The bromine radical is likely formed when hydrogen bromide reacts with NBS, resulting in the cleavage of the N – Br bond. The reaction takes place in a nonpolar solvent with relatively low concentrations of bromine. The reaction mechanism is illustrated below.

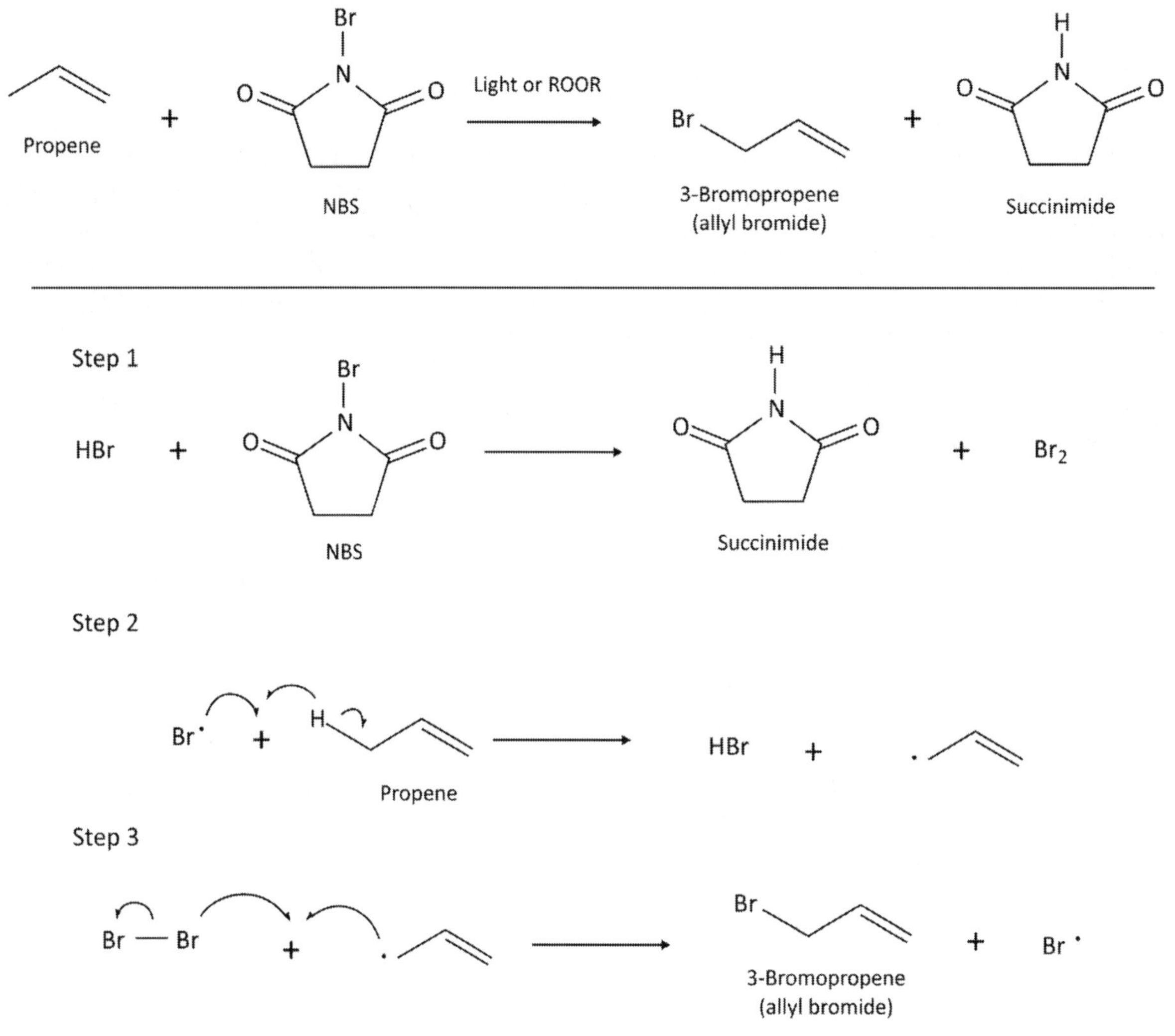

Propene + NBS —Light or ROOR→ 3-Bromopropene (allyl bromide) + Succinimide

Step 1

HBr + NBS → Succinimide + Br_2

Step 2

Br· + Propene → HBr + ·CH₂CH=CH₂

Step 3

Br — Br + ·CH₂CH=CH₂ → 3-Bromopropene (allyl bromide) + Br·

Figure 124. Bromination of propene

Benzylic Substitution Reactions

Benzylic groups contain groups or atoms bonded to an sp^3-hybridized carbon next to a benzene ring. The figure below shows several arrows that point to atoms that are benzylic. The chlorine and bromine atoms below are bonded at a benzylic position.

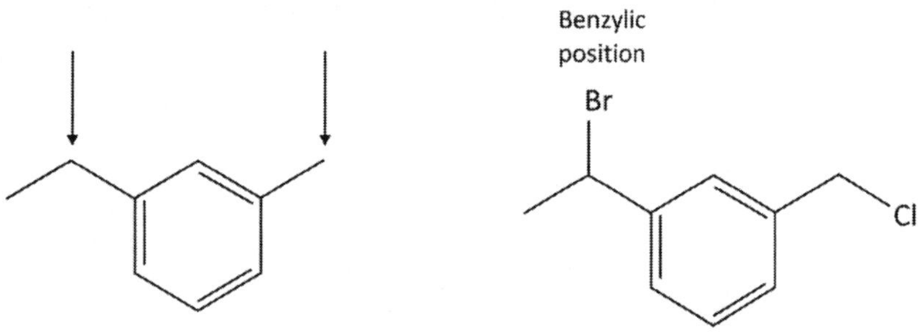

Figure 125. Benzylic atoms and positions

Benzylic hydrogens are generally considered the most reactive in a radical substitution reaction due to the delocalization of a benzylic radical. Some general chlorination and bromination reactions of benzylic hydrogens are shown in Figure 126. Chlorination is initiated by light energy, and bromination is initiated by NBS and light energy. The halogenations occur through a chain reaction radical mechanism.

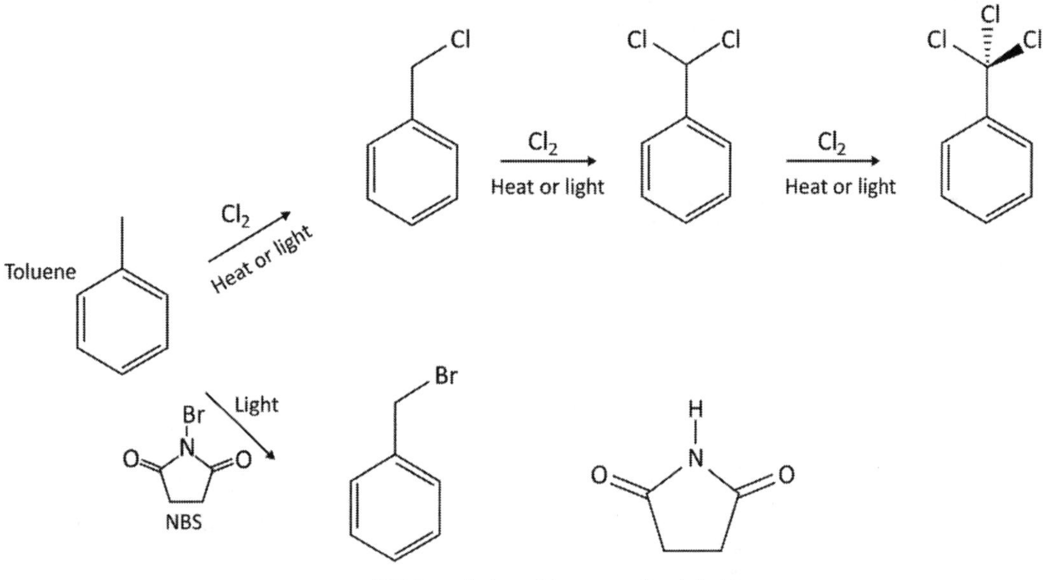

Figure 126. Chlorination and bromination of toluene (methylbenzene)

The chlorination of toluene takes place at temperatures of 400–600 °C or under ultraviolet light. Multiple chlorinations can occur at the side chain. Benzylic bromination is similar to allylic bromination but uses the reagent NBS to produce a low concentration of Br_2 or a bromine radical.

If the benzene ring contains longer chains (for example, ethylbenzene), halogenation leads to a stable 2° radical that will form readily and produce the major product 1-Halo-1-phenylethane. The least stable 1° radical will form more slowly and produce the minor product 1-Halo-2—phenylethane.

Radical Addition

The addition of hydrogen bromide (HBr) to an alkene in the presence of peroxides (for example, ROOR, ROOH) results in an anti-Markovnikov product. In the absence of any peroxides, a Markovnikov product is formed. The general reaction of HBr with propene under the presence and absence of peroxide is shown below.

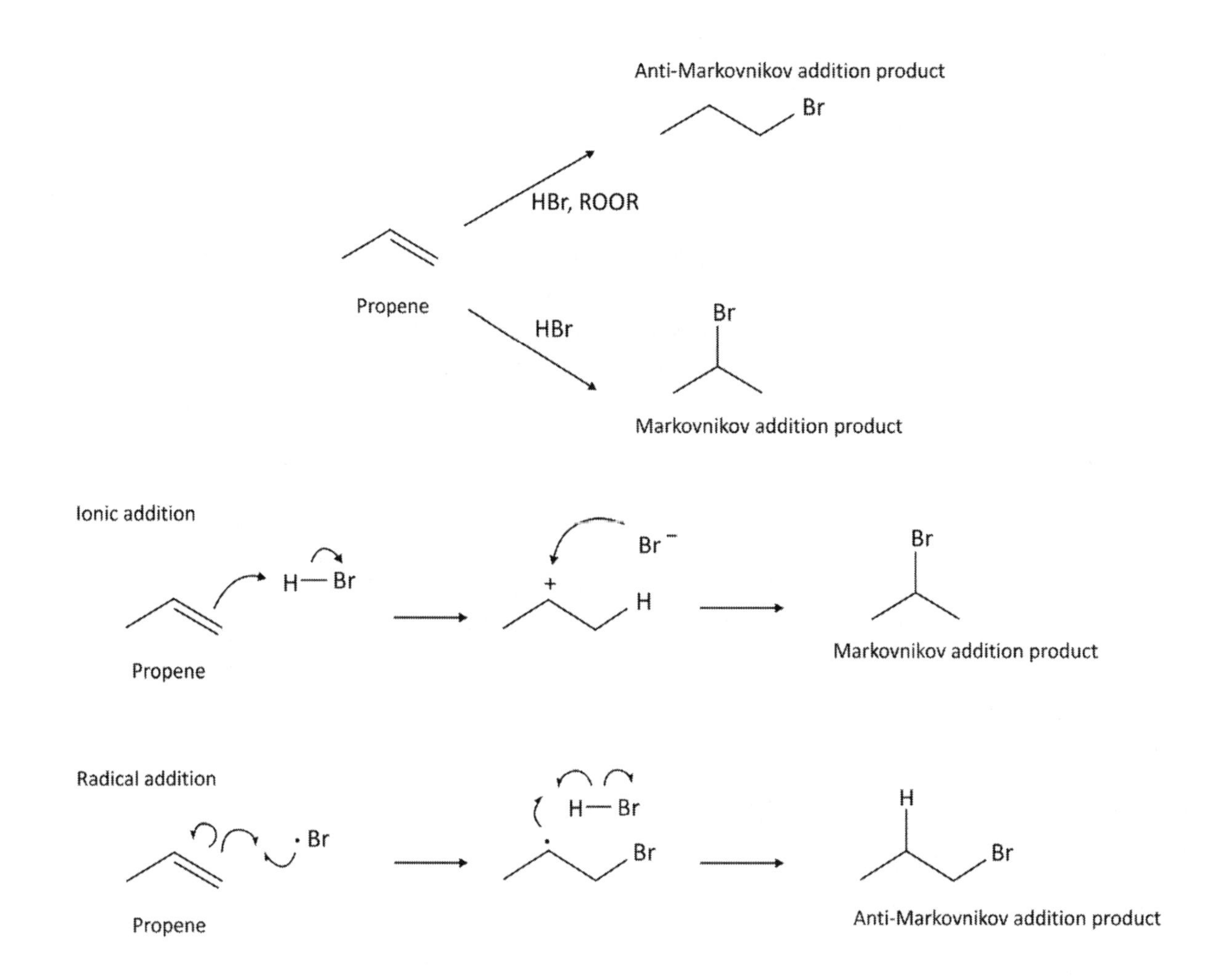

Figure 127. Anti-Markovnikov and Markovnikov addition of HBr to propene

Other hydrogen halides such as hydrogen iodide (HI), hydrogen chloride (HCl), and hydrogen fluoride (HF) will not give an anti-Markovnikov product in the presence of peroxides. Therefore, the anti-Markovnikov product is specific to the use of HBr. The general reaction mechanism of an anti-Markovnikov addition occurs by a radical chain reaction, as shown below.

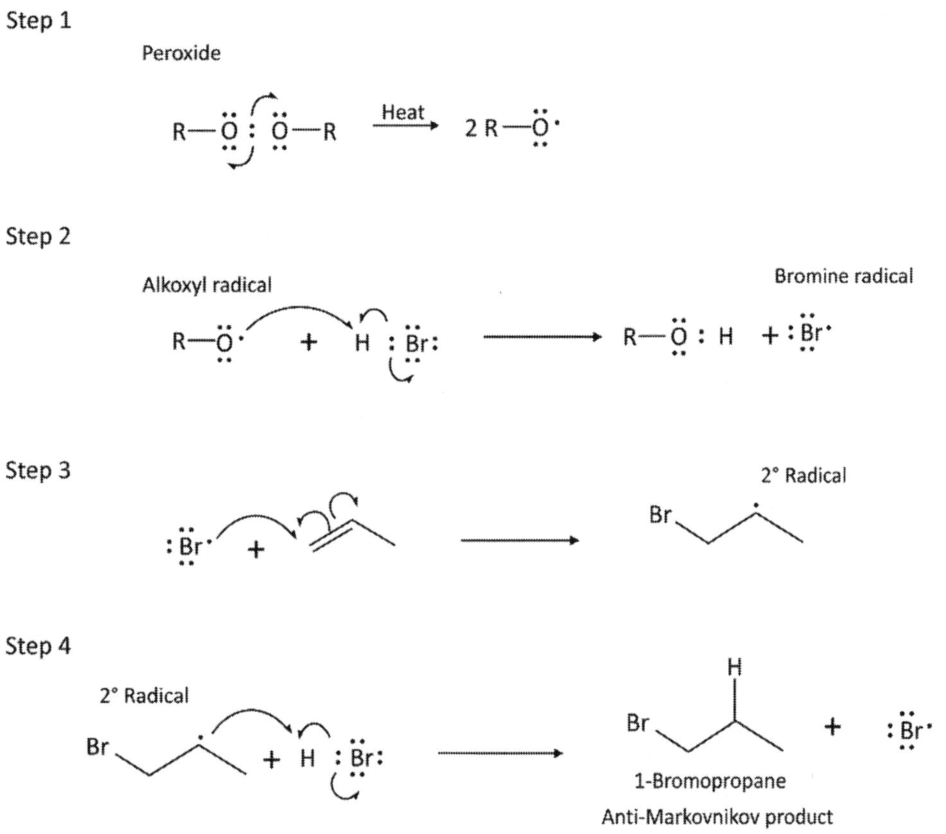

Step 1

Peroxide

$R-\ddot{O}:\ddot{O}-R \xrightarrow{\text{Heat}} 2\,R-\ddot{O}\cdot$

Step 2

Alkoxyl radical

Bromine radical

$R-\ddot{O}\cdot + H:\ddot{Br}: \longrightarrow R-\ddot{O}:H + :\ddot{Br}\cdot$

Step 3

2° Radical

:Br· + ⟶ Br

Step 4

2° Radical

Br + H :Br: ⟶ Br H + :Br·

1-Bromopropane

Anti-Markovnikov product

Figure 128. Anti-Markovnikov addition of HBr: reaction mechanism

In the first or initiation step, an organic peroxide undergoes homolytic cleavage at the oxygen-oxygen bond. In the second step, the alkoxyl radical removes a hydrogen atom from HBr to produce a bromine radical. The third step is a propagation step, in which the bromine radical adds to the $C = C$ bond to create a 2° alkyl radical (which is more stable). In the last or propagation step, the alkyl radical removes hydrogen from HBr. The formed product is 1-bromopropane; the bromine radical is also regenerated. The previous two steps repeat, leading to a chain reaction.

Radical Polymerization of Alkenes

Monomers such as ethylene or ethene ($CH_2 = CH_2$) can polymerize by a radical mechanism under high heat and pressure (1,000 atm) with an organic peroxide. An addition reaction initiates the polymerization of ethylene to produce polyethylene, and such polymers are called addition or chain-growth polymers. The general reaction mechanism follows the usual initiation, propagation, and termination steps.

Step 1 Chain initiation

$$R{-}C(=O){-}O{-}O{-}C(=O){-}R \longrightarrow 2\,R{:}C(=O){-}\dot{O} \longrightarrow 2\,CO_2 + 2\,R\cdot$$

Diacyl peroxide

Step 2 Chain initiation

$$R\cdot + H_2C{=}CH_2 \longrightarrow R{-}\overset{H_2}{C}{-}CH_2\cdot$$

Step 3 Chain Propagation

$$R{-}\overset{H_2}{C}{-}CH_2\cdot + n\ H_2C{=}CH_2 \longrightarrow R{\left(\overset{H_2}{C}{-}\overset{H_2}{C}\right)}_n\overset{H_2}{C}{-}CH_2\cdot$$

Step 4 Chain Termination

$$R{\left(\overset{H_2}{C}{-}\overset{H_2}{C}\right)}_n\overset{H_2}{C}{-}CH_2\cdot$$

Combination

$$\left[R{\left(\overset{H_2}{C}{-}\overset{H_2}{C}\right)}_n\overset{H_2}{C}{-}\overset{H_2}{C}\right]_2$$

Disproportionation

$$R{\left(\overset{H_2}{C}{-}\overset{H_2}{C}\right)}_n\underset{H}{C}{=}CH_2 + R{\left(\overset{H_2}{C}{-}\overset{H_2}{C}\right)}_n CH_2CH_3$$

Chain branching: back biting

$$R{-}CH_2CH(H)(CH_2CH_2)_nCH_2\dot{C}H_2 \longrightarrow R{-}CH_2\dot{C}H(CH_2CH_2)_nCH_2CH_3 \longrightarrow R{-}CH_2CH(\dot{C}H_2CH_2)(CH_2CH_2)_nCH_2CH_3$$

Figure 129. Radical polymerization of ethylene

In the propagation step, successive ethylene units are added until the growth is stopped by combination or disproportionation. The radical at the end of the chain can also remove a hydrogen atom from within the chain, a process called back-biting, resulting in chain branching.

Oxidations and Reductions

Carbonyl compounds ($C = O$) can serve as the gateway between the interconversions between other types of functional groups. These compounds include functional groups such as an aldehyde, a ketone, a carboxylic acid, an ester, and an amide. An important class of reactions involves the oxidation and reduction of carbonyl compounds and alcohols. **Oxidation** is the loss or decrease of hydrogen atoms and/or the increase in the number of oxygen atoms of a compound. **Reduction** is the opposite of oxidation: the hydrogen content is increased, and the oxygen content is decreased.

Primary (1°, alcohols) can be oxidized to aldehydes (propanol to propanal), and an aldehyde can be reduced to alcohols (propanal to propanol). The conversion of *n*-propanol ($CH_3CH_2CH_2OH$, alcohol) to propanal (CH_3CH_2CHO, aldehyde) is oxidation since the number of hydrogen atoms is decreased. If propanal is converted to propanoic acid (CH_3CH_2COOH, carboxylic acid), then the reaction is oxidation since the oxygen atom count has increased and is added to the carbon carbonyl group. Converting a carboxylic acid to an aldehyde (propanoic acid to propanal) is a reduction reaction since the oxygen content is decreased. Therefore, the reverse of each reaction, for example, propanoic acid to propanal and propanal to propanol, is a reduction since the hydrogen content is increased. The conversion of an alcohol to an alkane is a reduction (propanol to propane) since the oxygen content decreases.

Alkynes and alkenes may also undergo oxidation-reduction reactions. If a compound such as acetylene ($HC \equiv CH$) is hydrogenated to ethene ($CH_2 = CH_2$), the reaction is a reduction because more hydrogen atoms are added to the triple bond. Some organic reactions, such as alcohol dehydration and alkene hydration, are not considered oxidation-reduction reactions since water is removed or added. Some reagents used in reduction reactions include the reduction of carbonyl compounds with metal hydrides and the catalytic hydrogenation of alkenes and alkynes. Alkali metals in ammonia can also reduce alkynes. A summary of the oxidation-reduction reactions is given below.

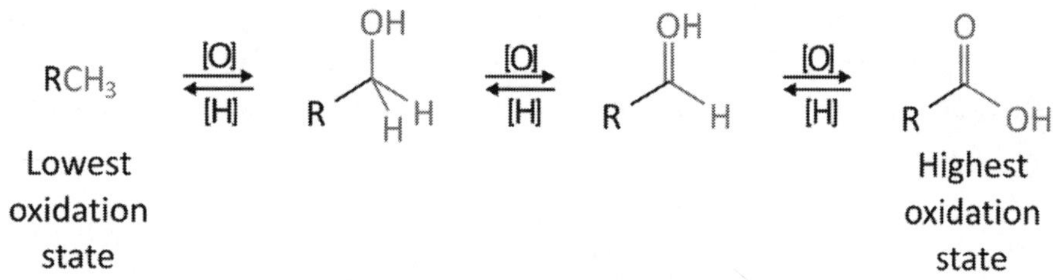

Figure 130. Oxidation and reduction states

The symbol [O] over a forward arrow (→) indicates oxidation of the organic molecule, and the symbol [H] followed by the backward arrow (←) indicates a reduction of the molecule. If the compound at the lowest oxidation state ($R - CH_3$) undergoes a reaction in which the hydrogen atoms are replaced with a halogen (for example, Cl), then the reaction is an oxidation since the hydrogen content decreases. If one organic compound is reduced, then another species must be the **reducing agent** or the species that is oxidized. If an organic compound is oxidized, another species, called the **oxidizing agent**, is reduced.

Reduction Reactions and Reagents

Producing Alcohols by the Reduction of Carbonyl Compounds: Carboxylic Acids and Esters

Given a carbonyl compound, a primary 1° and secondary 2° alcohol can be synthesized by reduction with a reducing agent. Lithium aluminum hydride (LAH or $LiAlH_4$) is a strong reducing agent and metal hydride that can reduce carboxylic acids and esters to primary 1° alcohols. In the first step, LAH may be combined with diethyl ether (Et_2O) or tetrahydrofuran (THF), followed by the addition of an acid such as sulfuric acid to create an acidic environment. For example, consider the reduction reaction of a primary 1° carboxylic acid with $LiAlH_4$ and tetrahydrofuran (THF)/hydronium ion (H_3O^+). The carbonyl reduction produces an alcohol.

1. $LiAlH_4$, ether
2. H_3O^+

Carboxylic acid → Alcohol

Figure 131. Reduction of a 1° carbonyl compound with a metal hydride

A tertiary 3° carboxylic acid, such as 2,2-dimethyl propanoic acid, can be reduced to 2,2-dimethyl propanol (92%) using LAH/Et_2O followed by treatment with sulfuric acid. The reduction of an ester compound with the same reagents (1. LAH/Et_2O, 2. H_2O/H_2SO_4) will produce two alcohols:

$$R-(C=O)-OR' \rightarrow R-CH_2-OH+R'-OH$$

Reduction using LAH must be done with extreme care since LAH can react violently with water or weakly acidic solvents. For example, the reaction of LAH with proton donors such as water is violent and results in the formation of hydrogen gas. Therefore, anhydrous solvents such as tetrahydrofuran (THF) and diethyl ether (Et_2O) are used with LAH. Water and acid are carefully added to neutralize the salts that are formed.

Producing Alcohols by the Reduction of Carbonyl Compounds: Aldehydes and Ketones

Sodium borohydride ($NaBH_4$) is commonly used to reduce aldehydes and ketones. The reagent $NaBH_4$ is not strong enough to reduce carbonyl compounds such as carboxylic acids and esters. Although LAH can be used to reduce aldehydes and ketones, $NaBH_4$ is preferred since it can be used safely in water and in an alcohol solvent (for example, methanol or MeOH). Butanal, an aldehyde, can be reduced to the primary 1° alcohol called 1-butanol (85%) using $NaBH_4$/MeOH. Butanone, a ketone, can be converted to the secondary 2° alcohol 2-butanol (87%) using $NaBH_4$/MeOH. A metal catalyst and hydrogen are other reagents that can be used to reduce an aldehyde or ketone to an alcohol. Reagents such as sodium metal in an alcohol solvent can also carry out the reduction.

An important step in the reduction of aldehydes or ketones is that both LAH and $NaBH_4$ allow a hydride ion to be transferred to the carbonyl compound. The hydride ion is the nucleophile. The general reaction mechanism is shown in the figure below.

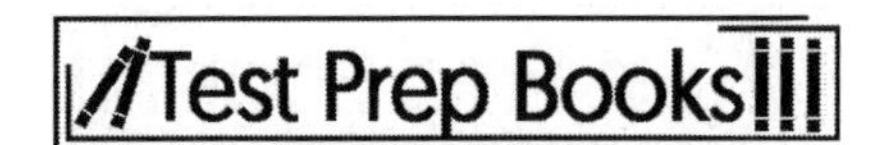

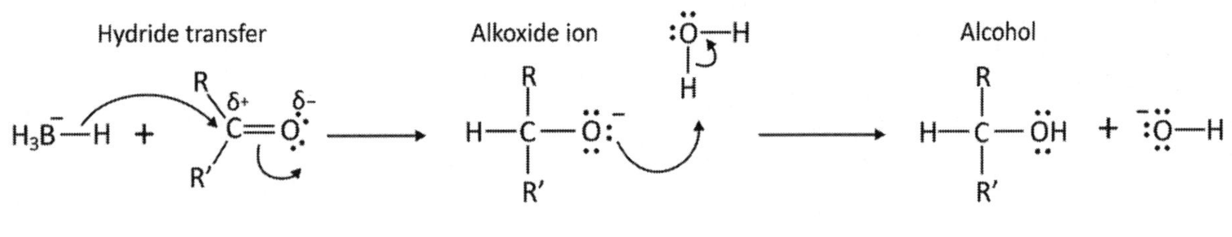

Figure 132. Hydride transfer mechanism

Reduction of Alkyl Halides to Hydrocarbons

If an alkyl halide is treated with LAH, the halogen atom will be replaced with a hydrogen atom. The reaction is a reduction since hydrogen has a higher oxidation state (+1) than the lower oxidation state of oxygen (-2) or a halogen (-1). Most tertiary 3°, secondary 2°, and primary 1° alkyl halides can be reduced with LAH or a deuterated form of LAH, for example, $LiAlD_4$.

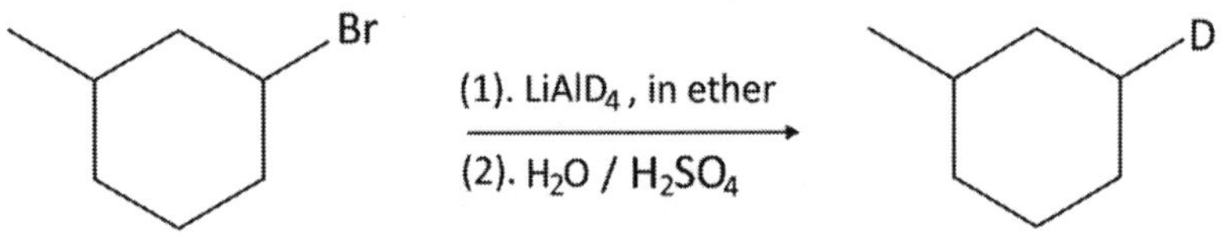

Figure 133. Reduction of alkyl halides

Clemmensen and Wolff-Kishner Reductions

An unbranched alkylbenzene can be prepared by reduction of a carbonyl group in an acylbenzene molecule. Recall that in a Friedel-Crafts acylation, an acyl group (for example, $CH_3CH_2 - (C = O)$) is substituted onto a benzene ring to form an acylbenzene ($Ar - (C = O) - CH_2CH_3$). In a Friedel-Crafts acylation, rearrangements of the carbon chain do not occur. The reason is the stabilized resonance form of the acylium ion; it is more stable than other types of carbocations. Since rearrangements don't occur, a Friedel-Crafts acylation followed by reduction is a good method to prepare a kind of unbranched alkylbenzene. The general reaction is shown below.

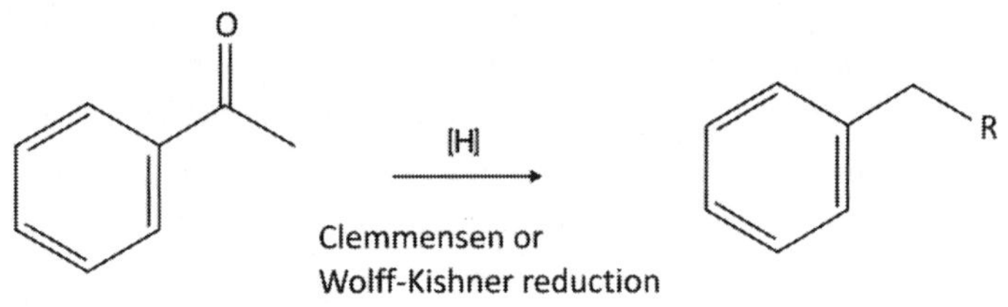

Figure 134. Reduction by Clemmensen or Wolff-Kishner

Suppose a chemist were planning to synthesize propylbenzene. Two approaches could be undertaken. In the first approach, benzene can undergo a Friedel-Crafts alkylation. However, a rearrangement will occur, and two products, two types of alkylbenzenes, will form. In contrast, the Friedel-Crafts acylation of benzene will produce a single ketone in high yield with an unarranged carbon chain. The second approach is more desirable since the ketone ($R_1 - (C = O) - R_2$) can be reduced to propylbenzene by either the Clemmensen method or the Wolff-Kishner method.

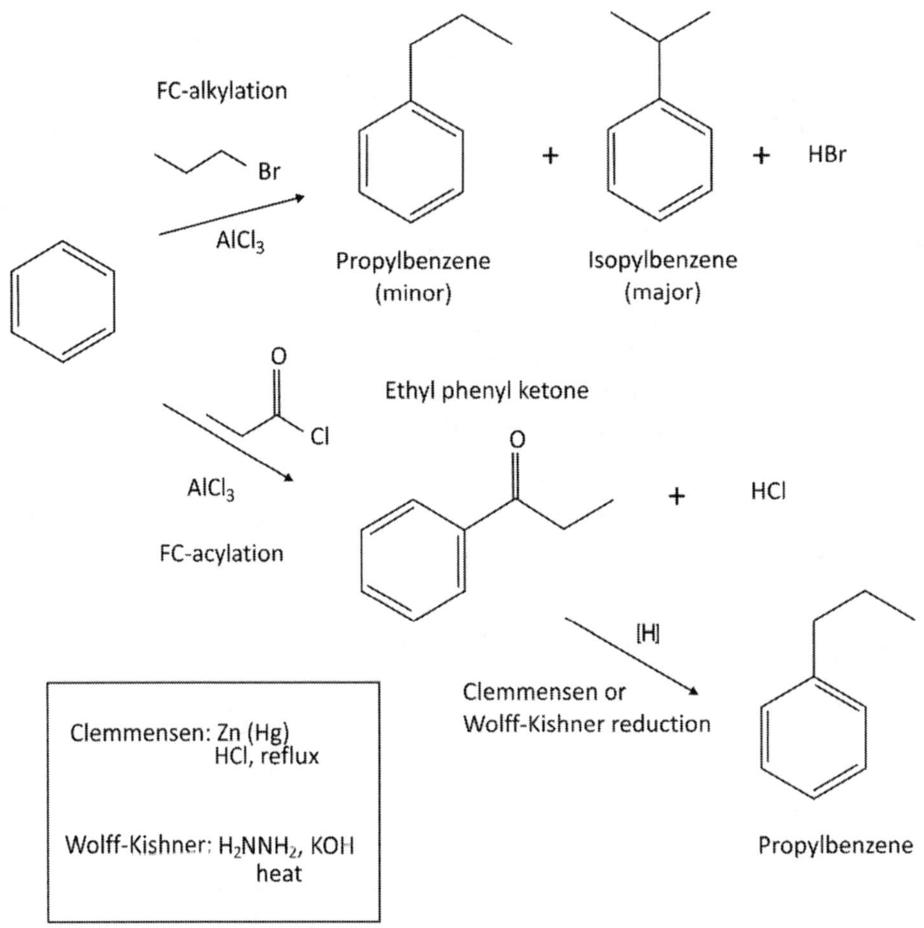

FC-alkylation
Br
$AlCl_3$
Propylbenzene (minor)
+
Isopylbenzene (major)
+ HBr
O
Cl
$AlCl_3$
FC-acylation
Ethyl phenyl ketone
O
+ HCl
[H]
Clemmensen or Wolff-Kishner reduction
Propylbenzene

Clemmensen: Zn (Hg)
HCl, reflux

Wolff-Kishner: H_2NNH_2, KOH
heat

Figure 135. Preparation of propylbenzene by Friedel-Crafts acylation followed by reduction

In a **Clemmensen reduction**, a synthetic method to convert a ketone to a methylene group, the ketone is refluxed with hydrochloric acid and amalgamated zinc. Ethyl phenyl ketone can be treated with the Clemmensen reagents to produce propylbenzene (80%). The **Wolff-Kishner reduction** can also reduce a ketone to a methylene group, but it uses hydrazine and a base under heat. As shown in Figure 136, a Clemmensen reduction is carried out under acidic conditions, whereas a Wolff-Kishner reduction is done under basic conditions. The Wolff-Kishner reduction initially results in the formation of a hydrazone intermediate. Ethyl phenyl ketone can be reduced to propylbenzene with a comparable yield (82%) through the Wolff-Kishner reduction.

Ethyl phenyl ketone

Hydrazone intermediate

Propylbenzene (82%)

Wolff-Kishner:

H_2NNH_2, KOH

heat

N_2, H_2O

Figure 136. Wolff-Kishner reduction

Reductions of Alkenes: Catalytic Hydrogenation with a Catalyst

Hydrogenation of alkenes gives a product that results in the syn addition of the hydrogen atoms (Figure 137). The hydrogen atoms are adsorbed on the metal surface. The π bond of the alkene is attracted to the metal or catalyst surface. The alkene interacts with the surface such that it picks up hydrogen atoms one after another. The alkene is then converted to an alkane. Since the alkane does not contain a π bond, it is not attracted to the surface, and it moves away. The final product is the result of the syn addition of H_2, and no trans product is formed. If one face of the double bond is more sterically hindered, that face cannot approach the surface. Therefore, it is less likely that the hydrogen atoms will attach to the hindered face of the double bond. The hydrogen atoms will add to the less sterically hindered side or face.

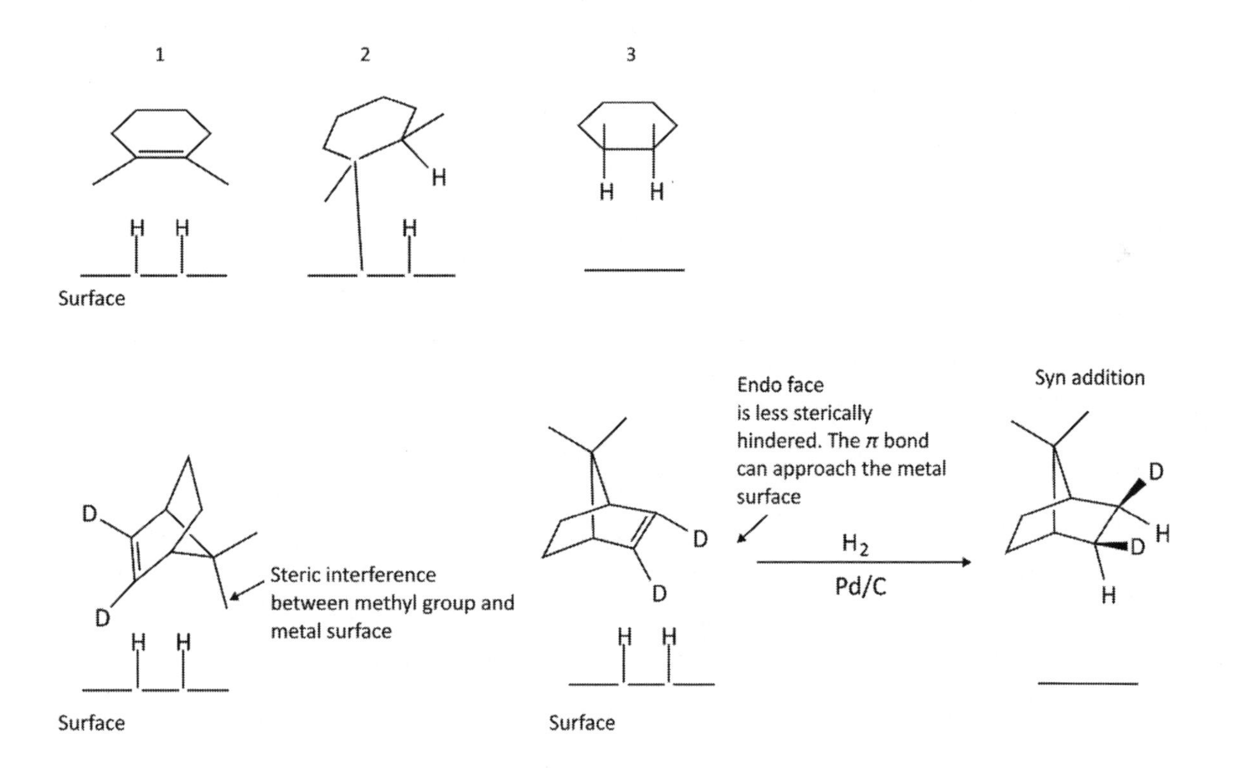

Figure 137. Catalytic hydrogenation: syn addition to alkenes and steric hinderance

Reductions of Alkynes to Alkenes: Reagents and Stereochemistry

Sodium and ammonia (Na, NH_3) are reducing reagents used to convert an alkyne to an alkene with a trans (*E*) geometry. Hydrogen gas can be used to reduce an alkyne to an alkene or an alkane, depending on the catalyst. If hydrogen gas is used with Pd, Pt, or Ni, then the alkyne will be converted to an alkane. If hydrogen gas is used in combination with Pd and $BaSO_4$, reduction will stop once the alkene forms. Barium sulfate, $BaSO_4$, acts as a deactivating agent and can prevent the alkene from being reduced to an alkane. When hydrogenation of the alkyne occurs with Pd and a deactivating agent, a cis or (*Z*)-alkene is formed. Other metal-deactivating agents are $Pd/BaCO_3$/quinoline and Lindlar's catalyst.

Oxidative Reactions and Reagents

Oxidation of Alcohols and Aldehydes

When oxidation occurs, a hydrogen atom is removed from the alcohol or aldehyde carbon. In general, a primary 1° alcohol can be oxidized to an aldehyde and subsequently oxidized into a carboxylic acid. A secondary 2° alcohol can be oxidized into a ketone. Tertiary 3° alcohols generally cannot be oxidized because there are no hydrogens on the alcohol carbon.

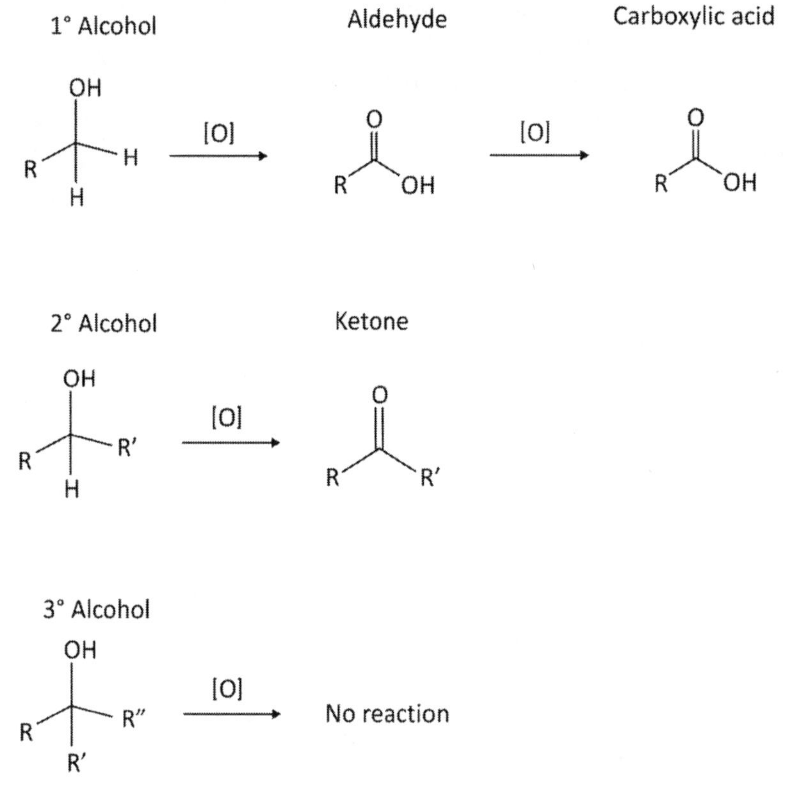

1° Alcohol → [O] → Aldehyde → [O] → Carboxylic acid

2° Alcohol → [O] → Ketone

3° Alcohol → [O] → No reaction

Figure 138. Oxidation of alcohols and aldehydes

Primary 1° and secondary 2° alcohol oxidation can occur by an elimination pathway when specific reagents are used. The reagents first add a leaving group to the alcohol on the hydroxyl oxygen atom in the initial reaction. Several concerted steps take place in the elimination step. A base will abstract the hydrogen atom from the alcohol carbon. A double bond or π bond between the alcohol carbon and

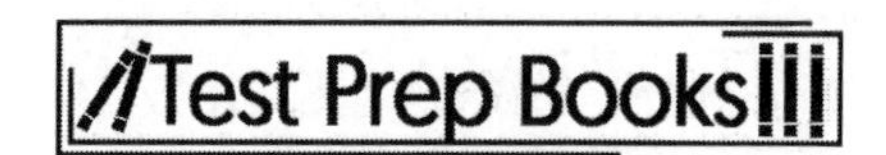

hydroxyl oxygen will form. The leaving group will also depart from the hydroxyl oxygen. The general reaction mechanism is shown below.

1° or 2° alcohol

Elimination step

-HA

LG=Leaving group

Figure 139. Alcohol oxidation: Elimination

If the oxidized alcohol produces an aldehyde, the aldehyde may be oxidized to a carboxylic acid in the presence of water. Through an addition reaction, the aldehyde is hydrated with a hydroxyl group at the carbonyl carbon and a hydrogen atom at the carbonyl oxygen. The aldehyde hydrate forms in low concentrations but contains the hydrogen atom (bonded to oxygen) required for elimination. When the hydrate is oxidized, a carboxylic acid will form. Based on Le Chatelier's principle, the reaction will proceed toward the right until all the aldehyde molecules are oxidized.

Chromic Acid Oxidation

Common oxidizing agents involving chromium (VI) reagents include potassium chromate (K_2CrO_4), potassium dichromate ($K_2Cr_2O_7$), and chromium trioxide (CrO_3). A secondary alcohol can be oxidized to a ketone using $K_2Cr_2O_7$ and sulfuric acid. The reagents can be used to create the chromic acid, the oxidizing agent. The chromium (VI) reagents are typically used in acidic mediums and can be converted to chromic acid (H_2CrO_4). Oxidation reactions involving chromium (VI) reagents involve the formation of chromate esters and follow an elimination step. The **Jones reagent** is a source of H_2CrO_4 and is prepared by mixing Na_2CrO_4 or CrO_3 with aqueous sulfuric acid, H_2SO_4. A Jones reagent can be added to non-oxidizing solutions such as alcohols, an aldehyde/acetone mixture, or acetic acid. Using a Jones reagent, primary 1° alcohols can be oxidized to carboxylic acids, and secondary 2° alcohols can be oxidized to ketones.

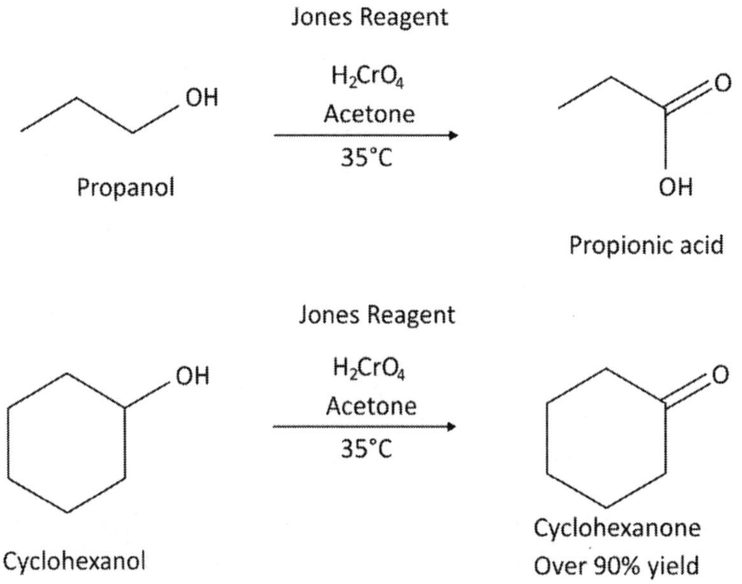

Jones Reagent

Propanol → (H_2CrO_4, Acetone, 35°C) → Propionic acid

Jones Reagent

Cyclohexanol → (H_2CrO_4, Acetone, 35°C) → Cyclohexanone Over 90% yield

Figure 140. Oxidation of 1° and 2° alcohols using a Jones reagent

The Jones reagent has the advantage of serving as a color-based functional group test. The color of chromic acid solutions is a clear orange-red color, but the product mixture of the alcohol and the Jones reagent is opaque greenish-blue since chromium (VI) is reduced to Cr (III). If the alcohol reactants are not present, then no color change occurs and the solution remains orange-red. The breathalyzer alcohol test makes use of the color-changing reaction whereby chromic acid reacts with a 1° or 2° alcohol (or aldehyde) to produce a green-blue solution. The general reaction mechanism of chromic acid oxidation is shown below.

Step 1: Chromate ester formation

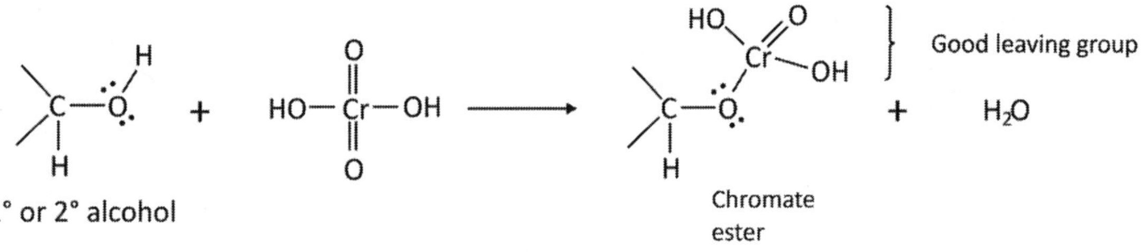

1° or 2° alcohol + HO—Cr(=O)(=O)—OH ⟶ Chromate ester + H_2O

Good leaving group

Step 2: Oxidation by elimination of H_2CrO_3

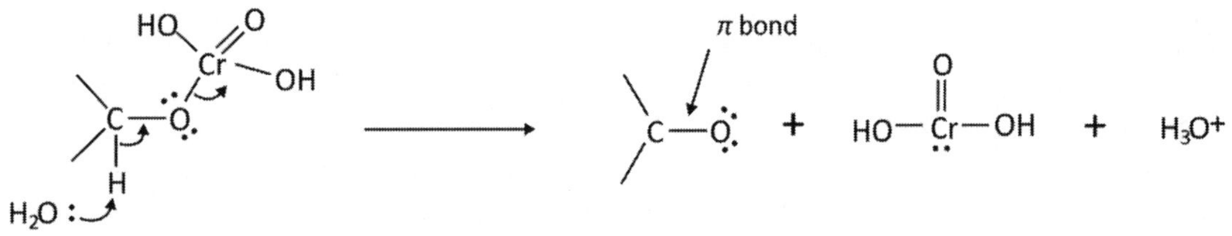

H_2O : ⟶ C=O (π bond) + HO—Cr(=O)—OH + H_3O^+

Figure 141. Chromic acid oxidation mechanism

Oxidation by the Swern Method

Due to the carcinogenic and environmental hazards that chromium (VI) reagents impose, the Swern oxidation method is a vital alternative for the oxidation of primary 1° and secondary 2° alcohols to aldehydes and ketones. The Swern reaction takes place in the absence of water. Primary 1° alcohols will form aldehydes (not carboxylic acids), and secondary alcohols can be oxidized to produce ketones. The Swern reaction is carried out sequentially. In the first step, oxalyl chloride ($\mathrm{Cl-COCO-Cl}$) is mixed with dimethyl sulfoxide (DMSO) at a low temperature to produce a chloro-dimethysulfonium salt. Other by-products such as carbon monoxide, carbon dioxide, and hydrochloric acid will form. In the second step, the alcohol substrate is added to the chloro-dimethysulfonium salt, thereby adding a leaving group or dimethylsulfonium group on the hydroxyl oxygen. In the last step, a base (for example, amine) is added to bring about an elimination reaction. A general Swern oxidation is shown below.

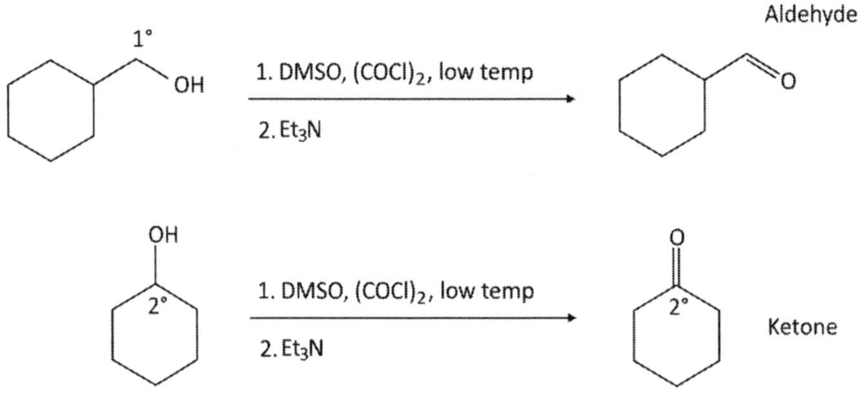

Aldehyde

1°

OH

1. DMSO, $(COCl)_2$, low temp

2. Et_3N

OH

2°

1. DMSO, $(COCl)_2$, low temp

2. Et_3N

O

2°

Ketone

Figure 142. Swern oxidation of a 1° and 2° alcohol

Oxidation with Pyridinium Chlorochromate (PCC)

Some oxidizing reagents such as potassium permanganate ($KMnO_4$) are used under basic conditions. The oxidizing reagents, such as chromic acid or permanganate, contain a relatively high number of oxygen atoms. When these oxidizers react with a hydrocarbon under heat, the reaction continues until all the hydrogen atoms on the compound are removed. Such reagents may not be desirable when producing a specific reaction product. For example, the oxidation of a primary alcohol ($CH_3CH_2 - OH$) with a chromium (VI) reagent does not necessarily produce an aldehyde ($CH_3 - COH$) because the reagent will continue to oxidize the compound. Instead, anhydrous chromium (VI) reagents such as pyridinium dichromate (PDC), trioxide-pyridine complex (CrO_3-2-pyridine), or pyridinium chlorochromate (PCC) are used. PCC is a chromium (VI) salt formed from the reaction of CrO_3, HCl, and pyridine (C_6H_5N). PCC, and PDC are stable solids, and each reagent is soluble in a specific organic solvent. For instance, PCC is soluble in a dichloromethane solvent. For conditions that exclude water or anhydrous conditions, PCC allows for the oxidation of a primary 1° alcohols to aldehydes without the formation of the aldehyde hydrate. In contrast, for an aqueous environment, a Jones reagent will oxidize primary 1° alcohols to carboxylic acids. Primary and secondary alcohols can be oxidized with PCC to produce an aldehyde and a ketone.

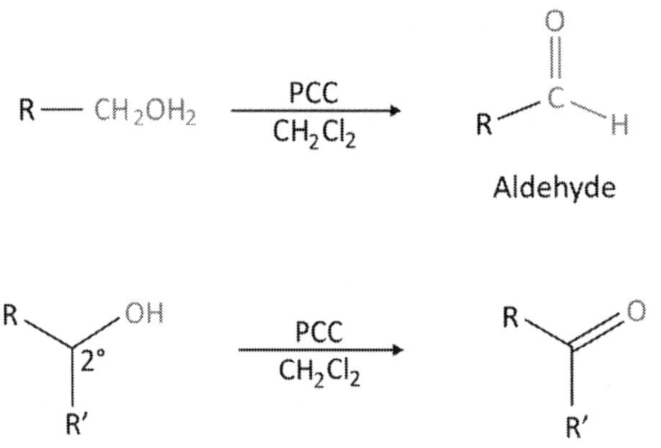

$R - CH_2OH_2$ $\xrightarrow[CH_2Cl_2]{PCC}$ R–C(=O)–H

Aldehyde

R, OH, 2°, R′ $\xrightarrow[CH_2Cl_2]{PCC}$ R, O, R′

Figure 143. Oxidation of a primary and secondary alcohol

Oxidation Using Potassium Permanganate ($KMnO_4$)

Oxidative reactions involving the use of $KMnO_4$ are usually carried out in basic aqueous solutions whereby MnO_2 precipitates during oxidation. The acidification of the filtrate converts the initial reactants to a carboxylic acid. In general, primary 1° alcohols and aldehydes are converted to carboxylic acids when oxidized with $KMnO_4$. Secondary 2° alcohols can be oxidized with $KMnO_4$ to produce a ketone. Hot chromic acid and hot basic permanganate can react with alkylbenzenes, alkenes, and alkynes to yield oxidative cleavage products. For instance, the reaction of sodium dichromate ($Na_2Cr_2O_7$) or $KMnO_4$ with butyl benzene will produce the carboxylic acid called benzoic acid ($Ar - COOH$).

$CH_2CH_2CH_2CH_3$ — $KMnO_4$ / H_2O → O, C, OH

Butylbenzene   Benzoic acid

Figure 144. Oxidation of an alkylbenzene

For oxidation of the alkylbenzene to benzoic acid, the oxidation will start at the benzylic carbon if there are one or more benzylic hydrogen atoms. No reaction occurs if a benzylic hydrogen is absent, for example, tert-butyl benzene.

Haloform Oxidations

Other oxidative cleavage reactions include the cleavage of methyl ketones with an alkaline solution of halogens. For example, the reagents I_2/KOH can initiate a haloform reaction whereby a methyl ketone is converted to a carboxylic acid.

O, C, CH_3 — I_2 / OH → O, C, OH

Figure 145. Oxidation-haloform reaction

Treatment of the methyl ketone can be carried out with a basic solution of I_2, Br_2, or with sodium hypochlorite (bleach $NaOCl$). The solution must be neutralized to produce the carboxylic acid. Depending on the halogen used, other side products such as CH_3I will form.

Oxidation of Diols with Periodic Acid (HIO_4)

The reaction of periodic acid (HIO_4) and vicinal diols is another example of an oxidative cleavage reaction. Periodic acid will cleave the $C - C$ bond of α-hydroxy aldehydes, ketones, α-dicarbonyl compounds, and 1,2-diols in which the OH groups are in cisoid formation (not a *trans*-1,2-diol). The following examples demonstrate the oxidative cleavage of a diol.

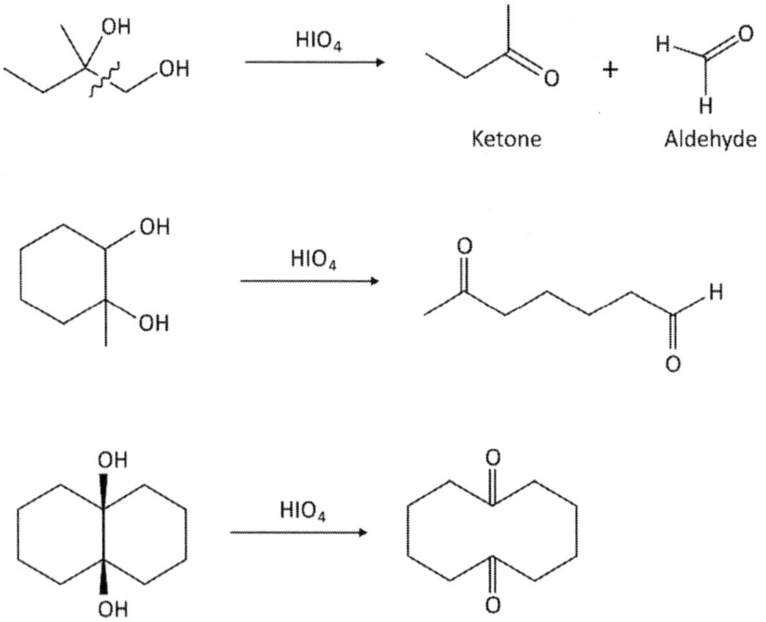

Figure 146. Oxidative cleavage using periodic acid

A tertiary 3° alcohol within the diol will cleave to form a ketone. A secondary 2 °and a primary 1° alcohol will cleave to form an aldehyde.

Alkene Oxidations: Ozonolysis and $KMnO_4$

The oxidative cleavage reaction of an alkene with ozone produces a carbonyl compound. The alkene must have at least one unsaturated disubstituted carbon or vinylic hydrogen. When the alkene is treated with a mixture of ozone and zinc in an acidic medium (hydronium ion, acetic acid), an aldehyde and a ketone form.

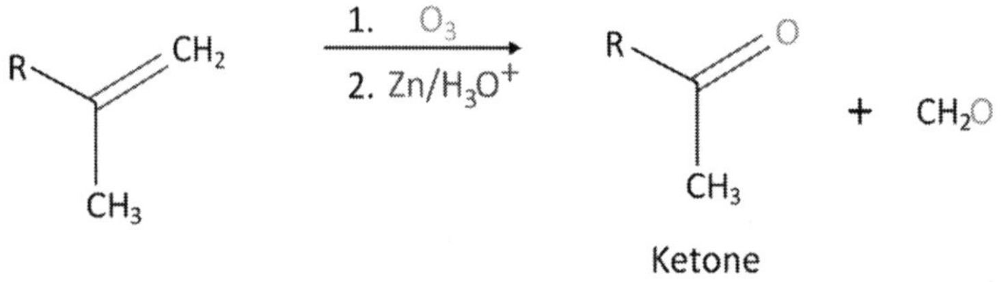

Figure 147. Oxidation by ozonolysis: alkene to a ketone and aldehyde

Ozonolysis of the $C = C$ bond results in two oxygen atoms becoming double-bonded to each carbon atom in the alkene: $H_2C = O$ and $R - (CO) - CH_3$. The vinyl carbon atom at the terminal alkene $(= CH_2)$ is oxidized to an aldehyde, for example, formaldehyde: $H_2C = O$. If the vinyl carbon atom is of the form $(= CHR)$, it will be converted to an aldehyde $(R - (CO) - H)$. If the vinyl carbon atom is disubstituted $(= CRR')$, then the carbon atom is oxidized to a ketone $(R - (CO) - R')$. In Figure 147, the molecule is an acyclic alkene and will form two molecules when it's oxidized with ozone. However, if the molecule is a cyclic alkene, then the product is acyclic (one product). A mnemonic way to think of the ozonolysis of a $C = C$ bond is to replace the $C1 = C2$ bond with $C1 = O$ and $O = C2$. The reaction

products will not contain any alkenes, and the substituents attached to the alkene carbons will remain unchanged.

Alkenes may also be treated with potassium permanganate ($KMnO_4$) to produce carbonyl groups such as a methyl ketone and a carboxylic acid. The double bond is broken to create the carbonyl compounds. For a terminal alkene, the $= CH_2$ group will be oxidized to carbon dioxide (CO_2). If the carbon atom is monosubstituted ($= CHR$), then the carbon atom is oxidized to a carboxylic acid group ($-(CO) - OH$). Carbon atoms that are disubstituted, for example, $= CRR'$, are converted to ketones ($R - (CO) - R$). Similar to the ozonolysis reaction, the double bond is broken, and two separate molecules can be created. If the alkene is located within a ring, then the ring will break.

For example, the oxidation of 1-methyl cyclopentene with $KMnO_4$ results in ring-opening with two carbonyl groups located at the terminal end (Figure 148). Carbon atom 1 is of the form $= CR'R$ and is converted to the ketone $CH_3 - (CO) - R$. Carbon atom 5 is of the form $= CHR$ and is converted to a carboxylic acid ($R - (CO) - OH$).

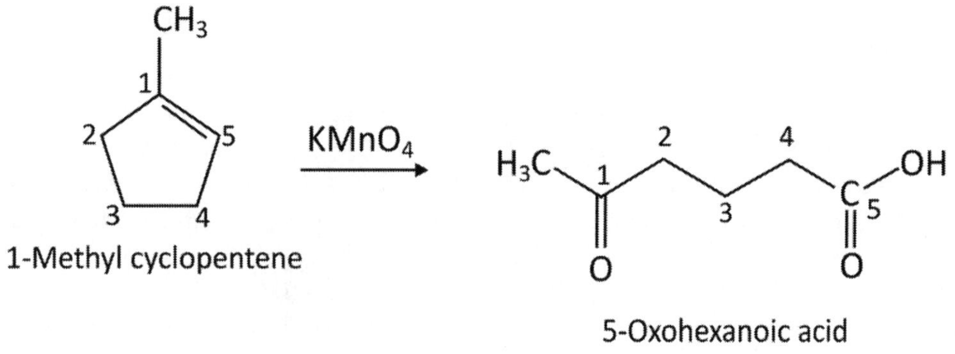

CH_3

1-Methyl cyclopentene

$KMnO_4$

H_3C OH

5-Oxohexanoic acid

Figure 148. Oxidation of an alkene to a carbonyl compound

Spectroscopy

There are several important instruments used in the study of organic chemistry that help identify unknown compounds or substances that are synthesized in the laboratory. Some of these instruments include mass spectrometry (MS), infrared spectroscopy (IR), and nuclear magnetic spectroscopy (NMR). In chemical synthesis, these characterization techniques confirm whether the produced products have the anticipated structures. For example, the halogenation of a benzene atom is anticipated to produce a product that contains a halogen-substituted benzene ring. Chemists need special instruments to help determine if the product does indeed contain a halogen. Each spectral method provides a unique fingerprint of the analyzed compound shown by a graph containing specific peaks or lines. As the structure of the compound becomes more complicated, the combination of these spectral methods makes it possible to analyze the structure of the compound correctly. Each spectral method is unique and can provide information that another instrument cannot. For example, mass spectroscopy can provide information on the molecular formula of a compound, unlike infrared and nuclear magnetic spectroscopy.

Mass Spectroscopy

Mass spectroscopy provides a way of determining the molecular formula of an unknown compound by detecting ions based on its mass to charge ratio. First, the molecules are injected into the mass spectrometer. Then the molecules are ionized in the gas phase under a high vacuum. A beam of electrons (70 eV) bombards and ionizes the molecules. Bombardment from the electron beam dislodges a valence electron from the gas molecule, producing a molecular ion with a charge +1 and an unshared electron. Note that the molecular ions will still have the same molecular mass as the original molecule because the mass of an electron is relatively small. The **radical cation or molecular ion** formed is represented as $\mathrm{M}\cdot^{+}$. The ionization of propane ($\mathrm{CH_3CH_2CH_3}$) by **electron impact ionization** within the mass spectrometer can be represented as:

$$\mathrm{CH_3CH_2CH_3} + \mathrm{e^-} \rightarrow \mathrm{CH_3CH_2CH_3}\cdot^{+} + 2\,\mathrm{e^-}$$

The radical propane cation is shown in brackets to indicate that the electron was removed from one of the atoms. When the molecular ion is represented, if the molecule contains O, N, or a π bond, the odd electron is placed at the nitrogen, oxygen, π bond, or halogen. Otherwise, the placement of the odd electron may be arbitrary, especially if the molecule contains $\mathrm{C-C}$ and $\mathrm{C-H}$ bonds. The ions that are produced pass through a magnetic or electric field and are deflected at some angle. When the deflections are measured, a mass spectrum is produced, in which ions are arranged based on their mass-to-charge (m/z) ratio. The mass spectrum is typically plotted or shown as the relative abundance against the mass-to charge-ratio. Specifically, the x-axis shows the formula weights of the ions that are detected. The x-axis is labeled "m/z" where m is the mass and z is the charge. The y-axis shows the abundance for each detected ion either as a percentage regarding the tallest peak (called the **base peak**) or as the number of detected ions present. The figure below shows a mass spectrum of propane.

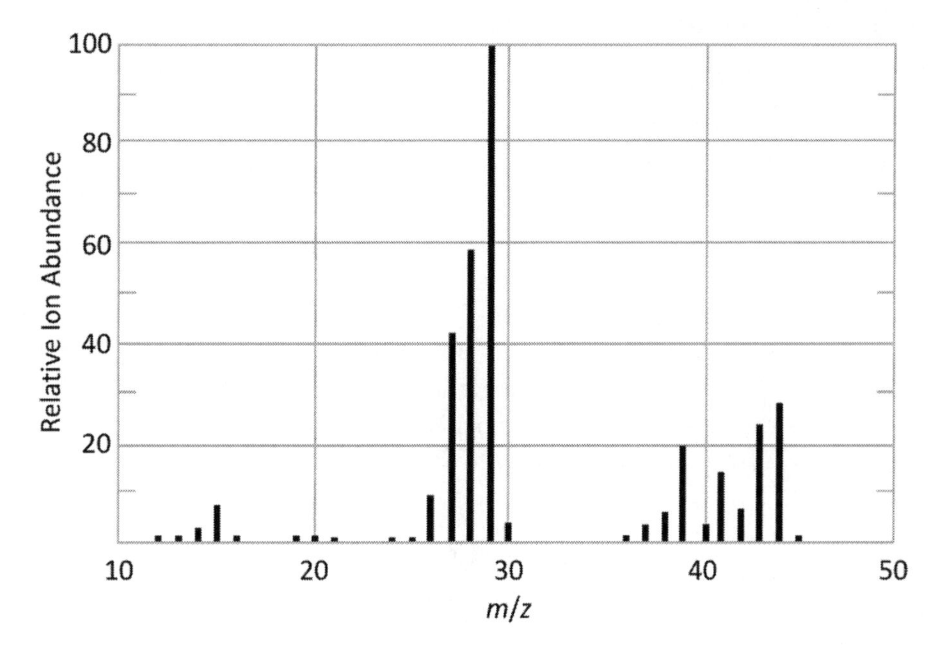

Figure 149. Area under the signal

The base peak in the middle of Figure 149 is the most easily formed and abundant fragment (29 m/z). The fragment corresponds to an ethyl fragment, $C_2H_5{}^+$. Molecular ions may also undergo additional fragmentation into smaller ions and neutral components, for example, radicals and neutral molecules (less than 30 m/z).

In some cases, the ion does not represent a molecular ion. For example, the peak on the right in Figure 149 with approximately 28% relative abundance may or may not be a molecular ion. The m/z value is equal to 44 and is closer to the molecular weight of a neutral propane molecule. Therefore, the species at $m/z = 44$ will not represent a base peak since the propane molecule will tend to fragment to form other peaks less than $m/z = 44$. Fragmentation patterns can manifest in a high-resolution mass spectrum and will allow the exact molecular formula to be found. Studying the abundance of fragment ions can help determine the stability of radicals and carbocations. For example, if a mass spectrum shows a higher abundance of $CH_3CH^+CH_3$ than $CH_3CH_2CH_2{}^+$, then it would indicate that 2° carbocations are more stable than 1° primary carbocations.

Infrared Spectroscopy

Infrared spectroscopy uses infrared radiation (500–4000 cm^{-1}) to determine the types of functional groups present in the compound. As the compound is exposed to infrared radiation, specific functional groups within the molecule will absorb the radiation at discrete energies, causing them to move into a vibrationally excited state. The molecule may have a vibrational motion that corresponds to wagging, stretching, or twisting. Bonds found in chemical functional groups, for example, $C = C$, $O - H$, $C = O$, will have a specific vibrational frequency. In other words, these groups will absorb IR radiation at specific frequencies or wavelengths. An IR spectrum will provide information on the various types of functional groups present or absent within the molecule. The IR spectrum may plot the %transmittance (or %absorbance) versus the wavelength (micro-meters) or wavenumbers (inverse centimeters or reciprocal of the wavelength).

The amount of energy (E) absorbed by the molecule is discrete and is given by the following equation:

$$E = hv; \quad v = \frac{c}{\lambda}$$

Planck's constant is given by $h = 6.626 \times 10^{-34}\ \mathrm{J} \times \mathrm{s}$, and the term v denotes the frequency of radiation absorbed or released by a molecule. Note that the frequency is proportional to the reciprocal of the wavelength λ: $v \propto 1/\lambda$. The speed of light is given by $c = 3.00 \times 10^{8}\ \mathrm{m/s}$. Units of the wavelength are in meters within the equation. For example, an sp^2 $\mathrm{C-H}$ bond will absorb at a wavelength equal to about 3.00×10^{-6} m or 3.00 μm or 3.00×10^{-4} cm. When expressed as wavenumber, the value is the inverse or reciprocal of the wavelength in centimeters: 3300 cm^{-1}. The frequencies of absorption refer to the wavenumbers. An IR spectrum will typically display the x-axis as the wavenumber. When deciphering an IR spectrum, it's useful to remember key absorption frequencies and the molecular vibrations that are associated with them. The table below lists several important frequencies.

Bond Type	**Frequency or wavenumber (cm^{-1}).**
$\mathrm{N-H}$ and $\mathrm{O-H}$	3,400
$\mathrm{C-H}$ (sp^3 carbon)	3,000–2,850
$\mathrm{C-H}$ (sp^2 carbon)	3,100–3,000
$\mathrm{C-H}$ (sp carbon)	3,300
$\mathrm{C \equiv N}$ and $\mathrm{C \equiv C}$	2,100
$\mathrm{C = O}$	1,700
$\mathrm{C = C}$, and $\mathrm{C-C}$ aromatic	1,600
$\mathrm{C-C}$ aromatic	1,500

Table 7. Infrared Absorption frequencies

The plot of an IR spectrum will typically show the wavenumber decreasing from left to right along the x-axis. Each wavenumber will correspond to a peak (pointing downward) that will be visible in a transmittance IR plot. The peaks may be broad or narrow, depending on the nature of the functional group. The OH band will be relatively broad and is generally recognizable in an IR spectrum. IR experiments are typically prone to moisture from the air, so the OH band tends to appear unless the analyze sample is kept dry. Importantly, the frequency of the OH band corresponds to the stretching or contraction of the oxygen-hydrogen bond ($\mathrm{O-H}$), not of the bond *to* the hydroxide group ($\mathrm{R-OH}$).

Nuclear Magnetic Spectroscopy (NMR)

Nuclei, such as $^{1}\mathrm{H}$ and $^{13}\mathrm{C}$, act as magnets and spin around an axis. The superscripts placed to the left of the proton and carbon atom refer to their respective isotopes. Both nuclei within a molecule can exhibit magnetic moments. In the presence of a strong magnetic field, the nuclei can simultaneously absorb electromagnetic radiation specific to the radio-frequency range. Magnetic resonance is the process in which nuclei in a compound absorb energy. Nuclear magnetic resonance (NMR) spectrometers vary the strength of the magnetic field, causing the intrinsic spin in the protons to align in two orientations. When the nuclei are irradiated at a specific frequency, the nuclei spin-flip to a higher energy state such that the nuclei all resonate with. An NMR instrument will use a detector to monitor the absorption frequency corresponding to resonance, and an electronic signal is measured. A nuclear magnetic spectrum is a graph that shows the corresponding signal intensity against a characteristic absorption frequency or chemical shift δ (ppm) that is specific to a nucleus in a magnetic field. NMR

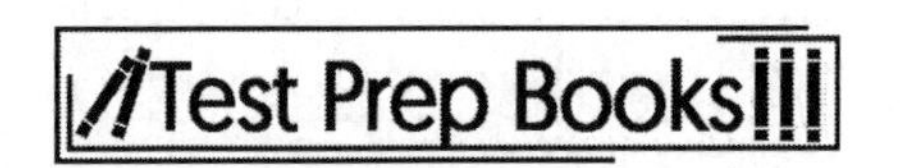

spectrometers use superconducting magnets that have high magnetic strengths (for example, 300 MHz) that are hundreds of thousands of times greater than the Earth's magnetic strength. Nuclei in different environments resonate at different field strengths, so there are unique peaks or chemical shifts within the spectrum. NMR spectroscopy can be categorized into ^{1}H NMR and ^{13}C NMR spectroscopy. Unlike IR and MS spectroscopy, NMR provides information on the number and type of carbon and hydrogen atoms in a molecule.

Proton Nuclear Magnetic Spectroscopy (^{1}H NMR)

For ^{1}H NMR, the spectrum for a specific compound will show a set of peaks that generally range from 1 to 12 ppm. The position of these peaks or signals along the x-axis is referred to as the chemical shift. The chemical shift is based on a delta scale and has units of parts per million (ppm). Each chemical shift corresponds to a particular type of proton and provides information about the structural environment. If the chemical shift of signal A lies on the left of the spectrum, relative to another signal, then signal A has a higher frequency. Conversely, if the chemical shift of signal A lies on the right of the spectrum, relative to some other signal, then signal A has a lower frequency. The table below shows six types of protons.

H type	**Chemical shift δ (ppm)**
An H bonded to an sp^3 carbon atom	1
An H bonded to an sp^3 carbon attached to a π system	2
An H bonded to a carbon attached to an oxygen atom.	3–4
An H bonded to an sp^2 carbon atom	5–6
An H bonded to an aromatic carbon atom	7–8
An H bonded to an aldehyde carbon atom	10
An H bonded to a carboxylic oxygen atom	11–12

Table 8. ^{1}H-NMR chemical shifts

Counting the number of signals in a ^{1}H NMR spectrum yields an approximate number of distinct proton environments for a given molecule. The electron density influences the magnetic environment for each signal. The physical meaning of the chemical shift is related to the frequency of the NMR signals that are created by the nuclei. Chemical shifts are important because they provide clues to the structure of a molecule.

There are four essential features that an NMR spectrum provides.

1. The types of proton atoms in ^{1}H NMR can be determined from the spectrum by examining the chemical shifts. In other words, the number of signals within the spectrum determines the number of different proton environments in a compound.

2. Where the signals lie along the x-axis provides information about the magnetic environment for each set of protons.

3. Integrating the area underneath a curve or respective peak/signal yields the relative number of equivalent protons.

4. The splitting pattern of each signal (doublet, triplet signals) or multiplicity provides the number of protons on an atom next to the atom whose signal is measured. Specifically, the $n + 1$ rule regarding

the spin-spin splitting (spin coupling of two adjacent protons) of signals provides a way to find the number of protons adjacent to the proton creating the signal.

Chemical Shift and Signal Patterns

The following NMR graph shows two main signals found in chloroethane.

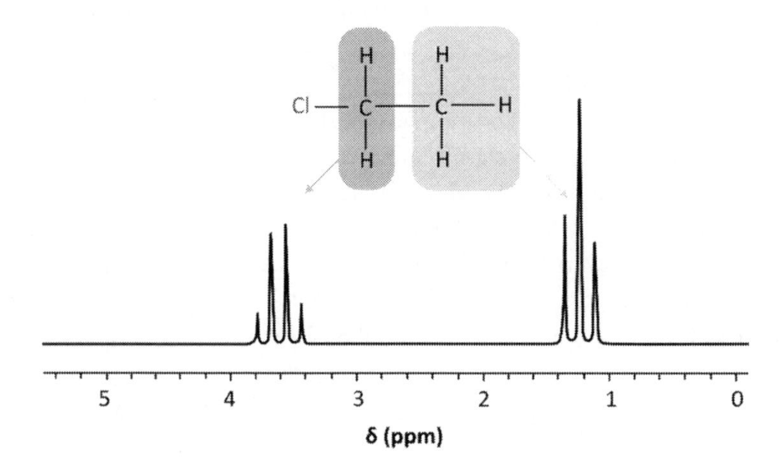

Figure 150. HNMR graph of chloroethane

The first signal on the left side consists of four peaks, and the second signal at the lower frequency end consists of three peaks. It would be incorrect to say the spectrum contains seven signals. A signal is not a peak. The four peaks found at the higher frequency are one signal split into four. There is another signal that is typically present at 0 ppm that comes from a compound called tetramethylsilane (TMS). The TMS compound is used for calibration; however, to avoid confusion, it's not shown in the spectrum. Because there are two distinct signals in the spectrum, there are two types of different proton environments (not two protons). The higher frequency signal lies between 3.5 and 4 ppm and the lower frequency between 1 and 1.5 ppm. As shown in the table above, the left signal may be attributed to protons within an alkyl chloride or protons bonded to a carbon atom that is connected to a chlorine atom. The right signal may be attributed to protons bonded to a 1° or sp^3 hybridized carbon atom. In chloroethane, the signal between 3.5 and 4 ppm is split into a quartet of peaks and represents the two alkyl chloride protons. The signal between 1 and 1.5 is split into a triplet and corresponds to three 1° alkyl protons.

The Area Under the Signal

For each respective signal, the integration of the signal area or area underneath the signals in a ^{1}H NMR spectrum is proportional to the number of hydrogen atoms associated with the signal.

In an NMR spectrum, you will likely notice curves called integrals, which resemble steps placed above each signal. The integral step height is proportional to the number of hydrogen atoms. The ratio of the integral step height from signal A (triplet) over the step height from signal B (quartet) will give the "area" ratio for the signals. The following figure shows the area under each signal peak for a spectrum similar to chloroethane.

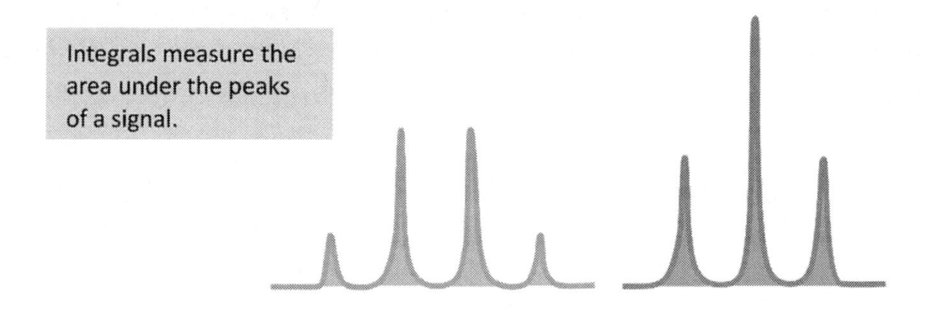

Figure 151. Area under the signal

The area under the signal is integrated (shaded area) for each signal. A ratio is taken between each signal area to determine the number of protons in the spectrum. Typically, an NMR spectrum will place a numerical value above the integral and signals to denote the number of hydrogens. The step heights for the quartet and triplet can be measured, either manually with a ruler or by computer software, and will provide a 1.0 (quartet) to 1.5 (triplet) ratio. Atoms cannot have a fraction, so the number of hydrogens for each signal may be multiplied by two to give 2 (quartet) and 3 (triplet).

Signal Splitting or Coupling

Signal splitting, also called coupling or signal multiplicity, provides specific information about the constitution or the identity of a compound. Signal splitting is predictable. Hydrogens that are not equivalent (for example, alkyl hydrogens and alkyl chloride protons) will create a magnetic field within 2–3 bonds of other hydrogens that are producing the signal. Therefore, there is a coupling effect between the different hydrogens (for example, alkyl protons and alkyl chloride protons). The coupling effect of nearby hydrogens splits the energy levels for the specific hydrogen signal that is observed. Multiple peaks are created. For example, the alkyl protons in chloroethane can couple with the signal corresponding to the alkyl chloride protons such that four peaks are formed. There are simple rules to predict the number of peaks due to coupling in a ^{1}H NMR spectrum. The number of peaks is equal to "$n + 1$," where n refers to the number of vicinal and geminal hydrogen atoms that are nonequivalent (for example, alkyl protons) to the hydrogens (for example, alkyl chloride protons) that create the signal. **Vicinal hydrogens** are hydrogens on adjacent carbons. Coupling is seen with vicinal hydrogens that are separated by three bonds from the hydrogens that create the signal. **Geminal hydrogens** are hydrogens bonded to the same carbon atom, and coupling can occur if the germinal hydrogens are in a chiral molecule.

Signals with one peak are called singlets. Signals with two, three, and four peaks are called doublets, triplets, and quartets. Consider the ^{1}H NMR spectrum of chloroethane shown previously. There are no cases where n is equal to zero because that would mean one of the signals would have one peak. The spectrum contains a quartet and a triplet. The signal for $Cl - CH_2 -$ (alkyl chloride protons) is a quartet because there are three hydrogen atoms on the adjacent carbon ($n = 3$). The signal for $CH_3 -$ (alkyl protons) is a triplet because there are two hydrogens on the adjacent carbon ($n = 2$).

Carbon-13 Nuclear Magnetic Spectroscopy (^{13}C NMR)

The spectra given by ^{13}C NMR will typically be shown as a broadband proton-decoupled spectrum. Whereas the signals in ^{1}H NMR are visible as peaks or cusps, ^{13}C NMR will contain signals that have a series of single lines. The number of lines in the ^{13}C NMR spectra will correspond to the number of different types of carbon atoms within a molecule. Like ^{1}H NMR, various chemical shifts are associated with the different kinds of carbon atoms. For every distinct carbon atom present, there is one corresponding signal that consists of one peak. Furthermore, the signal area in ^{13}C NMR is not relevant, and the splitting of ^{13}C signals into multiple peaks (triplet, etc.) is not seen.

Chemical Shifts

Chemical shifts in ^{13}C NMR that correspond to a carbon atom that has low electron density (carbon atoms bonded to electronegative atoms) are found further to the left in a spectrum at higher frequencies or larger chemical shifts. In contrast, a high electron density around an atom (alkyl carbons) results in a signal that lies further to the right in the spectrum at lower frequencies and smaller chemical shifts. The table below shows approximate carbon-13 chemical shifts.

C type	**Chemical shift δ (ppm).**
sp^3 alkyl carbon atom	10–30
sp^3 carbon attached to an O, N, or X	50–70
sp carbon atom	75–90
sp^2 carbon atom	100–150
Ester, amide, and carboxyl $(C = O)$	160–180
Aldehyde and ketone $(C = O)$	190–200

Table 9. ^{13}C-NMR chemical shifts

Carbon atoms bonded to electron-withdrawing functional groups such as halogens and hydroxyl groups are deshielded. Consequently, the ^{13}C NMR peaks will show up at higher frequencies or larger chemical shifts compared to unsubstituted carbon atoms. The figure below is a simulated ^{13}C NMR spectrum of chloroethane.

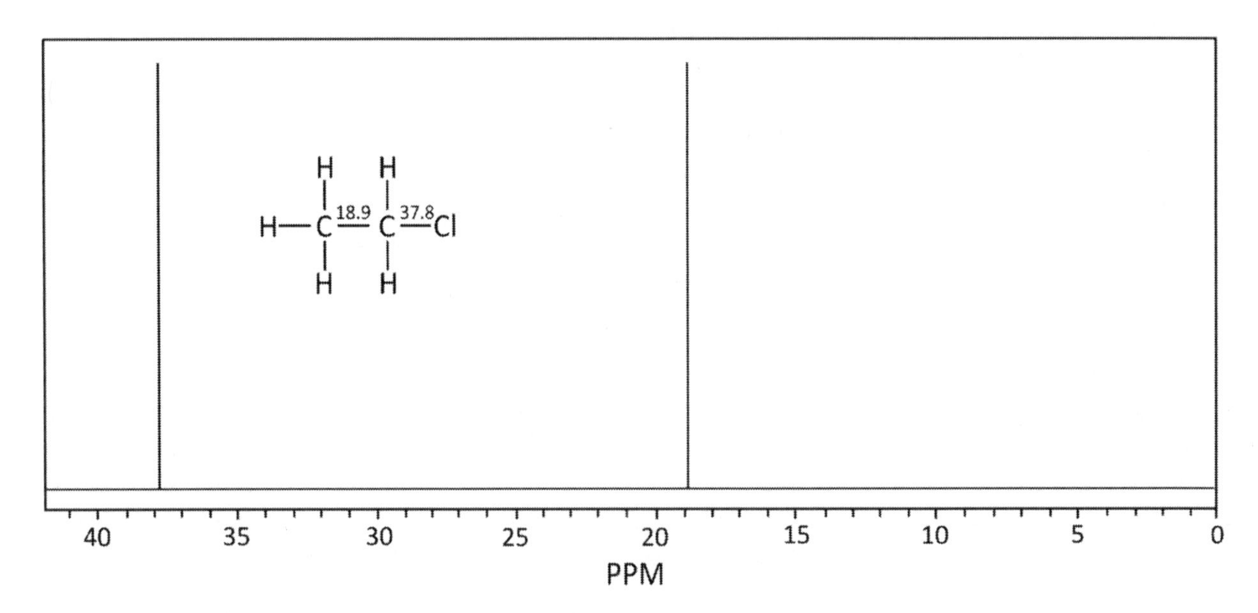

Figure 152. Simulated ^{13}C NMR spectrum

Chloroethane contains two carbon atoms in distinct environments and should produce two signals. The chemical shifts are found at 18.8 and 37.8 ppm. There is a clear separation between each peak that is due to the level of shielding around each carbon atom. The signal at 18.9 ppm corresponds to an alkyl carbon atom that has a relatively high electron density, and will, therefore, be found at lower frequencies and smaller chemical shifts. In contrast, the peak found at a higher frequency or larger chemical shift must be a carbon atom that has a lower electron density; it is less shielded and bonded to a chlorine atom.

Synthesis and Analysis

Organic synthesis requires predicting the products for several steps in a reaction. For a reaction that involves three steps, it's typically easier to visualize at the beginning the needed steps to produce a target molecule from known precursors. However, in some cases, it may be challenging to visualize the sequence of chemical transformations from beginning to end. If we know the desired molecule that will be synthesized but are unsure where to start, then we can think of the sequential steps needed to go backward. By going back one step at a time, we can identify the required precursors that react to form a product molecule. The backward thought process, referred to as **retrosynthetic analysis**, can be repeated such that we work backward to obtain simple compounds until the starting compound is obtained. The starting compound may be readily available in a laboratory. The concept of retrosynthetic analysis was coined by Nobel Laureate E.J. Corey and is illustrated in the figure below.

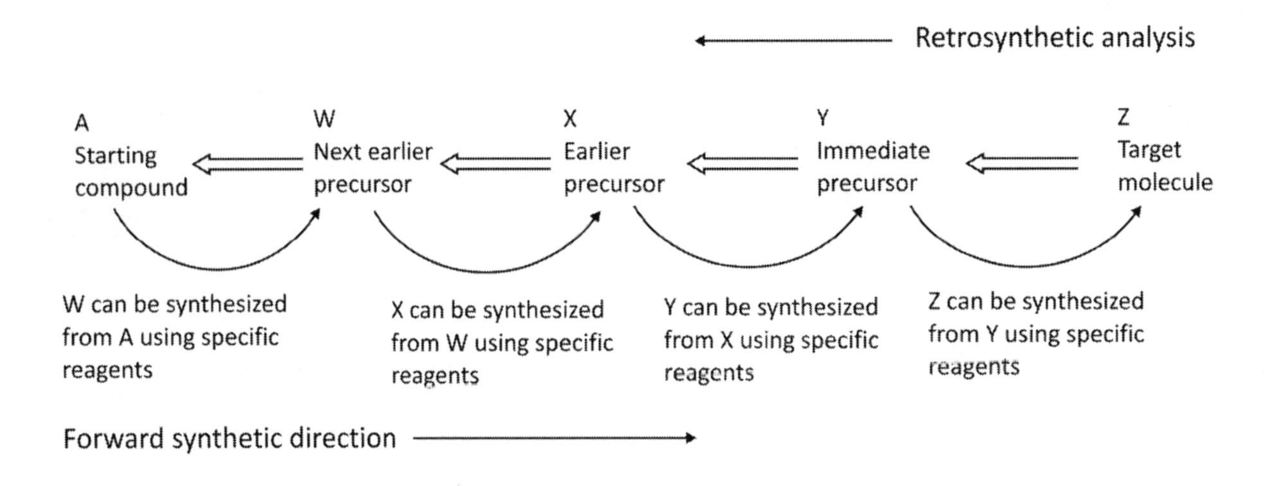

Figure 153. Retrosynthetic analysis

When performing a retrosynthetic analysis, it's helpful to think of the possible precursors and possible synthetic routes. The illustration shown above is not linear; it will not proceed through one synthetic route. Examining the numerous synthetic routes enables one to determine the most feasible route. Ideally, a chemist would pursue a synthetic route that requires fewer steps, is relatively safe, and makes use of readily available and low-cost reagents.

When outlining a retrosynthetic map, it's essential to know the chemistry of functional groups, how to pick reagents that will give a desired functional group, and how to use protecting groups to prevent another functional group from undergoing an unwanted reaction during the transformation of another functional group. Specific reagents must be used to create a precursor that has a specific regiochemistry and stereochemistry. In electrophilic aromatic substitution, in addition to knowing the reagents needed to introduce a substituent, the directing effects of the substituents must be considered such that the reactions are done in the correct order. In the laboratory, after the preparation and purification (for example, flash chromatography) of a precursor molecule, a routine spectroscopic analysis (for example, NMR) is typically performed to identify the compound.

Before applying a retrosynthetic analysis, let's consider some examples that require the determination of a target compound, beginning with a starting compound and several reagents. Determine the major product for the following reaction sequence.

Ethynylbenzene
or
phenyl acetylene

$\overset{+\ -}{Na:NH_2}$ → X; Br → Y; H_2, Lindlar catalyst → Z

Figure 154. Organic synthesis example 1

In the first reaction step, it should be recognized that the amide (or sodium amide) ion is a strong nucleophilic base and will attack the electrophilic ethynylbenzene. The organic molecule, ethynylbenzene, contains several acidic hydrogens. The question is which hydrogen is the most acidic such that when it's removed, it will give the most stable carbanion. The hydrogen-bonded to $C \equiv C$ will be most acidic, and when removed by the amide ion, it will create an ethynide carbanion ($Ar - C \equiv C:^{-}$, see acid and base chapter). The resulting carbanion will act as a nucleophile and will undergo an S_N2 reaction with propyl bromide. Catalytic hydrogenation with the H_2/Lindlar catalyst results in the reduction of the alkyne to an alkene. Usually, an alkyne would be reduced to an alkane if the usual Pd or Pt catalyst is used. The final product is 1-phenyl-1-pentene. The general reaction mechanism is shown below.

$C_6H_5-C\equiv C-H$ $:\bar{N}H_2$ → (NH_3) X: $C_6H_5-C\equiv \bar{C}:$ + Br → (NaBr) Y: $C_6H_5-C\equiv C-C_3H_7$

H_2, Lindlar catalyst

Catalytic hydrogenation is a syn addition, so the *Z* isomer will form

(*Z*)-1-Phenyl-1-pentene

Figure 155. Organic synthesis example 1 mechanism

Note that catalytic hydrogenation to the alkyne is a *syn* addition and will result in the formation of a cis or (*Z*) alkene.

Synthesis Using Diazonium Salts

The preparation of an intermediate arene diazonium salt $\left(\mathrm{Ar} - \mathrm{N_2}^{+}\right)$ is useful when synthesizing aromatic compounds. The diazonium group $(-\mathrm{N} \equiv \mathrm{N}^{+})$ can be replaced with a number of atoms or groups such as $-\mathrm{OH}$, $-\mathrm{Cl}$, $-\mathrm{Br}$, $-\mathrm{CN}$, $-\mathrm{I}$, $-\mathrm{F}$, and $-\mathrm{H}$. To prepare a diazonium salt, a primary aromatic amine $(\mathrm{Ar} - \mathrm{NH_2})$ must be diazotized with sodium nitrite ($\mathrm{NaNO_2}$ or HONO) at a temperature at 0–5 °C, since arene diazonium salts are unstable above 5–10 °C and can explode. An acid may be used with sodium nitrite at 0 °C. The addition of a reagent to the salt, such as CuCl or CuBr, will result in the replacement of the salt with the desired group, for example, ($\mathrm{Ar} - \mathrm{Cl}$ or $\mathrm{Ar} - \mathrm{Br}$). The replacement of molecular nitrogen from the diazonium ions, using copper salts, to aryl halides (specific to $\mathrm{Ar} - \mathrm{Cl}$, $\mathrm{Ar} - \mathrm{Br}$, and $\mathrm{Ar} - \mathrm{CN}$) are generally known as **Sandmeyer reactions**. The nature of the reactions are thought to occur by a radical aromatic nucleophilic substitution. The following figure shows how the addition of different reagents to the arene diazonium salt can form different aromatic compounds.

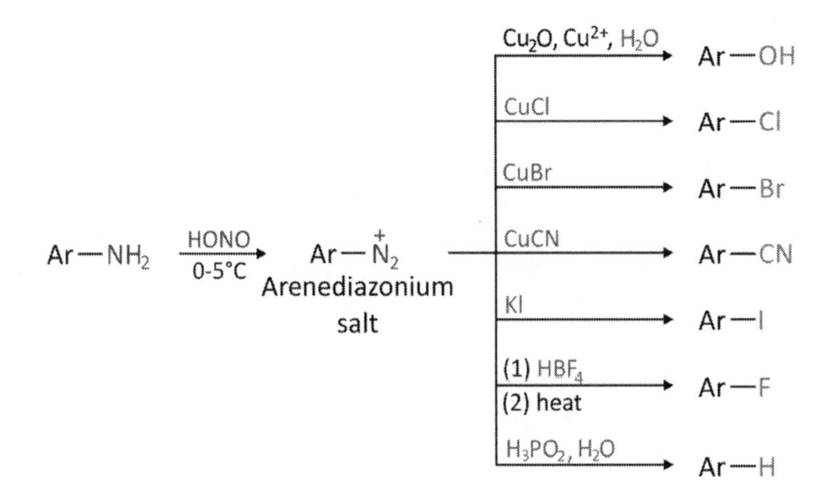

Figure 156. Arenediazonium salt reactions

Primary arylamines $(\mathrm{Ar} - \mathrm{NH_2})$ can be produced by the reduction of a nitrobenzene compound (for example, nitrobenzene $\mathrm{Ar} - \mathrm{NO_2}$) with hydrogen gas and a catalyst $(\mathrm{H_2/Pt})$. Nitrobenzene can be synthesized from a benzene using the nitrating reagents, nitric, and sulfuric acid $(\mathrm{HNO_3/H_2SO_4})$. Suppose that we wanted to produce *m*-iodochlorobenzene from benzene. What are the specific reagents needed and the possible precursors? Several key concepts are required to determine a likely reaction sequence. In addition to knowing the mechanism behind electrophilic aromatic substitution, the directing effects of electron-withdrawing and donating substituents must be considered. Halogen substituents such as chlorine and iodine are weak, deactivating ortho-para directors. Suppose we had benzene undergo chlorination with $\mathrm{Cl_2/FeCl_3}$ to obtain chlorobenzene. If subsequent halogenation with iodine were possible, then a mixture of *o*-chloroiodobenzene and *p*-chloroiodobenzene would be produced but not *m*-chloroiodobenzene. However, iodine does not react easily with benzene, and electrophilic aromatic substitution does not occur. A benzene ring containing iodine can be prepared by using diazonium salts. Therefore, one of our precursors must be nitrobenzene because, through a series of reduction steps followed by the preparation of a diazonium salt, iodine can be substituted onto the ring. The question regarding the initial reaction sequence is: Which occurs first, chlorination or nitration of the benzene ring? If chlorination of the benzene ring is carried out as the first reaction step, then the chlorine substituent would have an ortho-para directing effect and not a meta directing effect. If nitration occurred first, then the nitro group would have a meta directing effect regarding the

placement of the chlorine group. Therefore, nitration (HNO_2/H_2SO_4) occurs first, followed by chlorination ($Cl_2/FeCl_3$). After the reduction of the nitro group with H_2/Pt, a diazonium salt is prepared with $NaNO_2$/0–5 °C, followed by treatment with potassium iodide. The proposed reaction sequence is shown below.

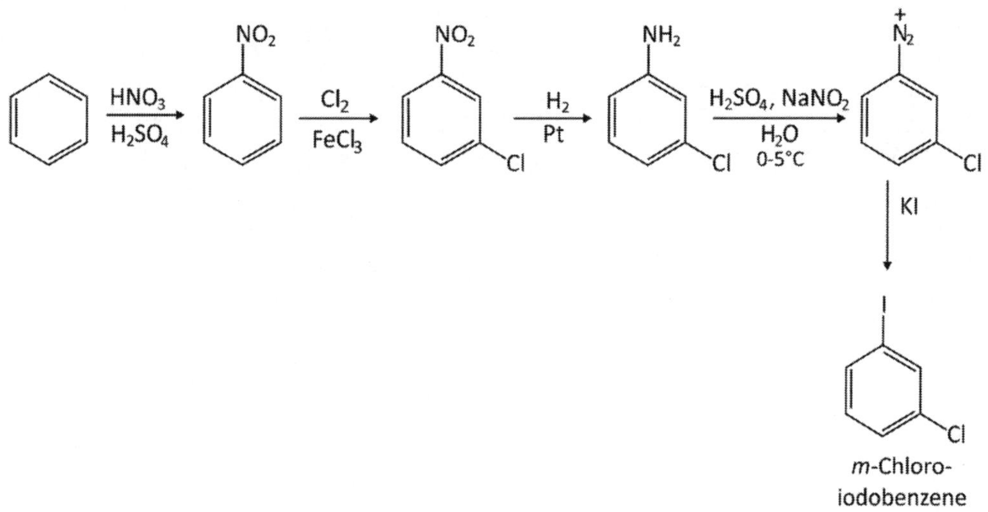

Figure 157. Synthesis of m-chloroiodobenzene

Synthesis by a Friedel-Crafts Acylation

Suppose you were synthesizing the 1,4-dipropyllbenzene from benzene. What are the possible reagents and precursors? Because of the presence of the alkyl groups on a benzene ring, the reaction sequence can involve a series of two Friedel-Crafts reaction alkylations. For example, two successive reactions of propyl chloride and aluminum chloride ($CH_3CH_2CH_2Cl/AlCl_3$) may be a possible route. However, the issue with Friedel-Crafts alkylations is that the initial carbocation will rearrange to the most stable carbocation. For example, removal of the chlorine group from *n*-propyl-chloride initially produces a primary 1° carbocation, although that carbocation will rearrange into a 2° carbocation. The reaction product that forms will be 1,4-diisopropylbenzene.

Furthermore, a Friedel-Crafts acylation reaction would be preferable if a disubstituted benzene ring were the target molecule. Friedel-Crafts alkylation can result in multiple polyalkylations since the alkyl groups are electron-donating. The rings may undergo further substitution in a Friedel-Crafts alkylation method. A more efficient way to attach an alkyl group to a benzene ring is to carry out a Friedel-Crafts acylation method followed by reduction of the carbonyl group to a CH_2 group on the added chain. The reduction reaction can be carried out either with a Wolff-Kishner (NH_2NH_2, $NaOH$, heat) or a Clemmensen ($Zn(Hg)$ and concentrated HCl) method. Because of the placement of the alkyl groups on the benzene ring (para position), the first substituent that is added to the benzene ring must be an ortho-para director or electron-withdrawing. A limitation of the Friedel-Crafts reaction is that once an acyl group is added to the ring, it will not undergo additional acylation since the added acyl group will be deactivating. Even if the reaction was possible, the acyl group will act as a meta-director and would not produce p-disubstituted benzene. However, if the acyl group were reduced to an alkyl chain, then the substituent would be electron-donating and an ortho-para-director. The first step would be to perform a Friedel-Crafts acylation with *n*-propyl chloride/$AlCl_3$, followed by reduction (Clemmensen or Wolff-

Kishner). The acylation/reduction method can then be repeated to produce the target molecule (Figure 158).

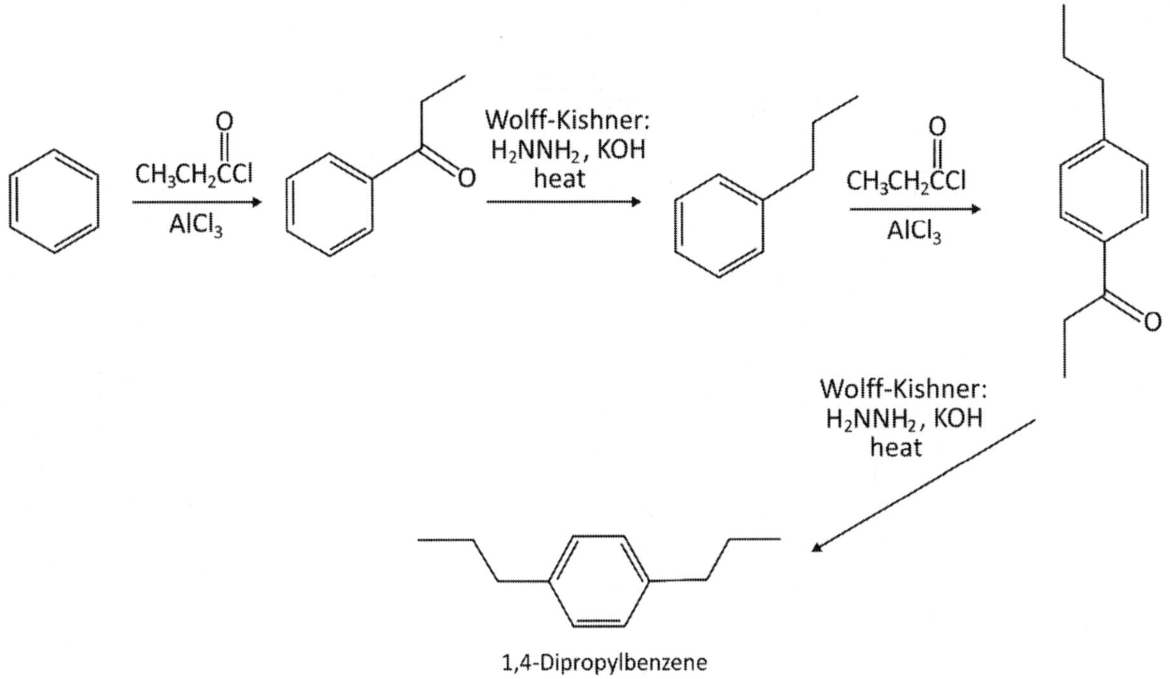

$CH_3CH_2\overset{O}{\overset{\|}{C}}Cl$, $AlCl_3$

Wolff-Kishner: H_2NNH_2, KOH, heat

$CH_3CH_2\overset{O}{\overset{\|}{C}}Cl$, $AlCl_3$

Wolff-Kishner: H_2NNH_2, KOH, heat

1,4-Dipropylbenzene

Figure 158. Synthesis of 1,4-dipropylbenzene

Synthesis of Ketones Involving β-dicarbonyl Compounds: Acetoacetic Ester Synthesis

β-dicarbonyls are compounds that contain an α acidic hydrogen and can be prepared by a Claisen condensation. For instance, the reaction of an ester compound such as ethyl acetate can react with a base (sodium ethoxide) to produce an enolate ion. Another compound of ethyl acetate can react with the enolate ion, followed by acid treatment, to form a β-dicarbonyl compound called ethyl acetoacetate or ethyl-3-oxobutanote. Therefore, ethyl acetoacetate is the Claisen condensation product from two ethyl acetate molecules. β-dicarbonyl compounds such as ethyl acetoacetate are considered active methylene compounds $(-\mathrm{CH_2}-)$ since two hydrogen atoms are adjacent to two electron-withdrawing carbonyl groups. Ethyl acetoacetate is one type of β-dicarbonyl compound that is referred to as β-ketoester. β-dicarbonyls have a relatively acidic α-proton $(\mathrm{p}K_\mathrm{a} = 11)$ due to the resonance stabilization of the enolate ion. In acetoacetic ester synthesis, ethyl acetoacetate can undergo a series of reactions that involve nucleophilic substitution and hydrolysis. For example, ethyl acetoacetate can easily react with a strong base such as sodium ethoxide to produce an enolate ion. Through a substitution reaction, the enolate ion can react with an alkyl halide such that an alkyl chain is added to the enolate ion. The resulting compound is hydrolyzed and decarboxylated to produce substituted ketone. Figure 159 shows

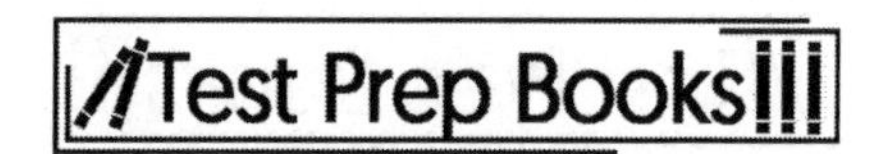

an example of an acetoacetic ester synthesis where ethyl acetoacetate undergoes a series of reactions that consists of three steps: alkylation, hydrolysis, and decarboxylation.

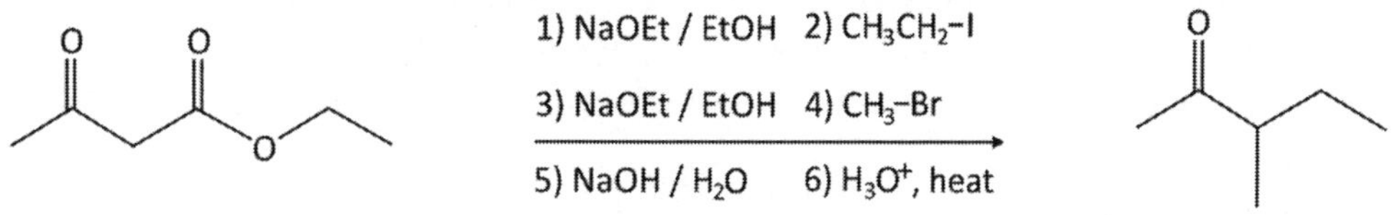
1) NaOEt / EtOH 2) CH3CH2-I
3) NaOEt / EtOH 4) CH3-Br
5) NaOH / H2O 6) H3O+, heat

Figure 159. Acetoacetic ester synthesis overview

Both α hydrogens can be substituted with an alkyl group, and the added alkyl groups don't have to be similar. In the first step, ethyl acetoacetate reacts with sodium ethoxide in an ethanol solvent. The ethoxide ion removes or deprotonates the alpha hydrogen on the β-ketoester to produce a reactive enolate ion. The resulting beta-keto ester anion can resonance-stabilize to several resonance structures. For example, the electrons on the carbanion can form a double bond with one of the carbonyl carbons. The π electrons from the carbonyl carbon-oxygen bond delocalize to the oxygen atom. Enolates are good nucleophiles and can react with an alkyl halide via a nucleophilic substitution bimolecular (S_N2) reaction. The general reaction mechanism for the three main steps is shown below.

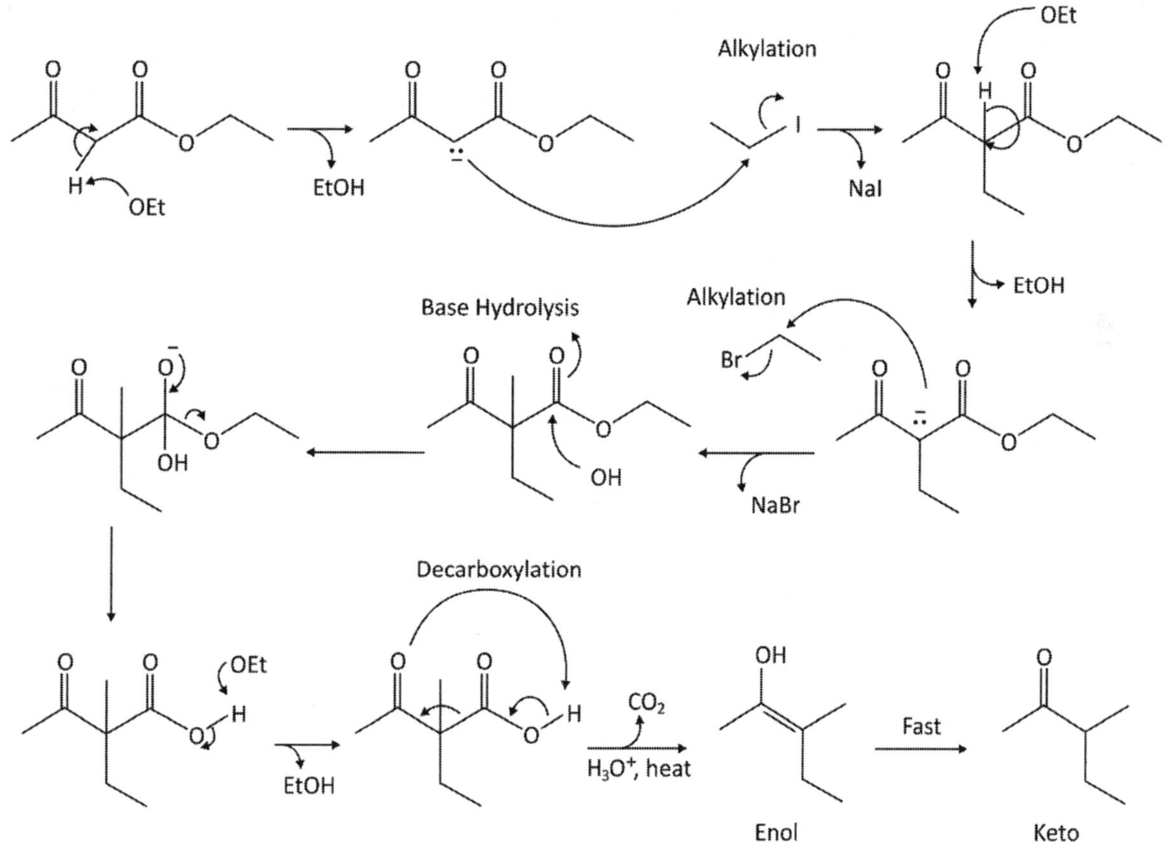
Alkylation
EtOH
NaI
EtOH
Base Hydrolysis
Alkylation
NaBr
Decarboxylation
EtOH
CO2
H3O+, heat
Fast
Enol
Keto

Figure 160. Acetoacetic ester synthesis mechanism

The enolate ion reacts with ethyl iodide, and the alkyl group is substituted at the α-position in place of the α -hydrogen that was removed. Recall that the most suitable halides are primary $1°$ and methyl halides (CH_3 > $1°$ > $2°$) in an S_N2 reaction. The order of a good leaving group is: $I > Br > Cl > F$. In theory, both α-hydrogens can be replaced with two alkyl groups, as shown in the reaction sequence in Figure 160. However, another molecule of sodium ethoxide must be used to abstract the remaining α -hydrogen. The resulting enolate reacts with a molecule of ethyl bromide (CH_3CH_2Br), thereby alkylating the ester.

Basic hydrolysis of the ester is carried out by adding sodium hydroxide /water and occurs in multiple steps. In the first step, the hydroxide ion attacks the electrophilic carbonyl carbon atom of the ester $C = O$. The π bond breaks and creates a tetrahedral intermediate. The intermediate reforms the $C = O$ bond such that the alkoxide ion becomes a leaving group (EtO^- or $CH_3CH_2O^-$), thereby forming a carboxylic acid. However, an acid-base reaction occurs where the alkoxide ion deprotonates the carboxylic acid. In the last reaction step, the addition of heat/acid results in a process called decarboxylation, whereby the carboxylic acid group separates or forms into carbon dioxide. Carboxylic acids located at the β position tends to decarboxylate easily under heat. The final product is an enol that rearranges to a substituted ketone.

Practice Test

1. What is the IUPAC name of the following compound?

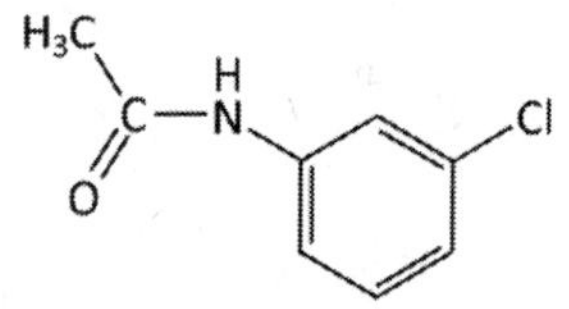

a. *m*-(3-chlorophenyl) ethanamide
b. *m*-(3-chlorophenyl) acetamide
c. *N*-(3-chlorobenzyl) acetamide
d. *N*-(3-chlorophenyl) ethanamide

2. Determine the correct IUPAC name for the following compound.

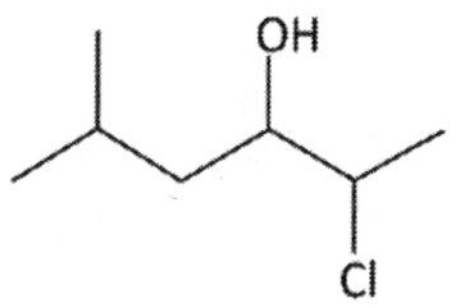

a. 2-chloro-5-methyl-3-hexanol
b. 2-chloro-5-methylhexanol
c. 5-chloro-2-methylhexanol
d. 2-chloro-5-methyl-3-hydroxyhexanol

3. Which structure below represents (*E*)-1,1-dibromo-2-pentene?

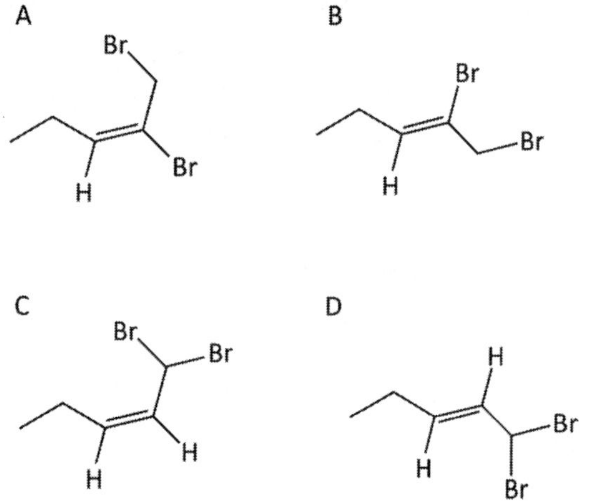

A

B

C

D

4. Which compound below contains an ester, an amide, and a carboxylic acid group?

A

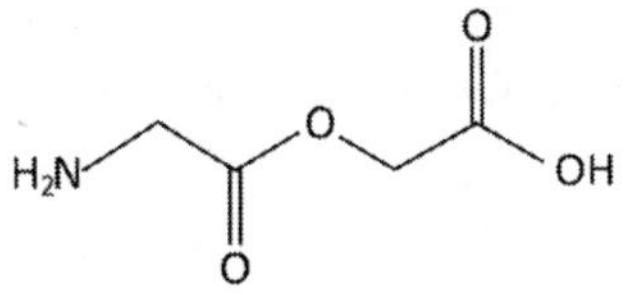

B

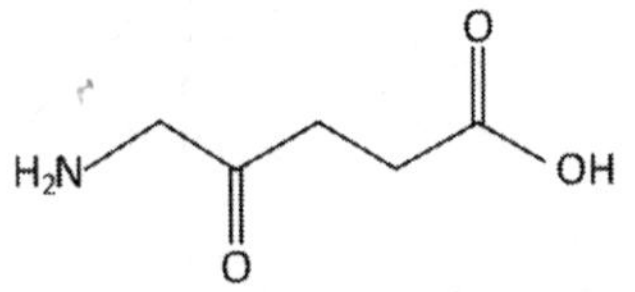

C

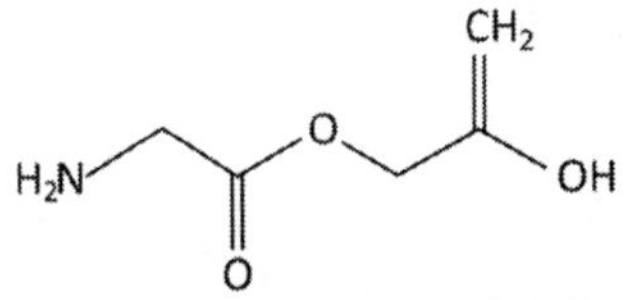

D

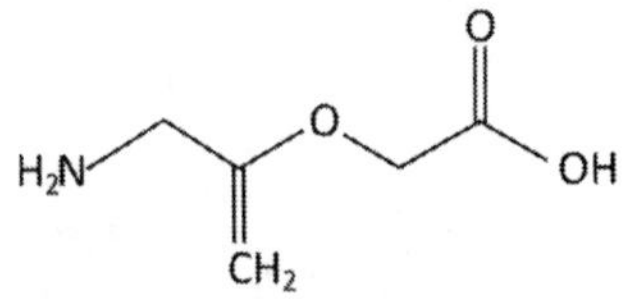

5. Which structure below corresponds to (*Z*)-3,5-dimethyl-3-decene?

A

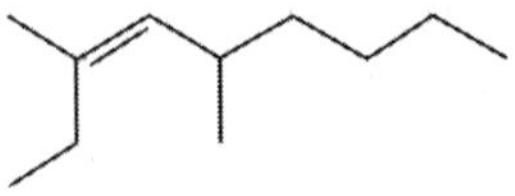

B

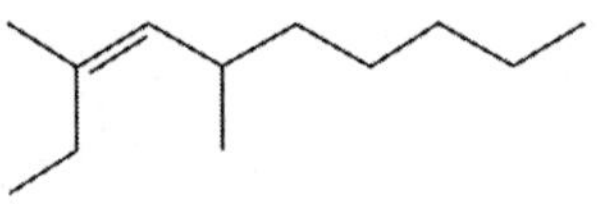

C

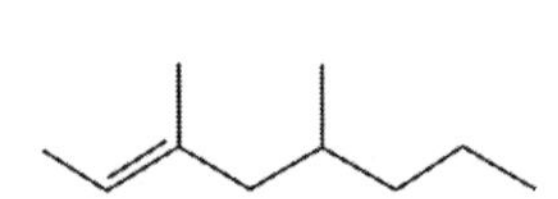

D

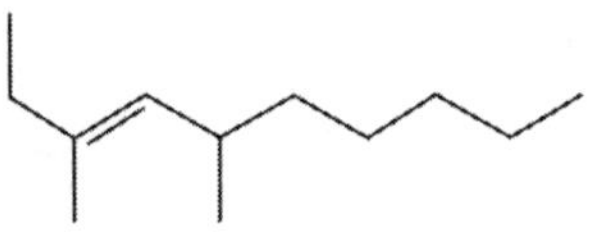

6. Which value below is closest to the bond angle in the $C-C=C$ bond in benzene?

a. 120°
b. 109.5°
c. 100°
d. 140°

7. Determine the correct hybridizations for the atoms that are marked I, II, III, and IV.

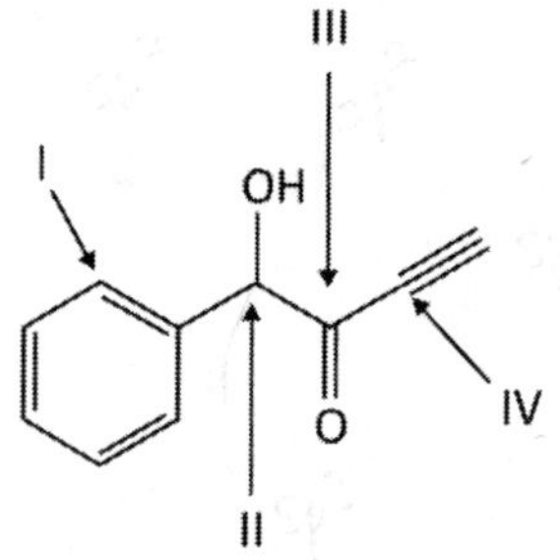

a. I=sp^3, II=sp^2, III=sp, IV=sp^3
b. I=sp^3, II=sp^2, III=sp, IV=sp^3
c. I=sp^2, II=sp^3, III=sp^2, IV=sp
d. I=sp^3, II=sp, III=sp^2, IV=sp^3

8. Which Lewis structure below contains a sulfur atom with a formal charge of +1?

A

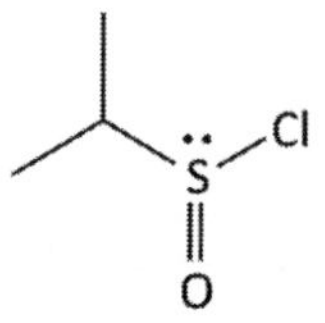

B

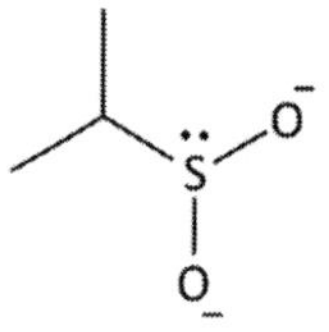

C

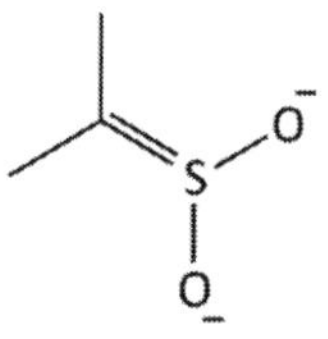

D

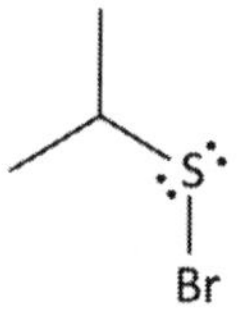

9. Which of the following carbocations is the most stable?

A

B

C

D

10. Which of the following structures is considered aromatic?

I

II

III

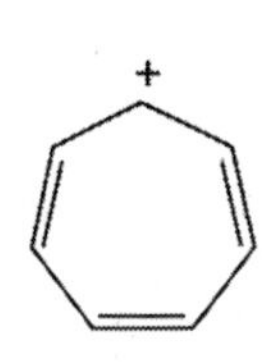

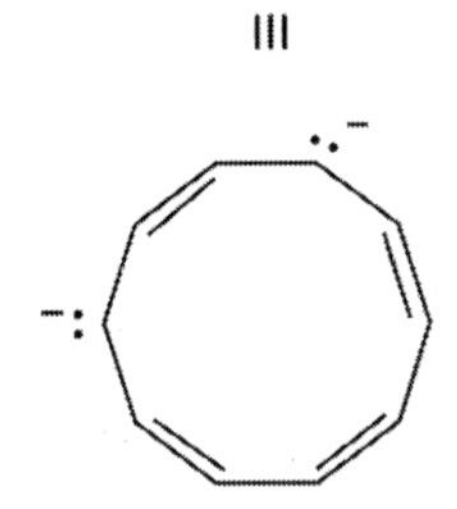

a. I, II, and III
b. II only
c. II and III
d. I and III

11. Which of the following is the strongest acid?

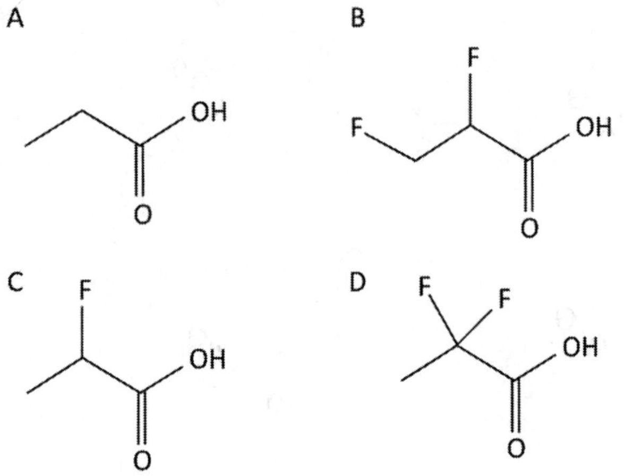

A B C D

12. Which of the protons below would have the smallest pK_a value?

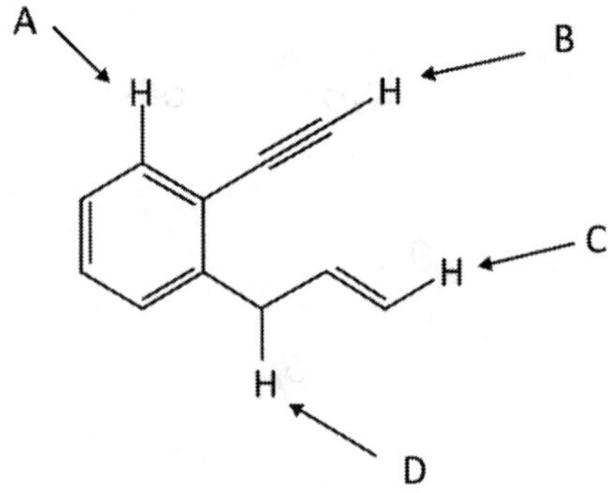

a. A
b. B
c. C
d. D

13. Consider the amino acid shown below. Which structure below corresponds to the predominant form at $\text{pOH} = 7$?

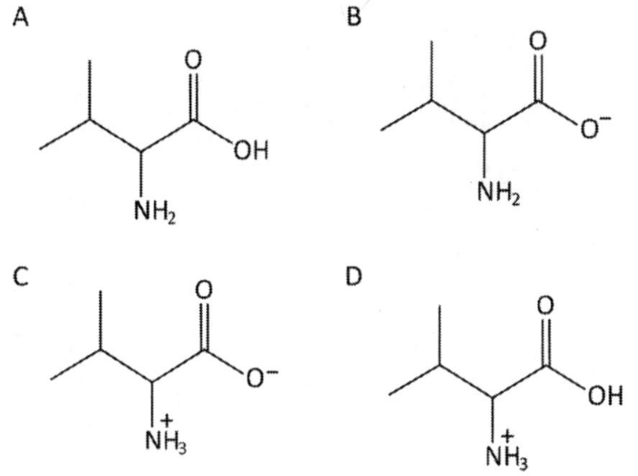

A
B
C
D

14. Which structure below explains why 4-hydroxybenzoic acid is more acidic than phenol?

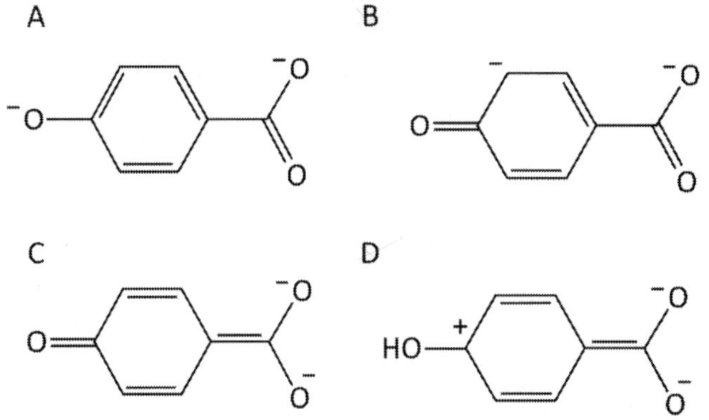

A
B
C
D

15. Below are four statements about the basicity of the two nitrogen atoms in the compound shown in the illustration. Which statement is true?

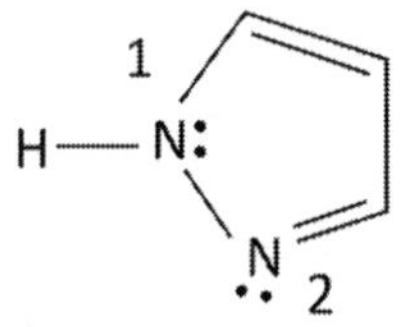

a. Both nitrogen atoms are not basic.
b. Nitrogen atom 2 is more basic than nitrogen atom 1.
c. Nitrogen atom 1 is more basic than nitrogen atom 2.
d. Both nitrogen atoms are strongly basic.

16. Which molecule below has an *R* configuration?

A

OH
C
H
CH_3
COOH

B

OH
C
O
C — H
H_3C
CH_2OH

C

OH
C
H
CH_2OH
COOH

D

OH
C
H
CH_3
C
CH

17. In the Fischer projection below, what are the stereochemistry configurations of the two chiral centers?

O
C — H
HO — 2 — H
HO — 3 — H
CH_2OH

a. 2*S*, 3*S*
b. 2*R*, 3*S*
c. 2*S*, 3*R*
d. 2*R*, 3*S*

18. Which molecule has an enantiomer?

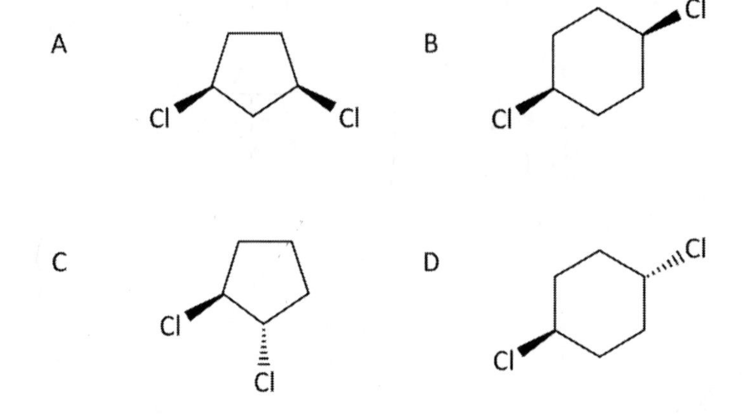

19. In the molecule below, how many stereocenters are present?

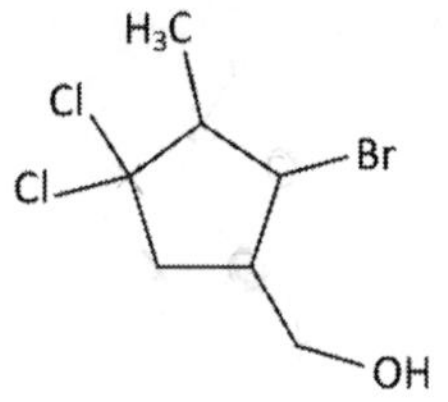

a. 2
b. 3
c. 4
d. 5

20. Which stereoisomer is the most stable?

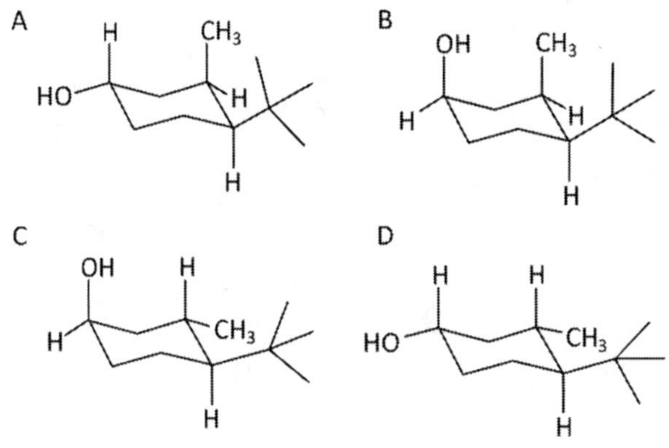

21. Which carbocation will NOT likely undergo carbocation rearrangement?

A

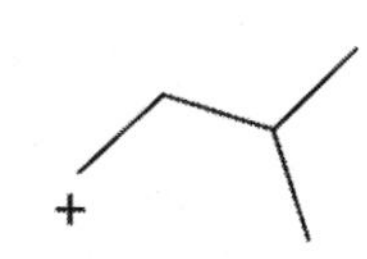

B

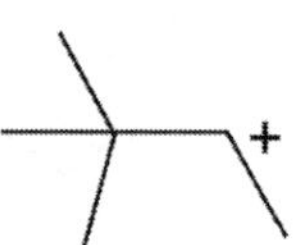

C

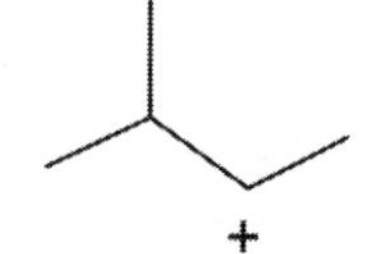

D

22. Predict the product for the following reaction.

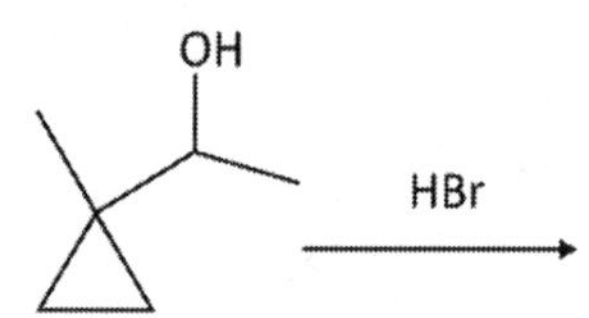

A

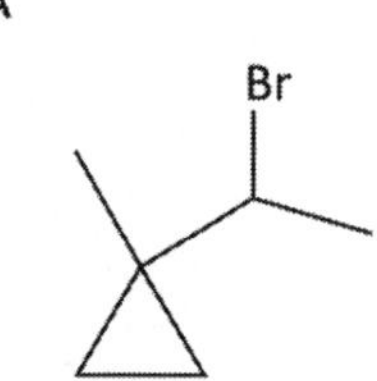

B

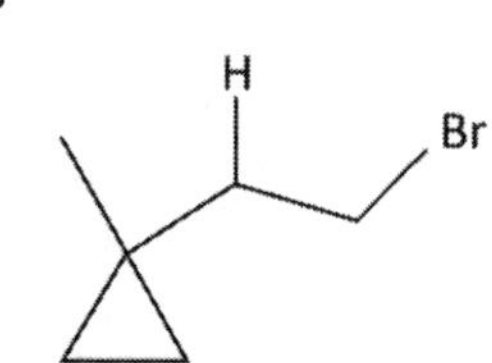

C

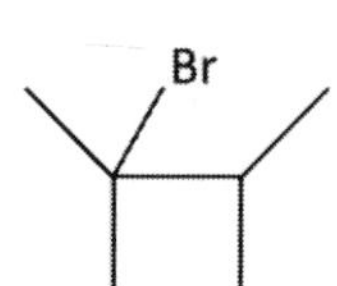

D

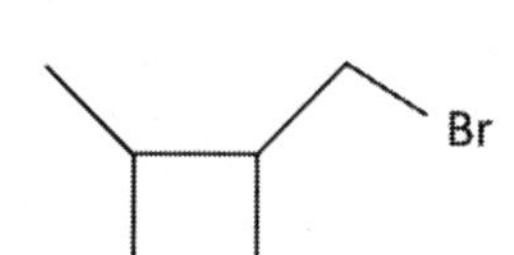

23. Predict the products for the following epoxide reaction.

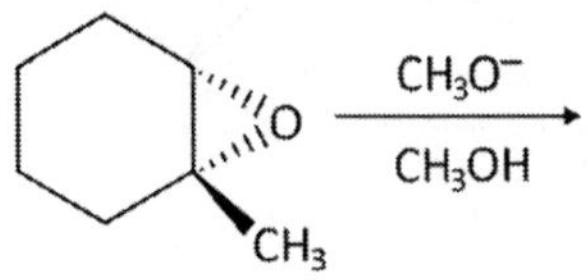

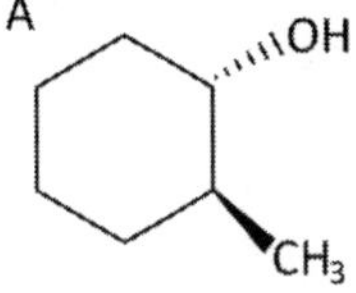

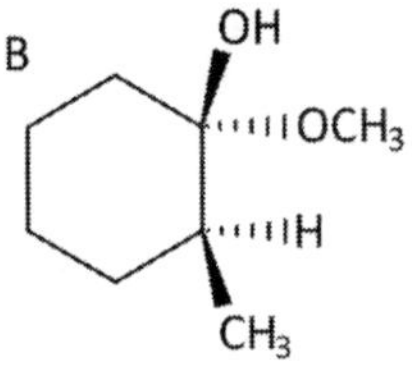

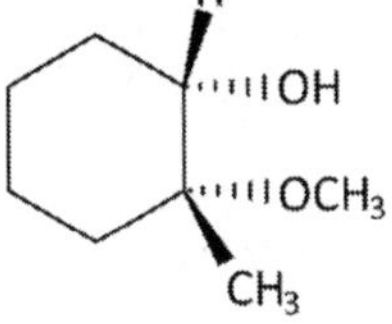

O, CH_3 — CH_3O^- / CH_3OH →

A OH, CH_3

B OH, OCH_3, H, CH_3

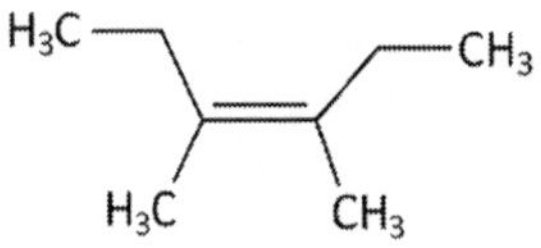

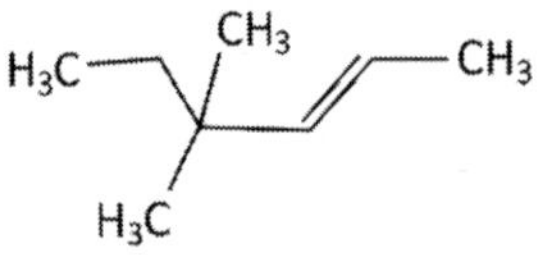

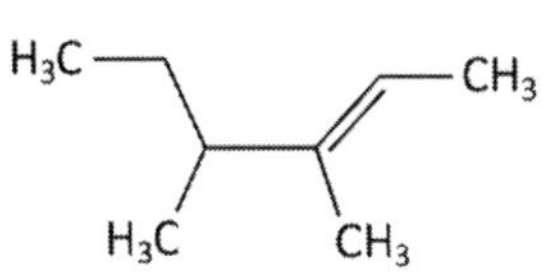

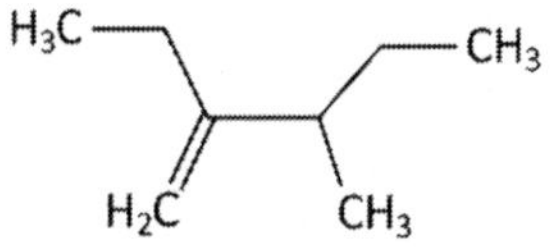

C H, OH, OCH_3, CH_3

D OCH_3, H, OH, CH_3

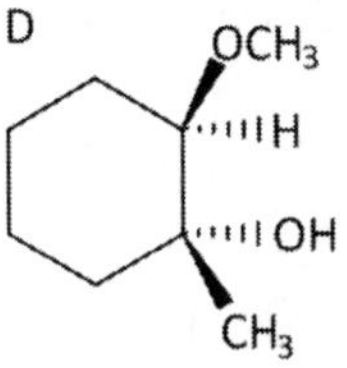

24. Predict the major alkene products for the following dehydration reaction of alcohol.

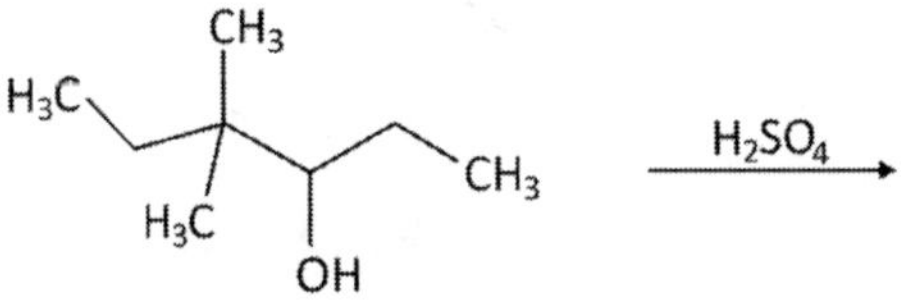

CH_3, H_3C, CH_3, H_3C, OH — H_2SO_4 →

A H_3C, CH_3, H_3C, CH_3

B H_3C, CH_3, CH_3, H_3C

C H_3C, CH_3, H_3C, CH_3

D H_3C, CH_3, H_2C, CH_3

25. What is the expected major pathway for the following reaction?

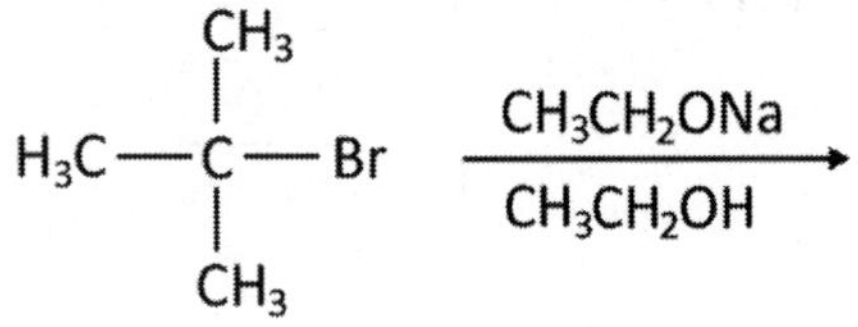

$$(CH_3)_3C{-}Br \xrightarrow[CH_3CH_2OH]{CH_3CH_2ONa}$$

a. S_N1
b. S_N2
c. E1
d. E2

26. Predict the final product from the reaction shown below.

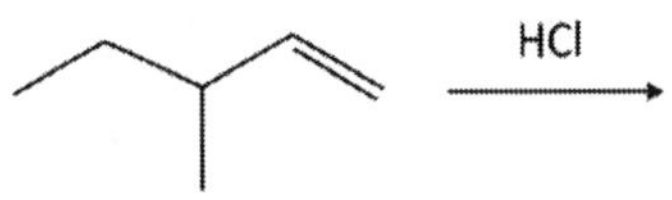

HCl

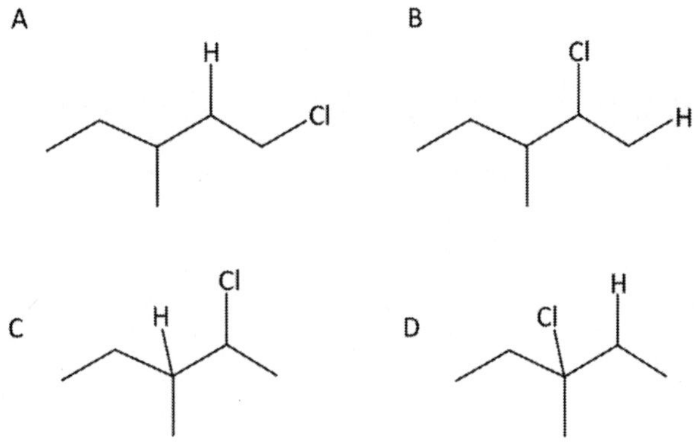

A

H

Cl

B

Cl

H

C

Cl

H

D

H

Cl

27. What are the products for the following acid-catalyzed hydration reaction?

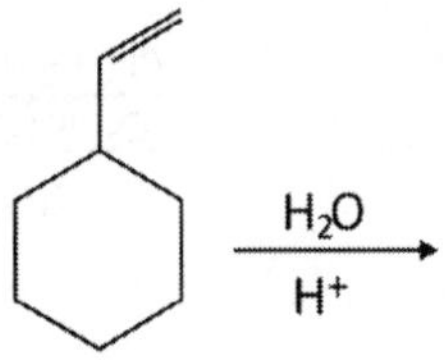

H_2O, H^+

A

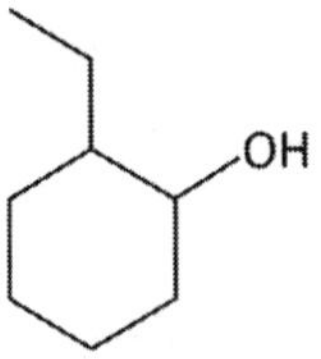

OH

B

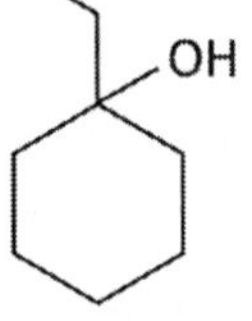

OH

C

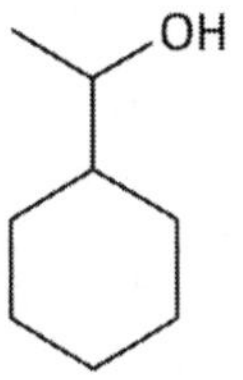

OH

D

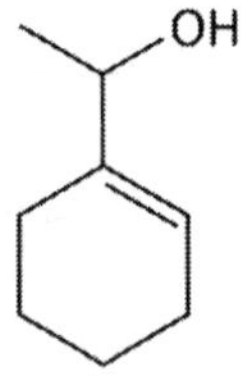

OH

28. For the oxymercuration reaction shown below, determine the correct reaction products.

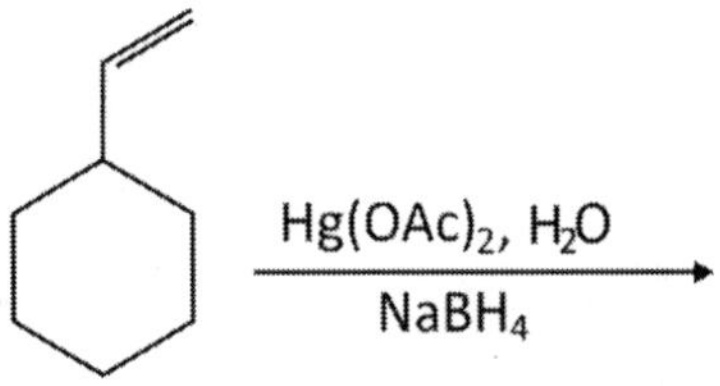

$Hg(OAc)_2$, H_2O
$NaBH_4$

A

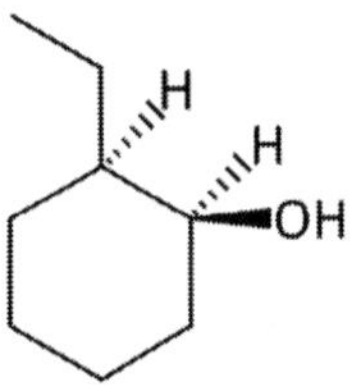

H H OH

B

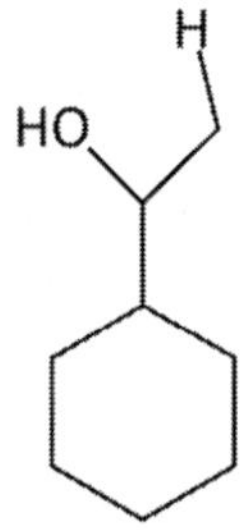

H HO

C

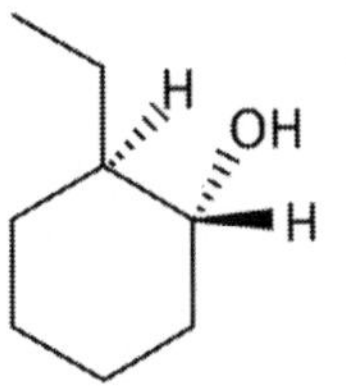

H OH H

D

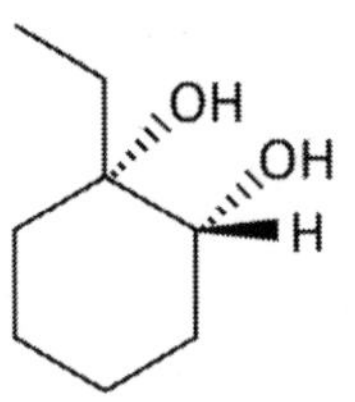

OH OH H

29. For the hydroboration reaction shown below, predict the correct reaction product.

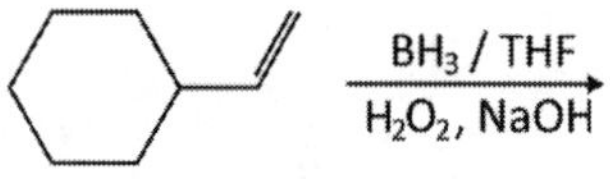

BH_3 / THF
H_2O_2, NaOH

A

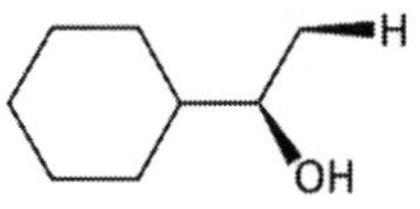

H
OH

B

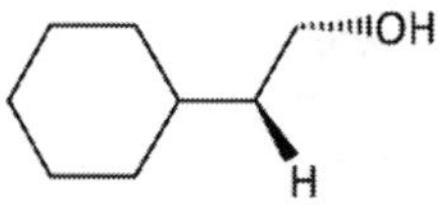

OH
H

C

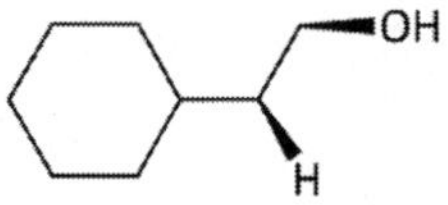

OH
H

D

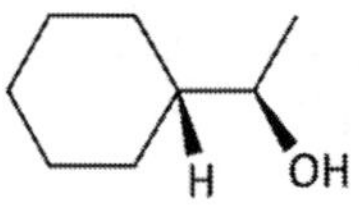

H OH

30. For the Diels-Alder reaction below, choose the correct product.

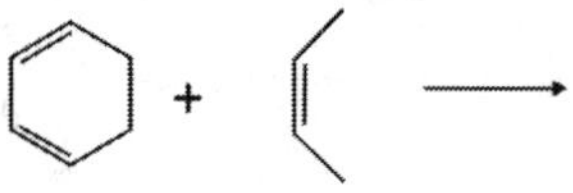

+

A

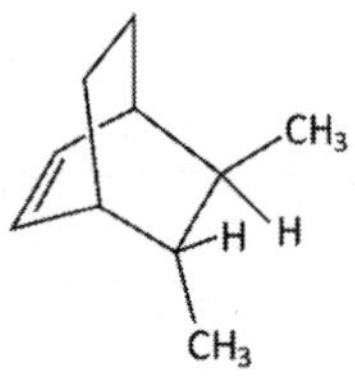

CH_3
H H
CH_3

B

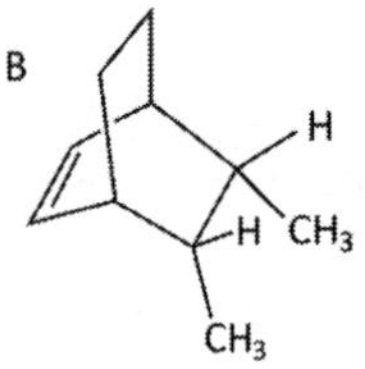

H
H CH_3
CH_3

C

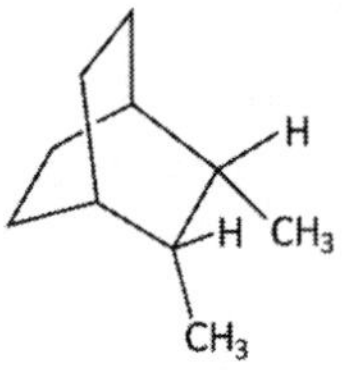

H
H CH_3
CH_3

D

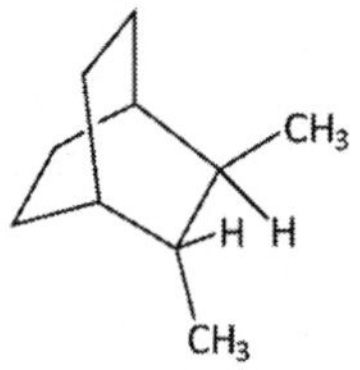

CH_3
H H
CH_3

31. Predict the products for the following reaction.

\+ BrMg $\xrightarrow{H_3O^+}$

A

OH

B

OCH_3

C

OCH_3

D

OH

32. Determine the product in the following reaction sequence.

$CH_3CH_2Br + P(C_6H_5)_3 \xrightarrow{C_4H_9Li} CH_3\overset{-}{C}H - \overset{+}{P}(C_6H_5)_3 \longrightarrow$

O

A

OCH_2CH_3

B

OH

CH_2CH_3

C

$CHCH_3$

D

CH_2CH_3

33. Which of the following reactions is a reversible nucleophilic addition?

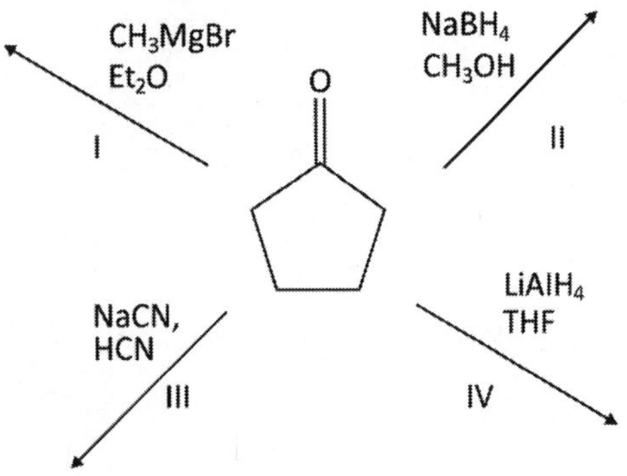
CH3MgBr
Et2O
I
NaBH4
CH3OH
II
O
NaCN,
HCN
III
LiAlH4
THF
IV

a. I
b. II
c. III
d. IV

34. What product is formed in the following reaction?

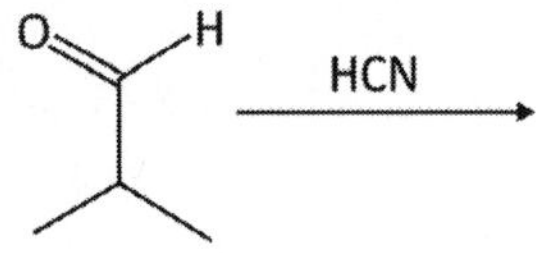
O
H
HCN

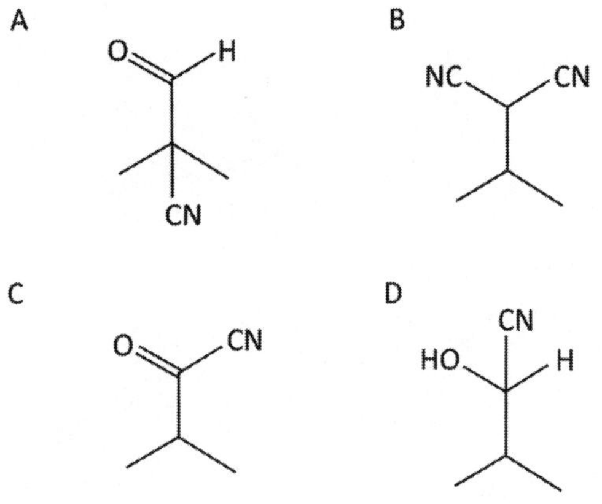
A
O
H
CN
B
NC
CN
C
O
CN
D
CN
HO
H

35. For the nucleophilic addition of an amine derivative shown below, what is the correct reaction product?

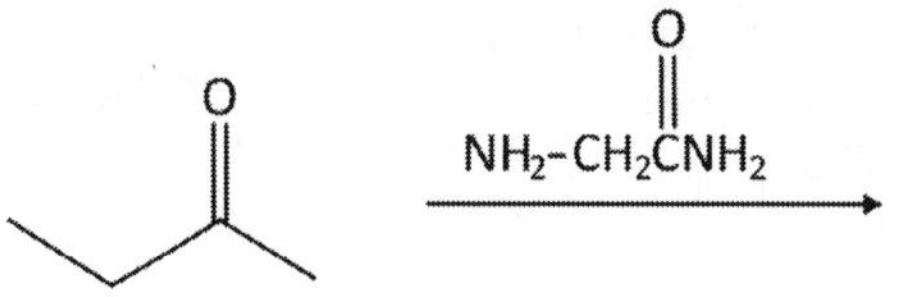

O
||
NH_2-CH_2CNH$_2$

A

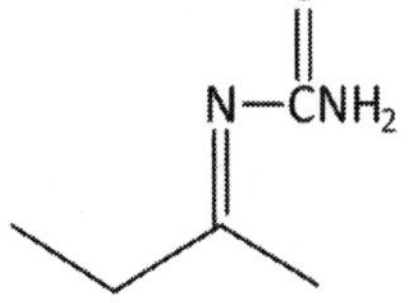

O
||
N—CNH$_2$

B

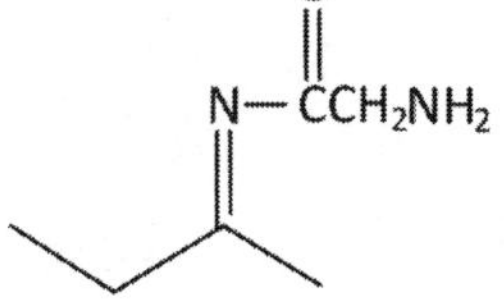

O
||
N— CCH$_2$NH$_2$

C

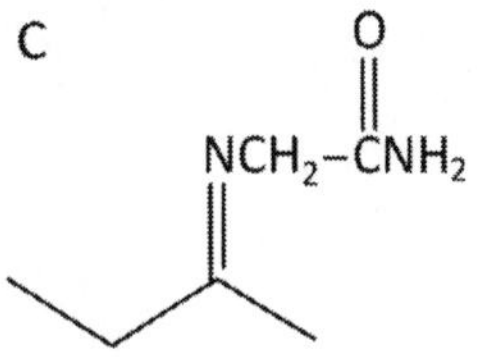

O
||
NCH$_2$–CNH$_2$

D

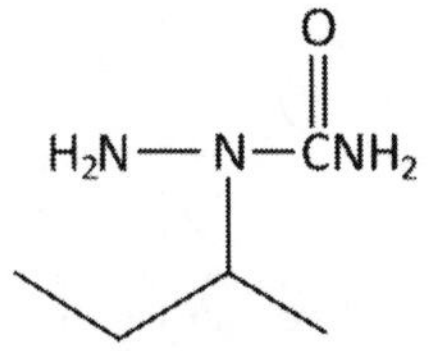

O
||
H$_2$N—N—CNH$_2$

36. Which product would be obtained when the following reactants are combined?

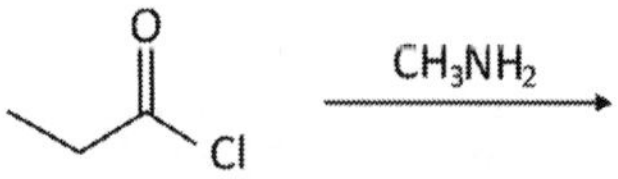

O
Cl
CH_3NH_2

A

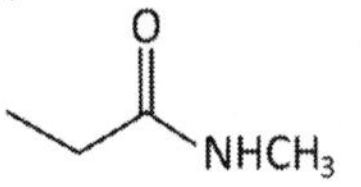

O
NHCH$_3$

B

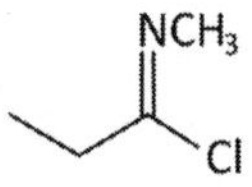

NCH$_3$
Cl

C

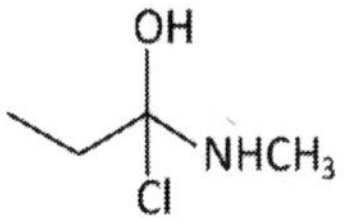

OH
NHCH$_3$
Cl

D

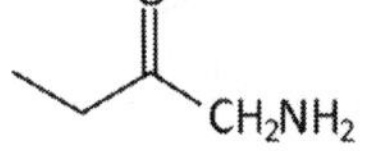

O
CH$_2$NH$_2$

37. Which reagent would produce the acid chloride shown below?

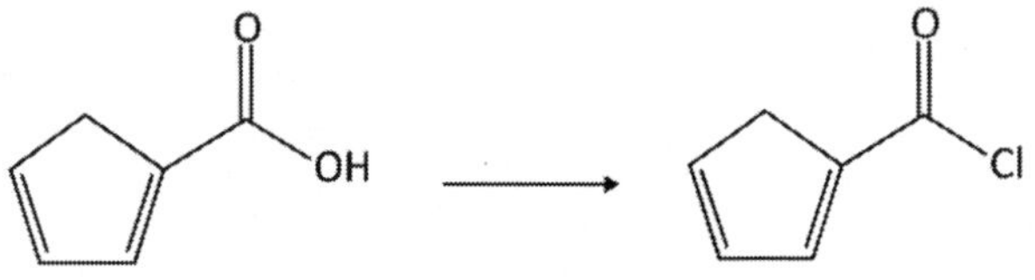

a. SO_2
b. $SOCl_2$
c. H_2SO_4
d. $SeCl_2$

38. What are the products for the following base hydrolysis reaction?

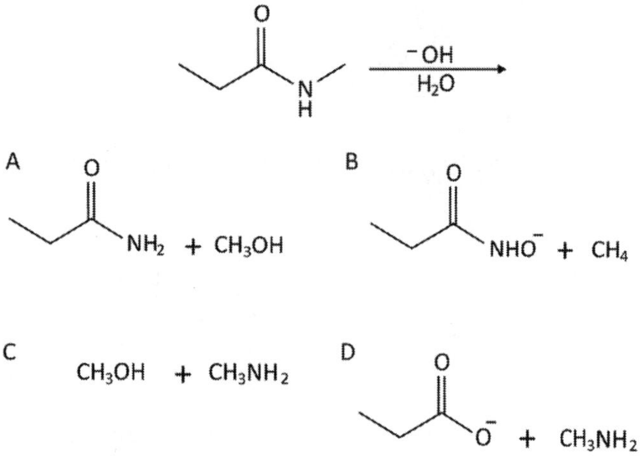

$\xrightarrow[H_2O]{^-OH}$

A NH_2 + CH_3OH

B NHO^- + CH_4

C CH_3OH + CH_3NH_2

D O^- + CH_3NH_2

39. The reaction sequence below leads to what final product?

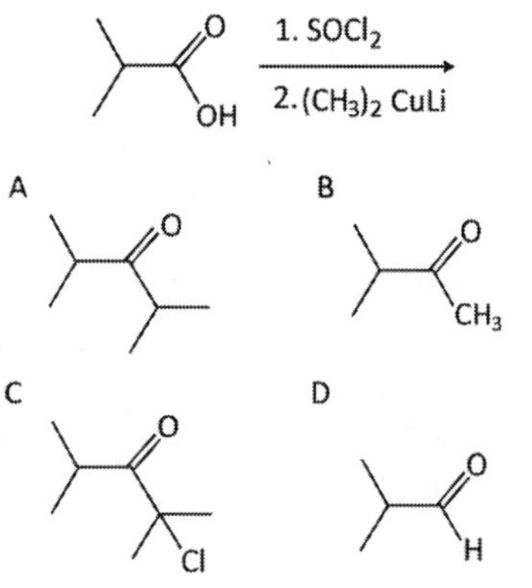

1. $SOCl_2$
2. $(CH_3)_2$ CuLi

A

B CH_3

C Cl

D H

40. What will be the correct intermediate for the following base-promoted hydrolysis reaction?

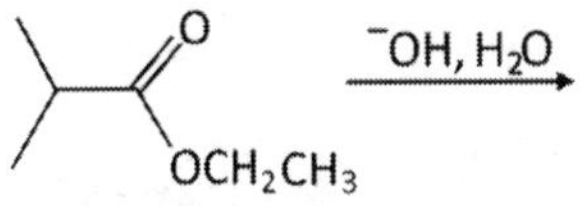

$^{-}OH, H_2O$

OCH_2CH_3

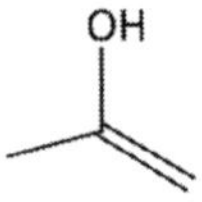

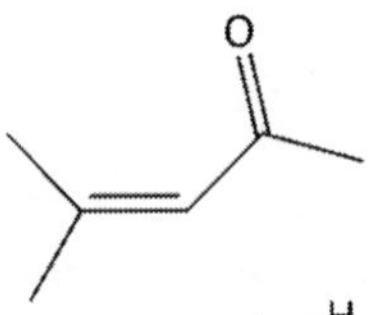

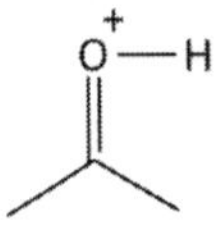

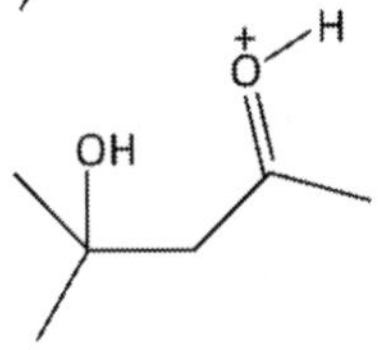

A

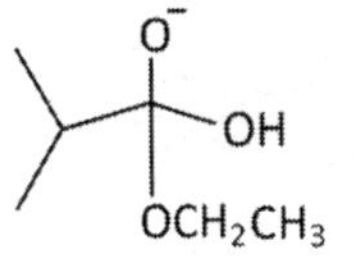

B

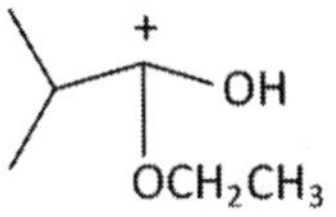

C

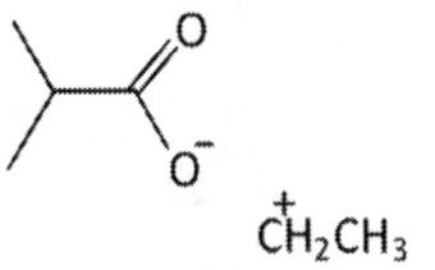

D

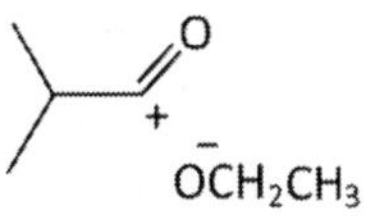

41. In an acid-catalyzed aldol condensation, what is the structure of the electrophilic species that the enol intermediate attacks?

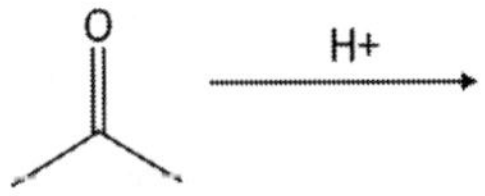

H+

A

B

C

D

42. What will be the products for the following reaction?

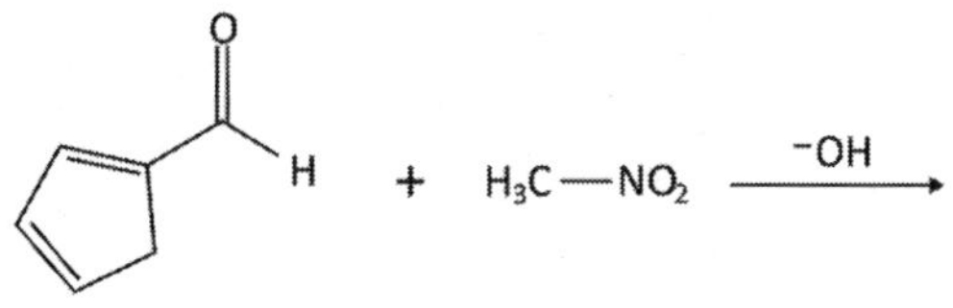

O H + $H_3C—NO_2$ $\xrightarrow{^{-}OH}$

A

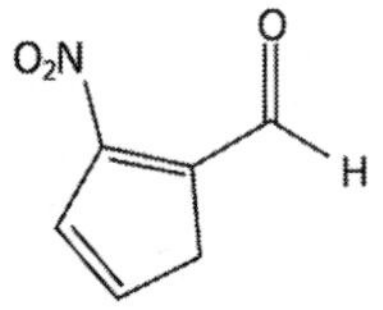

O_2N O H

B

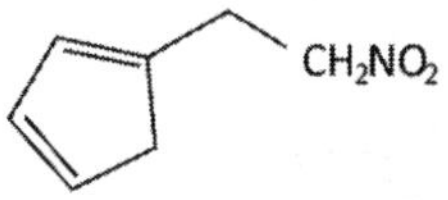

CH_2NO_2

C

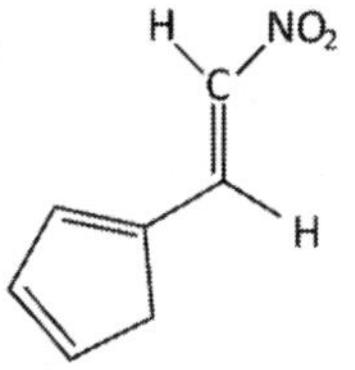

H NO_2 C H

D

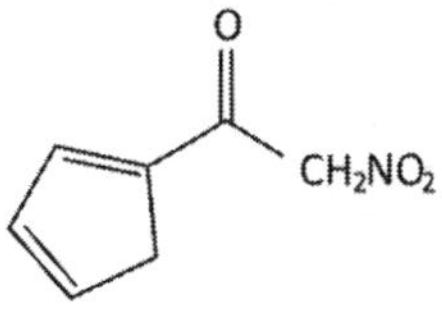

O CH_2NO_2

43. What will be the products for the ester and ketone reaction shown below?

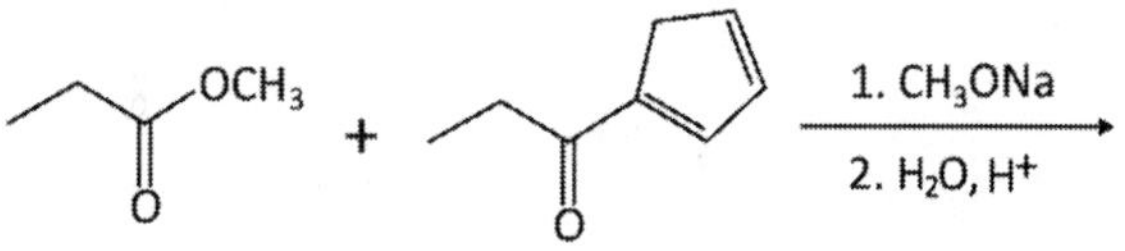

OCH_3 O + O

1. CH_3ONa

2. H_2O, H^+

A

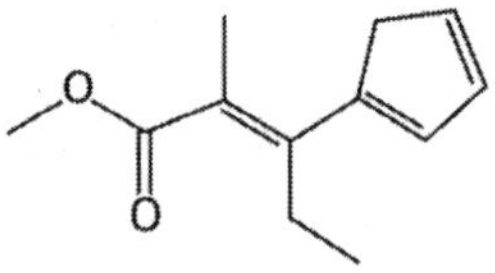

O O

B

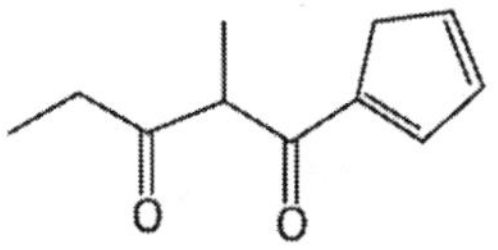

O O

C

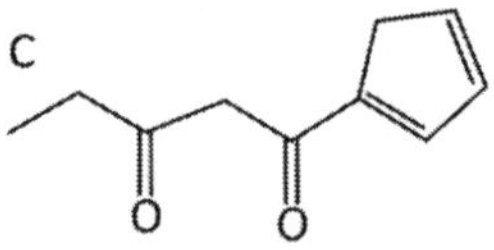

O O

D

O O

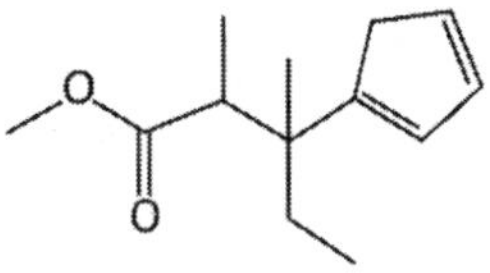

44. In an aldol reaction, two aldehyde molecules can react with one another, under basic conditions, to produce an addition product (for example, an aldol) and a dehydration product. What is the reason for the formation of the dehydration product that contains the $C = C$ bond?

a. Additional α hydrogens allow an additional reaction.
b. The aldol will readily undergo elimination of water to be stabilized by conjugation.
c. There is excess base.
d. Both aldehyde molecules are different.

45. What will be the reaction between the aldehyde and β-keto ester shown below?

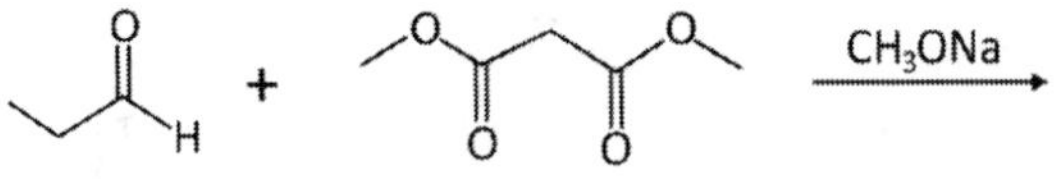

CH$_3$ONa

A

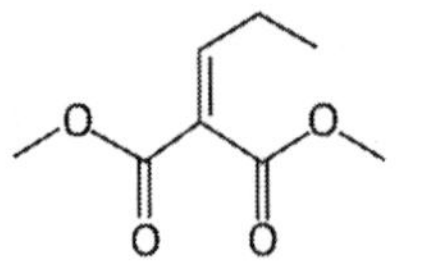

B

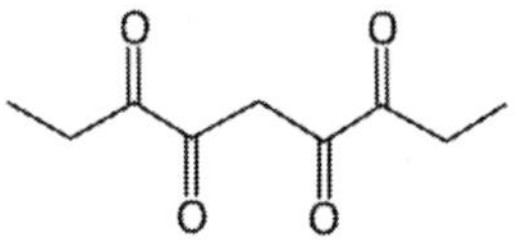

C

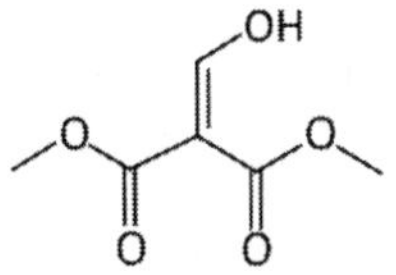

D

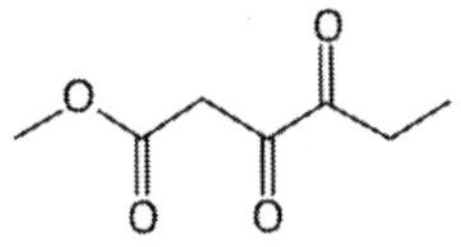

46. Which set of reagents will lead to the following transformation?

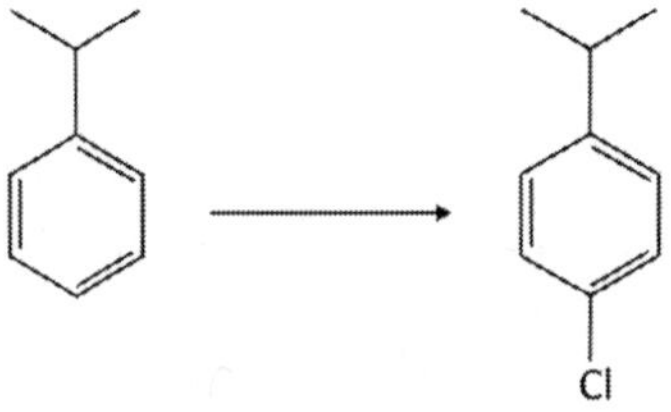

Cl

a. Cl_2 with UV light or heat
b. $NaCl$ and H_3O^+
c. Cl_2 and $FeCl_3$
d. Cl_2 in CCl_4

47. For the following reaction, which choice shows the correct sequence of reagents?

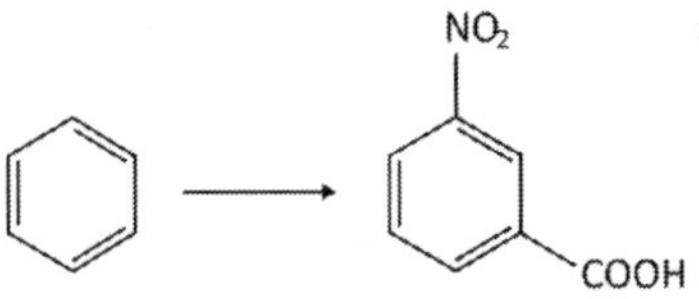

NO_2

COOH

a. First HNO_3/H_2SO_4 and heat, then $CH_3Cl/AlCl_3$, and finally $K_2Cr_2O_7/H_3O^+$ and heat
b. First $CH_3Cl/AlCl_3$, then $K_2Cr_2O_7/H_3O^+$ and heat, and finally HNO_3/H_2SO_4 and heat
c. First $CH_3COCl/AlCl_3$, then $K_2Cr_2O_7/H_3O^+$ and heat, and finally $NaNO_2$, HCl at 0 °C
d. First HNO_3/H_2SO_4 and heat, then $CH_3COCl/AlCl_3$, and finally $K_2Cr_2O_7/H_3O^+$ and heat

48. Determine the major product of the reaction below.

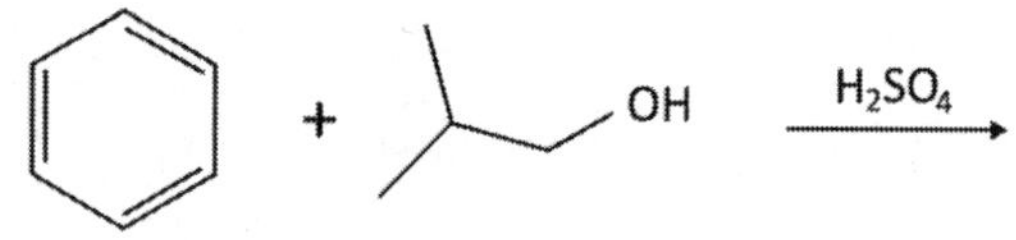

+ OH $\xrightarrow{H_2SO_4}$

A

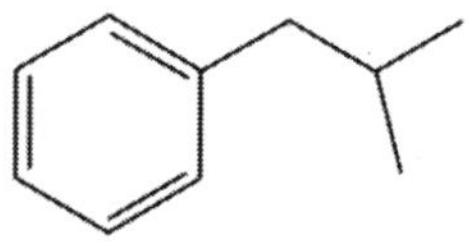

B

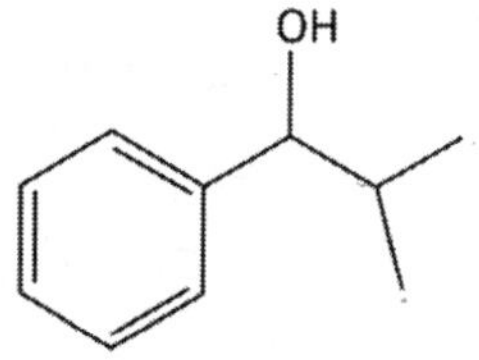

OH

C

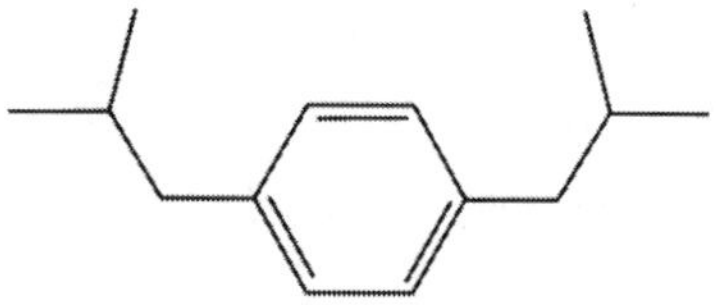

D

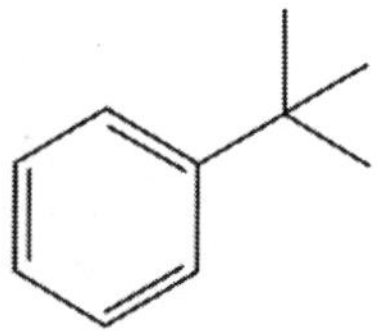

49. Which set of reagents below would produce isopropyl benzene from benzene?

a. $CH_3CH_2CH_2Cl$, $AlCl_3$
b. 1. Br_2, $FeBr_3$ 2. $CH_2CH_2CH_2MgBr$
c. 1. Cl_2, $FeCl_3$ 2. $CH_3CH = CHCl$, $AlCl_3$
d. 1. $CH_3CH_2 - (CO) - Cl$, $AlCl_3$ 2. Zn(Hg), conc., HCl

50. Consider the sulfonation of chlorobenzene below using SO_3/H_2SO_4. Which structure below explains why halogens are ortho-/para- directors?

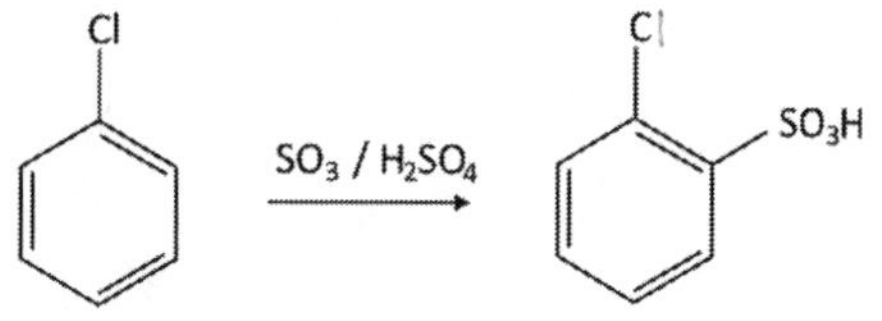

Cl $\xrightarrow{SO_3 / H_2SO_4}$ Cl, SO_3H

A

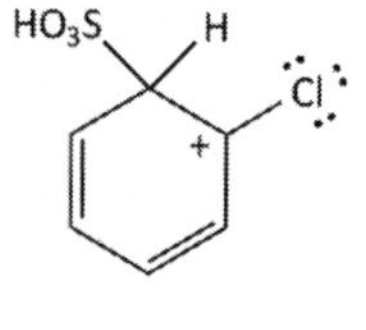

HO_3S H Cl +

B

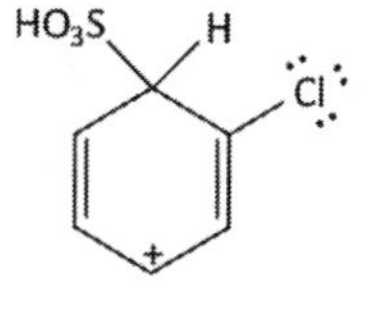

HO_3S H Cl +

C

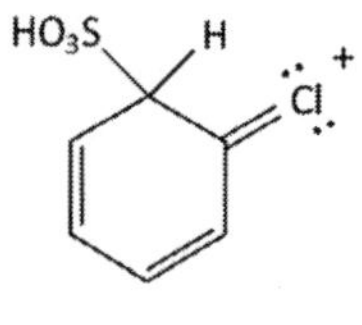

HO_3S H Cl +

D

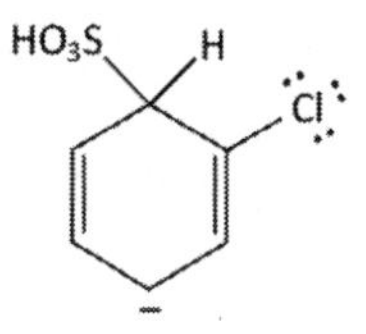

HO_3S H Cl −

51. What is the correct product for the reaction shown below?

HBr

Peroxides

A Br

B Br

C Br Br

D Br

52. Which of the following is the most stable radical?

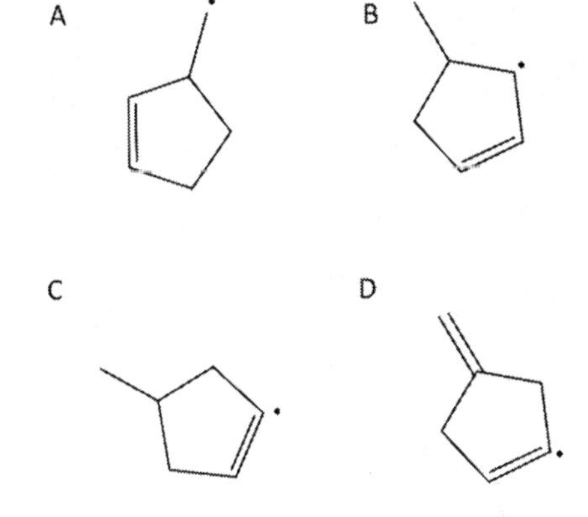

53. The copolymerization of the polymers shown below by free radical polymerization would produce what polymer?

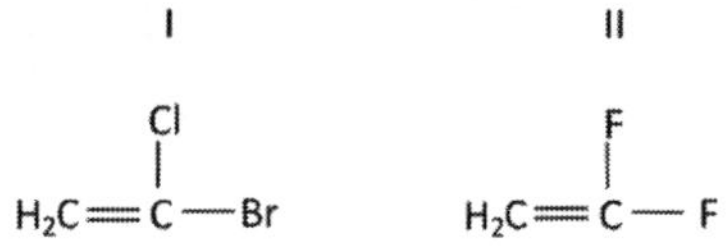

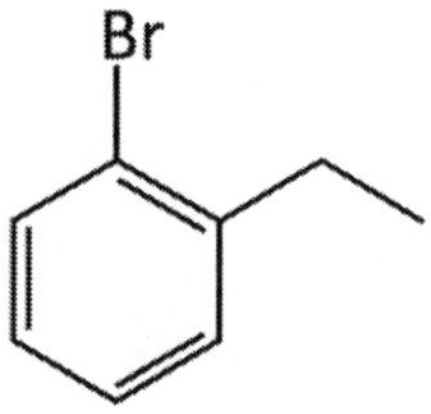

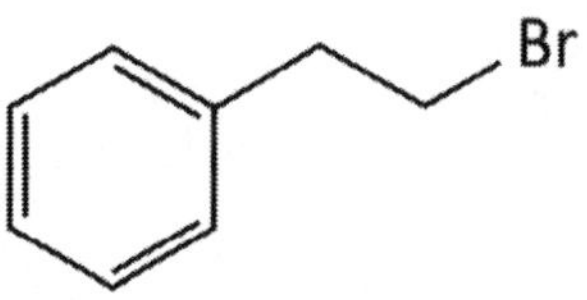

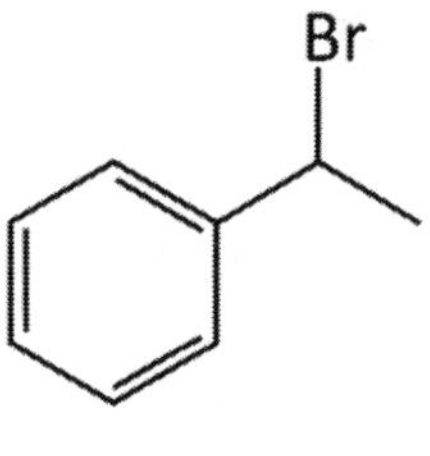

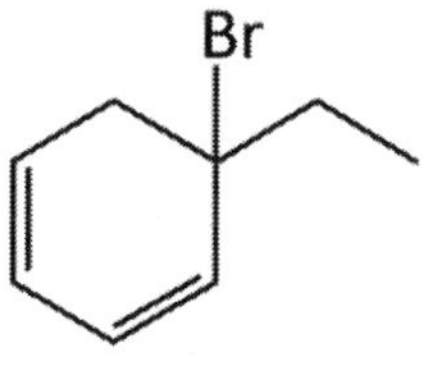

I: $H_2C{=}C(Cl)-Br$

II: $H_2C{=}C(F)-F$

A

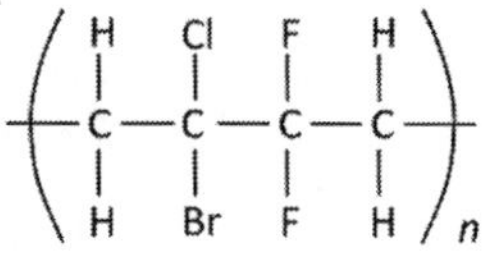

B

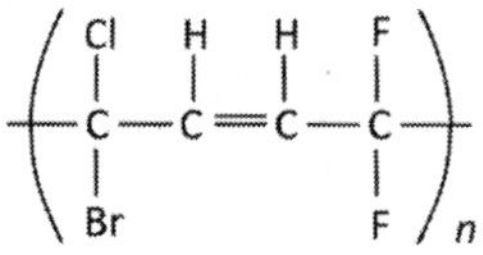

C

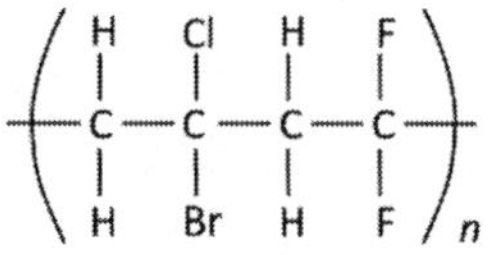

D

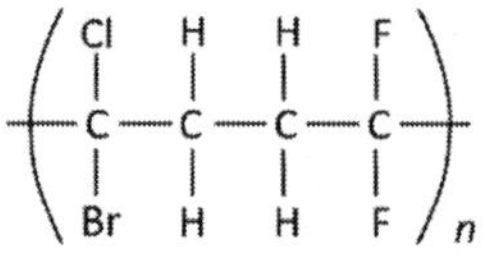

54. What is the most likely minor product that is formed in the following reaction?

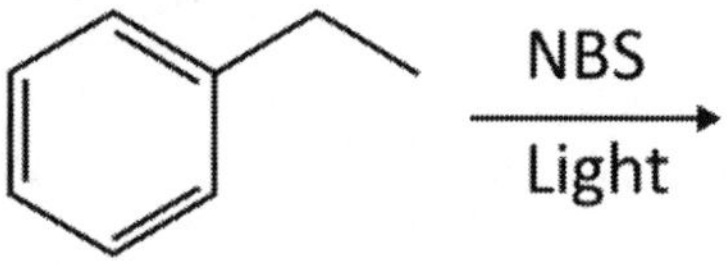

NBS

Light

A

B

C

D

55. Which of the following represents a propagation step in a free radical reaction?

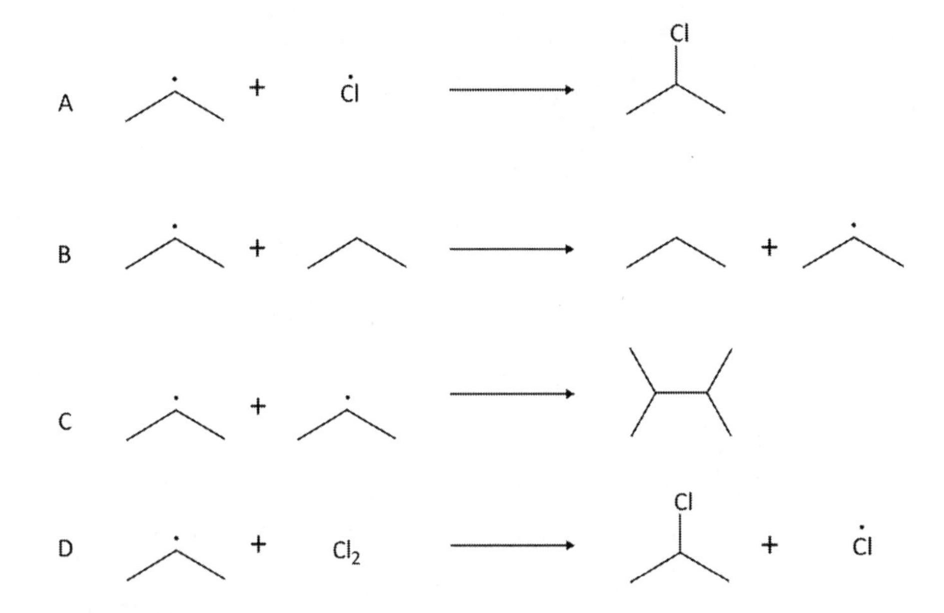

56. The following compound is subjected to an alkaline permanganate oxidation followed by neutralization. What is the final product?

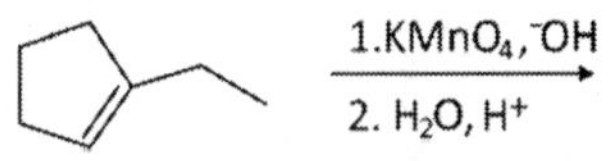

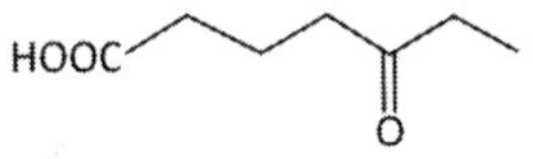

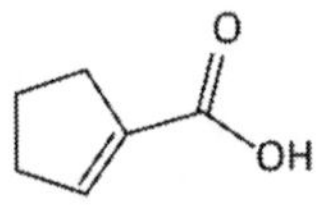

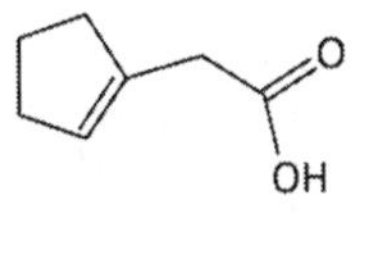

1. $KMnO_4$, ^{-}OH
2. H_2O, H^+

A HOOC O

B O OH

C O OH

D HOOC OH O

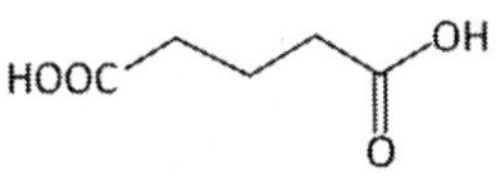

57. Which set of reagents is needed to produce the following product?

O

a. NH_2NH_2, KOH
b. $LiAlH_4$ and H_3O^+
c. $NaNH_2$, NH_3
d. H_2O, H^+

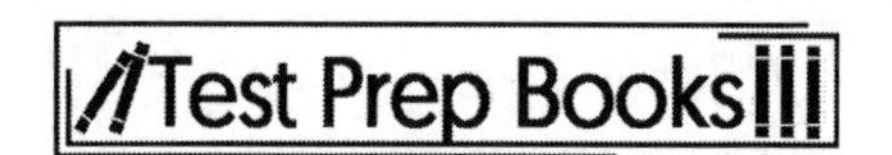

58. What are the products when the reactant below is treated with excess HIO_4?

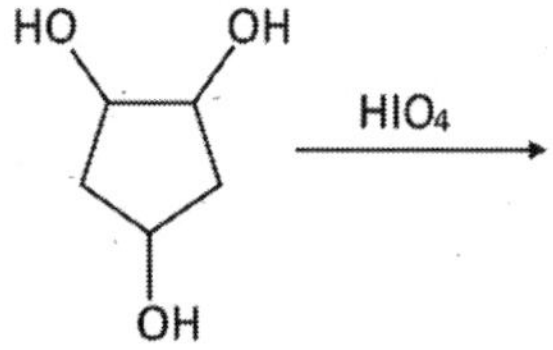

HO OH

HIO_4

OH

A

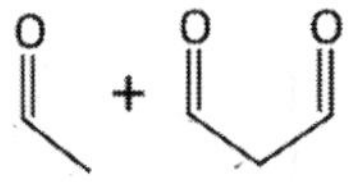

B

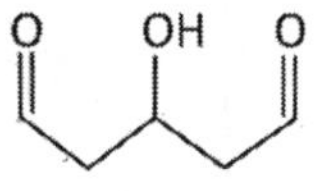

C

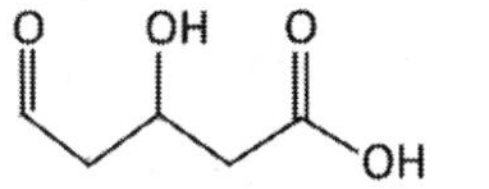

D

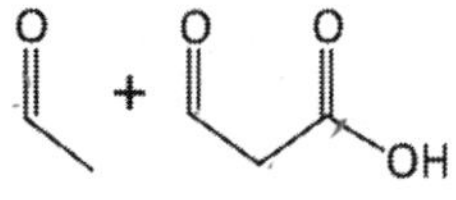

59. Which set of products is formed in the following oxidation reaction?

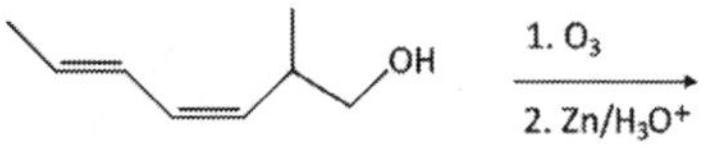

1. O_3
2. Zn/H_3O^+

A

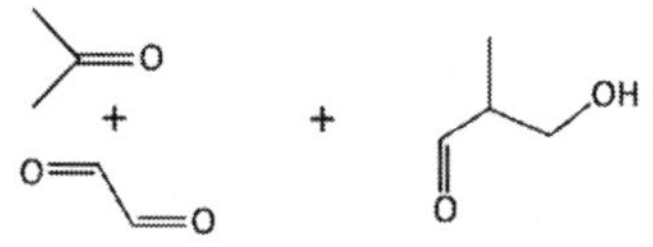

B

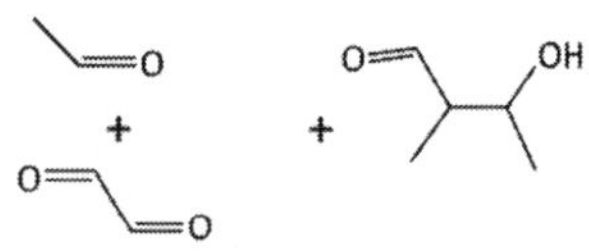

C

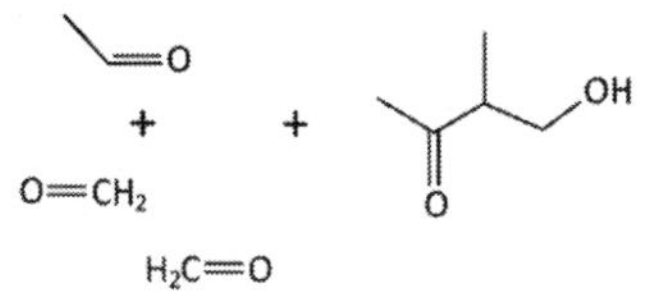

D

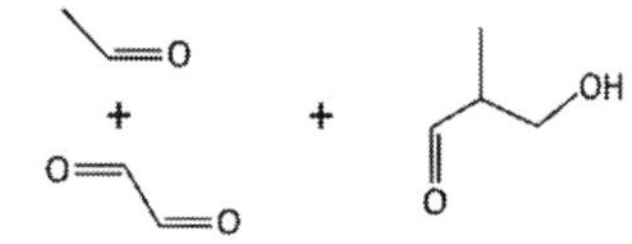

60. What set of reagents is needed for the reaction below?

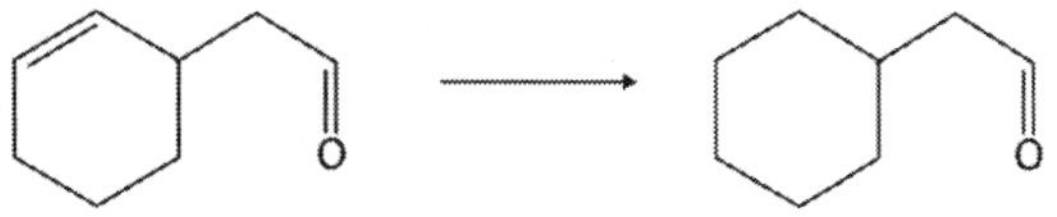

a. Jones reagent
b. Wolff-Kishner reagents
c. H_2, Pd/C
d. $LiAlH_4$ and H_3O^+

61. Which structure is consistent with the ^1_1H NMR spectrum below?

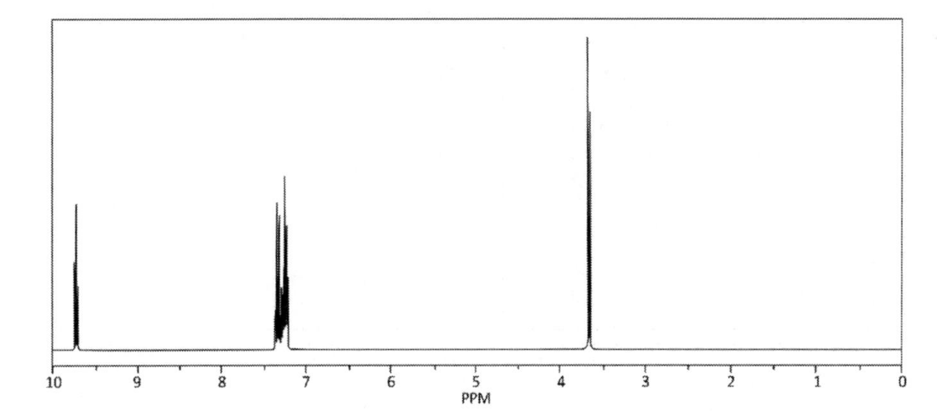

A

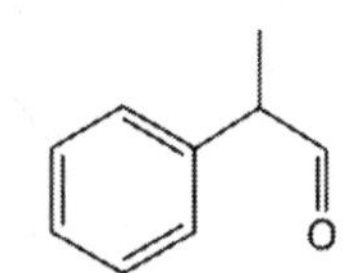

B

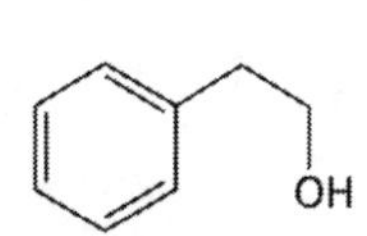

C

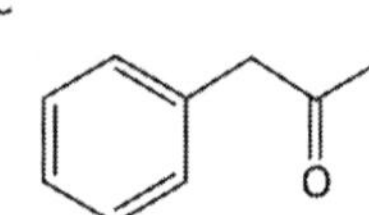

D

O

62. Which structure is consistent with the $^{13}_{6}C$ NMR spectrum below?

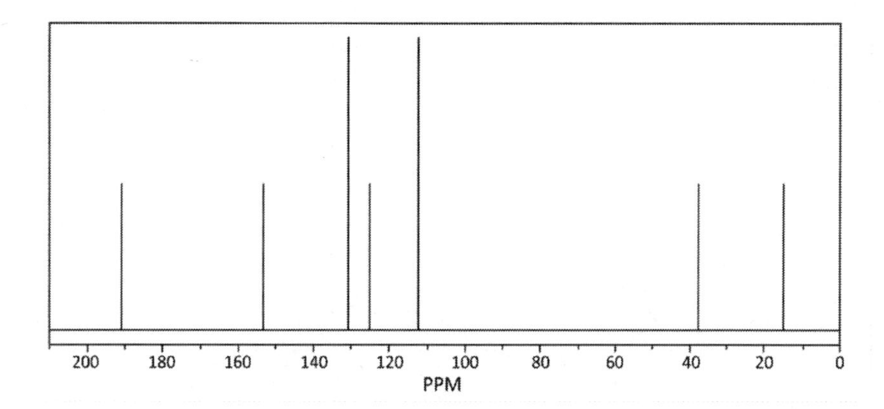

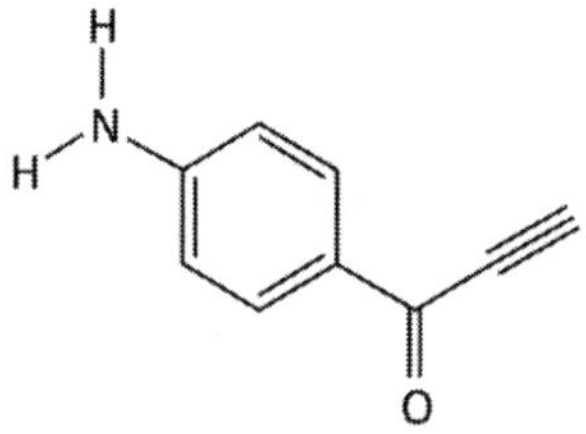

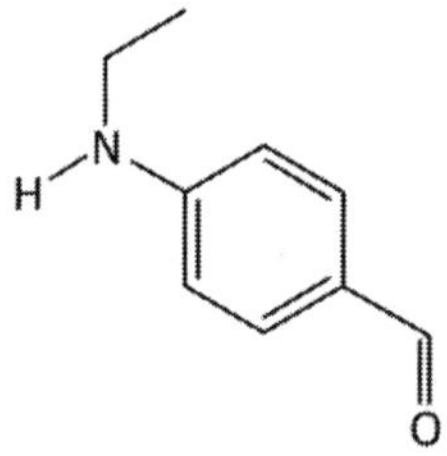

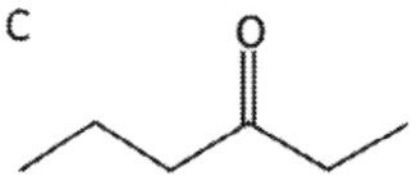

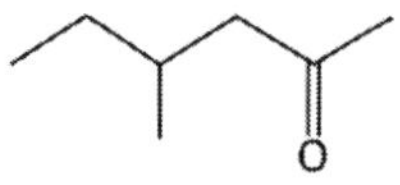

A

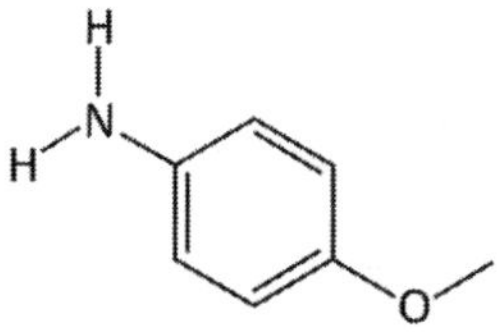

H
N
H

O

B

H
N
H

O

C

H
N

O

D

N
H

OH

O

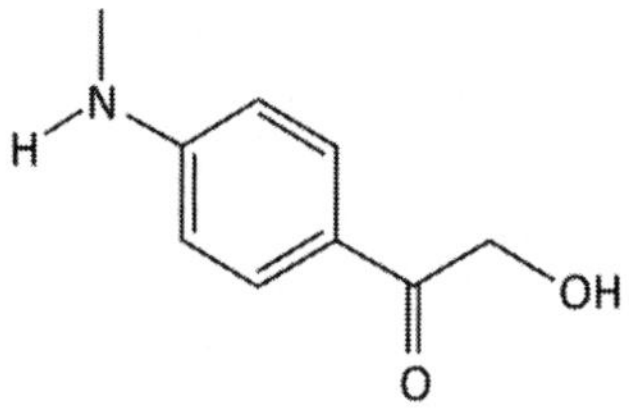

63. Which compound below will show a major fragment at $\frac{m}{z} = 100$ and 85 in its mass spectrum?

A

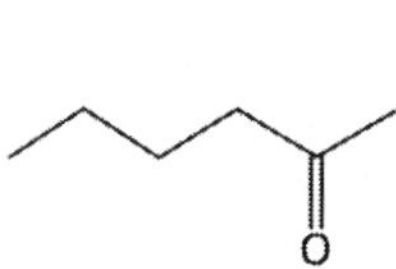

B

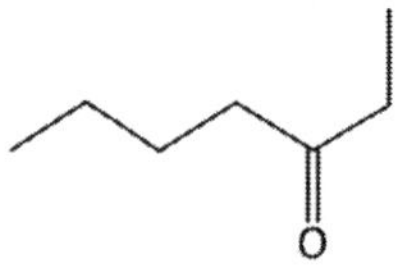

O

C

O

D

O

64. Which compound below corresponds to the following IR spectrum?

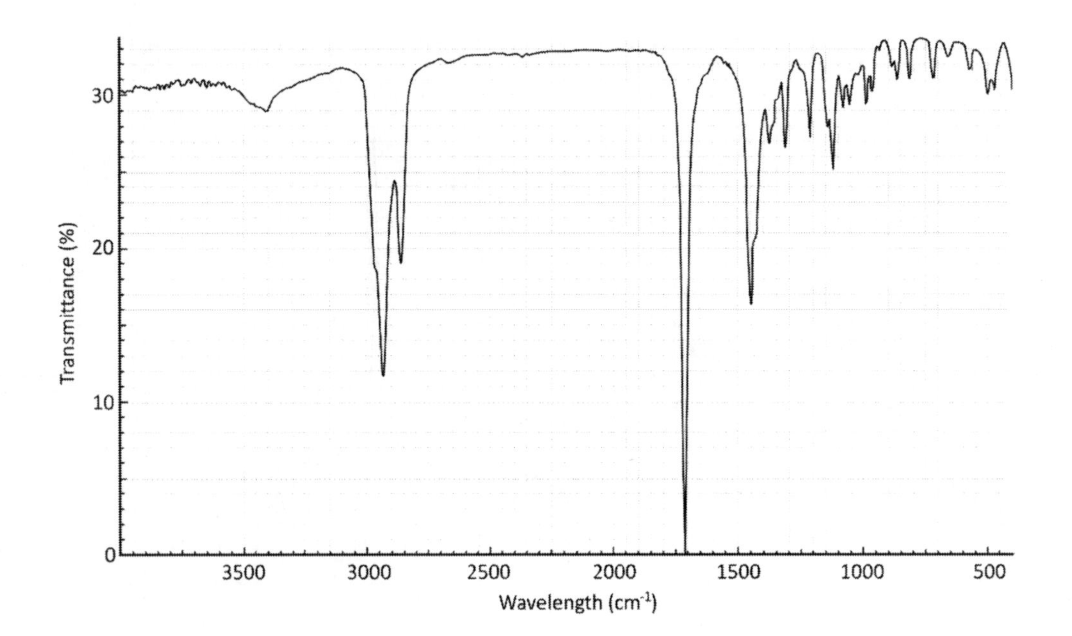

A

O=C–H (benzaldehyde)

B

O=C–OCH_3 (methyl benzoate)

C

(2-methylcyclohexanone)

D

O=C–OH (cyclohexene carboxylic acid)

65. Which structure is consistent with the following ^1_1H NMR spectrum?

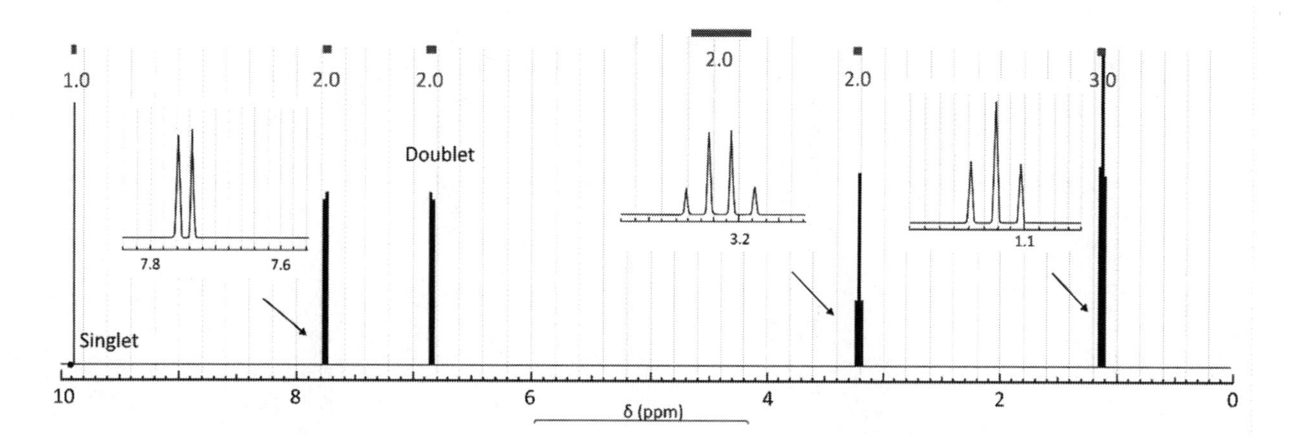

A

B

C

D

66. What will be the major product of the following reaction sequence?

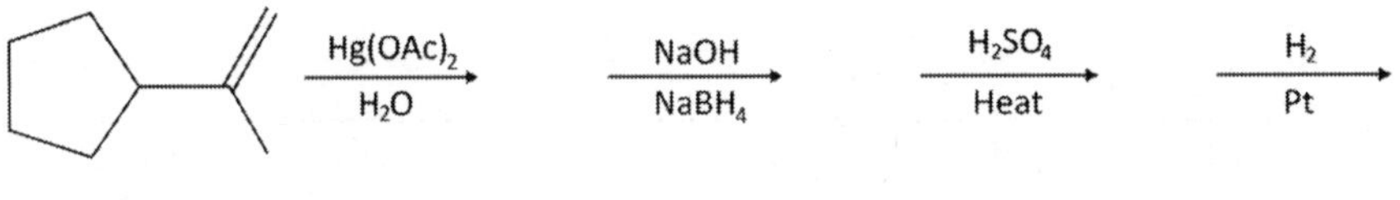

Reagents: $Hg(OAc)_2$, H_2O → NaOH, $NaBH_4$ → H_2SO_4, Heat → H_2, Pt

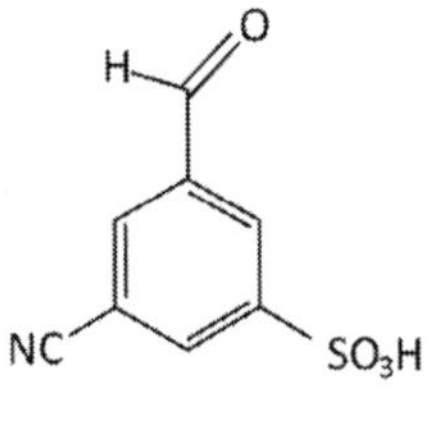

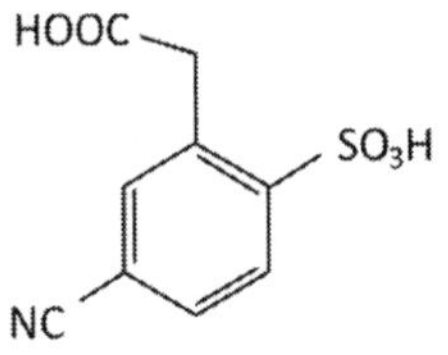

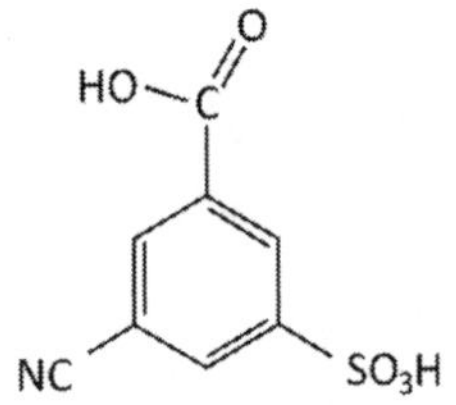

A

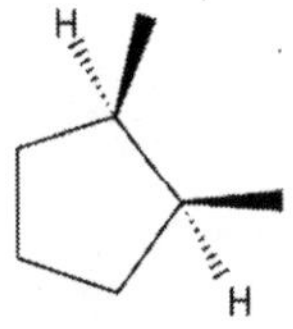

B

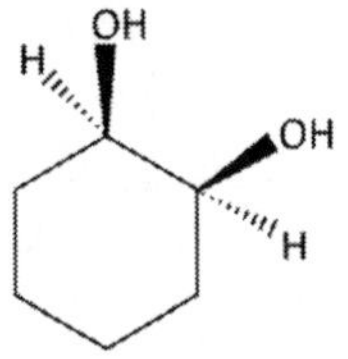

C

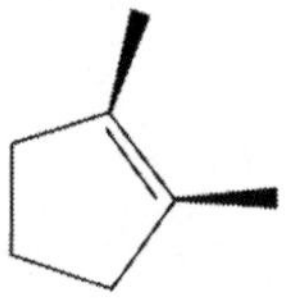

D

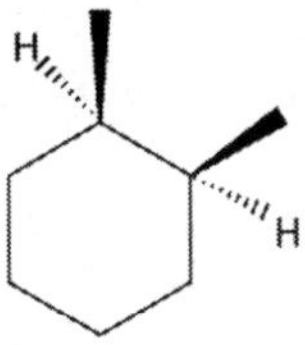

67. What will be the final product in the reaction sequence below?

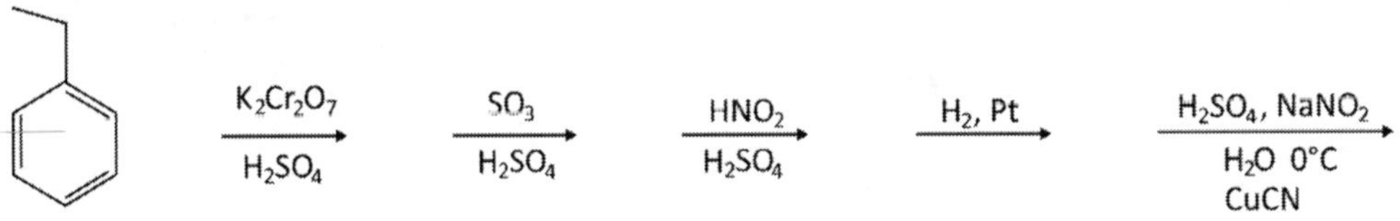

Reagents: $K_2Cr_2O_7$, H_2SO_4 → SO_3, H_2SO_4 → HNO_2, H_2SO_4 → H_2, Pt → H_2SO_4, $NaNO_2$, H_2O 0°C, CuCN

A

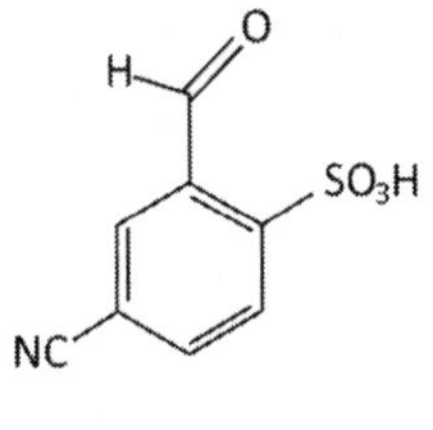

B

C

D

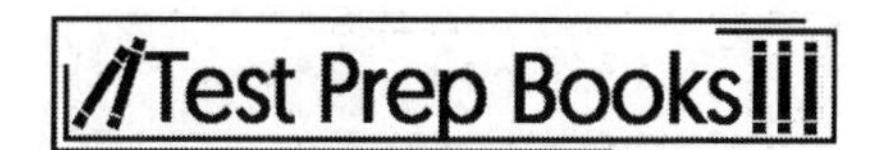

68. What is the correct reaction product for the following reaction?

$\xrightarrow[CCl_4]{Br_2}$ $\xrightarrow[110\text{-}160°C]{3\ NaNH_2}$ $\xrightarrow{NH_4Cl}$ $\xrightarrow[NH_3]{NaNH_2}$ $\xrightarrow{CH_3Br}$

A. $H_3C{-}C{\equiv}C{-}H$

B. $H_3C{-}C{\equiv}C{-}CH_3$

C. $H_3C(H)C{=}C(H)H$

D. $H_3C(H)C{=}C(H)CH_3$

69. An unknown alkene undergoes ozonolysis and produces the following compound.

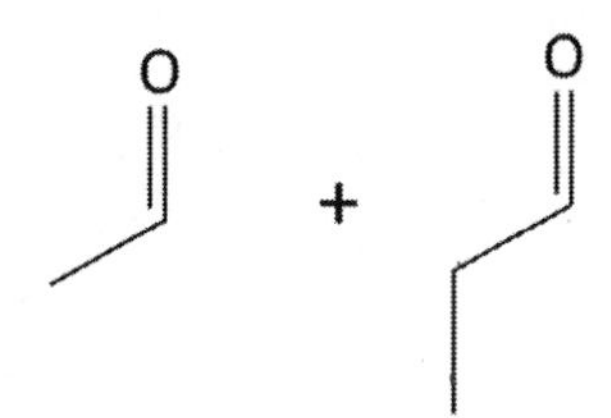

When the original compound is treated with Br_2/CCl_4, an optically inactive compound is produced, even when each isomer is isolated. Which of the following alkenes is consistent with previous observations?

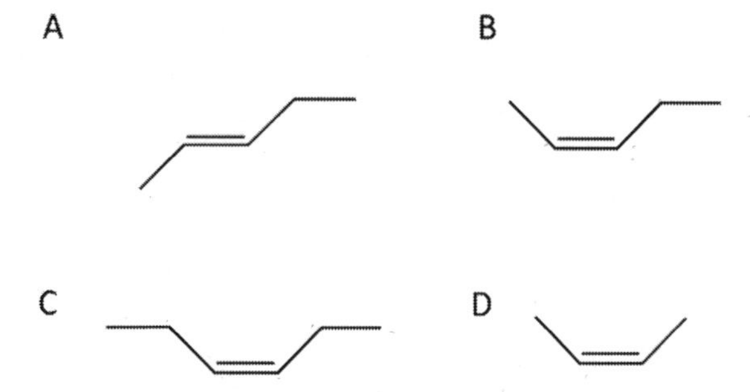

70. An optically active alcohol undergoes catalytical hydrogenation to produce an optically inactive compound. Which of the following molecules below corresponds to the starting alcohol?

A

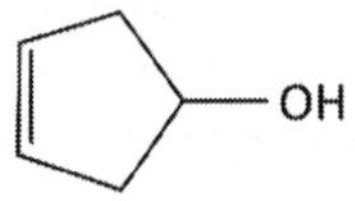

B

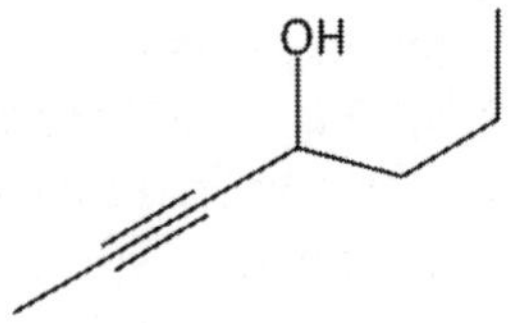

C

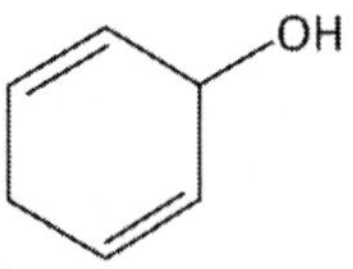

D

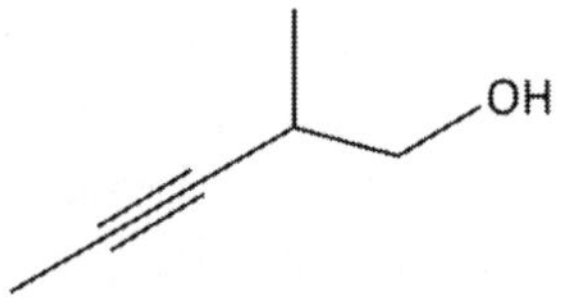

Answer Explanations

1. D The correct IUPAC name is N-(3-chlorophenyl) ethanamide. Two types of functional groups are present on the benzene ring: a halogen and an amide group. The IUPAC name for the amide group is ethanamide, and the common name is acetamide. The halogen is a chlorine atom and can have the prefix name "chloro." The "N-" means that a substituent is attached to nitrogen, for example, a chlorophenyl group, and is bonded to nitrogen on ethanamide (at the third position, in place of one of the nitrogens). Notice that the term "m" is not used in the IUPAC system. In addition, having an "m" and a "3" to indicate the position of ethanamide is redundant. Benzyl refers to a $C_6H_5 - CH_2$ or $Ar - CH_2$ group and is not to be confused with a phenyl group, C_6H_5.

2. A: The compound is an alcohol, and the IUPAC name will follow a convention where alcohols have the highest priority. The longest carbon chain consists of six carbon atoms, and the base name will be of the form hexanol. The hydroxyl group is located on the third atom (not the fourth). The base name can either be hexan-3-ol or 3-hexanol. The chlorine group is found at the second carbon atom and will be labeled as 2-chloro in the IUPAC name. A methyl group is located at the fifth carbon atom and will be labeled as 5-methyl. IUPAC names are listed in alphabetical order, for example, chloro before methyl. Therefore the IUPAC name is 2-chloro-5-methyl-3-hexanol or 2-chloro-5-methylhexan-3-ol.

3. D: The longest chain must consist of five carbon atoms with a double bond starting at the second carbon atom, for example, $C2 = C3$. Furthermore, there are two bromines bonded to the carbon one atom, thereby eliminating Choices *A* and *B* as the correct answers. Choice *C* is called (*Z*)-1,1-dibromo-2-pentene since the higher-priority groups are placed on the same side. The $-CH_2CH_3$ group is bonded to $C3$, and the $(Br)_2CH -$ group is bonded to $C2$. The $-CH_2CH_3$ and $(Br)_2CH -$ group are on the same side. The letter *Z* denotes the cis isomer. The correct answer is Choice *D* since it's an *E* isomer that contains the higher priority groups placed opposite or trans to one another.

4. A: Choice *A* contains the following functional groups found left to right on the molecule: an amide (NH_2), an ester group $(-(CO) - O)$, and a carboxylic acid group $(-(CO) - OH)$. Choice *B* contains an amide and carboxylic acid group but not an ester group. Choice *B* also contains a ketone. Choice *C* contains an amide, an ester, an alkene, and a hydroxyl group. Choice *D* contains an amide, an alkene, an ether, and a carboxylic acid group.

5. B: The base name decene indicates that the longest carbon chain is ten carbon atoms in length. Therefore Choices *A* and *C* are eliminated because the longest carbon chains consist of nine and eight atoms. The alkene group begins at the third carbon atom, for example, $C3 = C4$. Two methyl groups are located at the third and fifth carbon. The main difference between Choice *B* and Choice *D* occurs at carbon 3. Choice *D* is the *E* isomer since the higher priority groups about carbon 3 and 4 are opposite or trans to one another. In contrast, Choice *B* has the higher priority groups placed on the same side. Therefore, Choice *B* is the correct answer and corresponds to the name (*Z*)-3,5-dimethyl-3-decene.

6. A: The bond angle of a $C - C = C$ bond in benzene is similar to ethylene and has a bond angle of about 120 °C. The $H - C = C$ or $H - C - C$ bond angle in benzene is also roughly 120 °C. The three main hybridizations in a carbon atom are sp, sp^2, and sp^3. Acetylene is a molecule that contains two sp hybridized carbon atoms: $H - C \equiv C - H$. The bond angle for the $H - C \equiv C$ bond is 180° since acetylene has a linear geometry. Ethylene is a molecule that contains two sp^2 hybridized atoms: $H_2C = CH_2$. The bond angle at an $H - C = C$ bond is roughly 120° since ethylene has a trigonal planar geometry about the carbon atom. Methane is a molecule that contains one sp^3 hybridized carbon atom: CH_4. The $H - C - H$ bond angle is 109.5°.

7. C: Atoms I, II, III, and IV are sp^2, sp^3, sp^2, and sp hybridized. An sp^2 hybridized atom contains one double bond and two single bonds. An sp^3 hybridized atom contains four single bonds. For example, atom II is a carbon atom that is bonded to two different carbon atoms, a hydrogen atom, and an oxygen atom. Choices *A* and *B* are incorrect since atom II is designated as an sp^2 hybridized atom. Choice *D* is incorrect since an sp^3 hybridization state is designated for atom IV. Atom IV is sp hybridized, meaning that it contains one triple bond and one single bond.

8. B: The definition of a formal charge is given as follows.

$$\text{Formal charge } (FC) \text{ of an atom} = \#\text{ of valence e}^- - \left[\frac{1}{2}\#\text{ bonding e}^- + \#\text{nonbonding e}^-\right]$$

The number of valences electrons for an atom can be determined by looking at the group number of the atom within the periodic table. Sulfur belongs to group 6A and will have a total of six valence electrons. The number of valence electrons in the equation will remain fixed, but the number of bonding and nonbonding electrons will change. The formal charges for sulfur in Choices *A* through *D* are shown below.

Choice *A*:

$$FC = 6 - \left[\frac{1}{2}(8) + (2)\right] = 0$$

Choice *B*:

$$FC = 6 - \left[\frac{1}{2}(6) + (2)\right] = +1$$

Choice *C*:

$$FC = 6 - \left[\frac{1}{2}(8) + (0)\right] = +2$$

Choice *D*:

$$FC = 6 - \left[\frac{1}{2}(4) + (4)\right] = 0$$

Choice *B* represents a Lewis structure that contains a sulfur atom with a formal charge of +1.

9. A: The order of stability for carbocations is given as follows:

$$3°\ ((CH_3)_3C^+) > 2°((CH_3)_2CH^+) > 1°\left(CH_3CH_2{}^+\right) > \text{methyl}\left(CH_3{}^+\right) > \text{vinyl}\ (C - C = C^+)$$

Primary 1° allylic carbocations ($C = C - C^+$) have about the same stability as primary 1 ° benzylic carbocations $\left(C_6H_5 - CH_3{}^+\right)$ and may be less stable than or as stable as a tertiary 3° carbocation. Choices *A*, *B*, *C*, and *D* are aromatic carbocations. Choice *A* is a secondary 2° carbocation and is the most stable. Choice *B* resembles a vinyl or aryl carbocation and maybe the least stable. Choice *C* is an aromatic methyl carbocation and Choice *D* is an aromatic primary carbocation 1°. Choice *C* may have

greater stability since it's bonded to a carbon atom that is sp^2 hybridized and may undergo resonance. The general order of increasing stability is: B ≤ D < C < A.

10. B: The Hückel rule explains the criteria for aromaticity. For example, in benzene, there is a total of 6 π electrons. Based on the Hückel rule, the value of n must be a whole integer value such that it gives the total number of π electrons in the compound. For benzene, $n = 1$ since $4(1) + 2 = 6\,\pi$ electrons. In contrast, an anti-aromatic compound follows the $4n$ rule. Structures I, II, and III contain 12, 6, and 12 π electrons. Structures I and II are both anti-aromatic since $4n = 12, n = 3$. Based on the Hückel rule, $4n + 2$, only structure II is aromatic since $4n + 2 = 6, n = 1$.

11. D: As more electron-withdrawing groups are placed closer to the carboxylic acid functional group, the inductive effect becomes greater, and the proton on the acid group becomes more easily removed. Choice *A* is the weakest acid since it does not contain any electron-withdrawing groups close to the acid group (COOH). Choice *C* is a weaker acid than Choice *B*. Choice *D* is the strongest acid since it contains two fluorine groups that are closest to the acid group. If the question had asked for the strongest carboxylate base (for example, $\mathrm{CH_3 - CH_2 - COO^-}$), then Choice *A* would be the correct answer, and Choice *D* would be the weakest base (for example, $\mathrm{CH_3 - CF_2 - COO^-}$).

12. B: The larger the ionization constant K_a, the stronger the acid. Protons that have a large K_a will have a small $\mathrm{p}K_\mathrm{a}$. Removal of a proton from an acid will create a carbanion, for example, $\mathrm{HC \equiv CH}$ to $\mathrm{HC \equiv C{:}^-}$. Therefore, the most acidic proton will correspond to the most stable carbanion. The greater the 's' character in a carbanion, the more stable the carbanion. The protons bonded to ethyne $(\mathrm{HC \equiv CH}$, $\mathrm{p}K_\mathrm{a} = 25)$ will be more acidic than ethene $(\mathrm{H_2C = CH_2}, \mathrm{p}K_\mathrm{a} = 44)$, which is more acidic than ethane $(\mathrm{H_3C - CH_3}, \mathrm{p}K_\mathrm{a} = 50)$. Therefore, Choice *B* is the most acidic since it contains a proton with the smallest pK_a.

13. C: The pH scale generally ranges from zero to 14. Since $\mathrm{pH + pOH = 14}$, then $\mathrm{pOH = pH = 7}$. For a neutral solution, the amino and carboxylic groups must have opposite charges such that the overall charge of the molecule is neutral. The structure in Choice *C* is the predominant form of the amino acid when the solution is neutral. If the pH is less than 7, then the solution would be acidic, and the amino and carboxyl group would be protonated: $\mathrm{NH_2}$ to $\mathrm{NH_3}^+$ and $\mathrm{-O^-}$ to $\mathrm{-OH}$. The structure in Choice *D* would correspond to a structure where the $\mathrm{pH} < 7$. If the $\mathrm{pH} > 7$, the solution would be basic, and the amino and carboxyl group would be deprotonated: $\mathrm{NH_3}^+$ to $\mathrm{NH_2}$ and $\mathrm{-OH}$ to $\mathrm{-O^-}$. The structure in Choice *B* would correspond to a structure where the pH is greater than 7.

14. C: Choices *A*, *B*, and *C* represent possible resonance structures for a deprotonated molecule of 4-hydroxybenzoic acid. The structure in Choice *C* corresponds to the most stable resonance structure since the molecule is stabilized by conjugation, with the carboxylate group bearing the negative charge on both oxygen atoms. A deprotonated phenol (phenolate) is less acidic than 4-hydroxybenzoic acid since it cannot form a similar or more resonance stabilized structures. Phenolate $(\mathrm{Ar - OH})$ doesn't have an electron withdrawing substituent, for example, COOH, so it cannot form additional resonance-stabilized structures.

15. B: The molecule shown is called pyrazole and is similar in structure to imidazole but less basic. The decreased basicity of pyrazole is due to the closer proximity of the second nitrogen atom, which brings about a stronger inductive effect. Nitrogen atom 1 is not basic because its π electrons are part of the aromatic ring system. Therefore, its lone pairs are not readily donated. Nitrogen atom 2 is basic and can donate its lone pair of electrons to a proton. When the second nitrogen atom is protonated, the lone pair of electrons from nitrogen atom one will delocalize to form a resonance-stabilized ion.

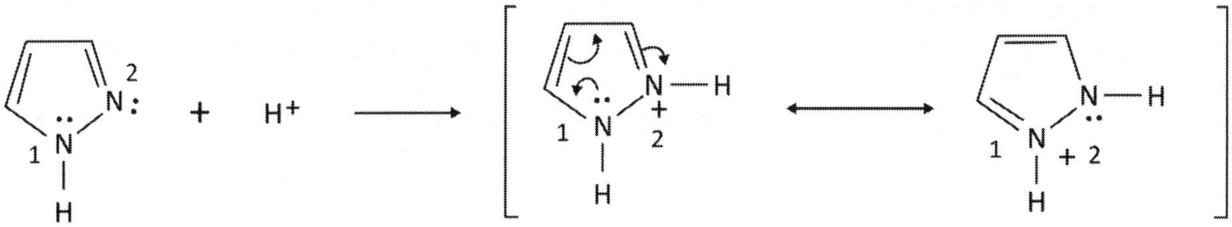

16. B: To determine whether a molecule has an *R* or *S* configuration, direct the lowest priority group away from you, as shown below. The order of the priority groups from lowest to highest in the structure in Choice *B* is CH_3, CH_2OH, $-(CO) - H$, and OH.

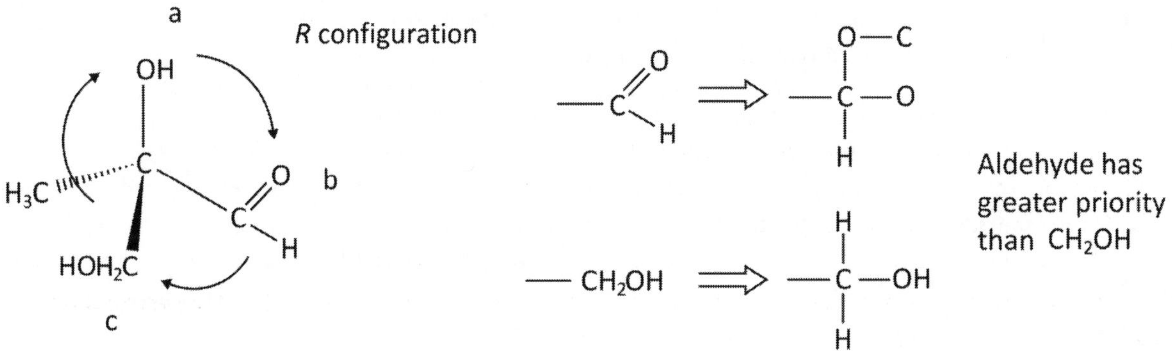

R configuration

Aldehyde has greater priority than CH_2OH

17. A: The Fischer projection can be represented by the following wedge and dash structure.

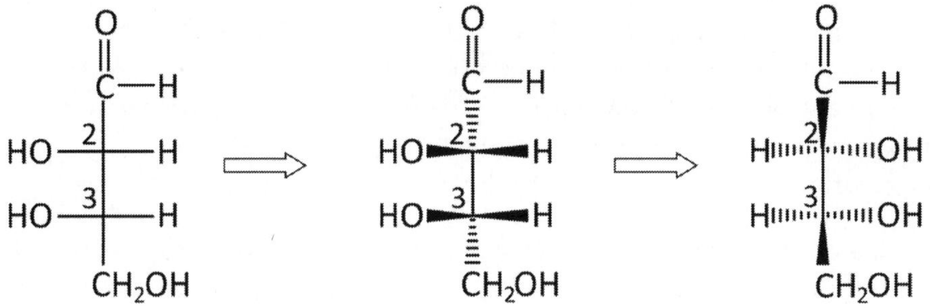

The stereochemistry configurations can be determined by orienting the lowest priority group away for each stereogenic carbon. If we look closely at carbon 2, with the lowest priority group pointed away, the configuration is *S*. Similarly, carbon 3 has an *S* configuration.

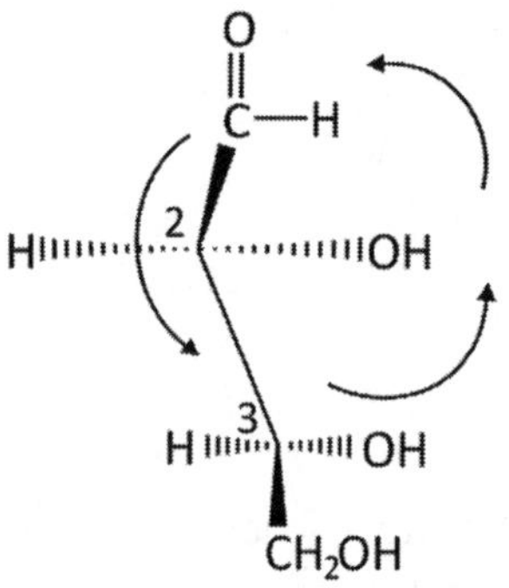

S configuration

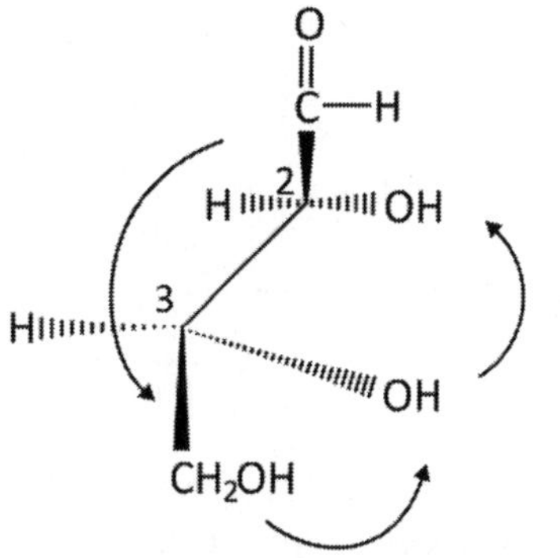

S configuration

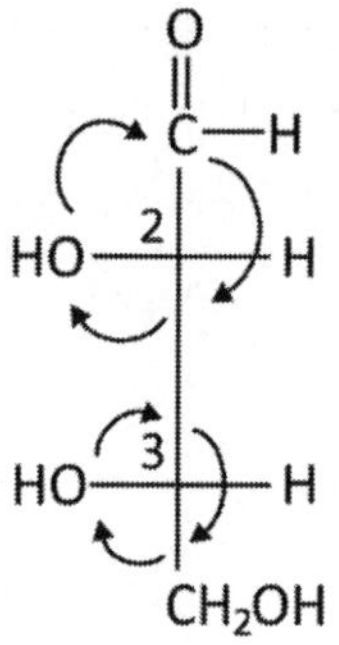

Appears to be *R* but is *S*

Appears to be *R* but is *S*

The correct answer choice is Choice *A*: 2*S*, 3*S*.

18. C: Enantiomers are stereoisomers that are mirror images of one another but not superimposable. The mirror image of the structure in Choice *C* is not superimposable.

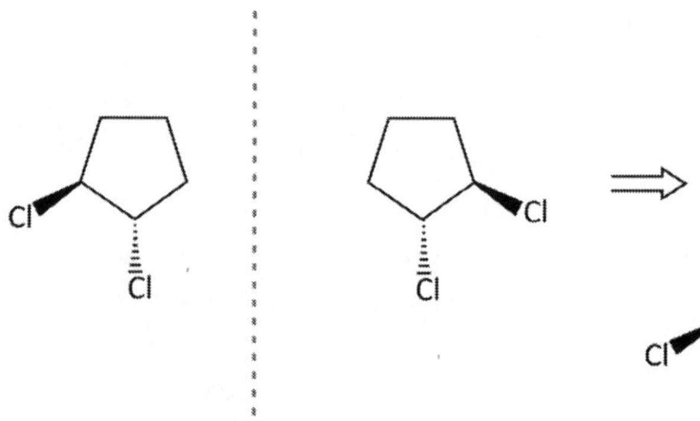

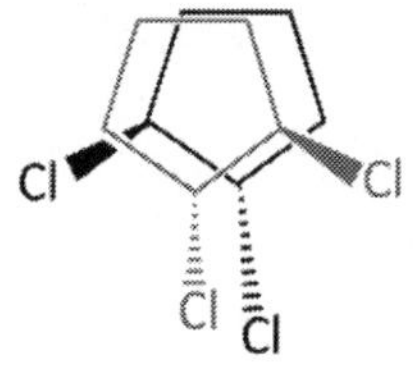

Mirror image: horizontal flip

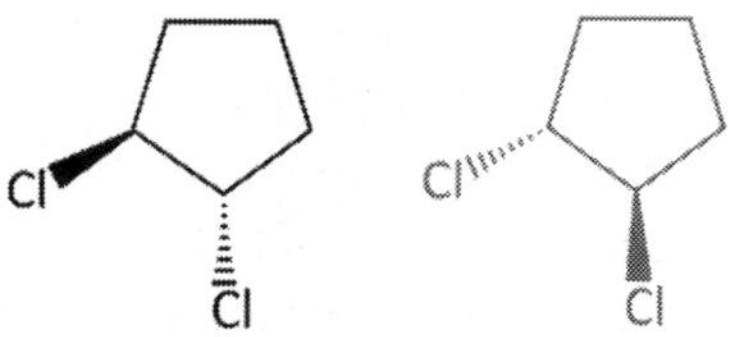

Not superimposable

The mirror images of Choices *A*, *B*, and *D* are superimposable. The mirror image of Choice *D* can be rotated such that it is superimposable.

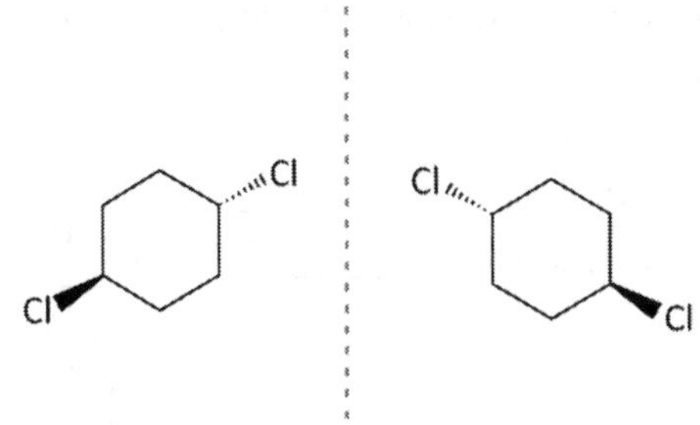

19. B: To determine the number of stereocenters, identify the number of carbon atoms that are bonded to four different substituents. Each stereocenter is shown on the right side of the figure below.

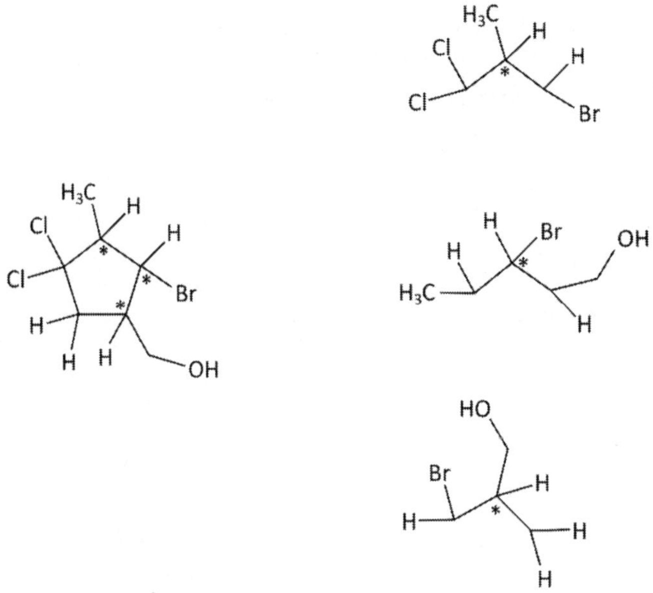

Three carbons are bonded to four substituents, represented by an asterisk in the figure above. Two carbon atoms are not stereogenic. For example, one carbon atom is bonded to two chlorine atoms, and another carbon atom is bonded to two hydrogen atoms.

20. D: Each cyclohexane structure adopts a chair conformation. The placement of the substituents, either in the axial or equatorial position, determines the stability of the molecule. The structures in Choices *A* and *B* are not stable since a methyl group (axial) and the tert-butyl group (equatorial) group are not only adjacent to one another but placed on the same face. The structure in Choice *B* is less stable than Choice *A* since the hydroxyl group is in an axial position. Choices *C* and *D* are more stable than Choices *A* and *B* because the methyl and tert-butyl groups occupy an equatorial position that is on opposite faces of the ring. However, Choice *D* is more stable than Choice *C* since the hydroxyl group is placed in an equatorial position that minimizes steric interaction.

21. D: The carbocations in Choices *A*, *B*, and *C* will undergo rearrangement; Choice *D* does not. Choice *A* is a primary 1° carbocation that can rearrange into a 2° and subsequently into a 3° carbocation. Choice *B* is a secondary carbocation, but a methyl group can be transferred or shifted to the carbocation to create a 3° at the adjacent carbon atom.

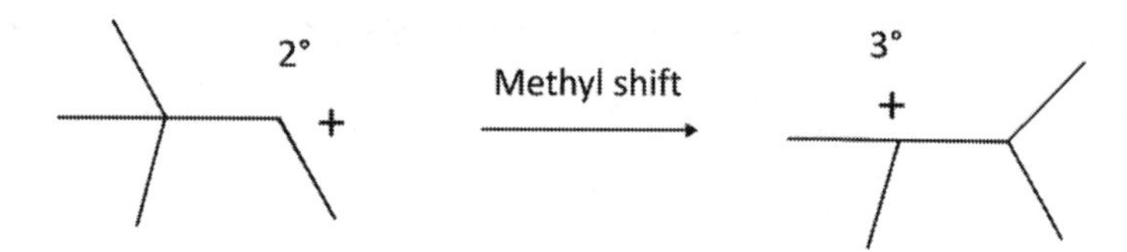

Choice *C* is a 2° carbocation that will rearrange into a 3° carbocation. Choice *D* is 3° and will not undergo further rearrangement.

22. C: Secondary 2° and 3° alcohols ($-\mathrm{OH}$) can react with hydrogen halides (for example, HBr) by an S_N1 reaction mechanism. A 1,2 alkyl or 1,2 hydride rearrangement can occur to form a more stable carbocation. The alkyl halide is derived from the more stable carbocation. From the given structure, a 1,2 alkyl rearrangement can occur when the hydroxyl group is removed.

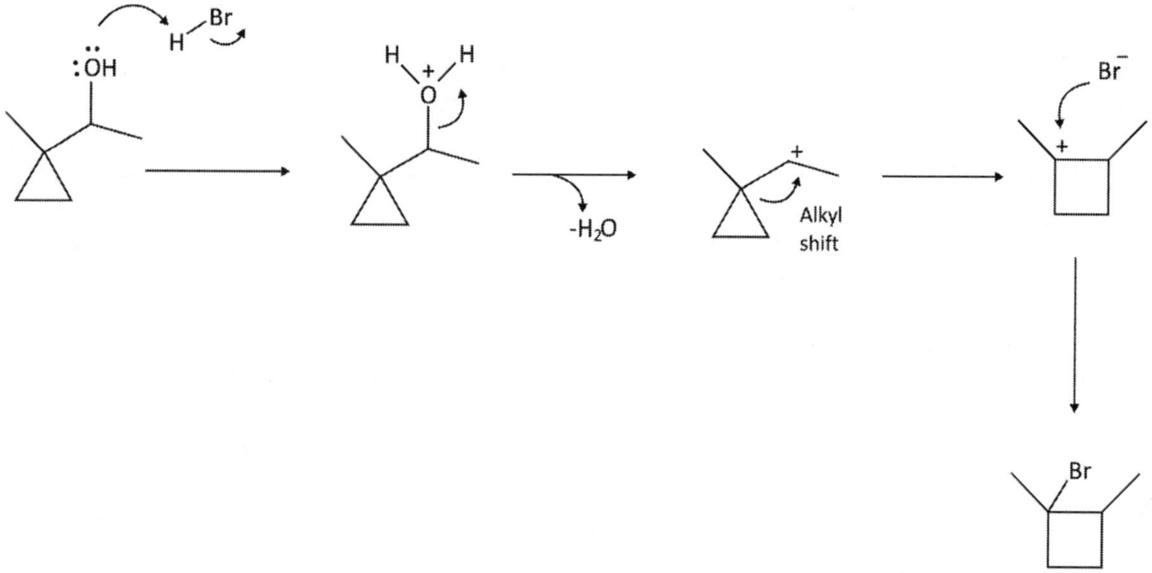

A new ring structure is formed with a 3° carbocation. The bromine atom then attacks the carbocation to form a halogenated substituted product. The possibility of the cyclopropane opening to a cyclopentane is excluded here since the 2° carbocation would have to form a less stable 1 °carbocation.

23. D: Epoxides will be under ring strain and consequently undergo nucleophilic attack at one of the $\mathrm{C}-\mathrm{O}$ bonds, thereby cleaving the $\mathrm{C}-\mathrm{O}$ bond. Epoxide reactions can take place in a basic or acidic medium. Ring-opening will occur by an S_N2 mechanism regardless of whether the oxygen atom is protonated or not. But the regiochemistry will differ and depend on whether or not the O atom is protonated before the nucleophilic attack. Under basic conditions, when the O atom is not protonated, a normal S_N2 reaction will occur. The less substituted carbon will be attacked. Under acidic conditions, when the O atom is protonated, the highly substituted carbon will be attacked, for example, 3° carbon atom. Nucleophilic attack will occur on the backside of the $\mathrm{C}-\mathrm{O}$ bond. The reaction results in an inversion of configuration at the reaction site. The site at which the alcohol forms retains its configuration. A ring-type epoxide will provide a product whereby the $-OH$ group and nucleophile (for example, CH_3O^-) are trans to each other. Choices *B* and *D* represent structures where the nucleophile is substituted at the less substituted carbon. Choice *B* is incorrect since the hydroxyl group does not retain its configuration, nor is it trans to $-OCH_3$. Choice *D* has the correct regiochemistry since the $-OH$ group retains its configuration and is trans to the $-OCH_3$ group.

24. A: The mechanism for alcohol dehydration is shown below.

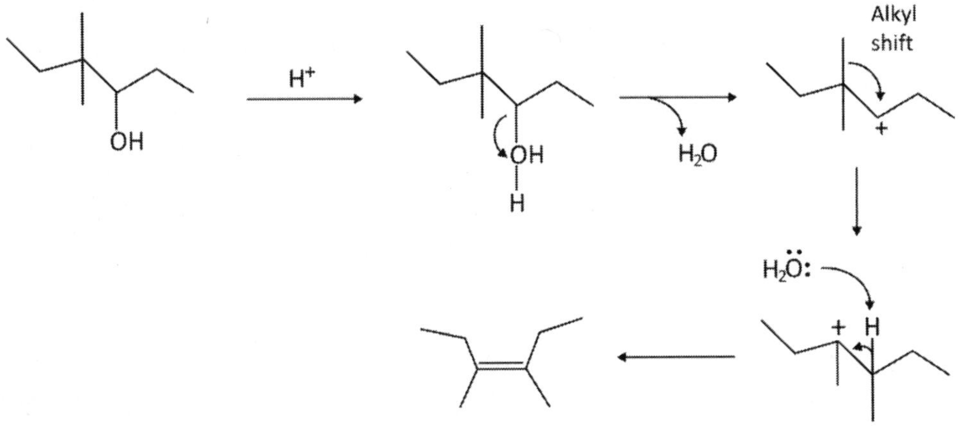

An alkyl shift (methanide shift) occurs after the second step, causing the 2° carbocation to rearrange to a 3° carbocation. A water molecule acts as a base and abstracts a proton from the original carbon atom that was a carbocation. Recall that Zaitsev's rule says that the more substituted alkene forms more favorably since they are more stable than less substituted alkenes.

25. D: The tertiary 3 °alkyl halide will proceed through an E2 reaction. An E2 elimination, unlike an E1, is promoted by a strong base such as sodium ethoxide. The base is involved in the rate-determining step and involves second-order kinetics since the two molecules must combine for the reaction to take place. For steric reasons, the reaction cannot proceed through a substitution reaction. Therefore, it's easier for the unhindered base to attack a β hydrogen. As the hydrogen atom is removed, the alkene double bond begins to form, and the halogen leaves simultaneously. The general reaction mechanism is shown below.

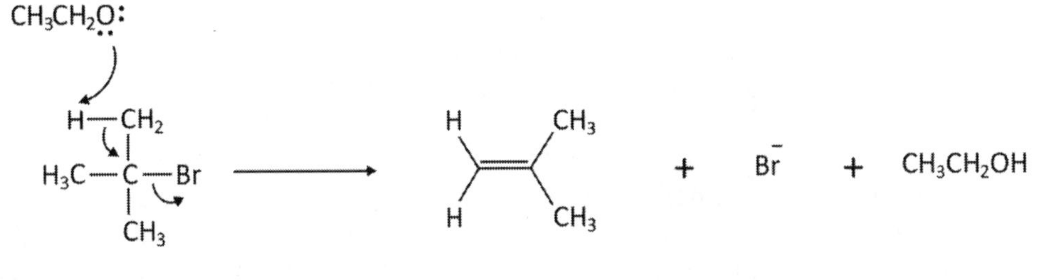

26. D: The reaction involves hydrogen halide addition to an unsymmetrical alkene. Based on Markovnikov's rule, when HCl is added to an unsymmetrical alkene, the electrophilic hydrogen atom is attached to the carbon atom, in $C = C$, that is bonded to more hydrogen atoms. Hydrohalogenation is regioselective but is nonstereoselective. The hydrogen atom will bond to the carbon that contains more hydrogen atoms. The halogen will bond to the carbon atom that has fewer hydrogen atoms. In the

hydrohalogenation of alkenes, carbocation rearrangements can occur and will determine where the halogen atom bonds.

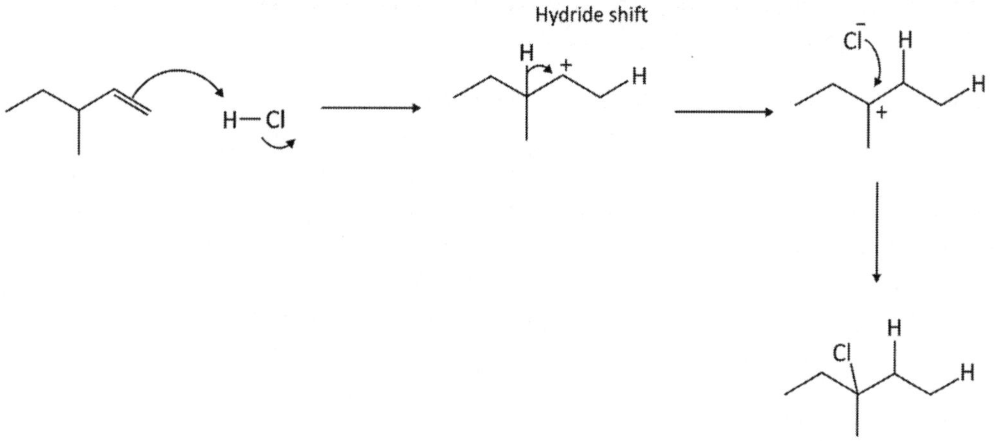

Choice *C* represents a product where a 2° could have reacted with the chlorine atom. But a halide shift occurs, and a 3° carbocation is formed. Choice *D* represents the correct structure that is obtained when the halogen attacks at the 3° site.

27. B: Like hydrohalogenation of alkenes, acid-catalyzed hydration is a Markovnikov addition. Hydration can also result in carbocation rearrangement. The general reaction mechanism is shown below.

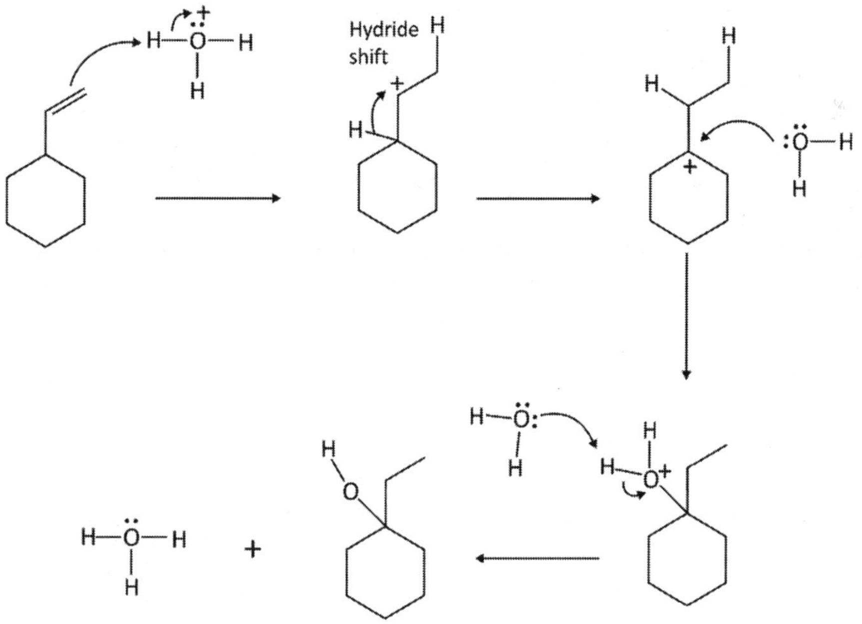

Choice *C* is incorrect since carbocation rearrangement from a 2° to 3° occurs. Choice *B* is the correct answer choice.

28. B: Unlike acid-base catalyzation, carbocation rearrangement does not occur in oxymercuration reactions. The addition of HgOAc forms an intramolecular coordinate covalent bond with the terminal carbon 2 in $C1 = C2$. Carbon 1 of the original double bond will then bond to $HgOAc$ to form a mercurinium ion. The addition of a water molecule will occur at the slightly positive carbon $(C1)$. Treatment with $NaBH_4$ removes the mercury component, $HgOAc$, to form an alcohol located at the 2° carbon atom. In other words, a hydroxyl group is added at carbon 1 of the double bond. Choice *B* represents the final product.

29. C: Oxymercuration-demercuration reactions involves a Markovnikov addition of water to an alkene with no carbocation or carbon skeleton rearrangement. In contrast, hydroboration involves an anti-Markovnikov addition of water to an alkene. Hydroboration is a stereoselective syn addition. Therefore, a hydroxyl group will be added at the terminal end of the alkene $(-C_1 = C_2 - H)$ onto carbon atom 2. A hydrogen atom will be attached to carbon atom 1. Both additions are in a syn fashion. Choice *C* is the correct answer choice. Choice *B* is incorrect since the addition is not syn. Choice *A* and D would represent the Markovnikov products in an oxymercuration-demercuration reaction.

30. B: The Diels-Alder reaction is a 4+2 cycloaddition alkene type reaction that occurs under heat conditions. The reaction mechanism is concerted and involves a pericyclic reaction or a reaction that takes place in one step without intermediates. There is a cyclic redistribution of the bonding electrons. The reaction occurs between a diene (for example, 1,3-butadiene) and a dienophile (ethene). The general reaction is shown below.

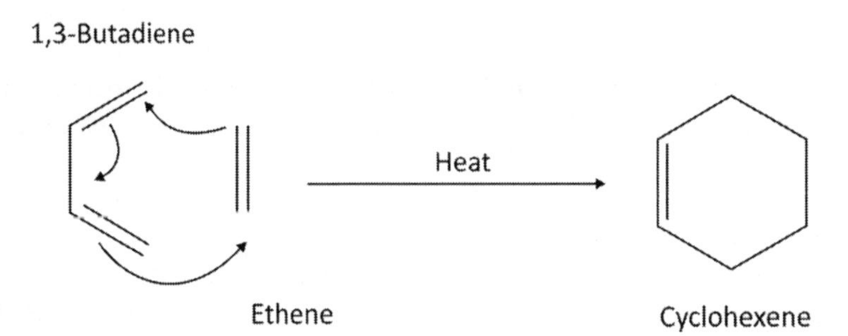

The diene (1,3-butadiene) must be in an s-cis conformation for the reaction to occur. Electron groups on the dienophile (ethene) can facilitate the reaction. Electron releasing groups on the diene will also make the Diels-Alder reaction occur readily. Diels-Alder reactions will also occur to form bicyclic systems like in the given problem. The endo orientation of the dienophile will be favored, and its configuration will be retained. The general reaction for the stated problem is shown below.

H
H CH_3
CH_3

Notice that dienophile configuration stays the same. The methyl groups from the dienophile will be in the endo position (pointing downward). Choices *C* and *D* are incorrect since there is no C=C double bond present from the diene. Choice *A* is incorrect since the methyl groups of the dienophile have the wrong configuration. Choice *B* is the correct answer since the double bond is present and the endo orientation is formed.

31. A: The reaction is an example of a 1,2 nucleophilic addition using a Grignard reagent. The alkyl group from the Grignard reagent attaches to the carbon carbonyl group on the other molecule. MgBr will bond to the oxygen atom of the carbonyl group but can be replaced with a hydrogen atom by the addition of an acid such as hydronium ion. The general reaction is shown below.

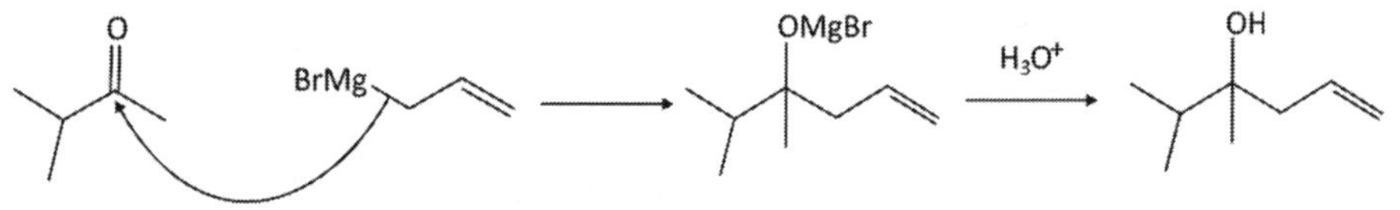

32. C: The reaction sequence is a Wittig reaction and is important in the synthesis of alkenes. The reaction results in the transformation of a carbon-oxygen double bond to a carbon-carbon double bond. A ketone or aldehyde must react with a phosphonium ylide. The first step shows the preparation of the phosphonium ylide and involves the reaction of ethyl bromide (a desired alkyl halide) and a trivalent phosphorous compound. A phosphonium salt is formed but then becomes deprotonated when it reacts with $R - Li$. The phosphonium ylide that forms contains a positive and negative charge that makes it nucleophilic. The ylide attacks the carbonyl carbon of the ketone aldehyde, and a new carbon-carbon bond is formed that eventually becomes a carbon-carbon double bond. The removal of the phosphorus /oxygen component results in the formation of an alkene. Choices *A* and *B* are not correct since the products are not alkenes. Choice *D* is incorrect since a double bond is shown within the ring. Choice *C* is correct since the oxygen atom from the carbonyl group is removed and replaced with a carbon chain that comes from the desired alkyl halide.

33. C: The Grignard reagent shown in I allows the addition of an alkyl and hydroxyl group to a carbonyl carbon. However, the reaction is not reversible, as indicated by the forward arrows in the reaction mechanism. $NaBH_4$ is a reducing agent used for the conversion of ketones and aldehydes to alcohols. $LiAlH_4$ (LAH) is a stronger reducing agent that can reduce a carboxylic acid or ester into an alcohol. However, these reducing agents do not involve a reversible nucleophilic addition. The only reagent that makes the reaction reversible is $NaCN/HCN$. $NaCN$ is considered a weak nucleophile.

Consequently, the forward reaction will shift to the right to a certain extent. Because CN is a good leaving group (it can be removed from the product), nucleophilic addition will be reversible, and an equilibrium will be established. The cyanide nucleophile can also undergo a 1,4 addition that will result in the formation of an enolate ion. The 1,4 addition results in a thermodynamically favored product, and tautomerization can occur.

34. D: The weak acid, HCN, catalyzes the nucleophilic addition reaction. The general reaction mechanism results in protonation of the oxygen atom on the carbonyl group.

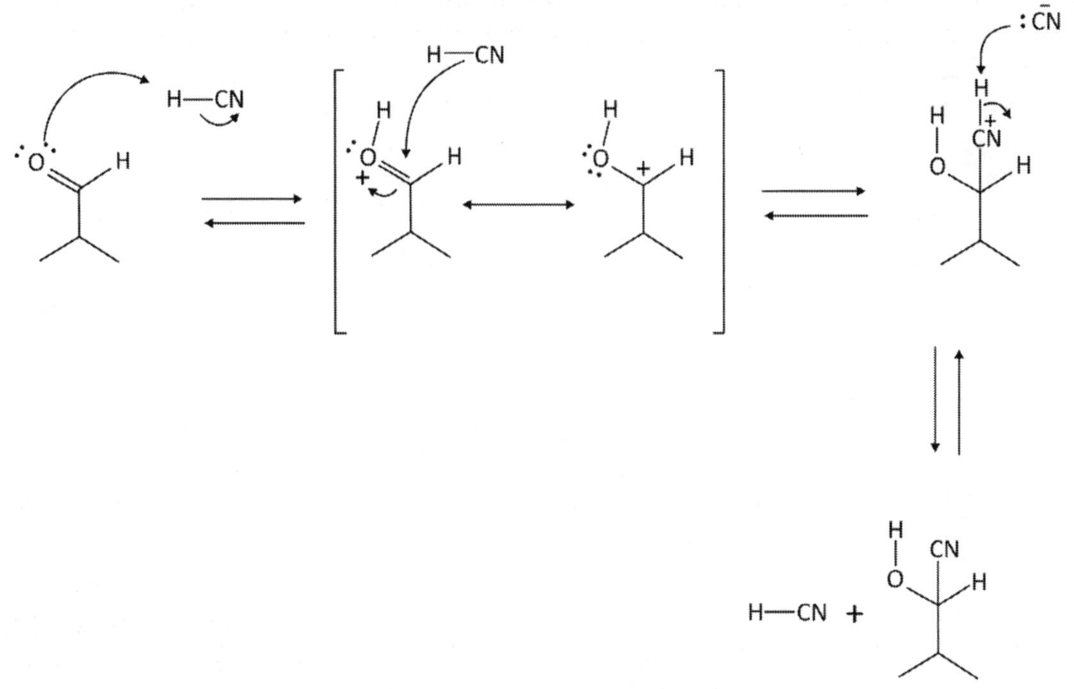

35. C: Nucleophilic addition of an amine results in the formation of an imine $(R'R''C = N - R)$. Two amine groups are present in one reactant. One of the amines is closer to the carbonyl group and will be less basic. The other terminal primary amine is more basic and is expected to be a stronger nucleophile. The reaction will result in the more basic terminal nitrogen forming a double bond to the carbonyl carbon of the other reactant (carbon 2). Through a series of reactions, several intermediates will form, such as the dipolar intermediate, an amino alcohol, a protonated amino-alcohol, an iminium ion, and the formation of an imine (*E* and *Z* isomers). The oxygen atom is removed as a water molecule when converted from an amino-alcohol to an iminium ion. Choice *A* is incorrect since the substituent added to the carbon 2 double bond is missing a methylene group (CH_2). Choice *B* would likely represent a minor product since the less basic nitrogen is attached to the carbon 2 double bond. Choice *D* is incorrect since there is an additional nitrogen atom on the added substituent and does not represent the initial primary amine structure. Choice *C* is the correct answer choice and shows the more basic nitrogen atom double-bonded to carbon 2.

36. A: Nucleophilic acyl substitution occurs in two main steps: nucleophilic addition and elimination. The general reaction mechanism is shown below. Methylamine acts as the nucleophile and attacks the carbonyl carbon atom.

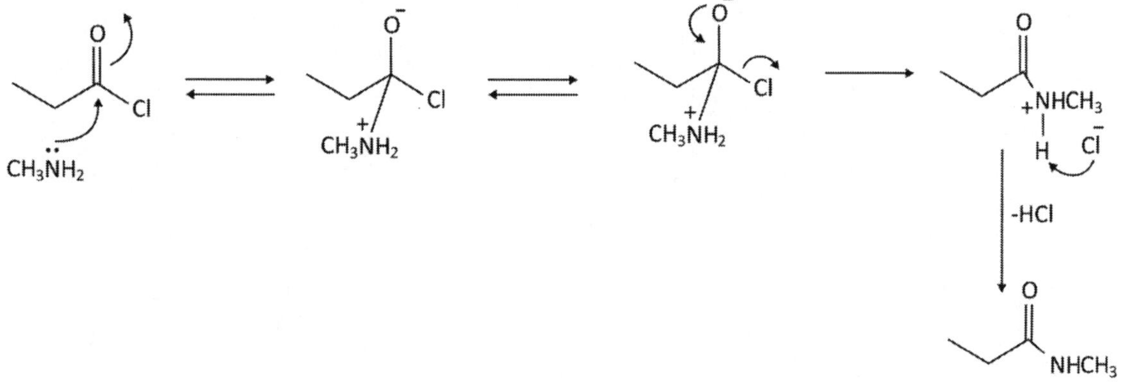

Choice *A* is the correct answer choice. Choices *B* and *C* are incorrect since they still contain the leaving group and also contain functional groups that should not be present. Choice *D* is not correct since the CH_2 group, bonded to the carbon carbonyl group, does not act as a nucleophile at the beginning of the reaction.

37. B: Carboxylic acids can react with inorganic acid chlorides such as thionyl chloride ($SOCl_2$), phosphorus trichloride (PCl_3), and phosphorus pentachloride (PCl_5) to form acyl chlorides. The mechanism follows a nucleophilic addition-elimination reaction mechanism. Choice *B* is the only answer choice that lists a reagent that leads to the conversion of a carboxylic acid to an acyl chloride.

38. D: The amide will undergo a basic hydrolysis acyl type substitution with a strong base such as sodium hydroxide. The resulting molecule will be a carboxylate ion and an amine. Choice *D* is the only answer choice that contains a carboxylate. The general reaction mechanism is shown below.

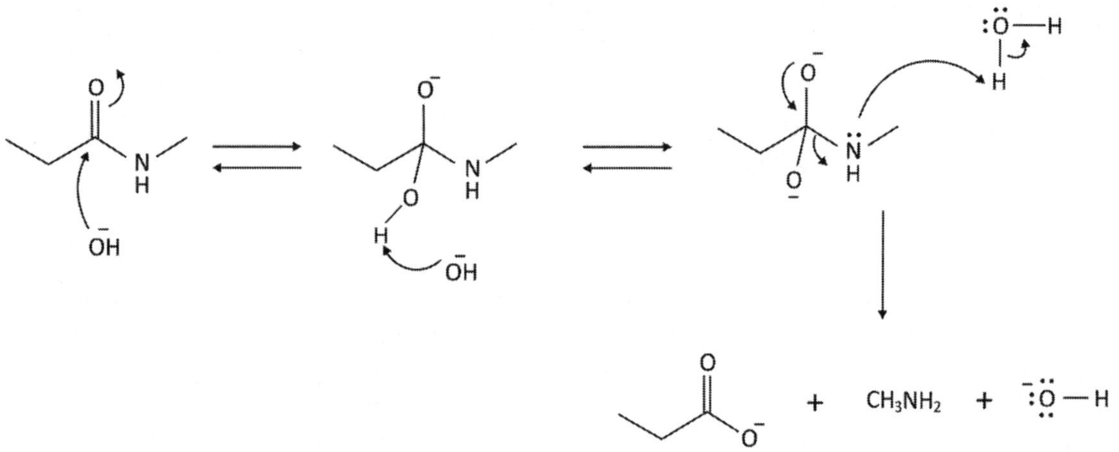

39. B: The first step of the reaction will transform the carboxylic acid into an acyl chloride. The second reagent is a weak Grignard reagent that reacts with the acyl chloride to form a ketone. One equivalent of the Grignard reagent will convert the acyl compound into a ketone. The general reaction mechanism is shown below.

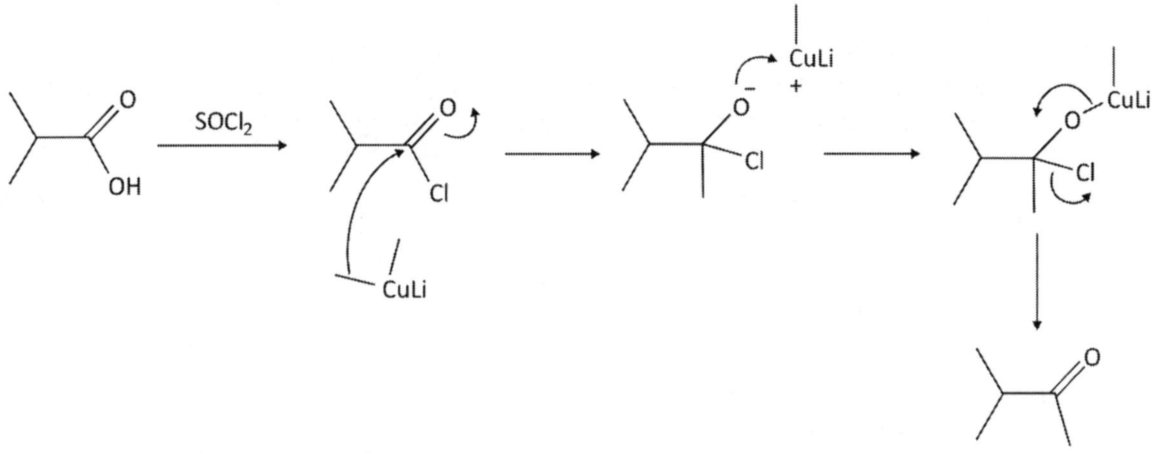

40. A: Saponification of an ester (nucleophilic acyl substitution by based promoted hydrolysis of an ester) produces a carboxylate and an alcohol. The intermediate that is formed contains a tetrahedral carbon atom. In other words, the carbon carbonyl atom should transition from sp^2 to sp^3. Therefore, Choices *C* and *D* cannot be correct. Choice *B* contains a carbocation that will be sp^2 hybridized with a trigonal planar geometry around the carbon atom. Choice *A* contains a carbon atom (originally the carbonyl carbon) that is sp^3 hybridized and is the correct answer choice. The general reaction scheme is shown below.

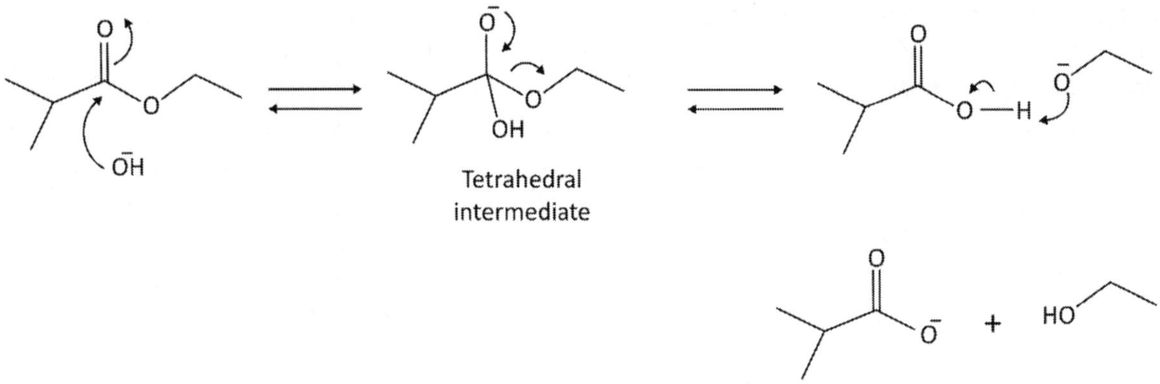

Tetrahedral intermediate

41. C: In an aldol condensation reaction, two molecules of the carbonyl reactant can combine to produce an aldol product. Since the reaction occurs under acidic conditions, the initial reactant will become protonated at the carbonyl oxygen atom. The reactant, acetone, will become a protonated acetone molecule and will break down into an enol when attacked by the conjugate base of the acid. The produced enol attacks and combines with another protonated acetone molecule (the intermediate). Therefore, to determine the correct answer choice, take the initial reactant, and add a hydrogen atom to the carbonyl oxygen atom to make it protonated. Choice *C* is the correct answer choice. Choices *A* and *B* are incorrect since these structures are not protonated, nor do they correspond to the correct structural intermediate. The structure in Choice *B* corresponds to the final product, and the structure in

Choice *D* corresponds to an intermediate that is produced when the enol and protonated acetone combine.

42. C: The reaction is an example of a nitroalkane condensation. The carbon atom in nitromethane (CH_3NO_2) will replace the carbonyl oxygen atom and form a carbon-carbon double bond. Choices *A*, *B*, and *D* are incorrect because all these structures lack the addition of a new carbon-carbon double bond. Choice C is the correct answer choice. The general reaction mechanism is shown below.

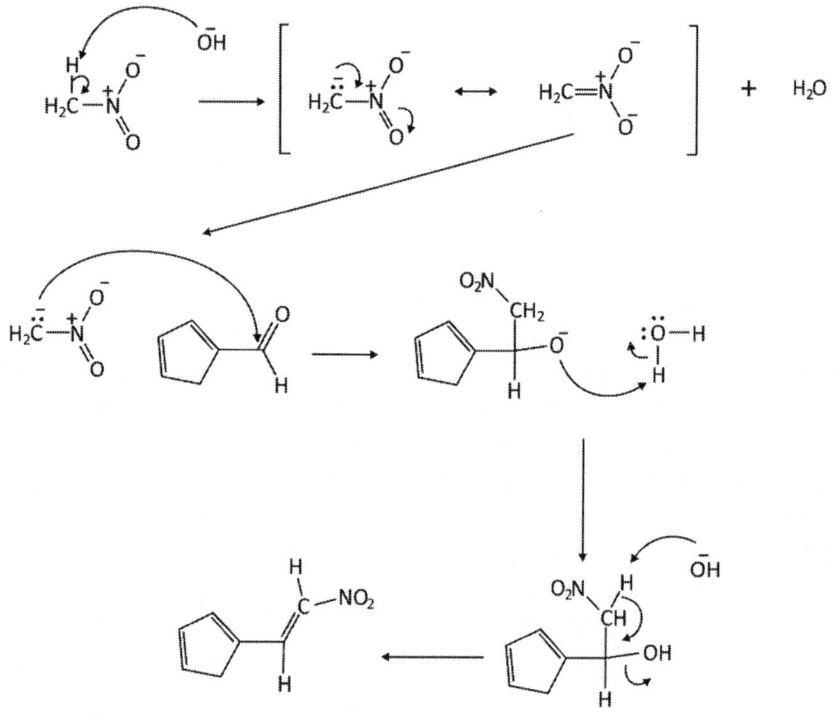

43. B: The reaction is an example of a crossed Claisen condensation between an ester and a ketone. The resulting compound is called a β-diketone. Both the ketone and the ester contain α acidic hydrogens, and when a base abstracts the α hydrogen from the ester and ketone, there will be two nucleophilic carbanions. The carbanion produce from the ketone is expected to be more nucleophilic since the inductive effect is smaller than the ester carbanion. Therefore, to a greater extent, the ketone carbanion will attack the carbon carbonyl atom on the ester. The general reaction mechanism is shown below.

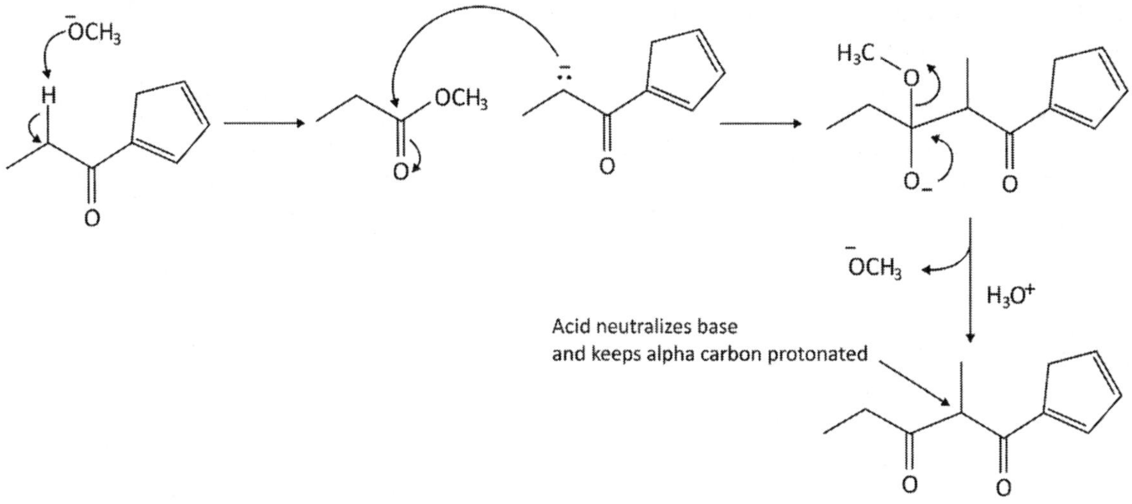
OCH3
H
O
OCH3
O
O
H3C
O
O
O
OCH3
H3O+
Acid neutralizes base
and keeps alpha carbon protonated
O
O

44. B: In an aldol reaction, an alkoxide ion forms and reacts with water. The alkoxide is a strong base, and water is the weak acid. The reaction will proceed toward the weaker base and weaker acid: the hydroxide ion and the aldol. Under basic conditions, the hydroxide ion attacks the α hydrogen located between the carbonyl group and the alcohol group of the aldol. The abstraction of the α hydrogen will form water, and the hydroxyl group on the aldol will act as a leaving group. The process can be described as an intermolecular elimination of water. An alkene will subsequently form, and the molecule becomes more stabilized by conjugation from the $C = O$ and $C = C$ bond. Choice *B* is correct. Choice *A* is not the best choice since only one α hydrogen needs to be present in the aldol. Choice *C* is not correct since the base is regenerated in aldol formation and dehydration. Therefore an additional base is not needed. Choice *D* is not correct since an aldol reaction will still occur if both aldehyde molecules are the same.

45. A: The aldehyde and β-keto ester reaction is an example of a crossed aldol-Claisen condensation reaction. The β -carbonyl system contains the more acidic α -hydrogen and will form the carbanion that attacks the carbon carbonyl of the aldehyde. The reaction will retain the β -keto ester structure, but the alcohol group will be removed and undergo a dehydration reaction to form an alkene.

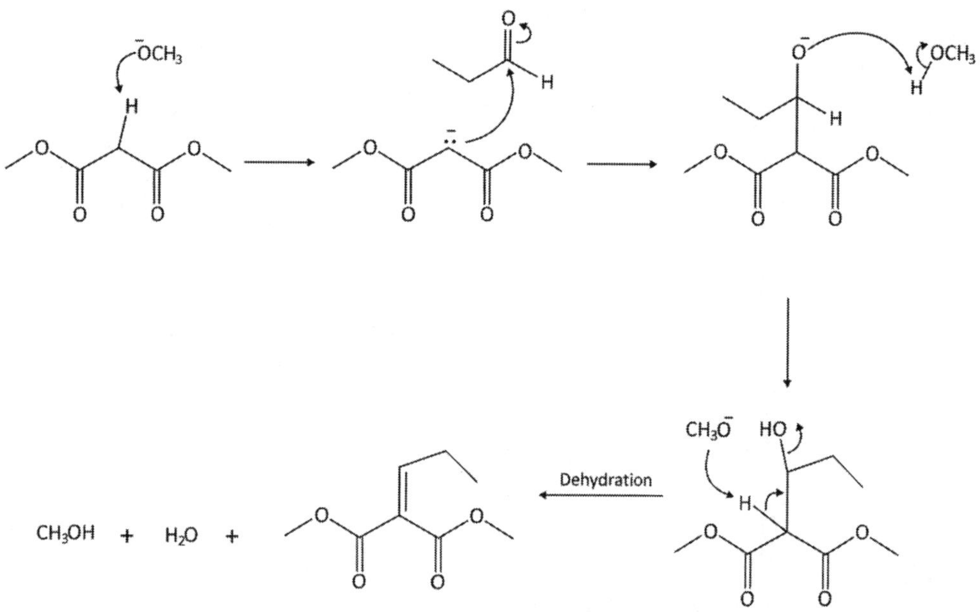

Dehydration

CH_3OH + H_2O +

46. C: The reaction is an example of electrophilic aromatic substitution. The benzene ring contains an electron releasing substituent group and will direct the next added substituent to either the ortho or para position. Choice *C* is the correct answer choice, containing the reagents ($Cl_2/FeCl_3$) used to chlorinate a benzene ring. Choice *D* represents reagents used in the halogen addition to alkenes, and Choice *A* represents reagents used to chlorinate an alkane under UV conditions.

47. B: In Choices *A* and *D*, the second step of the reaction involves a Friedel-Crafts alkylation but will not occur since an electron-withdrawing group is present on the benzene ring. In Choice *C*, the reagents, $NaNO_2/HCl$, do not lead to nitration of the benzene ring since these reagents are used for the preparation of a diazonium salt, for example, converting $-NH_2$ to $N_2{}^+$. The correct answer choice is Choice *B*. A Friedel-Crafts alkylation places a methyl group on the benzene ring. The methyl group is oxidized to a carboxylic acid with $K_2Cr_2O_7$/acid. The carboxylic acid is electron-withdrawing and will direct the nitro group (added with HNO_3/H_2SO_4) to the meta position.

48. D: The reaction is similar to a Friedel-Crafts alkylation and to a nitration reaction except that the alcohol is protonated by sulfuric acid. The protonated alcohol will then dehydrate and form a carbocation. The carbocation can undergo rearrangement from a secondary 2° to a more stable tertiary 3° carbocation. The benzene ring attacks the carbocation and forms tert-butylbenzene.

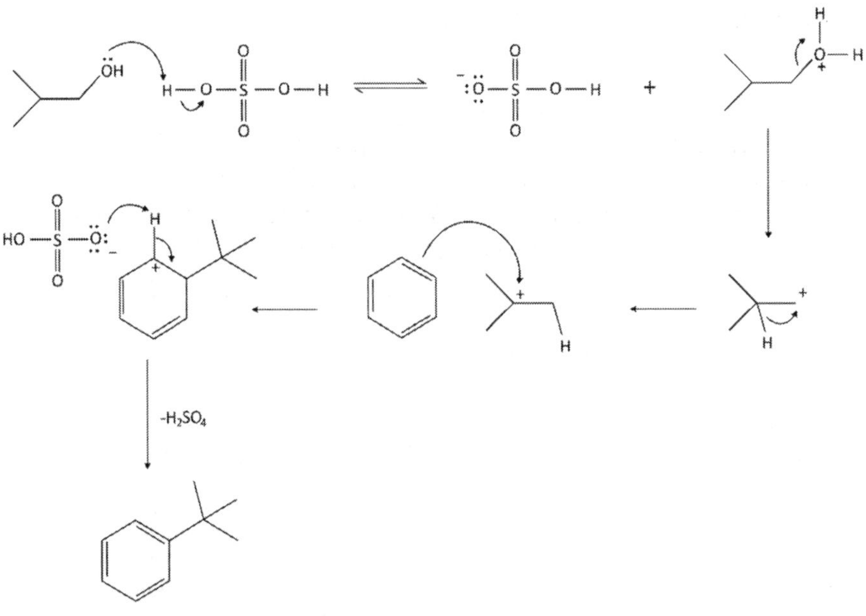

49. A: Choice *B* is incorrect because Grignard reagents are typically added to carbonyl compounds. Even if the alkyl chain were to be added, the chain would be *n*-propyl. Choice *C* is incorrect because it will result in the addition of two substituents to the benzene ring. Choice *D* involves a Friedel-Crafts acylation followed by reduction but would give *n*-propyl benzene instead of isopropyl benzene. Choice *A* is a Friedel-Crafts alkylation reaction that will result in carbocation rearrangement of $CH_3CH_2CH_2{}^+$ to $CH_3CH^+CH_2$ (1° to 2°). When the 2° carbocation is added to benzene, isopropyl benzene will form. Therefore, Choice *A* is the correct answer choice.

50. C: The answer choices represent different ortho resonance forms of sulfonated benzene before abstraction of the adjacent hydrogen. A para substituted structure, with the SO_3H group in the para position, would result in similar resonance structures. The stability of the resonance structures can explain the substitution of the SO_3H group at the ortho position. Some structures will be more stabilized than others. Choices *A* and *B* represent resonance structures of sulfonated benzene that have similar stabilities. Choice *D* is not a possible resonance structure since it is not consistent with the mechanism for sulfonation, for example, there is a pair of electrons located at the para position that should not be present. Choice *C* represents the most stable resonance structure of ortho sulfonated benzene. The lone pair from the weakly deactivating chlorine atom is donated to the carbon atom and thereby creates a stabilized conjugated structure. In other words, the structure is stabilized by conjugation.

51. A: The example reaction illustrates the radical addition of hydrogen bromide to an alkene. When peroxides are used in the reaction, an anti-Markovnikov product is produced, and the bromine atom is added to the carbon that is the least substituted or contains the greater number of hydrogen atoms. Choice *A* represents an anti-Markovnikov addition. If the bromine atom were added to the more substituted carbon, then the reaction would be a Markovnikov addition; however, that is not the case here since peroxides are added. Choice *C* is incorrect because it implies that another double bond would need to be present for an additional radical reaction to occur. Choice *B* is incorrect since the product represents the result of a Markovnikov addition. If the initial reactant contained a triple bond, then Choice *D* would be an alternative answer.

52. B: The order of radical stability is shown below.

$$benzylic/allylic > 3° > 2° > 1°\ alkyl > methyl > aryl/vinylic$$

Choice *A* represents a methyl radical, and Choice *D* represents a secondary 2° radical. Choice *B* represents an allylic radical, and choice C is a vinylic radical. Vinylic radicals are highly unstable, so choice C is the least stable. Choice *B* is a secondary 2° allylic radical and is more stable than Choices *D* and *A*. The order of increasing stability, from least to most, is Choice *C*, Choice *A*, Choice *D*, Choice *B*. Therefore, Choice *B* is the correct answer choice.

53. C: Both polymers will be connected by a single bond from each terminal carbon atom. The double bond for each polymer will be replaced by a single bond between the adjacent polymers. The monomer will consist of structures I and II and will make up the repeating unit within the polymer. The following figure illustrates how to construct the polymer from the individual polymers.

I: $H_2C{=}C(Cl){-}Br$ II: $H_2C{=}C(F){-}F$

Remove double bond
and connect terminal carbons
with a single bond

Enclose in brackets
with a subscript of '*n*' to
indicate that the monomer
is a repeating unit

$$\left(-CH_2-CClBr-CH_2-CF_2- \right)_n$$

54. C: Benzylic hydrogens are the most reactive in a radical substitution reaction. When treated with N-bromosuccinimide (NBS), light, and peroxide, the benzylic hydrogen atom will be replaced with a bromine atom. The reaction produces a secondary 2° benzylic radical that reacts readily with bromine. The reaction will continue until all the benzylic hydrogens are removed. Choice *C* is the correct answer choice.

55. D: Choice *B* shows the transfer of one electron between the same molecule and is not considered an actual reaction step in a radical reaction. The propagation of a radical (radical propane) occurs; however, it does not result in the formation of a new radical. Choices *A* and *C* represent a termination step since two radicals come together and terminate to form a neutral molecule. Choice *D* represents a propagation step whereby chlorine gas dissociates homolytically when reacting with a radical. The products of the reaction are 2-chloropropane and a chlorine radical. Choice *D* is the correct answer choice.

56. A: Oxidation using a basic permanganate solution followed by acidic treatment can be performed on an alkene or benzylic compound. Since the compound is an alkene, the double bond will be cleaved. One of the carbon atoms in the double bond is bonded to a hydrogen atom (carbon 1), and the other is disubstituted (carbon 2). After oxidation, each carbon in the original double bond, $\mathrm{C1 = C2}$, will be bonded to an oxygen atom, for example, $\mathrm{C1 = O}$ and $\mathrm{C2 = O}$. However, carbon 1 will become a carboxylic acid, and carbon 2 will become a ketone. Choice *A* represents the best answer choice. In Choice *D*, the number of carbon atoms changes (from seven to six), and carbon atom 2 becomes a carboxylic acid. However, the reaction in Choice *D* is not correct and mimics benzylic oxidation, where the entire alkyl chain is replaced with a COOH group. Choice *B* is incorrect since the initial reactant is not benzylic, and, like Choice *D*, the entire alkyl chain is removed and replaced with COOH. Like Choice *B*, the product in Choice *C* does not result in oxidative cleavage at the alkene bond.

57. A: The example illustrates a reduction reaction since the ketone is reduced to a methylene group $(-\mathrm{CH_2}-)$. In Choice *B*, $\mathrm{LiAlH_4}$, followed by acid treatment is used to reduce a primary carboxylic acid to an alcohol. Choice *C* is not a reagent used in reduction but is used in the removal of halogen groups in an alkane (for example, germinal dihalide or vicinal dihalide) to produce an alkene or alkyne. The reagents in Choice *C* can be used to remove a proton from an alkyne, thereby creating a carbanion, for example, $\mathrm{HC \equiv C{:}^-}$ In Choice *A*, the Wolff-Kishner reduction uses hydrazine and a base ($\mathrm{NH_2NH_2}$, KOH, and heat) to convert a ketone into a methylene group. Choice *A* is the correct answer choice. Choice *D* would be one reagent used in a Clemmensen reaction but is missing $\mathrm{Zn(Hg)}$.

58. B: Periodic acid $(\mathrm{HIO_4})$ is primarily used to oxidize vicinal diols (cis- 1,2 diols) and other types of compounds. The oxidation of ring structures that contain the diols will result in one compound; otherwise, more than one compound will form. If one of the carbon atoms bonded to the -OH group is bonded to two alkyl groups not within a ring structure, one of the products will be a ketone. If the carbon atom in an acyclic molecule is bonded to one alkyl group (in addition to a hydrogen and an $-\mathrm{OH}$ group), an aldehyde is produced. In the case of cyclic compounds, if the carbon atom bearing the hydroxyl group is bonded to three other carbons, oxidation will result in the formation of a ketone. If the carbon atom bearing the hydroxyl group is bonded to only two other carbons, oxidation will result in the formation of an aldehyde. The reactant in the presented problem is cyclic and contains three hydroxyl groups; however, there is only one pair of vicinal diols or two hydroxyls adjacent to one another. The remaining hydroxyl group will not react. One product is expected to form since the diols are on a ring structure, thereby eliminating Choices *A* and *D*. Two aldehydes are expected to form within the chain of the final compound since each vicinal diol carbon atom is also bonded to a hydrogen atom. Therefore, Choice *B* is correct.

59. D: Ozonolysis reactions will cleave the $\mathrm{C = C}$ double bond in a compound and replace one of the carbon atoms with an oxygen atom to make a $\mathrm{C = O}$ bond. There are two alkenes in the compound: $\mathrm{C1 = C2}$ and $\mathrm{C3 = C4}$ (left to right). Three reaction products are expected to form due to the oxidative cleavage. The expected products after oxidation should be of the form $\mathrm{CH_3 - C1H = O, O = C2H - C3H = O}$, and $\mathrm{O = C4H - CH(CH_3)CH_2OH}$. Choice *D* is the correct answer choice.

One compound will contain two carbonyl bonds. Choice *A* is incorrect since carbon 1 is a ketone instead of an aldehyde. Choice *B* is incorrect since the placement of the carbonyl bond at carbon 4 is at the wrong site and because there is an added methyl group. Choice *C* is not the right answer choice because the compounds containing carbon 2 and 3 should exist as one compound.

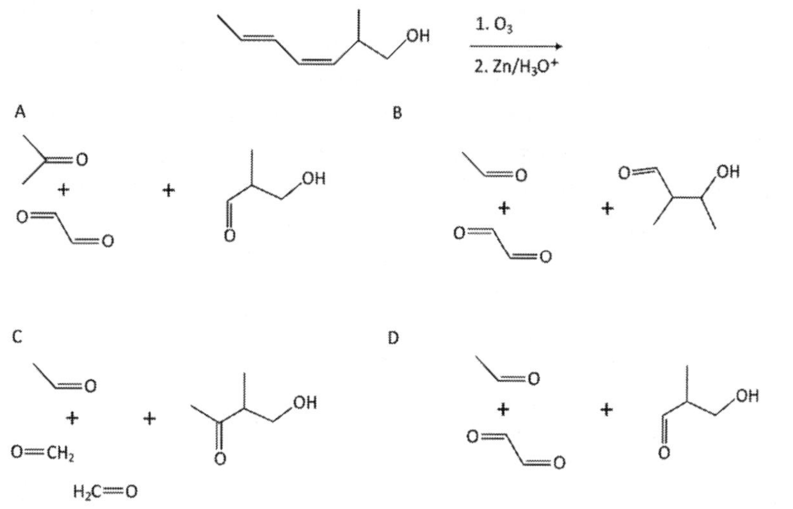

1. O_3
2. Zn/H_3O^+

A

B

C

$O{=}CH_2$

$H_2C{=}O$

D

60. C: A Jones reagent, H_2CrO_4, is an oxidizing agent that will convert a primary 1° alcohol into a carboxylic acid and a secondary 2° alcohol in a ketone, so Choice *A* is incorrect. Choice *B* is also incorrect since a Wolff-Kishner reduction uses hydrazine and a base ($NH_2NH_2/KOH/heat$) to convert a ketone into a methylene group. Choice *D* is also not a suitable choice since $LiAlH_4/H_3O^+$ is used to reduce a primary carboxylic acid to an alcohol. Choice *C* is the correct answer choice since catalytic hydrogenation of an alkene (H_2, Pd/C) results in syn addition of hydrogen to each carbon in the alkene.

61. D: The ^1H NMR spectrum shows three primary signals at 9.7, 7.3, and 3.7 ppm. Each signal contains multiple peaks and corresponds to three different types of hydrogens. Based on the table below, the signal at 7.3 most likely corresponds to an aromatic carbon or hydrogens found on the benzene ring. The multiple peaks found with that signal indicate that there are multiple aromatic hydrogens. The signal at 9.7 may be attributed to a proton bonded to a carbonyl carbon, for example, an aldehyde. The result would indicate that Choices *B* and *C* cannot be correct since an aldehyde functional group is missing. The signal at 3.7 is assigned to a hydrogen that is bonded to a carbon attached to an oxygen.

H type	**Chemical shift δ (ppm)**
An H bonded to an sp^3 carbon atom	1
An H bonded to an sp^3 carbon attached to a π system	2
An H bonded to a carbon attached to an oxygen atom.	3–4
An H bonded to an sp^2 carbon atom	5–6
An H bonded to an aromatic carbon atom	7–8
An H bonded to an aldehyde carbon atom	10
An H bonded to a carboxylic oxygen atom	11–12

^1H-NMR chemical shifts

If we examine each structure, it can be determined that the structure in Choice *A* should have four types of hydrogens: an aromatic H, H bonded to methyl C, H bonded to 3° C, and an aldehyde H. The structure in Choice *B* should have four types of hydrogens: an aromatic H, a methylene H next to the ring, a methylene H next to $-OH$, and an H in $-OH$. The structure in Choice *C* should have three hydrogen types: an aromatic hydrogen, a methylene H, and an H bonded to a methyl group. Lastly, the structure in Choice *C* would also have three hydrogens: an aromatic hydrogen, a methylene hydrogen, and an aldehyde hydrogen. Choices *A* and *B* would not be possible choices since the spectrum does not show four different signals. The structure in Choice *C* does not have an aldehyde hydrogen. Therefore, the structure in Choice *D* is the best answer choice. The figure below shows the predicted chemical shifts for each hydrogen.

A
1.54
7.29 3.81
7.40 9.72
7.27 7.29 O
7.40

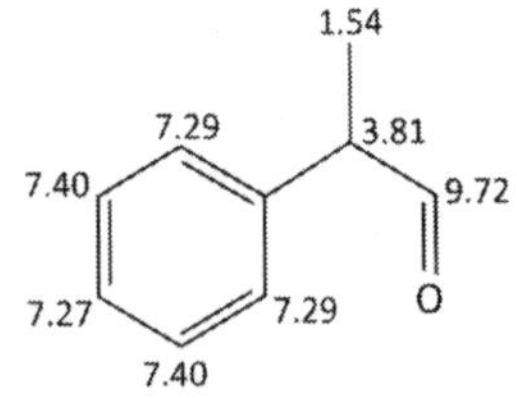

B
7.29 2.77
7.40 3.66
7.27 7.29 OH
7.40 3.65

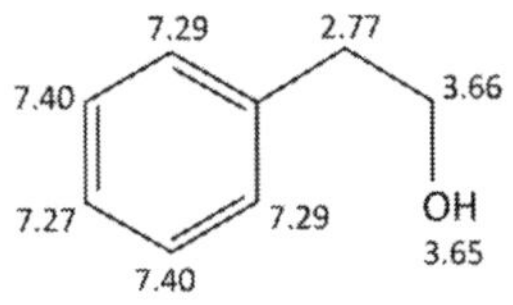

C
7.23 3.45 1.89
7.33
7.26 7.23 O
7.33

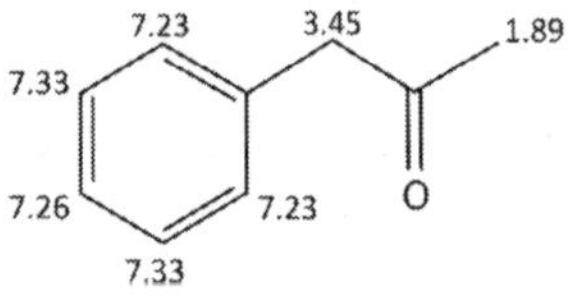

D
7.23 3.66
7.33 9.72
7.26 7.23 O
7.33

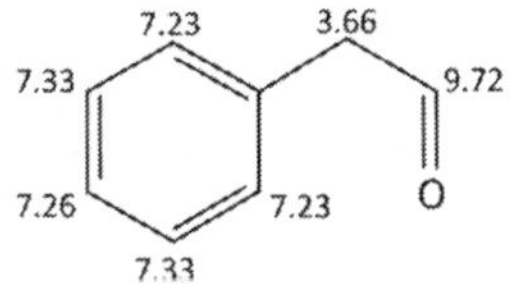

62. C: The ^{13}C NMR spectrum indicates seven signals, two of which are twice the height of other signals (around 113 and 131 ppm). The signals that are twice the height of the other signals may be interpreted as a signal corresponding to two equivalent carbons, for example, carbon atoms in the middle of the aromatic ring. Therefore, we are looking for a structure that has seven types of carbon atoms. In Choice *A*, there are three types of carbons within the aromatic ring: one $C-N$, four aromatic $C-H$, one aromatic $C-O$, and one methylene carbon. The signals at about 113 and 131 ppm would correspond to two carbons for each signal since they are doubled in height. Choice *A* is predicted to have five signals and is not consistent with the spectrum.

In Choice *B*, the carbon types are: one aromatic $C-N$, four aromatic H (two signals), one aromatic C bonded to a carbonyl carbon, one $C=O$, one $C\equiv$ bonded to a carbonyl carbon, and one $C\equiv$ bonded to hydrogen. Therefore, the total number of carbon signals should be seven.

For Choice *C*, there is one H_3C, one methylene bonded to N, one $C-N$, four aromatic H (two signals), one aromatic C bonded to a carbonyl carbon, and one carbonyl carbon. Choice *C* is predicted to have seven signals.

Choice *D* contains one H_3C-N, one aromatic $C-N$, four aromatic $C-H$ (two signals), one aromatic carbon bonded to a carbonyl, one carbonyl carbon, and one methylene carbon. Choice *D* is also predicted to have seven signals. Because Choices *B*, *C*, and *D* are possible choices, we must examine the associated chemical shifts. The peak between 190 and 200 is associated with a ketone or aldehyde, so it

makes it difficult to choose between Choices *B*, *C*, and *D* since they all have ketones or aldehydes. We can examine the signal shifts associated with other functional groups. If our answer choice were Choice *B*, there would be two signals associated with the triple bond at 75–90 ppm. However, these signals are not present, thereby eliminating Choice *B*. Choice *D* should have a signal associated with an sp^3 hybridized methylene carbon bonded to oxygen (50–70 ppm). However, there are no peaks between 40 and 110 pm. The structure in Choice *D* is not a likely choice. The structures in Choices *B* and *C* should have a signal associated with an sp^3 hybridized carbon bonded to nitrogen. The structure in Choice *C* should contain two signals associated with a methyl group (7–30 ppm) and a methylene carbon (18–50 ppm). The methyl signal would be absent in Choices *B* and *D* but present in Choice *C*. The spectrum shows two sp^3 hybridized carbon signals at about 18 and 38 ppm. Choice *C* is the best answer choice.

63. A: A molecule containing a carbonyl group (for example, ketone, aldehyde) can fragment at the carbon-carbon bond at either side of the $\mathrm{C}-(\mathrm{C}=\mathrm{O})$, for example, for either alkyl group attached to $\mathrm{C}=\mathrm{O}$. Fragmentation of ketones is called α-cleavage since the bond between the α carbon and carbon carbonyl carbon is broken. Alcohols, amines, and other types of carbonyl compounds will undergo alpha-fragmentation. The radical stabilities and carbocation will determine how fragmentation will occur. In general, the mass-to-charge ratio for the molecular ion can be the same as the molecular mass. Choices *A* and *C* have a molecular mass equal to 100, but Choices *B* and *D* don't. Choices *B* and *D* will not give a molecular ion at $m/z = 100$ and can be eliminated as a possible choices. For Choice *C*, the loss of an ethyl (mass of 29 amu) or *n*-propyl radical (mass of 43) would produce two acyl cations at $m/z = 57$ and $m/z = 71$. For Choice *A*, the loss of a methyl (mass of 15 amu) or *n*-butyl radical (mass of 57) would produce two acyl cations at $m/z = 43$ and $m/z = 85$. Choice *A* is the correct answer.

64. C: Each answer choice contains specific types of functional groups. These functional groups will vibrate at a particular frequency and give rise to a specific peak or fingerprint on the spectrum. Choice *A* should have a sharp peak corresponding to an aldehyde $\mathrm{C}=\mathrm{O}$ stretching vibration from an aldehyde (1690–1740 cm^{-1}). Choice *B* should have a sharp peak associated with an ester $\mathrm{C}=\mathrm{O}$ stretching vibration at 1735–1750 cm^{-1}. Choices *A* and *B* will also have an $\mathrm{Ar}-\mathrm{H}$ vibration stretch at about 3030 cm^{-1} and an aromatic $\mathrm{C}=\mathrm{C}$ stretch at 1450–1600 cm^{-1}. Choice *C* contains a ketone and should have a peak associated with a sharp $\mathrm{C}=\mathrm{O}$ stretching vibration at 1680–1750 cm^{-1}. In addition, a medium to sharp peak corresponding to an sp^3 $\mathrm{C}-\mathrm{H}$ stretching vibration at 2850–3000 cm^{-1} should be present. Choice *D* contains a carboxylic acid and should have a peak corresponding to a sharp peak at 1710–1780 cm^{-1}. The carboxylic acid will also have a broad peak corresponding to an $\mathrm{O}-\mathrm{H}$ stretch at 2500–3000 cm^{-1}. The alkene $\mathrm{C}=\mathrm{C}$ stretch would have a sharp peak ranging from 1620 to 1680 cm^{-1}

The spectrum shows two medium sharp peaks between 2750 and 3000 cm^{-1}, a strong, sharp peak at about 1700 cm^{-1}, and a medium sharp peak at about 1400 cm^{-1}. There are no sharp peaks at 3030 cm^{-1} due to an $\mathrm{Ar}-\mathrm{H}$ stretch, thereby eliminating choices A and B. Regarding Choice *D*, the spectrum lacks a broad peak, corresponding to the $-\mathrm{OH}$ group, between 2500 and 3000 cm^{-1}. The alkene $\mathrm{C}=\mathrm{C}$ peak is also not found between 1620 and 1680 cm^{-1}. Choice *D* is not a possible choice. Choice *C* is the best possible choice since there is a sharp C=O stretching vibration at 1680–1750 cm^{-1}, and a medium to sharp peak corresponding to an sp^3 $\mathrm{C}-\mathrm{H}$ stretching vibration ranging from 2850 to 3000 cm^{-1}.

65. B: The spectrum indicates there are five types of hydrogens since there are five signals. Using the $n+1$ splitting rule, we can predict the splitting pattern for each hydrogen type. For The structure in Choice A, the methyl group would give a triplet ($n+1=3, n=2$ neighboring hydrogens), the methylene group would give a quartet ($n+1=4, n=3$ neighboring hydrogens), an alkene H would produce a doublet ($n+1=2, n=1$ neighboring hydrogens), the hydrogens bonded to the sp^3 carbon on the ring give a singlet ($n + 1 = 1$, 0 neighboring hydrogens), and the aldehyde hydrogen would give a singlet ($n + 1 = 1, n = 0$ neighboring hydrogens). Structure A would indicate that there are at least six different types of hydrogens: one triplet, one quartet, two doublets ($\mathrm{C = C - H}$), and two singlets. The spectrum only shows one singlet, so Choice *A* is not a likely answer choice.

Choices *B* and *C* both contain five different types of hydrogens. For Choice *B*, the methyl group would give a triplet ($n + 1 = 3, n = 2$ neighboring hydrogens), the methylene group would give a quartet ($n + 1 = 4, n = 3$ neighboring hydrogens), an aromatic H would produce a doublet ($n + 1 = 2, n = 1$ neighboring hydrogens), and the aldehyde hydrogen would give a singlet ($n + 1 = 1, n = 0$ neighboring hydrogens). There are two doublets in the spectrum, so Choice *B* is consistent with the spectrum.

For Choice *C*, the methyl group would give a triplet ($n + 1 = 3, n = 2$ neighboring hydrogens), the methylene group would give a quartet ($n + 1 = 4, n = 3$ neighboring hydrogens), an aromatic H would produce a doublet ($n + 1 = 2, n = 1$ neighboring hydrogens), and the terminal hydrogens on the methyl group would give a singlet ($n + 1 = 1, n = 0$ neighboring hydrogens). Choice *C* contains five hydrogen types and would give four signals: one triplet, one quartet, two doublets (aromatic H), and one singlet. Choice *C* may also be a possible answer choice.

For Choice *D*, an aromatic H would produce a doublet ($n + 1 = 2, n = 1$ neighboring hydrogens), the methylene group would give a singlet ($n + 1 = 1, n = 0$ neighboring hydrogens), and the terminal hydrogens on the methyl or methoxy group would give a singlet ($n + 1 = 1, n = 0$ neighboring hydrogens). Choice *D* contains four hydrogen types that would give four signals: two doublets (aromatic H) and two singlets (methylene and methyl hydrogens). Signals relating to triplets or quartets would not be seen, so Choice *D* is not a possible choice.

Between Choices *B* and *C*, we can relate each signal with the hydrogen type. Choices *B* and *C* contain hydrogens bonded to an sp^3 carbon and should have a signal around 1 ppm. Choice *B* contains an aldehyde hydrogen and should have a signal at around 10 ppm. The spectrum shows a signal corresponding to an aldehyde. Furthermore, if Choice *C* were the answer choice, there would be a signal around 2 ppm corresponding to a hydrogen bonded to an sp^3 carbon (methylene hydrogen) that is attached to a π system; however, no such signal is present. Therefore, Choice *B* is the best answer choice.

66. D: Oxymercuration results involve a Markovnikov addition of water to an alkene with no carbocation rearrangement. The addition of HgOAc forms an intramolecular coordinate covalent bond with the terminal carbon in the alkene (at $\mathrm{CH_2} =$). The disubstituted carbon atom in the alkene will then bond to HgOAC to form a mercurinium ion. Water is added to the disubstituted carbon. Treatment with $\mathrm{NaOH/NaBH_4}$ in step two removes the mercury component, HgOAc, to create an alcohol located at the 3° carbon atom. In step 3, the alcohol is dehydrated and initially forms a 3° carbocation. However, ring-opening occurs, and an alkyl group is bonded to the 3° carbocation, thereby forming a more stable six-

membered ring. The remaining steps of the dehydration reaction result in alkene formation. In step 4, catalytic hydrogenation results in syn addition of the hydrogen atoms to the alkene.

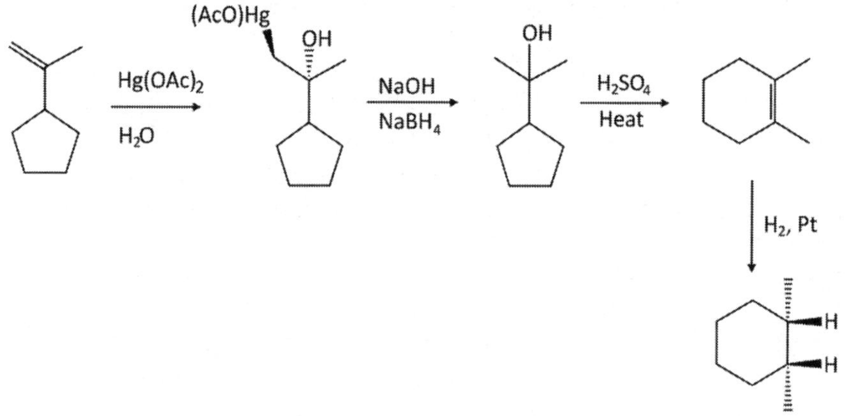

Step 3 carbocation rearrangement:

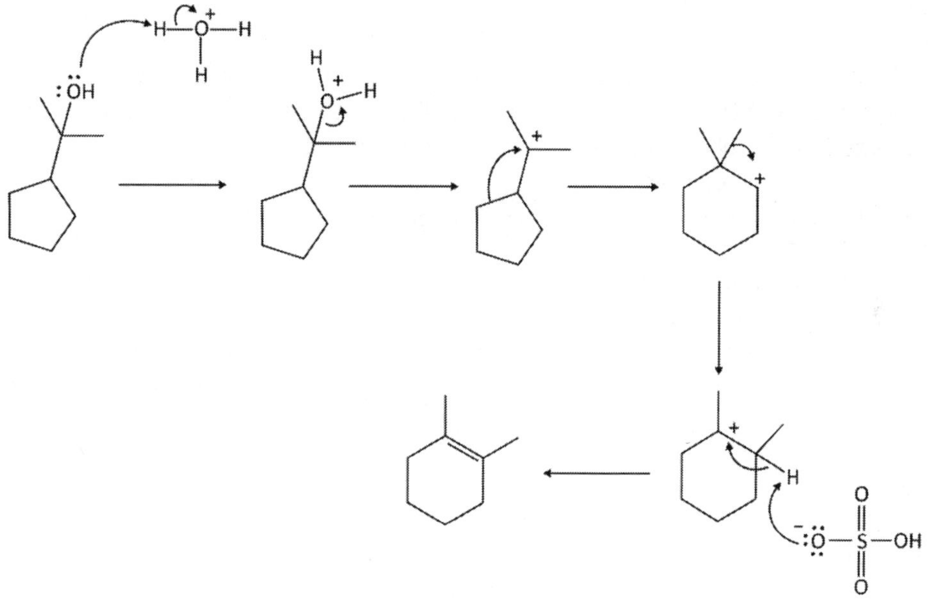

67. D: In step 1, the alkyl group of benzene is oxidized to a carboxylic acid. A benzylic hydrogen must be present for the oxidation to occur. In step 2, the carboxylic acid directs the SO_3H group to the meta position on the benzene ring. In step 3, nitration results in the addition of a nitro group meta to each electron-withdrawing group (COOH, and SO_3H). In step 4, a hydrogen/platinum catalyst can reduce the nitro group to an amine, NH_2. In the last step, treatment with sulfuric acid and sodium nitrite in water at

0 °C creates a diazonium salt ($-NO_2$ to N_2^+). Treatment with CuCN converts the salt from $-N_2^+$ to $-CN$.

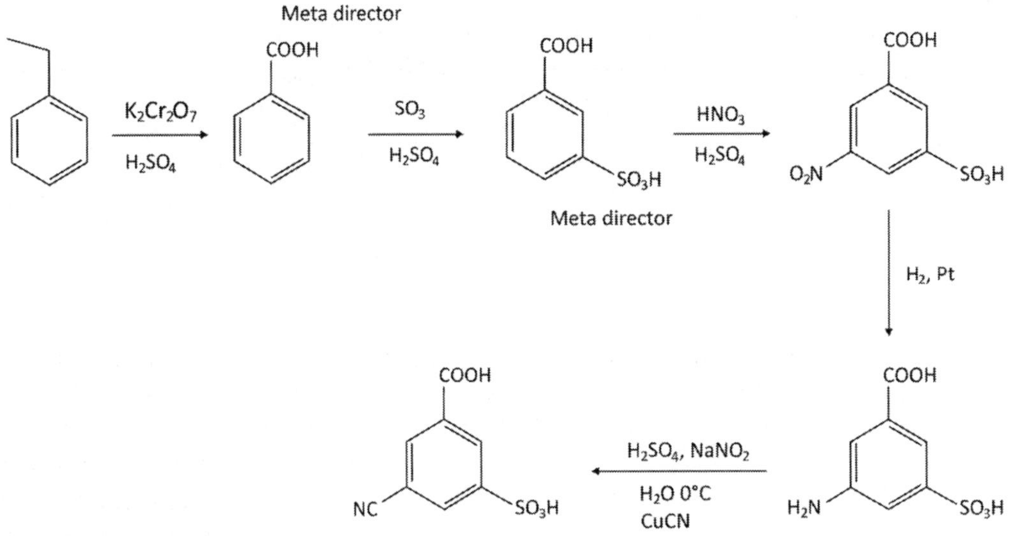

68. **B:** In step 1, the bromination of the alkene results in the formation of a vicinal dihalide. Treatment with one equivalent of $NaNH_2$ results in the removal of hydrogen atom followed by double bond formation and bromine removal. Treatment with a second equivalent of $NaNH_2$ removes another hydrogen atom, thereby creating a triple bond and removing the last bromine atom. An acetylide carbanion is produced after treatment with the third equivalent of $NaNH_2$.

Step 2 reaction mechanism:

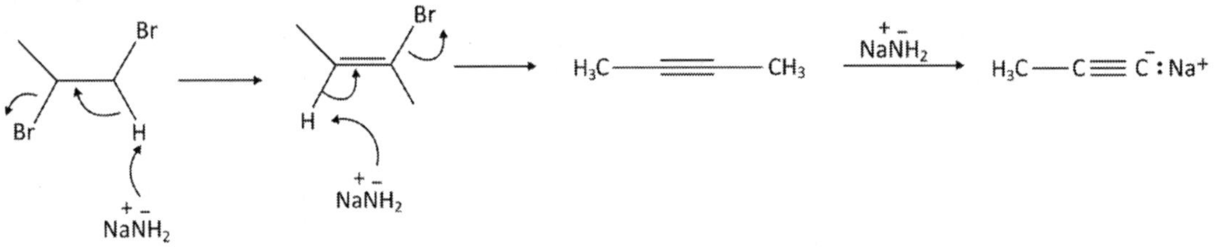

In the third step, ammonium chloride is used to protonated the carbanion. But in step 4, $NaNH_2$ is used again to remove the acidic terminal hydrogen to form an acetylide ion or carbon nucleophile. The last step is a nucleophilic substitution reaction whereby the carbanion reacts with the electrophilic carbon in CH_3Br. Bromine acts as the leaving group, and a new $C-C$ bond is formed.

$$\text{propene} \xrightarrow[CCl_4]{Br_2} \text{1,2-dibromopropane} \xrightarrow[110\text{-}160°C]{3\ NaNH_2} H_3C-C\equiv \ddot{C}^{-}\ Na^+ \xrightarrow[NH_3]{NH_4Cl} H_3C-C\equiv C-H$$

$$H_3C-C\equiv C-H \xrightarrow[\text{liq } NH_3]{NaNH_2} H_3C-C\equiv \ddot{C}^{-}\ Na^+ \xrightarrow{CH_3Br} H_3C-C\equiv C-CH_3$$

69. A: Choices *C* and *D* are not the correct answer choices since they do not have the correct number of carbon atoms. Choices *A* and *B* contain five carbon atoms and are the possible reactants. However, treatment with Br_2/CCl_4 would lead to an optically inactive compound for one of the products. The addition of bromine to an alkene is stereospecific. For example, bromination of cis-2-butene will produce (2*R*,3*R*)-2,3-dibromobutane and (2*S*,3*S*)-2,3-dibromobutane. But treatment of trans-2-butene would produce two optically inactive meso compounds (2*R*,3*S*)-2,3-dibromobutane. Similarly, the bromination of Choice *B* (cis isomer) would result in two optically active compounds. The bromination of Choice *A* (trans-isomer) would result in an optically inactive compound since each isomer is a meso compound. Therefore, Choice *A* is the correct answer choice.

70. B: Catalytic hydrogenation (without being poisoned) of an alkene or alkyne will convert the unsaturated hydrocarbon to an alkane. A molecule with one chiral center is optically active. The initial reactant is initially optically active (chiral) but becomes optically inactive when treated with H_2/Pt. Therefore, we can exclude reactants that are optically inactive. Choices *A* and *B* are reactants that are optically inactive since they don't have a chiral or stereogenic center. Therefore, Choices *A* and *B* can be eliminated. Choice *D* is a reactant that is optically active and remains active after catalytic hydrogenation since it still contains a stereogenic carbon. Choice *D* does not contain a chiral center after hydrogenation. Choice *B* contains a stereogenic center and is optically active. Catalytic hydrogenation creates an optically inactive product. The chiral center becomes achiral since it is now bonded to two *n*-propyl chains.

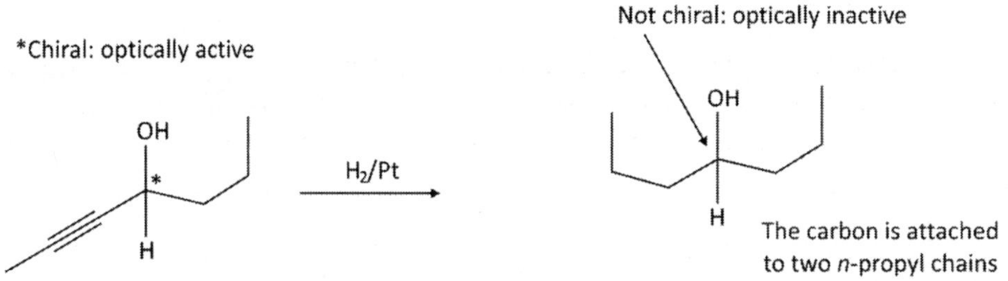

*Chiral: optically active

OH
*
H

H_2/Pt

Not chiral: optically inactive

OH
H

The carbon is attached to two *n*-propyl chains

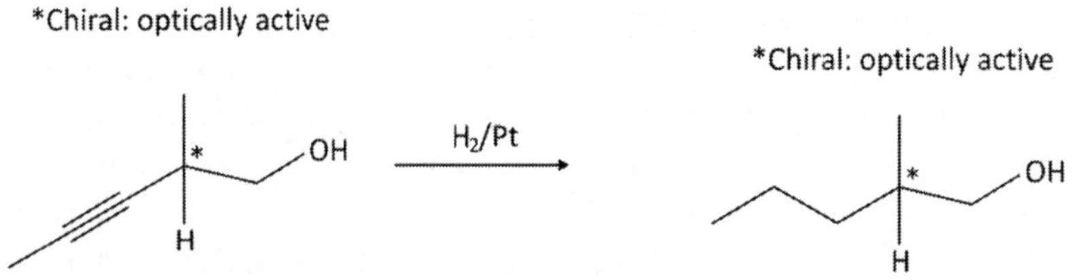

*Chiral: optically active

*
OH
H

H_2/Pt

*Chiral: optically active

*
OH
H

Dear ACS Organic Chemistry Test Taker,

Thank you again for purchasing this study guide for your ACS Org Chem exam. We hope that we exceeded your expectations.

Our goal in creating this study guide was to cover all of the topics that you will see on the test. We also strove to make our practice questions as similar as possible to what you will encounter on test day. With that being said, if you found something that you feel was not up to your standards, please send us an email and let us know.

We would also like to let you know about other books in our catalog that may interest you.

ACS Gen Chem

This can be found on Amazon: amazon.com/dp/1637759223

GRE

This can be found on Amazon: amazon.com/dp/1637752261

We have study guides in a wide variety of fields. If the one you are looking for isn't listed above, then try searching for it on Amazon or send us an email.

Thanks Again and Happy Testing!
Product Development Team
info@studyguideteam.com

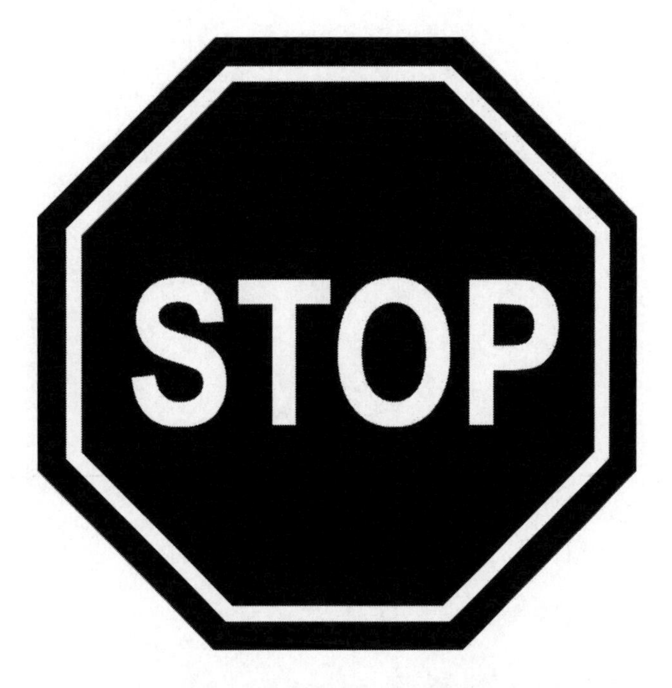

FREE Test Taking Tips Video/DVD Offer

To better serve you, we created videos covering test taking tips that we want to give you for FREE. **These videos cover world-class tips that will help you succeed on your test.**

We just ask that you send us feedback about this product. Please let us know what you thought about it—whether good, bad, or indifferent.

To get your **FREE videos**, you can use the QR code below or email freevideos@studyguideteam.com with "Free Videos" in the subject line and the following information in the body of the email:

a. The title of your product

b. Your product rating on a scale of 1-5, with 5 being the highest

c. Your feedback about the product

If you have any questions or concerns, please don't hesitate to contact us at info@studyguideteam.com.

Thank you!

Made in the USA
Las Vegas, NV
05 December 2024